T0302137

Well-being and Wellness: Psychosocial Risk Management

Well-being and Wellness: Psychosocial Risk Management is a companion to *Health and Safety: Risk Management* that describes the techniques and background knowledge for preventing injury and ill health in the workplace. The new book instead describes the techniques and background knowledge for preventing impairment of worker well-being and wellness.

These techniques differ from those required for the prevention of injury and ill health because of the need to take into account individual differences in susceptibility to psychosocial risk sources, and the fact that psychosocial risk sources can provide opportunities as well as threats. The book is divided into two parts: Part I describes the required background knowledge, including the nature of psychosocial harms to individuals, what can trigger these harms, and what can be done to mitigate these harms, and also deals with the necessary psychological background and the role of individual differences in reactions to psychosocial risk sources. Part II describes an outline psychosocial management system based on the ISO 45001 specification and the guidance in ISO 45002 and ISO 45003. However, the nature of the psychosocial risk sources being dealt with means that the ISO 45001 requirements must be extended in a number of ways, for example, by having threat and opportunity assessment, rather than risk assessment.

Written primarily for OH&S professionals who wish to extend the scope of their management system to include well-being and wellness issues, the book is also directly beneficial to human resources (HR) professionals who have the responsibility for managing psychosocial hazards such as bullying and harassment. Additionally, it can be understood and applied by managers in all sectors who want to improve the well-being and wellness of their team, and it will be a relevant reading for students on OH&S, HR, or management courses.

Dr Tony Boyle was a freelance consultant specialising in research and development aspects of health and safety. He has extensive consultancy, lecturing, and training experience in Europe, and has also worked in Hong Kong, Thailand, and the USA. Tony is a Chartered Fellow of IOSH, a Chartered Psychologist, a Registered Occupational Psychologist, and a Certified Risk Professional. He has held various occupational safety and occupational psychology research and lecturing posts.

Until 1998, he was the Chairman of the Health and Safety Consultancy, Hastam, and remained a non-executive director of the company until 2022.

Dr Fiona Charlton has more than 20 years' experience in operational and strategic health and safety positions. She holds a Master's in Occupational Health and Safety from Queens University, Belfast, and a professional doctorate from Sunderland University that examined the impact of workplace cultures on health and safety management. Fiona continues to work full time in the private sector, is a Chartered Member of IOSH, and sits on viva panels for doctoral students at Sunderland University.

Well-being and Wellness: Psychosocial Risk Management

Dr Tony Boyle and Dr Fiona Charlton

Routledge
Taylor & Francis Group

LONDON AND NEW YORK

Designed cover image: RossHelen/Getty Images ®

First published 2025
by Routledge
4 Park Square, Milton Park, Abingdon, Oxon OX14 4RN

and by Routledge
605 Third Avenue, New York, NY 10158

Routledge is an imprint of the Taylor & Francis Group, an informa business

British Library Cataloguing-in-Publication Data
A catalogue record for this book is available from the British Library

ISBN: 9781032791104 (hbk)
ISBN: 9781032791098 (pbk)
ISBN: 9781003490555 (ebk)

DOI: 10.4324/9781003490555

Typeset in Times New Roman
by Newgen Publishing UK

Contents

Figures[1]

1 *All figures created in PowerPoint by Tony Boyle specifically for this book.*

Tables

The authors

Tony Boyle was a freelance consultant specialising in research and development aspects of health and safety. He has extensive consultancy, lecturing, and training experience in Europe and has also worked in Hong Kong, Thailand, and the USA. He is now a full-time author.

Tony began his career with the National Institute of Industrial Psychology (NIIP) in 1968. He left the NIIP to do the research for his PhD on *The statistical theory of accident causation*. He has held various occupational safety and occupational psychology research and lecturing posts. Until 1998, he was the Chairman of the Health and Safety Consultancy, Hastam. He remained a non-executive director of the company until 2021.

With a Masters degree in Computer Expert Systems, he has developed several computer programs for use in health safety and environmental management. He has also produced audit and evaluation systems for a number of organisations.

Tony has carried out expert witness work, including work on high-profile cases, such as the Buncefield explosion and the Potters Bar derailment.

Tony is an author of *Health and Safety: Risk Management* and has published over 50 papers, articles, and chapters on accident causation, statistics in accident analysis, computer applications, and human factors aspects of safety. He was a frequent contributor to the Hastam blog at Hastam.co.uk.

He is a Chartered Fellow of IOSH, a Chartered Psychologist, a Registered Occupational Psychologist, and a Certified Risk Professional.

Fiona Charlton is a chartered health and safety professional with more than 20 years' experience in operational and strategic health and safety positions. While working in the Northern Ireland Civil Service (NICS), Fiona moved through the administrative ranks and into management, completed a BA (Hons) in Business Studies at the University of Ulster at Jordanstown, and began a Masters in Occupational Health and Safety at Queens University, Belfast.

Following a career break from the NICS, Fiona worked in the National Health Service (NHS), during which time she completed her Masters and started her professional doctorate at Sunderland University.

Following redundancy from the NHS, Fiona entered the private sector and completed her professional doctorate, which included 'an investigation of the impact of workplace cultures on health and safety management: a case study in a large PLC'.

Fiona continues to work in the private sector, and in addition to her full-time role, she enjoys sitting on viva panels for doctoral students in Sunderland University. Fiona has co-authored a chapter in a book *Deconstructing Doctoral Discourses* for doctoral students.

Acknowledgements

Permission to reproduce extracts from British Standards is granted by BSI Standards Limited (BSI). No other use of this material is permitted. British Standards can be obtained from BSI Knowledge knowledge.bsigroup.com.

Contains public sector information licensed under the Open Government Licence v3.0.

1 Preliminaries

Introduction

Since Tony Boyle has already published a book dealing with health and safety risk management,[1] it is helpful to begin by explaining why a separate book on psychosocial risk management is necessary.

The earlier book was principally about what will be referred to as 'traditional' health and safety risk management, and the terms 'psychosocial' and 'well-being' are not included in its index. The health and safety risk management principles described in this earlier book are based on ISO 45001:2018 *Occupational health and safety management systems – Requirements with guidance for use*[2] and the additional guidance in ISO 45002:2023 *Occupational health and safety management systems – General guidelines for the implementation of ISO 45001:2018.*[3]

In ISO 45001, the *intended outcomes of the OH&S management system are to prevent work-related injury and ill health to workers and to provide safe and healthy workplaces.* This is done primarily by eliminating hazards or, when this is not possible, controlling the OH&S risks arising from the hazards. However, hazards can have adverse effects other than injury and ill health. Figure 1.1 shows the main adverse effects of hazards on individuals and the interactions between these effects.

The adverse effects shown in Figure 1.1, and their interactions, are discussed in detail in Chapter 3, but, for now, all you need to know is that well-being can be considered as sub-clinical mental ill health, and reduced wellness can be considered as sub-clinical physical ill-health. For example:

Impaired well-being in the form of occasional feelings of sadness for no obvious reason can be considered as sub-clinical depression.
Impaired wellness in the form of being overweight can be considered as sub-clinical obesity.

ISO 45001 management systems deal with the top two levels in Figure 1.1, but the ISO 45001 *Scope* clause includes the following.

DOI: 10.4324/9781003490555-1

Figure 1.1 Adverse effects of hazards on individuals.

> *This document enables an organization, through its OH&S management system, to integrate other aspects of health and safety, such as worker wellness/ wellbeing.*

The present book describes a psychosocial risk management system that integrates worker well-being and wellness into the ISO 45001 framework, that is, it deals with the third level in Figure 1.1. It does this by taking into account the effects on worker well-being and wellness of all the types of hazard listed in ISO 45001, that is, *physical, chemical, biological, psychosocial, mechanical, electrical, or based on movement and energy.* For example:

Noise is a form of energy and traditional health and safety risk management focuses on noise levels that can damage the hearing mechanisms in the ear. Psychosocial risk management extends this to effects on well-being such as reduced opportunities for conversation due to background noise, and effects on wellness such as headaches.

Chemical hazards are many and varied and traditional health and safety risk management focuses on those chemical hazards that can damage workers' health. Psychosocial risk management extends this to effects on well-being such as annoyance over contaminated clothes, and effects on wellness such as nasal and eye irritation.

Although ISO 45001 and ISO 45002 deal with the management of all categories of hazard, it has been recognised that additional guidance on the management of psychosocial hazards is required, and this has been provided by ISO 45003:2021 *Occupational health and safety management – Psychological health and safety at work – Guidelines for managing psychosocial risks.*[4]

ISO 45003 provides extensive lists of psychosocial hazards (reproduced in Chapter 5) and valuable guidance on preventing injury and ill health arising from these hazards. However, ISO 45003 does not provide guidance on managing the effects of psychosocial hazards on worker well-being and wellness. This is not a criticism of ISO 45003, simply a statement of fact that makes clear why the present book is needed. It is intended for those who wish to extend an existing management system to include worker well-being and/or wellness, or to set up a stand-alone management system to deal with worker well-being and/or wellness.

When the term 'psychosocial risk management' is used in this book, it means the risk management processes required to maintain and, where appropriate, improve worker well-being and/or wellness.

There are various reasons why a psychosocial risk management might be needed, but an important one is to ensure the effective management of well-being and wellness initiatives. It is often the case that organisations wish to improve the well-being and/or wellness of their workers and set up processes to do this. However, if there is no management system to support these processes, they usually fall into disuse. This, of course, is also true of health and safety or environmental processes, which is why management systems are so important.

ISO 45001 and its supporting documents ISO 45002 and ISO 45003 provide an excellent basis for the management of the top two levels of adverse effects shown in Figure 1.1, that is, injury and ill health, and the psychosocial management system described in this book is based on this specification and its guidance. This is allowed explicitly in ISO 45001, where one of the opportunities for improvement is *promotion of well-being at work* (clause 6.1.1.1), and in ISO 45002, which lists as one of the opportunities for improving OH&S performance as *improving well-being even where no significant risks have been determined* (clause 6.1.2.3).

However, when the intention is to focus on well-being and wellness, rather than injury and ill health, two additional topics have to be addressed.

The psychosocial hazards described in ISO 45003 can have beneficial effects as well as harmful effects. For example, not everyone facing redundancy will see it as a threat, some individuals will see it as an opportunity. For this reason, it is preferable to think of psychosocial hazards as psychosocial risk sources that create opportunities and threats, rather than simply psychosocial hazards that create psychosocial risks.

There are factors that affect well-being and wellness that are not work-related. For example, a good diet and exercise outside work can improve an individual's performance at work, and bereavement and relationship difficulties can impair well-being and have an adverse effect on individual's performance at work. In this book, these factors are referred to as improvers (beneficial effect) and triggers (adverse effect). These work-relevant factors should be taken into account in a comprehensive psychosocial management system.

These two topics, and the links between them, are illustrated in Figure 1.2. Note the following points about Figure 1.2:

The increasing and decreasing well-being, referred to in the large arrows, can refer to a single individual, a group of individuals such as the members of a work

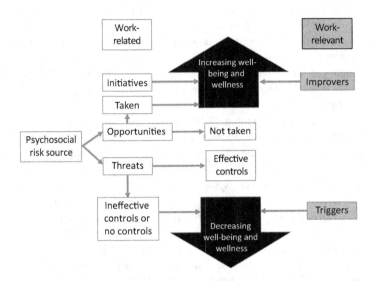

Figure 1.2 Influences on well-being and wellness.

team, or a larger set of individuals such as those taking part in a well-being and wellness survey.

The right-hand side of the diagram shows the influence of the work-relevant triggers and improvers.

The left-hand side of the diagram deals with work-related issues and illustrates the following.

A psychosocial risk source can give rise to psychosocial opportunities and/or psychosocial threats.

If a psychosocial opportunity is taken, it results in an increase in the well-being and/or wellness of the individual(s) concerned.

If a psychosocial opportunity is not taken, then the psychosocial risk source has no effect on the well-being and/or wellness of the individual(s) concerned.

Organisations can increase individuals' well-being and wellness by using psychosocial initiatives.

If a psychosocial risk source gives rise to a threat – that is, it becomes what ISO 45003 refers to as a psychosocial hazard – then psychosocial risk control is required.

If a psychosocial risk control is not implemented, or it is not effective, this results in a decrease in the well-being and/or wellness of the individual(s) concerned.

If a psychosocial risk control is implemented effectively, the psychosocial risk source has no effect on the well-being and/or wellness of the individual(s) concerned.

All of the work-related and work-relevant issues are dealt with in detail in Part I of this book, and the actions organisations can take with regard to these issues are dealt with in Part II.

The principal audiences for this book are as follows:

OH&S professionals who wish to extend the scope of their OH&S management system to include well-being and wellness issues.

Human resources (HR) professionals who have responsibility for managing psychosocial hazards such as bullying and harassment.

Managerial workers who want to improve their management of the well-being and wellness of their team.

Students on courses intended for members of the first three categories.

These audiences need background information on a number of topics that are not normally dealt with traditional health and safety risk management, and this background information is provided in Part I of this book.

The second part of this book is about the practicalities of implementing a psychosocial risk management system. The chapters in Part II, taken together, describe the authors' view of what 'good' might look like in the context of this type of psychosocial risk management. Taken together, these chapters provide a step-by-step guide to developing a psychosocial management system.

References

1   Boyle T. *Health and safety: Risk management* (5th edition). Routledge 2019.
2   British Standards Institution. *Occupational health and safety management systems – Requirements with guidance for use*, BSI ISO 45001, 2018. BSI 2018.
3   British Standards Institution. *Occupational health and safety management systems – General guidelines for the implementation of ISO 45001:2018*, BSI ISO 45002, 2023. BSI 2023.
4   British Standards Institution. *Occupational health and safety management – Psychological health and safety at work – Guidelines for managing psychosocial risks*, BSI ISO 45003, 2021. BSI 2021.

Part I

The background information

2   Part I overview

Setting up a psychosocial management system requires background information that is not required for a traditional health and safety management system. Part I of this book provides this background information and it is set out in the following chapters.

3 **The harms.** This chapter describes what is meant by injury, mental and physical ill health, and well-being and wellness, and how these harms vary in severity and how they interact with each other. It also describes the nature and effects of harms that occur outside work but have an effect on worker performance.

4 **The disorders.** This chapter deals with the main mental and physical disorders of relevance to well-being and wellness, for example, anxiety and stress. For each disorder, the chapter provides definitions, describes symptoms, and gives information on how the disorder is measured and treated.

5 **The hazards and risk sources.** This chapter deals with the definition and classification of hazards and the effects hazards can have. There is a description of what is meant by psychosocial hazards, and why these hazards are better described as risk sources. The chapter ends with a discussion of the implications of having to deal with risk sources, and the framework for hazard creation in organisations.

6 **The elimination and control.** This chapter deals with the various things an organisation may have to do to eliminate or control the hazards and risk sources.

7 **The triggers.** This chapter describes the various events that can happen during an individual's life that can impair well-being and wellness, for example, bereavement and financial difficulties.

8 **The improvers.** This chapter describes the actions that individuals can take to improve their own well-being and wellness, and the resources that individuals can access to improve their well-being and wellness. The chapter also deals with treatment of impaired well-being and wellness.

9 **The psychology.** This chapter deals with those aspects of human psychology that are important in psychosocial risk management but rarely have an impact on traditional health and safety. These aspects are individual differences, personality, self-selecting populations, and the power of the mind.

DOI: 10.4324/9781003490555-3

10 The people. This chapter discusses the roles of workers involved in the causes and effects of psychosocial hazards, that is, perpetrators, victims, beneficiaries, and the immune. There is also a section dealing with interested parties.

11 The psychosocial management system terminology. This chapter sets out the management system terminology to be used in the rest of the book. In particular, it explains why some of the terminology used in ISO 45001[1] and ISO 45003[2] is not used in this book.

12 The documented information. This chapter begins by describing the ISO 10013[3] guidance on quality management system documented information and the various types of documented information including the management system manual, procedures, work instructions, forms, and checklists. The chapter also deals with the media and the structure to be used for documented information.

Each of the chapters in Part I begins with a *Crash course* section that summarises the key points contained in the chapter. These crash courses are all you need to read if you just want an overview of the topic covered by the chapter. The body of each chapter gives the detailed information, and you should study the whole chapter if you wish to have a better understanding of the topics covered.

References

1   British Standards Institution. *Occupational health and safety management systems – Requirements with guidance for use*, BSI ISO 45001, 2018. BSI 2018.
2   British Standards Institution. *Occupational health and safety management – Psychological health and safety at work – Guidelines for managing psychosocial risks*, BSI ISO 45003, 2021. BSI 2021.
3   British Standards Institution. *Quality management systems – Guidance for documented information,* BSI ISO 10013, 2021. BSI 2021.

3   The harms

Crash course

When you are setting up a psychosocial management system, you will have to explain to workers and interested parties what you mean by well-being and wellness, and how well-being and wellness differ from mental and physical ill health. This chapter provides the necessary information.

The World Health Organization (WHO) provides detailed definitions of injury, mental ill health, and physical ill health, and, where necessary, these are the definitions used in this book. The WHO also published a *Well-being Index* for measuring well-being, and this index is used for illustration throughout this book. There are straightforward ways of measuring many aspects of wellness, including waist size, pulse rate, and blood pressure. These measures are described at relevant points in later chapters.

Harms vary in severity and are interlinked in various ways as shown in Figure 3.1.

Crash course Figure 3.1 presents adverse effects of hazards on individuals.

The important points to note from Figure 3.1, reading upwards from the bottom of the figure, are as follows:

Figure 3.1 Adverse effects of hazards on individuals.

DOI: 10.4324/9781003490555-4

Reduced well-being can result in reduced wellness and *vice versa*. For example, a depressed individual may indulge in comfort eating, resulting in weight gain, or an individual may get depressed because they are gaining weight as a result of unhealthy eating habits. This can lead to a vicious circle where both depression and weight gain increase.

Significant reductions in well-being can result in mental ill health, and significant reductions in wellness can result in physical ill health.

Mental ill health can reduce well-being, and physical ill health can reduce wellness.

There can be crossovers between mental ill health and wellness and physical ill health and well-being, as shown by the dotted arrows.

Mental ill health can result in physical ill health, and physical ill health can result in mental ill health. As with well-being and wellness, there can be vicious circles where the mental ill health causes increases in the physical ill health and *vice versa*.

Reduced well-being, reduced wellness, mental ill health, and physical ill health can all result in injury via self-harm. This ranges from minor harm such as nail biting to suicide.

Sustaining an injury can result in reduced well-being, reduced wellness, mental ill health, and physical ill health.

Introduction

When you are setting up a psychosocial management system, you will have to explain to workers and interested parties what you mean by well-being and wellness, and how well-being and wellness differ from mental and physical ill health. This chapter provides the necessary information.

Traditional health and safety usually deals mainly with injury and physical ill health, although some aspects of mental health, such as stress, are increasingly being included. However, the nature and extent of these three types of harm are never, in the authors' experience, defined by health and safety practitioners. For example, there is rarely a clarity around how injuries sustained outside work should be dealt with – despite the fact that they may have an impact on the organisation's bottom line.

Harm to individuals' well-being and wellness is not usually taken into account in traditional health and safety, although ISO 45001[1] states

> *This document enables an organization, through its OH&S management system, to integrate other aspects of health and safety, such as worker wellness/ wellbeing.*

However, *wellness/well-being* are not defined in ISO 45001, and the authors' experience is that different organisations use different definitions, and that what is wellness in one organisation is well-being in another and *vice versa*.

This chapter provides formal definitions of the five types of harm: injury, physical ill health, mental ill health, reduced well-being, and reduced wellness. It also describes how these harms vary in severity, and how they interact with each other in the real world. There is also a section on harms sustained away from work that includes a discussion on how these might be managed.

Injury

The World Health Organization (WHO) publishes the *International Classification of Diseases* (ICD-11),[2] which is *The global standard for diagnostic health information*. Where possible, this document and other WHO documents are used as sources of definitions since this enables the use of definitions that are not country specific.

Despite its title, ICD-11 deals with more than diseases, and chapter 22 deals with *Injury, poisoning or certain other consequences of external causes*. This chapter includes the following:

> *In the ICD, injury means physical or physiological bodily harm resulting from interaction of the body with energy (mechanical, thermal, electrical, chemical or radiant, or due to extreme pressure) in an amount, or at a rate of transfer, that exceeds physical or physiological tolerance. Injury can also result from lack of vital elements, such as oxygen. Poisoning by and toxic effects of substances are included, as is damage of or due to implanted devices.*

This is the definition of injury used in this book.

The WHO definition describes qualitatively different injuries – cuts, burns, poison, etc. – but injuries also differ in severity. Most people have an intuitive idea of what would be a minor cut or a major cut, but medics need clear definitions. These are definitions of *clinical severity*, and there are typically three or four levels. Table 3.1 shows an example of each.

Medics will provide descriptions for the nature of harm at each level, and an example you may have heard used is the four degrees of burn severity, that is:

First-degree burns. These affect only the outer layer of skin, the epidermis. The burn site is red, painful, dry, and with no blisters. Mild sunburn is an example.
Second-degree burns. These involve the epidermis and part of the lower layer of skin, the dermis. The burn site looks red, blistered, and may be swollen and painful.

Table 3.1 Three- and four-level scales of clinical severity of injuries

Four level	Three level
Minor	Minor
Moderate	Moderate
Major	Severe
Extreme	

Source: Prepared by Tony Boyle for this book.

Third-degree burns. These destroy the epidermis and dermis. They may go into the innermost layer of skin, the subcutaneous tissue. The burn site may look white or blackened and charred.

Fourth-degree burns. These go through both layers of the skin and underlying tissue, as well as deeper tissue, possibly involving muscle and bone. There is no feeling in the area since the nerve endings are destroyed.

Scales for the severity of injury are often used in health and safety risk management but the clinical descriptions are not. Severity scales are dealt with in Chapter 23 'Psychosocial threat and opportunity assessment'.

Physical ill health

As with injuries, there are qualitatively different types of physical ill health. These are described in the various chapters of ICD-11, and these descriptions are summarised in Table 3.2. Note that chapter 6 has been omitted from the table

Table 3.2 WHO classification of types of physical ill health

Classification	Chapter	
	No	Title
By causes of ill health	01	Organisms such as parasites and bacteria
	02	Neoplasms *Neoplasms are uncontrolled multiplication of cells as in cancer*
By parts of body affected	03	Blood and blood-forming organs
	04	Immune system
	05	Endocrine and nutritional *The endocrine system produces hormones*
	08	Nervous system
	09	Visual system
	10	Ear and mastoid process *The mastoid process is the part of the skull behind the ear*
	11	Circulatory system
	12	Respiratory system
	13	Digestive system
	14	Skin
	15	Musculoskeletal system and connective tissue *Connective tissue includes sinews and tendons*
	16	Genitourinary system
Other	07	Sleep–wake disorders
	17	Sexual health
	18	Pregnancy, childbirth the puerperium *The puerperium is the six weeks or so after delivery*
	19	Perinatal period *The perinatal period is the few weeks before and after birth*
	20	Developmental anomalies
	21	Symptoms, signs, or clinical findings, not elsewhere classified

because it deals with *Mental, behavioural or neurodevelopmental disorders* which are the subject of the next section of the present chapter. Text in italics in Table 3.2 is the authors' explanatory notes.

Abstracted by Tony Boyle from World Health Organization. *International Classification of Diseases* 11th Revision. WHO 2022. Available online at https://icd.who.int/en. Last accessed 21 November 2023.

You can see from Table 3.2 that there is a wide range of things that can go wrong with the human body, and traditional health and safety risk management only deals with a fraction of them. This is because traditional health and safety risk management deals with physical ill health arising from work-related activities, and these types of ill health usually arise from injuries. For example:

Noise-induced hearing loss is a result of physical damage to the hair cells in the ear – it is not a disease.

Cancer caused by asbestos fibres in the lungs (mesothelioma) is a disease, but it occurs because of an injury – asbestos fibres penetrating the lungs.

Action with regard to the musculoskeletal system is to prevent injuries or disorders, not diseases such as arthritis.

In some organisations, there are actions for preventing ill health, but these are usually the responsibility of the human resources (HR) personnel – not the health and safety personnel. This is because information on the physical health of workers in an organisation is confidential and health and safety personnel are not normally authorised to access such information. The role of confidentiality in psychosocial risk management is dealt with in later chapters.

As with injuries, individual types of physical ill health vary in severity, and the scales for the clinical severity of physical ill health are similar to those shown in Table 3.1.

Mental ill health

As was mentioned earlier, chapter 6 of ICD-11 is *Mental, behavioural or neurodevelopmental disorders*, which it describes as

> *syndromes characterised by clinically significant disturbance in an individual's cognition, emotional regulation, or behaviour that reflects a dysfunction in the psychological, biological, or developmental processes that underlie mental and behavioural functioning. These disturbances are usually associated with distress or impairment in personal, family, social, educational, occupational, or other important areas of functioning.*

The information contained in chapter 6 is comprehensive and highly specialised in places, but it is possible to give an overview of the content. Table 3.3 shows the framework of the disorders listed in ICD-11 chapter 6 with, where appropriate, examples of the disorders included in each part of the framework. The examples in

Table 3.3 WHO ICD-11 – Chapter 6 framework

Codes	Title	Examples and notes
6A00–6A06	Neurodevelopmental disorders	6A02 Autism spectrum disorder 6A05 Attention deficit hyperactivity disorder
6A20–6A25	Schizophrenia or other primary psychotic disorders	6A20 Schizophrenia 6A23 Acute and transient psychotic disorder *Psychotic disorders involve loss of contact with external reality* 6A24 Delusional disorder
6A40–6A41	Catatonia *Co-occurrence of several symptoms of decreased, increased, or abnormal psychomotor activity.*	6A40 Catatonia associated with another mental disorder 6A41 Catatonia induced by substances or medications
Mood disorders		
6A60–6A62	Bipolar or related disorders	Bipolar disorders *Occurrence of manic, mixed or hypomanic episodes or symptoms*
6A70–6A73	Depressive disorders	6A70 Single episode depressive disorder 6A71 Recurrent depressive disorder 6A72 Dysthymic disorder p*ersistent depressed mood lasting more than two years* 6A73 Mixed depressive and anxiety disorder
6A80	Symptomatic and course presentations for mood episodes in mood disorders	6A80.0 Prominent anxiety symptoms in mood episodes 6A80.1 Panic attacks in mood episodes 6A80.2 Current depressive episode persistent 6A80.3 Current depressive episode with melancholia 6A80.4 Seasonal pattern of mood episode onset 6A80.5 Rapid cycling *at least four mood episodes in the last 12 months*
6B00–6B06	Anxiety or fear-related disorders	6B00 Generalised anxiety disorder 6B01 Panic disorder 6B02 Agoraphobia *Fear of open spaces* 6B03 Specific phobia 6B04 Social anxiety disorder 6B05 Separation anxiety disorder 6B06 Selective mutism *Children not speaking in certain situations, e.g., at school*
6B20–6B25	Obsessive-compulsive or related disorders	6B20 Obsessive-compulsive disorder 6B21 Body dysmorphic disorder *Preoccupation with perceived faults in body or appearance*

Table 3.3 (Continued)

Codes	Title	Examples and notes
		6B22 Olfactory reference disorder *Mistakenly believing you are emitting an offensive odour* 6B23 Hypochondriasis *Mistakenly believing you have a life-threatening illness* 6B24 Hoarding disorder 6B25 Body-focused repetitive behaviour disorders, *e.g., hair-pulling, skin-picking, lip-biting*
6B40–6B45	Disorders specifically associated with stress	6B40 Post-traumatic stress disorder 6B41 Complex post-traumatic stress disorder 6B42 Prolonged grief disorder 6B43 Adjustment disorder *A maladaptive reaction to an identifiable psychosocial stressor or multiple stressors, e.g., divorce or illness*
6B60–6B66	Dissociative disorders *Dissociative disorders are characterised by involuntary disruption or discontinuity in the normal integration of one or more of the following: identity, sensations, perceptions, affects, thoughts, memories, control over bodily movements, or behaviour. They are highly technical conditions*	6B60 Dissociative neurological symptom disorder 6B61 Dissociative amnesia 6B62 Trance disorder 6B63 Possession trance disorder 6B64 Dissociative identity disorder 6B65 Partial dissociative identity disorder 6B66 Depersonalisation–derealisation disorder
6B80–6B85	Feeding or eating disorders	6B80 Anorexia nervosa *characterised by significantly low body weight* 6B81 Bulimia nervosa *characterised by frequent, recurrent episodes of binge eating followed by compensatory action such as self-induced vomiting* 6B82 Binge eating disorder *characterised by frequent, recurrent episodes of binge eating but not followed by compensator* 6B83 Avoidant-restrictive food intake disorder *characterised by avoidance or restriction of food intake resulting in, e.g., weight loss and impairment of family life*

(Continued)

Table 3.3 (Continued)

Codes	Title	Examples and notes
		6B84 Pica *characterised by the regular consumption of non-nutritive substances*
		6B85 Rumination-regurgitation disorder *characterised by the intentional and repeated bringing up of previously swallowed food*
6C00–6C01	Elimination disorders	6C00 Enuresis *Repeated voiding of urine into clothes or bed*
		6C01 Encopresis *Repeated passage of faeces in inappropriate places*
6C20–6C21	Disorders of bodily distress or bodily experience	6C20 Bodily distress disorder *Excessive attention to bodily symptoms often resulting in repeated contact with health care providers*
		6C21 Body integrity dysphoria *desire to become physically disabled in a significant way, e.g., major limb amputee*
Not coded	Disorders due to substance use or addictive behaviours	Disorders due to substance use Disorders due to addictive behaviours
6C70–6C73	Impulse control disorders	6C70 Pyromania *Strong impulse to start fires*
		6C71 Kleptomania *Strong impulse to steal*
		6C72 Compulsive sexual behaviour disorder
		6C73 Intermittent explosive disorder *Brief episodes of verbal or physical aggression or destruction of property*
6C90–6C91	Disruptive behaviour or dissocial disorders	6C90 Oppositional defiant disorder *Defiant, disobedient, provocative, or spiteful behaviour*
		6C91 Conduct-dissocial disorder *Rights of others or societal norms, rules, or laws are violated*
6D10–6D11	Personality disorders and related traits	6D10 Personality disorder
		6D11 Prominent personality traits or patterns *applied to describe types of personality disorder*
6D30–6D36	Paraphilic disorders *Disorders involving abnormal sexual desires*	6D30 Exhibitionist disorder *Exposing genitals in public places*
		6D31 Voyeuristic disorder *Observing individuals who are naked, undressing, or engaging in sexual activity*
		6D32 Paedophilic disorder
		6D33 Coercive sexual sadism disorder
		6D34 Frotteuristic disorder *Touching or rubbing against a non-consenting person in crowded public places*

Table 3.3 (Continued)

Codes	Title	Examples and notes
		6D35 Other paraphilic disorder involving non-consenting individuals 6D36 Paraphilic disorder involving solitary behaviour or consenting individuals
6D50–6D51	Factitious disorders *Falsifying medical, psychological, or behavioural signs and symptoms*	6D50 Factitious disorder imposed on self 6D51 Factitious disorder imposed on another
6D70–6D72	Neurocognitive disorders	6D70 Delirium *Disturbance of attention, orientation, and awareness* 6D71 Mild neurocognitive disorder 6D72 Amnestic disorder *Prominent memory impairment*
6E20–6E21	Mental or behavioural disorders associated with pregnancy, childbirth, or the puerperium	6E20 Mental or behavioural disorders associated with pregnancy, childbirth, or the puerperium without psychotic symptoms 6E21 Mental or behavioural disorders associated with pregnancy, childbirth, or the puerperium with psychotic symptoms

Table 3.3 have been chosen because they are the more commonly known disorders, and some of them will be used later in the book to illustrate various points about psychosocial risk management. Italic text in Table 3.3 is the authors' explanatory notes. The table includes all of the chapter 6 codes and the gaps in table, for example, there is no code 6A30, are gaps in chapter 6, not inadvertent omissions.

Abstracted by Tony Boyle from World Health Organization. *International Classification of Diseases* 11th Revision. WHO 2022. Available online at https://icd.who.int/en. Last accessed 21 November 2023.

As with physical ill health, the various disorders listed in Table 3.3 vary in severity. The three- and four-level scales shown in Table 3.1 are also used in various forms to describe the severity of mental ill health.

However, many types of mental ill health, including depression, can occur at a severity below the level that would justify classification as clinical. These low levels of disorders are dealt with in the next section.

Reduced well-being

An individual's well-being is how, in general, they feel. The WHO published a simple five-item *Well-being Index*, and this is shown in Table 3.4. This index no

Table 3.4 WHO 5 Well-being Index

Please respond to each item by marking one box per row, regarding how you felt in the last two weeks.	*All of the time*	*Most of the time*	*More than half the time*	*Less than half the time*	*Some of the time*	*At no time*
WHO 1 I have felt cheerful in good spirits.	5	4	3	2	1	0
WHO 2 I have felt calm and relaxed.	5	4	3	2	1	0
WHO 3 I have felt active and vigorous.	5	4	3	2	1	0
WHO 4 I woke up feeling fresh and rested.	5	4	3	2	1	0
WHO 5 My daily life has been filled with things that interest me.	5	4	3	2	1	0

longer appears on the WHO websites, but it has been widely used, and copies in various formats are available on the internet. It is used here because it serves as a simple and straightforward way to demonstrate that well-being can easily be measured.

WHO (no longer available on WHO websites). Available in multiple formats on internet. Table 3.4 adapted for use in book by Tony Boyle.

When individuals complete the WHO 5 *Well-being Index*, they get a score between 0 and 25, with a score above 12 indicating an 'acceptable' level of well-being. However, a score of 0 on any of the five items indicates a problem with their well-being.

The WHO 5 *Well-being Index* illustrates the following points about well-being.

The feelings referred to are not included in the injury, physical ill health, and mental ill health categories described earlier in this chapter. In theory, a person could be in recovery from a serious disease or disorder and still have a high level of well-being.

Very low scores could indicate that the person is approaching mental ill health levels. For example, long periods of not feeling *cheerful in good spirits* could be a prelude to depression, and not feeling *calm and relaxed* could be a prelude to anxiety disorder.

There are other ways of measuring well-being and these are described in Chapter 25 'Psychosocial measurement, analysis, and evaluation', together with the implications of well-being numerical scores.

For the purposes of this book, well-being will be treated as a range of mental processes that are related to mental health processes but occur in ways, and at severity levels, that do not constitute mental illness.

Reduced wellness

As with well-being, there are many definitions of wellness. In addition, some sources make no distinction between well-being and wellness, while others define wellness as what was described as well-being in the previous section.

For the purposes of this book, wellness has been treated as the physical equivalent of well-being. That is, reduced wellness is impaired physical conditions below the level that would justify classifying them as clinical. For example:

Occasional insomnia reduces wellness, but it would have to happen very frequently over a period of time for it to became a sleep–wake disorder (chapter 7 in Table 3.2).

Indigestion reduces wellness, but it would have to be severe and prolonged for it to became a disorder of the digestive system (chapter 13 in Table 3.2).

Mild rashes and dry skin reduce well-being and wellness, but they are not a skin disorder (chapter 14 in Table 3.2).

All of the conditions causing reduced wellness can, in theory, be measured, and it is possible to construct a 'wellness index' to match the WHO 5 *Well-being Index*. A number of measures that could be used in such an index are available as self-measures because they require only simple equipment and little expertise. These self-measures include the following:

Waist measurement.[i] The British Heart Foundation[3] has the following information on waist circumference as a measure of wellness.

The recommended waist measurements are:

* *below 37 inches (94cm) for men*
* *below 31.5 inches (80cm) for women.*

People with waist sizes bigger than these are more likely to develop certain health problems, such as type 2 diabetes, high blood pressure, heart disease and stroke.

Adults from certain ethnic backgrounds, including South Asian, Chinese, other Asian, Middle Eastern, Black African or African-Caribbean, with waist sizes higher than 90cm for men and 80cm for women are at greater risk of developing ... health problems.

Body mass index (BMI). This is a number calculated using an individual's weight and height and there are various online BMI calculators, for example on the UK's NHS website.[4] These calculators are usually accompanied by guidance on what constitutes a healthy BMI, and what to do to maintain a healthy BMI.

Resting heart (pulse) rate. A healthy resting heart rate, or pulse rate, for an adult is between 60 and 100.

Blood pressure measures. These measures require a blood pressure monitor but these items of equipment are readily available and not expensive. The instructions for using the monitor should also give guidance on what constitutes healthy measures of blood pressure. Note that ISO 45002[5] refers to a tensimeter in its discussion of calibration of measuring instruments. In the context of OH&S, this can be taken to mean an instrument for measuring blood pressure.

Lung function (spirometry test). There are various instruments for measuring lung function but the simplest ones measure how forcibly an individual can breathe out (exhale). Some of these instruments are also lung exercisers that can be used by individuals to help improve their lung function.

There is also a range of wellness measures involving tests on a sample of an individual's blood. Self-test kits are available for purchase online but the advertising and selling of these test kits are not regulated, so care is needed when purchasing and using them. The best approach is to use a regulated service such as the one run by the United Kingdom's National Health Service.[6] This organisation sells a *Full Screen* test kit that enables individuals to test their blood sugar, vitamin D, cholesterol levels, and various aspects of their thyroid function.

Other measures of wellness are described in Chapter 25 'Psychosocial measurement, analysis, and evaluation'. Chapter 25 also describes how organisations can construct a composite wellness index with numerical scores that can be used in similar ways to the WHO well-being index described in the previous section.

Mental and physical links

Injury, mental ill health, physical ill health, well-being, and wellness have been dealt with as separate topics but in real life they are interrelated. These interrelationships are illustrated in Figure 3.1.

The important points to note from Figure 3.1, reading upwards from the bottom of the figure, are as follows.

Reduced well-being can result in reduced wellness and *vice versa*. For example, a depressed individual may indulge in comfort eating, resulting in weight gain,

Figure 3.1 Adverse effects of hazards on individuals.

or an individual gets depressed because they are gaining weight as a result of unhealthy eating habits. This can lead to a vicious circle where both depression and weight gain increase.

Significant reductions in well-being can result in mental ill health, and significant reductions in wellness can result in physical ill health.

Mental ill health can reduce well-being and physical ill health can reduce wellness.

There can be crossovers between mental ill health and wellness and physical ill health and well-being, as shown by the dotted arrows.

Mental ill health can result in physical ill health and physical ill health can result in mental ill health. As with well-being and wellness, there can be vicious circles where the mental ill health cause increases in the physical ill health and *vice versa.*

Reduced well-being, reduced wellness, mental ill health, and physical ill health can all result in injury via self-harm. This ranges from minor harm such as nail biting to suicide.

Sustaining an injury can result in reduced well-being, reduced wellness, mental ill health, and physical ill health.

While recognising the complexity of the interrelationships of harms, the types of harm will be dealt with separately throughout the book, and interrelationships will only be mentioned when it is necessary to do so.

Work-related and work-relevant harms

In traditional health and safety risk management, practitioners refer to 'work-related harms', that is, harms caused by some aspect of the work being done, the tools, equipment and materials being used, or the environment in which the work is done. However, it is recognised that harms that occur outside work can have an effect on the organisation – it does not matter whether a person breaks their leg falling down stairs at work or playing football in their own time, they are still 'off work' and having a detrimental effect on the organisation's productivity and its bottom line.

Because of this, some organisations also tackle 'work relevant harms', that is, harms that occur outside work but affect the organisation in some way. Typical examples are providing workers with personal protective equipment (PPE) for use during work at home, and allowing workers to have influenza (flu) vaccinations during their work hours.

Workers suffering impaired well-being or wellness will be at work and working, but may not producing their optimal performance. This is obviously detrimental to the organisation, but it will not show up in traditional measures of health and safety performance. Since there are many causes of impaired well-being or wellness that do not involve work, this detrimental effect can be extensive. For this reason, it is important to take work-relevant psychosocial harms into account in a psychosocial management system. Work-relevant psychosocial harms are dealt with in detail in Chapter 7 'The triggers'.

ISO 45001 and ISO 45003[7]

ISO 45001 defines injury and ill health as

adverse effect on the physical, mental or cognitive condition of a person.

It is not clear to the authors why *cognitive condition* is identified separately in the ISO 45001 definition since cognition is a mental process. The relevant definitions from the Oxford Dictionary of English (ODE[8]) are

mental *relating to the mind*
cognitive *relating to cognition*
cognition *the mental action or process of acquiring knowledge and understanding through thought, experience, and the senses*
emotional *instinctive or intuitive feeling as distinguished from reasoning or knowledge*

Using 'emotional or cognitive' in the ISO 45001 definition would make more sense. However, it can be argued that 'physical or mental' would have been adequate.

ISO 45003 uses the ISO 45001 definition of injury and ill health. However, although *well-being at work* is defined, there is no separate definition of well-being. *Well-being at work* is discussed in Chapter 11 'The psychosocial management system terminology'. The term 'wellness' does not occur in ISO 45003.

It is possible that ISO 45003 would be improved by providing a definition of well-being and a note on how well-being differs from wellness.

Note

i Organisations that provide their workers with uniforms may already have data available on workers' waist measurements.

References

1   British Standards Institution. *Occupational health and safety management systems – Requirements with guidance for use*, BSI ISO 45001, 2018. BSI 2018.
2   World Health Organisation. *International Classification of Diseases* 11th Revision. WHO 2022. Available online at https://icd.who.int/en. Last accessed 21 November 2023.
3   www.bhf.org.uk/informationsupport/risk-factors/obesity. Last accessed 26 January 2024.
4   www.nhs.uk/live-well/healthy-weight/bmi-calculator/. Last accessed 26 January 2024.
5   British Standards Institution. *Occupational health and safety management systems – General guidelines for the implementation of ISO 45001:2018*, BSI ISO 45002, 2023. BSI 2023.
6   https://monitormyhealth.org.uk/our-purpose. Last accessed 26 January 2024.
7   British Standards Institution. *Occupational health and safety management – Psychological health and safety at work – Guidelines for managing psychosocial risks*, BSI ISO 45003, 2021. BSI 2021.
8   MobiSystems, Inc. *Oxford Dictionary*, version 15.8. Last accessed 17 January 2024

4 The disorders

Crash course

Since well-being and wellness are, respectively, sub-clinical forms of mental and physical ill health, that is, mental and physical disorders, you may have to explain key points about these disorders to workers and interested parties. This chapter provides the necessary information about the disorders that are of particular relevance to psychosocial risk management, that is:

Well-being – depression, anxiety, stress, panic, and fatigue.
Wellness – obesity, blood disorders, cardiac disorders, and loss of lung function.

There are various definitions of these disorders, and each disorder has a characteristic set of symptoms. There are also various ways of measuring the severity of these disorders and different ways of treating them.

Introduction

As was seen in Chapter 3, reduced well-being is typically a sub-clinical occurrence of a mental disorder, for example, 'feeling low' is a sub-clinical occurrence of depression. Similarly, reduced wellness is typically a sub-clinical occurrence of a physical disorder, for example, being overweight is a sub-clinical occurrence of obesity.

Since this is the case, you may have to explain to workers and interested parties key points about these disorders. This chapter provides the necessary information about the disorders that are of particular relevance to psychosocial risk management, that is:

Well-being – depression, anxiety, stress, panic, and fatigue.
Wellness – obesity, blood disorders, cardiac disorders, and loss of lung function.

The next two sections deal with the main well-being disorders and the main wellness disorders.

DOI: 10.4324/9781003490555-5

Well-being disorders

The well-being disorders dealt with in this section are depression, anxiety, stress, panic, and fatigue. For each of the disorders, there is the following information.

The dictionary definition of the disorder. This is the sort of definition that most individuals will use for their understanding of the disorder. The Oxford Dictionary of English (ODE)[1] definitions have been used for illustration, with definitions from other dictionaries where appropriate.

The medical definitions of the disorder. These are the technical definitions used by medical and other professionals. These definitions are expressed in ways that enable the disorder to be measured and treated.

The symptoms of the disorder. Each of the disorders has a number of effects on an individual's behaviour and feelings and these effects are known as symptoms. The pattern of symptoms is characteristic of the disorder, but there are major overlaps with different disorders having the same symptom.

How the disorder is measured. The main methods of measurement use checklists of symptoms, and individuals are rated on whether, and to what extent, they are suffering from each of these symptoms. Some of the checklists are designed for use by the individuals themselves – usually described as self-reporting – and other checklists are designed for use by medical professionals who interview and observe the individual and complete the checklist based on their findings.

How the disorder is treated. Treatment options depend on the nature and severity of the symptom. However, typical treatments for psychosocial disorders include medication and so-called 'talking treatments' such as cognitive behavioural therapy (CBT). The last section of this chapter is a summary of the main talking therapies.

Depression

Dictionary definitions

The ODE defines depression as *feelings of severe despondency and dejection*. This only helps if you know what despondency and dejection mean. They are defined as follows:

despondency – *low spirits from loss of hope or courage: dejection.*
dejection – *a sad and depressed state; low spirits.*

This is all a bit circular. However, the overall impression is that depression is sadness and low spirits. This is confirmed by other dictionaries, for example

feelings of severe despondency and dejection

(Cambridge).[2]

a state of feeling sad: low spirits

(Merriam-Webster).[3]

Medical definitions

Medical definitions of depression are expressed in terms of the main symptoms. Two examples are given below:

> *Depression is a common illness characterized by persistent sadness and a loss of interest in activities that one normally enjoys, accompanied by an inability to carry out daily activities, for at least two weeks. Other symptoms include loss of energy; change in appetite; sleeping more/less; anxiety; reduced concentration; indecisiveness; restlessness; feelings of worthlessness, guilt or hopelessness; and thoughts of self-harm or even committing suicide.*

(WHO).[4]

> *Depression is extreme sadness or despair that lasts more than days. It interferes with the activities of daily life and can cause physical symptoms such as pain, weight loss or gain, sleeping pattern disruptions, or lack of energy. People with depression may also experience an inability to concentrate, feelings of worthlessness or excessive guilt, and recurrent thoughts of death or suicide.*

(American Psychological Association).[5]

However, there are more detailed lists of symptoms of depression available, and a sample list is given in the next subsection.

Symptoms

There are numerous classifications and listings of the symptoms of depression and a typical example taken from the website of the UK's National Health Service[6] is reproduced below.

Psychological symptoms
The psychological symptoms of depression include:

- *continuous low mood or sadness*
- *feeling hopeless and helpless*
- *having low self-esteem*
- *feeling tearful*
- *feeling guilt-ridden*
- *feeling irritable and intolerant of others*
- *having no motivation or interest in things*
- *finding it difficult to make decisions*
- *not getting any enjoyment out of life*

- *feeling anxious or worried*
- *having suicidal thoughts or thoughts of harming yourself.*

Physical symptoms
The physical symptoms of depression include:

- *moving or speaking more slowly than usual*
- *changes in appetite or weight (usually decreased, but sometimes increased)*
- *constipation*
- *unexplained aches and pains*
- *lack of energy*
- *low sex drive*
- *changes to menstrual cycle*
- *disturbed sleep – for example, finding it difficult to fall asleep at night or waking up very early in the morning.*

Social symptoms
The social symptoms of depression include:

- *avoiding contact with friends and taking part in fewer social activities*
- *neglecting hobbies and interests*
- *having difficulties in home, work or family life.*

It can be seen from this list that the various symptoms are all measurable, although a range of techniques will be required. These techniques are discussed in the next subsection.

Measurement

The principles behind measuring depression are straightforward.

Decide on which symptoms you are going to include in your measuring instrument.
Devise a numerical scale for each symptom, for example, 0–5, with a low score being 'good'.
Measure an individual on each of your scales.
Add the individual's scores on all of your scales to give an overall measure of their depression.

However, there are – as might be expected – many complications associated with this approach. The main ones are as follows:

Which symptoms to include in a particular measuring instrument. Different researchers and clinicians will have different views on which are the important symptoms to include. This has led to a range of measuring instruments being developed, and some of these are described later in this subsection.

How the data should be collected. There are two main options – self-report and collection by relevant professionals such as medical researchers, clinical psychologists, and psychiatrists. Self-report instruments range from simple questionnaires that are available online for you to check your own level of depression to detailed questionnaires that require some time to fill in. Collection by relevant professionals involves the professional interviewing and observing the individual being measured and either completing a detailed questionnaire similar to those used for self-report or preparing a free-format report. Examples of instruments using these various data collection techniques are described later in this subsection.

What the 'scores' mean in practice. In general, low scores indicate no depression or mild depression, and very high scores indicate severe depression. However, there is often a debate about where the boundaries are between one level of depression and another. In addition, since all the measuring instruments rely, to some extent, on self-reporting, they rely on individuals being self-aware and truthful.

Whether depression should be measured in isolation. Depressed individuals are often suffering from other disorders such as anxiety. There is, therefore, an argument to be made for having multidimensional measuring instruments for psychological health, and examples of these measuring instruments are given later in this chapter.

Despite these complications, measuring instruments for depression are widely used and the list below contains examples, with brief notes on their nature and use.

Beck Depression Inventory (BDI).[7] This is a detailed self-report measuring instrument that can also be self-scored. However, it has to be purchased.

Center for Epidemiologic Studies Depression Scale (CES-D).[8] This is in the public domain and no permission is required for its use. The instructions for its use are directed at an interviewer, but it could be used and self-scored by individuals. The CES-D 20 is reproduced in Table 4.1, and there is also a ten-scale version.

Hamilton Depression Rating Scale.[9] This is also in the public domain and no permission is required for use. However, the instructions for use include *To be administered by a health care professional.*

Montgomery-Åsberg Depression Rating Scale.[10] This is also in the public domain and the *rating is based on a clinical interview*. There are guidance notes for the interviewer.

All of the instruments listed above are questionnaire based, but there is another approach that does not use questionnaires. This approach involves competent assessors investigating an individual's state with regard to depression and related conditions. This is described in, for example, the UK's National Institute for Health and Care Excellence (NICE): *Depression in adults: Recognition and management Clinical guideline* (NICE 222).[11]

Table 4.1 Center for Epidemiologic Studies Depression Scale (CES-D 20)

0 = Rarely or none of the time (< 1 day) 1 = Some or a little of the time (1–2 days) 2 = Occasionally or a moderate amount of time (3–4 days) 3 = Most or all of the time (5–7 days)				
During the Past Week	*0*	*1*	*2*	*3*
1 I was bothered by things that usually don't bother me.				
2 I did not feel like eating; my appetite was poor.				
3 I felt that I could not shake off the blues even with help from my family or friends.				
4 I felt I was just as good as other people.				
5 I had trouble keeping my mind on what I was doing.				
6 I felt depressed.				
7 I felt that everything I did was an effort.				
8 I felt hopeful about the future.				
9 I thought my life had been a failure.				
10 I felt fearful.				
11 My sleep was restless.				
12 I was happy.				
13 I talked less than usual.				
14 I felt lonely.				
15 People were unfriendly.				
16 I enjoyed life.				
17 I had crying spells.				
18 I felt sad.				
19 I felt that people dislike me.				
20 I could not get 'going'.				

SCORING: 0 for answers in the first column, 1 for answers in the second column, 2 for answers in the third column, 3 for answers in the fourth column. The scoring of positive items is reversed. Possible range of scores is 0–60, with the higher scores indicating the presence of more symptomatology. A score of 16 or higher is the start of the *mild depression* range.

Source: cesd-r.com

Treatment

The recommended treatments for depression vary according to the severity of the depression. The main options for the mild, moderate, and severe depressions just described are given next.

MILD DEPRESSION

Watchful waiting. Many cases of mild depression 'clear up' without any treatment. However, they should be monitored by an appropriate medical professional, such as a general practitioner, who does the watchful waiting to check that the depression is clearing up.

Exercise. Various types of exercise can help depression, including walking and gardening, and exercising in groups may be more effective than exercising alone.

Talking about depression. Talking to friends, relatives, or colleagues about the symptoms being experienced can help with mild depression and, as with exercise, group activity may be more effective than one-to-one conversations.

Online resources. There is a wide range of online resources available for help with depression. These include the following:

Online support groups. These may be specific mental health support groups or more general social media groups. The specific mental health support groups generally have a higher level of content moderation and for this reason they are the preferred option.

Chatbots. There are artificial intelligence-based computer programs that are designed to hold conversations with human beings, and there are chatbots specifically intended to help with mental health problems. Some people are more willing to give detailed information about how they feel when they know they are not talking to a 'real person'.

Apps. There are various apps that are designed to help with mental health. They can cover general mental health, for example, *Moodfit*,[12] or be specific to a mental health topic, for example, the *Depression Self-help Guide*.[13]

MODERATE DEPRESSION

There are two options for the treatment of moderate depression.

Talking treatments. These include counselling by a counsellor with the relevant competences and CBT. These treatments can be conducted online or face-to-face. Because these two treatments can be used to treat all of the disorders described in this chapter, they are described in detail in a separate section at the end of this chapter, together with the other main talking therapies.

Medication. The most usual type of medication is one of the many types of anti-depressant. Typically, these medicines are prescribed by general practice medical professionals.

At the upper end of the moderate depression scale a combination of talking therapies and medication may be used.

SEVERE DEPRESSION

Treatment for severe depression is an extension of the combined treatments used at the upper end of the moderate depression scale. The main differences are as follows.

A wider range of talking therapies may be used, including interpersonal therapy (IPT) and psychotherapy.

Stronger antidepressants are used. The use of these is avoided for moderate depression because of their potential for adverse side effects.

Treatment may be carried out by a team of professionals. This team will include those responsible for prescribing the medication and delivering the talking treatments, with assistance from psychiatric nurses and additional therapists such as physiotherapists and occupational therapists.

Anxiety

Dictionary definitions

The ODE defines anxiety as *a feeling of worry, nervousness, or unease about something with an uncertain outcome.* However, it can be argued that an individual can be anxious about something that has a certain outcome – not just something that is uncertain. This view is confirmed by definitions from other dictionaries, for example

> *an uncomfortable feeling of nervousness or worry about something that is happening or might happen in the future*
>
> (Cambridge)

> *apprehensive uneasiness or nervousness usually over an impending or anticipated ill*
>
> (Merriam-Webster)

Medical definitions

In medical terminology, there are various *anxiety disorders* that are characterised by fear, worry, or nervousness. These include panic disorder (which is discussed in a later section of this chapter), various phobias, and generalised anxiety disorder (GAD), which is the subject of the present section.

As with other disorders, medical definitions of GAD concentrate on the symptoms. For example, the Mayo Clinic defines GAD as *excessive, ongoing anxiety and worry that can interfere with your daily activities.*[14] The Mayo Clinic also gives a detailed list of possible symptoms, and this list is reproduced in the next subsection.

Symptoms

The Mayo Clinic[15] provides separate lists of examples of psychological and physical symptoms as follows.

Psychological symptoms

- *Persistent worrying or anxiety about a number of areas that are out of proportion to the impact of the events*

- *Overthinking plans and solutions to all possible worst-case outcomes*
- *Perceiving situations and events as threatening, even when they aren't*
- *Difficulty handling uncertainty*
- *Indecisiveness and fear of making the wrong decision*
- *Inability to set aside or let go of a worry*
- *Inability to relax, feeling restless, and feeling keyed up or on edge*
- *Difficulty concentrating, or the feeling that your mind 'goes blank'*

Physical symptoms

- *Fatigue*
- *Trouble sleeping*
- *Muscle tension or muscle aches*
- *Trembling, feeling twitchy*
- *Nervousness or being easily startled*
- *Sweating*
- *Nausea, diarrhoea or irritable bowel syndrome*
- *Irritability*

Measurement

Measurement of the severity of GAD uses similar techniques to those described earlier for measuring depression, and the same caveats apply. A frequently used instrument for measuring GAD is the *Generalised Anxiety Disorder Assessment (GAD-7)*.[16] This is a seven-item instrument – hence GAD-7 – and each item asks the individual to rate the severity of their symptoms over the past two weeks. The instrument is reproduced in Table 4.2.

The scoring scheme for the GAD-7 is reproduced in Table 4.3.

Table 4.2 GAD-7 measuring instrument

0 = Not at all; 1= Several days; 2 = More than half the days; 3 = Nearly every day				
Over the *last 2 weeks*, how often have you been bothered by the following problems?	*0*	*1*	*2*	*3*
1 Feeling nervous, anxious, or on edge				
2 Not being able to stop or control worrying				
3 Worrying too much about different things				
4 Trouble relaxing				
5 Being so restless that it is hard to sit still				
6 Becoming easily annoyed or irritable				
7 Feeling afraid as if something awful might happen				

Source: www.cgakit.com

Table 4.3 GADS-7 scoring scheme

Score	Anxiety severity
0–4	None – Minimal
5–9	Mild
10–14	Moderate
15–21	Severe

Source: www.cgakit.com

There are other instruments for measuring anxiety, and an online search will produce numerous examples.

Treatment

There are various self-help treatments for GAD, and people suffering from milder forms can be taught various techniques such as using a CBT workbook and relaxation. With more severe symptoms, as with severe depression, assistance from a range of specialists will be required.

Medication for GAD include some antidepressants, but anticonvulsants and sedatives are also used in some circumstances.

Stress

Dictionary definitions

The ODE defines stress as *a state of mental or emotional strain or tension resulting from adverse or demanding circumstances.* However, stress is also *something that causes a state of strain or tension.* This dual use of the word stress occurs in other dictionaries, for example,

> *great worry caused by a difficult situation or something that causes this disorder*
> (Cambridge)

> *a physical, chemical, or emotional factor that causes bodily or mental tension and may be a factor in disease causation: a state resulting from a stress especially one of bodily or mental tension resulting from factors that tend to alter an existent equilibrium*
> (Merriam-Webster)

To avoid confusion, in this book *stress* will be used to mean the mental or emotional state, and *stressor* will be used to mean the factor that causes the mental or emotional state. This usage occurs in medical definition of stress, as will be seen in the next section.

Medical definitions

Medical definitions of stress tend to be similar to the dictionary definitions, and they can be summed up as the physiological or psychological response to internal or external stressors. However, the detail in the various definitions makes one or more of the following points about stress.

Small amounts of stress may be beneficial as a motivator.

Stress can be a one-off occurrence when a severe stressor produces the so-called *fight or flight* response. This type of acute stress can be a health and safety hazard, but it is not usually a psychosocial hazard, and it is not dealt with in this section.

Long-term exposure to stressors results in the chronic stress response, and these exposures create a wide range of symptoms as described in the next subsection.

Symptoms

As with depression and anxiety, there are numerous classifications and listings of the symptoms of chronic stress. The example reproduced below is taken from the website of the UK's National Health Service.[17]

Physical symptoms

- *headaches or dizziness*
- *muscle tension or pain*
- *stomach problems*
- *chest pain or a faster heartbeat*
- *sexual problems*

Mental symptoms

- *difficulty concentrating*
- *struggling to make decisions*
- *feeling overwhelmed*
- *constantly worrying*
- *being forgetful*

Changes in behaviour

- *being irritable and snappy*
- *sleeping too much or too little*
- *eating too much or too little*
- *avoiding certain places or people*
- *drinking or smoking more.*

Measurement

As with depression and anxiety, there are various self-report measures of stress, many of them freely available online. A typical example, the Perceived Stress Scale, is a ten-point scale that asks questions about an individual's reactions in the previous month. Items on the scale cover control, personal problems, and anger. Copies of the full scale are available on the internet, as are various other self-report measures of stress.

Treatment

Chronic stress can be caused by a clearly identifiable stressor, and in these circumstances, the preferred option is to tackle the stressor. For example, if a person is suffering chronic stress because of too high workloads or too tight deadlines, reorganising what has to be done and when can remove the stressor.

When stressors cannot be removed, the various self-help activities, including mindfulness and contact with the natural world, can be used to manage the symptoms. In addition, the talking treatments such as CBT can be used to treat chronic stress.

There are no specific medical treatments for chronic stress, but medication is used to deal with symptoms such as difficulty sleeping and digestive disorders.

Panic

Dictionary definitions

The ODE defines panic as a *sudden uncontrollable fear or anxiety, often causing wildly unthinking behaviour* and a panic attack as *a sudden overwhelming feeling of acute and disabling anxiety.* Other definitions of panic include

a sudden strong feeling of fear that prevents reasonable thought and action
(Cambridge)

a sudden overpowering fright
(Merriam-Webster)

Panic attacks that occur in response to a frightening event are not a mental disorder, they are a natural, if unhelpful, reaction. Panic attacks that occur repeatedly and in the absence of frightening events are what constitute panic disorder.

Medical definitions

The American Psychological Association's definition of a panic attack is *a sudden surge of overwhelming fear that comes without warning and without any obvious reason.*[18]

Symptoms

The example of panic disorder symptoms reproduced below is taken from the website of the UK's National Health Service.[19] However, there are many variants of the list of panic disorder symptoms.

Symptoms include:

Physical symptoms

- *faster, irregular or more noticeable heartbeat*
- *feeling lightheaded and dizzy*
- *headaches*
- *chest pains*
- *loss of appetite*
- *sweating*
- *breathlessness*
- *feeling hot*
- *shaking*

Mental symptoms

- *feeling tense or nervous*
- *being unable to relax*
- *worrying about the past or future*
- *feeling tearful*
- *not being able to sleep*
- *difficulty concentrating*
- *fear of the worst happening*
- *intrusive traumatic memories*
- *obsessive thoughts*

Measurement

As with the disorders already described, there are various measurement techniques for panic disorder. One of the American Psychological Association questionnaires has the following ten items.[20]

During the PAST 7 DAYS, I have...

1. *felt moments of sudden terror, fear or fright, sometimes out of the blue (i.e., a panic attack)*
2. *felt anxious, worried, or nervous about having more panic attacks*
3. *had thoughts of losing control, dying, going crazy, or other bad things happening because of panic attacks*
4. *felt a racing heart, sweaty, trouble breathing, faint, or shaky*

5. *felt tense muscles, felt on edge or restless, or had trouble relaxing or trouble sleeping*
6. *avoided, or did not approach or enter, situations in which panic attacks might occur*
7. *left situations early, or participated only minimally, because of panic attacks*
8. *spent a lot of time preparing for, or procrastinating about (putting off), situations in which panic attacks might occur*
9. *distracted myself to avoid thinking about panic attacks*
10. *needed help to cope with panic attacks (e.g., alcohol or medication, superstitious objects, other people)*

There is a scoring system used with this questionnaire that is similar to the ones used for the questionnaires described in earlier sections.

Treatment

The treatments for panic disorder are similar to those for anxiety. For example, mild panic disorder is treated with self-help tools such as online CBT, while severe panic disorder requires medication and interventions by a range of medical professionals.

Fatigue

Dictionary definitions

The ODE defines fatigue as *extreme tiredness resulting from mental or physical exertion or illness.* Other definitions include

extreme tiredness

(Cambridge)

weariness or exhaustion from labor, exertion, or stress

(Merriam Webster)

Medical definitions

The medical definitions of fatigue are very similar to the dictionary definitions.

Symptoms

Fatigue is often discussed in health and safety because it is a causal factor in errors and accidents. Great Britain's Health and Safety Executive lists the following effects of fatigue[21]:

slower reactions
reduced ability to process information

memory lapses
absent-mindedness
decreased awareness
lack of attention
underestimation of risk
reduced coordination.

However, fatigue also has symptoms of less relevance to errors and accidents, including,

Headaches and dizziness
Sore muscles and muscle weakness
Irritability
Apathy

Measurement

There are three ways of measuring fatigue.

Behavioural. For example, by measuring error rates, reaction times, and attention span.

Physiological. For example, measuring blood sugar levels and brain activity (using an electroencephalogram (ECG).

Psychological. There are numerous checklists for measuring fatigue, and they are in the same format, and used in the same ways, as the checklists already described for measuring such things as stress and anxiety. There is a high degree of similarity, and some overlap, among these checklists but one of them, the *Fatigue assessment scale,*[i] copies of which are widely available on the internet, has ten items. Users of the scale rate each item from 1 – *Never* to 5 – *Always*.

I am bothered by fatigue
I get tired very quickly
I don't do much during the day
I have enough energy for everyday life
Physically, I feel exhausted
I have problems starting things
I have problems thinking clearly
I have no desire to do anything
Mentally, I feel exhausted
When I'm doing something I can concentrate quite well

Treatment

The appropriate treatment for fatigue will depend on its causes. Fatigue caused by physical ill health, such as thyroid problems, is treated by medical professionals, as is fatigue caused by mental ill health. However, fatigue caused by impaired well-being or wellness can be treated with lifestyle changes. For example, adopting a healthier diet, drinking less alcohol, taking more exercise, and dealing with poor patterns of sleep.

Multi-disorder measures

There are many measuring instruments that use a single set of questions or statements to measure two or more of the disorders described so far, and some of these instruments also measure disorders other than the ones described so far.

The multi-disorder measuring instrument are of two types – those for use by relevant professionals during interviews and those primarily intended for self-reporting. Examples of both types can be found on the internet.

Wellness disorders

The wellness disorders dealt with in this section are obesity, blood disorders, cardiac disorder, and loss of lung function. These are a small subset of the possible wellness disorders, but they are dealt with here because they are the ones that can be measured by the individual concerned, and where self-help improvement actions are possible.

Obesity

Medical definitions

The World Health Organization[22] gives the following definitions.

A body mass index (BMI) over 25 is considered overweight, and over 30 is obese.

How BMI is measured is described in a later subsection.

However, people who are very muscular may have a high BMI but very little fat. For this reason, waist size or circumference is also used. The British Heart Foundation[23] information on waist circumference was given in chapter 3, but it is repeated below for ease of reference.

The recommended waist measurements are:

- *below 37 inches (94cm) for men*
- *below 31.5 inches (80cm) for women.*

People with waist sizes bigger than these are more likely to develop certain health problems, such as type 2 diabetes, high blood pressure, heart disease and stroke.

Adults from certain ethnic backgrounds, including South Asian, Chinese, other Asian, Middle Eastern, Black African or African-Caribbean, with waist sizes higher than 90cm for men and 80cm for women are at greater risk of developing ... health problems.

Effects

Obesity has obvious effects such as reduced mobility; however long-term obesity can have severe mental and physical ill effects. Mental ill effects include lowered self-esteem and depression, and physical ill effects include diabetes, cardiac problems, strokes, and breast and bowel cancer.

Measurement

Waist circumference is simply measured using a tape measure, but body mass index (BMI) calculation is more complex.

BMI is a number calculated using an individual's weight and height. This can be done using a BMI chart that has weight on one axis and height on the other axis, and individuals check their BMI by identifying the point on the chart where their weight and height measures cross. Examples of BMI charts are freely available on the internet.

However, these charts do not take into account individual differences, such as gender, age, and ethnicity. A more accurate measure of BMI can be obtained by using an online BMI calculator, such as the one provided by the UK's National Health Service.[24]

Treatment

In general, obesity is caused by taking in more energy than is used, typically by eating and drinking too much and not doing enough exercise. Initial treatments for obesity, therefore, focus on restoring the input–output balance. These may be self-help treatments, or assisted by support groups or dietary and exercise specialists. Other types of treatment include the following:

Prescribing orlistat – this is a lipase inhibitor, that is, it reduces the absorption of dietary fat which reduces energy intake.
Prescribing other weight loss medications that operate by making the person who takes them feel full.
Weight-loss surgery – also known as bariatric or metabolic surgery. There are two main types.

Surgery intended to reduce the capacity for food intake, for example, putting bands around the stomach (gastric bands) or removing part of the stomach (sleeve gastrectomy).
Surgery to remove fat (liposuction) – usually from around the abdomen.

Blood disorders

There are two blood disorders to consider: low levels of oxygen in the blood and high and low levels of sugar in the blood.

Blood oxygen level

Oxygen in the bloodstream is essential for life, and a reduced level of oxygen in the bloodstream impairs wellness. Blood oxygen level is measured using an oximeter. This is a small device that clips over the end of a finger and measures the oxygen level in the individual's blood, and their heart rate. There is an optimum level for blood oxygen, and the oximeter reading is the percentage of this optimum level. A reading over 95% shows a healthy level of blood oxygen.

Symptoms of low blood oxygen level include shortness of breath, chest pains, confusion, headaches, and a rapid pulse. Self-help methods for improving blood oxygen level include breathing exercises, taking a walk outside, improving ventilation, regular exercise, and having a well-balanced diet.

Blood sugar level

Too high a sugar level in the blood, or too low a level, reduces wellness, and for people with diseases such as diabetes it can be a life-threatening disorder.

Common symptoms of high blood sugar levels include the following:

Feeling very thirsty
Urinating a lot
Feeling weak or tired
Blurred vision
Losing weight

Common symptoms of low blood sugar levels include the following:

Sweating
Feeling tired
Dizziness
Feeling hungry
Tingling lips
Feeling shaky or trembling
A fast or pounding heartbeat (palpitations)
Becoming easily irritated, tearful, anxious, or moody
Turning pale

There are two methods that can be used to measure blood sugar level. The first involves pricking a finger to produce a drop of blood for testing; the second, less accurate, method is a meter held next to the skin. Irrespective of the method used, the result is the concentration of glucose in the blood expressed in millimoles per litre (mmol/l). There are good reasons for using this generally unfamiliar measure, but there is no need to go into the complexities. All that you needed to know is that the healthy range is a blood glucose level between 4 mmol/l and 7 mmol/l. Less than 4 mmol/l is considered hypoglycaemia and greater than 7 mmol/l is considered hyperglycaemia. Diabetes is a common cause of hyperglycaemia.

Treatments for unhealthy levels of blood sugar range from exercise and a well-balanced diet for mild disorders to medical interventions for severe disorders, for example, insulin injections for diabetes.

Cardiac disorders

There are two cardiac disorders to consider: heart rate and blood pressure.

Heart rate

A healthy resting heart rate, or pulse rate, for an adult is a steady beat at between 60 and 100 beats per minute. The three disorders associated with heart rate that can be self-diagnosed without specialised equipment are as follows:

An irregular pulse (arrhythmia). This can be dangerous if it results in blood not being properly pumped around the body.
Too fast a heart rate (tachycardia). This can result in fainting, feeling very tired, dizziness, or palpitations.
Too slow a heart rate (bradycardia). This can also result in fainting and feeling very tired. Note that people who are very fit, for example, professional athletes, can have very slow resting heart rates – down to 40 per minute in some cases.

The problem with heart rate is that there may be no obvious symptoms, so regular measurement is required to detect problems at an early stage. All three disorders, arrhythmia, tachycardia, and bradycardia, require medical intervention to determine the causes and identify appropriate treatments.

Blood pressure

There are two measures of blood pressure:

Systolic blood pressure. This is the pressure when your heart beats and pushes blood through your arteries.
Diastolic blood pressure. This is the pressure when your heart rests between beats.

Blood pressure is measured using a monitoring machine, and the units of pressure are millimetres of mercury (mmHg).[ii] The two pressures are usually quoted together as, for example, 140 over 90 mmHg or just 140/90. By convention, the systolic pressure is given first and the diastolic pressure second.[iii]

Healthy blood pressure values are between 90/60 mmHg and 120/80 mmHg. High blood pressure is 140/90 mmHg or higher, and low blood pressure is less than 90/60 mmHg. High blood pressure is more common than low blood pressure.

As with heart rate, there may be no obvious symptoms of high or low blood pressure, so that regular monitoring is required if problems are to be detected at an early stage. Both high and low blood pressure require medical intervention to determine the causes and identify appropriate treatments.

Loss of lung function

An important job the lungs do is to get oxygen into the bloodstream, and one of the causes of low blood oxygen level is poor lung function. There are various ways of measuring lung function but the simplest is to measure how strongly an individual can breathe out (exhale). This is known as the 'peak flow,' and there are simple devices for measuring this, known as spirometers. The person being tested exhales into the spirometer as hard as they can, and this measures the strength of their breathing out.

Other tests include lung volume tests that measure how well the lungs expand with each breath, and whether they empty normally, and gas transfer tests measure how well the lungs extract oxygen from the air.

Loss of lung function can cause a range of problems including trouble with breathing, shortness of breath, decreased ability to exercise, a persistent cough, and discomfort when breathing in or out.

If an individual's peak flow is too low, they can use a breathing exercise machine to improve their lung function, but medical intervention is required to determine the causes of the loss of function and identify appropriate treatments.

The main talking therapies

As was pointed out in the *Treatment* sections earlier in this chapter, talking therapies are used for a range of disorders, and to avoid repetition this separate section briefly describes the main talking therapies.

Cognitive behavioural therapy

CBT aims to help individuals understand their thoughts and behaviours, and how these affect them. While CBT recognises that events in an individual's past may have shaped them, it concentrates on how the individual can change the way they think, feel, and behave in the present. This is done by teaching the individual how to overcome negative thoughts.

A typical course of CBT consists of 5 to 20 weekly sessions with a therapist, with each session lasting 30 to 60 minutes. However, group CBT and online CBT are also available.

Cognitive therapy, which helps individuals learn how to manage their thoughts and how their thoughts make them feel, is also available.

Interpersonal therapy

IPT focuses on an individual's relationships with others and the problems they may be having in their relationships, such as difficulties with communication or coping with bereavement.

Psychoanalysis

Psychoanalysis, also known as psychodynamic psychotherapy or psychoanalytic psychotherapy, is the classic free association talking therapy. A psychoanalyst encourages individuals to say whatever is going through their mind in the hope that this will help them become aware of hidden meanings or patterns in what they do or say that may be contributing to their problems.

Counselling

Counselling helps individuals think about the problems they are experiencing in ways that enable them to find new ways of dealing with these problems.

Counsellors support individuals and offer practical advice, but they do not tell individuals what to do. Counselling is useful for individuals who need help coping with a current crisis, such as anger, bereavement, redundancy, or relationship issues.

Mindfulness-based cognitive therapy

Mindfulness-based therapies help individuals focus on their thoughts and feelings as they happen, moment by moment. Mindfulness-based cognitive therapy (MBCT) combines mindfulness techniques such as meditation and breathing exercises with cognitive therapy.

Notes

i   Published by the World Association for Sarcodosis and Other Granniomarous Disorders. Sarcodosis is a disease involving abnormal collections of inflammatory cells that form lumps known as granulomata.

ii Hg is the chemical symbol for mercury. It is Hg because the Latin name for mercury is hydrargyrum – literally, liquid silver. Mercury is also known as quicksilver.

iii There are also instruments available for measuring other aspects of cardiac function. For example, monitors that enable you to check for atrial fibrillation.

References

1 MobiSystems, Inc. *Oxford Dictionary*, version 15.8. Last accessed 17 January 2024.

2 https://dictionary.cambridge.org. Last accessed 17 January 2024.

3 www.merriam-webster.com. Last accessed 17 January 2024.

4 www.who.int/india/health-topics/depression. Last accessed 24 January 2024.

5 www.apa.org/topics/depression. Last accessed 24 January 2024.

6 www.nhs.uk/mental-health/conditions/depression-in-adults/symptoms/. Last accessed 24 January 2024.

7 www.apa.org/pi/about/publications/caregivers/practice-settings/assessment/tools/beck-depression. Last accessed 25 January 2024.

8 www.apa.org/depression-guideline/epidemiologic-studies-scale.pdf. Last accessed 27 January 2024.

9 www.apa.org/depression-guideline/hamilton-rating-scale.pdf. Last accessed 27 January 2024.

10 www.apa.org/depression-guideline/montgomery-asberg-scale.pdf. Last accessed 25 January 2024.

11 www.nice.org.uk/guidance/ng222. Last accessed 27 January 2024.

12 Robie Ridge Software, *Moodfit*, version 2.37. Last accessed 27 January 2024.

13 www.nhsinform.scot/illnesses-and-conditions/mental-health/mental-health-self-help-guides/depression-self-help-guide/. Last accessed 27 January 2024.

14 www.mayoclinic.org/diseases-conditions/search-results?q=GAD. Last accessed 27 January 2024.

15 www.mayoclinic.org/diseases-conditions/generalized-anxiety-disorder/symptoms-causes/syc-20360803. Last accessed 27 January 2024.

16 Spitzer RL, Kroenke K, Williams JB, et al; *A brief measure for assessing generalized anxiety disorder: the GAD-7*. Archives of Internal Medicine. 2006. Available online at https://patient.info/doctor/generalised-anxiety-disorder-assessment-gad-7. Last accessed 27 January 2024.

17 www.nhs.uk/mental-health/feelings-symptoms-behaviours/feelings-and-symptoms/stress/. Last accessed 27 January 2024d.

18 www.apa.org/topics/anxiety/panic-disorder. Last accessed 28 January 2024.

19 www.nhs.uk/mental-health/feelings-symptoms-behaviours/feelings-and-symptoms/anxiety-fear-panic/. Last accessed 28 January 2024.

20 www.psychiatry.org/File%20Library/Psychiatrists/Practice/DSM/APA_DSM5_Severity-Measure-For-Panic-Disorder-Adult.pdf. Last accessed 28 January 2024.

21 www.hse.gov.uk/humanfactors/topics/fatigue.htm. Last accessed 28 January 2024.

22 www.who.int/health-topics/obesity/#tab=tab_1. Last accessed 28 January 2024.

23 www.bhf.org.uk/informationsupport/risk-factors/obesity. Last accessed 28 January 2024.

24 www.nhs.uk/live-well/healthy-weight/bmi-calculator/. Last accessed 28 January 2024.

5 The hazards and risk sources

Crash course

Your workers and interested parties will be familiar with the idea of hazards and how hazards can cause injury and ill health. However, you will have to explain to them that the effects of hazards on well-being and wellness are now going to be taken into account. You will also have to explain how your organisation is going to define psychosocial hazards.

Hazards are classified in various ways, but for the purposes of psychosocial risk management, you need classifications that include well-being hazards such as discrimination and overwork, and wellness hazards such as sedentary work and lack of sleep.

For the majority of psychosocial hazards, the extent of their effect on individuals depends on the dose the individuals receive. This means that these hazards must be treated in similar ways to the ways in which noise and chemicals in the atmosphere are treated in traditional health and safety.

ISO 45003[1] uses the terms *hazards of a psychosocial nature* and *psychosocial hazards* without defining either term. It appears that in ISO 45003, these terms are synonymous.

The *hazards of a psychosocial nature* in ISO 45003 are divided into three categories: *aspects of work organization, social factors at work*, and *work environment, equipment, and hazardous tasks*. Examples of each category are given in three tables in ISO 45003, and these tables are reproduced as Tables 5.2, 5.3, and 5.4 in the body of this chapter.

The ISO 45003 lists are extensive, but they do not take into account the fact that various categories of workers' behaviour can have a detrimental effect on other workers' well-being and wellness. For the purposes of this book, these categories are referred to as 'prohibited behaviours' and, in addition to discrimination and victimisation, they are as follows.

Illegal activities. These include theft, fraud, bribery, and damaging property.
Activities that breach contractual arrangements. These include poor timekeeping, taking unauthorised leave, not following reasonable instructions, and disclosure of confidential information.

DOI: 10.4324/9781003490555-6

Nonconformity with an organisation's procedures and work instructions.

In addition, ISO 45003 does not take into account the effects of the absence of various categories of workers' behaviour that can have a detrimental effect on other workers' well-being, and for the purposes of this book, these are referred to as 'required behaviours'. Required behaviours include using appropriate management styles and treating fellow workers with respect.

ISO 45003 is also restricted to well-being hazards – there is no consideration of wellness hazards.

In addition to these limitations, ISO 45001[2] and ISO 45003 assume that the various hazards of a psychosocial nature have, by definition, only negative effects. This is not the case, and redundancy is used in this chapter to explain why this is so. Because hazards of a psychosocial nature can have beneficial effects, they are better referred to as risk sources, the term used in business risk management systems.

Introduction

Traditional health and safety risk management deals with the identification, elimination, and control of hazards, which ISO 45001 defines as a *source with a potential to cause injury and ill health*. However, so far as this book is concerned, this approach has the following limitations.

Psychosocial hazards are rarely dealt with, although this is allowed for in ISO 45001. Only injury and ill health are taken into account, not well-being and wellness. It is assumed that hazards will affect different individuals in the same way and to the same extent. No account is taken of the fact that some psychosocial hazards may create opportunities for some individuals.

In order to overcome these limitations, it is preferable to adopt business risk management terminology and refer to risk sources which can have positive results (opportunities) or negative results (threats). However, since the hazard terminology is so embedded in ISO 45001 and ISO 45003, the chapter begins by using this terminology before discussing the use of the risk source terminology.

This chapter has the following structure.

Hazards
    Hazard classification
    Effects of hazards
    Psychosocial hazards

Risk sources
Implications of risk sources and the framework for hazard creation and effects

Table 5.1 Classification of hazards

Discipline	Hazard type	Hazard examples	Principal harm
Health and safety	Injury hazards	Electricity	Shock
		Hot objects	Burns
		Sharp objects	Cuts
	Physical health hazards	Asbestos	Mesothelioma
		Rats' urine	Weil's disease
		Mineral oils	Scrotal skin cancer
Human resources	Mental health hazards	Traumatic event	PTSD*
		Alcohol abuse	Dementia
		Body shaming	Anorexia
Psychosocial risk management	Well-being hazards	Discrimination	Depression
		Redundancy	Anxiety
		Overwork	Stress
	Wellness hazards	Sedentary job	Loss of muscle mass
		Poor diet at work	Weight gain
		Lack of sleep	Fatigue

* Post-traumatic stress disorder.
Source: Prepared by Tony Boyle for this book.

Hazard classification

There are various classifications of hazards, for example, Annex A of ISO 45001 gives the following classification in paragraph A.6.1.2.1 – *Hazards can be physical, chemical, biological, psychosocial, mechanical, electrical, or based on movement and energy.* There are few examples given to illustrate the categories, but clause 6.1.2.1 *Hazard identification* does include the following examples: *social factors (including workload, work hours, victimization, harassment, and bullying).*

For the purposes of this book, hazards are classified by the discipline that typically deals with them, and the nature of the harm they principally cause. Table 5.1 shows the classification to be used and gives examples of each class.

Effects of hazards

The effects of a particular hazard can vary in two ways: the nature of the harms they produce and the severity of those harms. Traditional health and safety only deals with hazards with effects that

Can result in injury and ill health.
Can have a severity above a certain, usually unspecified, level.

Here are two examples:

Noise. An individual's exposure to noise is measured, and the 'dose' calculated using the level of noise and the duration of the exposure. Action is taken only if the dose exceeds the predetermined level for 'acceptable' doses. No account is taken of the effects of lower doses of noise, although these can be beneficial in some circumstances by, for example, increasing alertness. However, they can also have detrimental effects on well-being (stress and social isolation) and wellness (headaches and increased blood pressure).

Chemicals. For many airborne chemicals, dose measurements are made and, as with noise, action is taken only if the dose exceeds a predetermined level. No account is usually taken of the effect of doses lower than the predetermined level, although these may be having detrimental effects on well-being, for example, stress, and wellness, for example, irritation of the throat or eyes.

Psychosocial risk management, so far as this book is concerned, deals with the effects on well-being and wellness of the hazards typically considered in traditional health and safety management. This is done by extending the scope of traditional risk assessment processes and the techniques involved are described in Chapter 23 'Psychosocial threat and opportunity assessment'.

Obviously, psychosocial risk management also deals with the hazards that affect well-being and wellness that are not typically covered by traditional health and safety risk assessment – that is, psychosocial hazards. These hazards also have a relationship between the dose and the harms caused and this is illustrated in Figure 5.1.

Note the following points about Figure 5.1.

Day-to-day well-being symptoms are such things as slight and transient periods of anxiety and 'feeling low'.

Day-to-day wellness symptoms are such things as slight and transient periods of insomnia and indigestion.

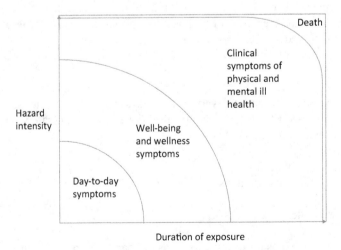

Duration of exposure

Figure 5.1 Hazard intensity, duration of exposure, and symptoms caused.

A single exposure to a high-intensity hazard, or extended exposure to a low-intensity hazard, can have very serious effects, including death – typically from suicide.

The magnitude of the hazard's effect is a combination of its intensity and the duration of exposure. This will be referred to this as the 'dose' because it is similar to the dose measures for things such as exposure to noise and airborne chemicals. In general, increases in the dose result in more severe symptoms.

Psychosocial hazards are discussed in more detail in the next section.

Psychosocial hazards

As was mentioned earlier, ISO 45001 includes *psychosocial* hazards in its list of hazard types. However, there is no further reference to psychosocial in this Standard.

It was also mentioned earlier that ISO 45003 uses the terms *hazards of a psychosocial nature* and *psychosocial hazards* without defining either term. It appears that in ISO 45003 these terms are synonymous.

The *hazards of a psychosocial nature* in ISO 45003 are divided into three categories: *aspects of work organization, social factors at work,* and *work environment, equipment, and hazardous tasks.* Examples of each category are given in three tables in ISO 45003, and these tables are reproduced next as Tables 5.2, 5.3, and 5.4.

While these three tables make up an extensive list, it is not a complete list. For example, discrimination does not appear in any of the three tables, although it is mentioned twice in the body of ISO 45003 in clause 7.3 *Awareness.*

Table 5.2 Aspects of how work is organised

Examples	
Roles and expectations	— Role ambiguity
	— Role conflict
	— Duty of care for other people
	— Scenarios where workers do not have clear guidelines on the tasks they are expected to do (and not do)
	— Expectations within a role that undermine one another (e.g., being expected to provide good customer service, but to not spend a long time with customers)
	— Uncertainty about, or frequent changes to, tasks and work standards
	— Performing work of little value or purpose
Job control or autonomy	— Limited opportunity to participate in decision-making
	— Lack of control over workload
	— Low levels of influence and independence (e.g., not being able to influence the speed, order, or schedule of work tasks and workload)

(*Continued*)

Table 5.2 (Continued)

Examples	
Job demands	— Underuse of skills — Continual work exposure to interaction with people (e.g., the public, customers, students, patients) — Having too much to do within a certain time or with a set number of workers — Conflicting demands and deadlines — Unrealistic expectations of a worker's competence or responsibilities — Lack of task variety or performing highly repetitive tasks — Fragmented or meaningless work — Requirements for excessive periods of alertness and concentration — Working with aggressive or distressed people — Exposure to events or situations that can cause trauma
Organisational change management	— Lack of practical support provided to assist workers during transition periods — Prolonged or recurring restructuring — Lack of consultation and communication about workplace changes, or consultation and communication which is of poor quality, untimely, or not meaningful
Remote and isolated work	— Working in locations that are far from home, family, friends, and usual support networks (e.g., isolated working or 'fly-in-fly-out' work arrangements) — Working alone in non-remote locations without social/human interaction at work (e.g., working at home) — Working in private homes (e.g., providing care or domestic roles in other people's homes)
Workload and work pace	— Work overload or underload — High levels of time pressure — Continually subject to deadlines — Machine pacing — High level of repetitive work
Working hours and schedule	— Lack of variety of work — Shift work — Inflexible work schedules — Unpredictable hours — Long or unsociable hours — Fragmented work or work that is not meaningful — Continual requirements to complete work at short notice
Job security and precarious work	— Uncertainty regarding work availability, including work without set hours — Possibility of redundancy or temporary loss of work with reduced pay — Low-paid or insecure employment, including non-standard employment — Working in situations that are not properly covered or protected by labour law or social protection

Source: British Standards Institution. *Occupational health and safety management – Psychological health and safety at work – Guidelines for managing psychosocial risks*, BSI ISO 45003, 2021. BSI 2021.

Table 5.3 Social factors at work

Examples	
Interpersonal relationships	— Poor communication, including poor information sharing
	— Poor relationships between managers, supervisors, co-workers, and clients or others that workers interact with
	— Interpersonal conflict
	— Harassment, bullying, victimisation (including using electronic tools such as email and social media), third-party violence
	— Lack of social support
	— Unequal power relationships between dominant and non-dominant groups of workers
	— Social or physical isolation
Leadership	— Lack of clear vision and objectives
	— Management style unsuited to the nature of the work and its demand
	— Failing to listen or only casually listening to complaints and suggestions
	— Withholding information
	— Providing inadequate communication and support
	— Lack of accountability
	— Lack of fairness
	— Inconsistent and poor decision-making practices
	— Abuse or misuse of power
Organisational/ workgroup culture	— Poor communication
	— Low levels of support for problem-solving and personal development
	— Lack of definition of, or agreement on, organisational objectives
	— Inconsistent and untimely application of policies and procedures, unfair decision-making
Recognition and reward	— Imbalance between workers' effort and formal and informal recognition and reward
	— Lack of appropriate acknowledgement and appreciation of workers' efforts in a fair and timely manner
Career development	— Career stagnation and uncertainty, under-promotion or over-promotion, lack of opportunity for skill development
Support	— Lack of support from supervisors and co-workers
	— Lack of access to support services
	— Lack of information/training to support work performance
Supervision	— Lack of constructive performance feedback and evaluation processes
	— Lack of encouragement/acknowledgement
	— Lack of communication
	— Lack of shared organisational vision and clear objectives
	— Lack of support and/or resources to facilitate improvements in performance
	— Lack of fairness
	— Misuse of digital surveillance

(Continued)

Table 5.3 (Continued)

Examples	
Civility and respect	— Lack of trust, honesty, respect, civility, and fairness — Lack of respect and consideration in interactions among workers, as well as with customers, clients, and the public
Work/life balance	— Work tasks, roles, schedules, or expectations that cause workers to continue working in their own time — Conflicting demands of work and home — Work that impacts the workers' ability to recover
Violence at work	— Incidents involving an explicit or implicit challenge to health, safety, or well-being at work; violence can be internal, external, or client initiated, for example: — Abuse — Threats — Assault (physical, verbal, or sexual) — Gender-based violence
Harassment	— Unwanted, offensive, intimidating behaviours (sexual or non-sexual in nature), which relate to one or more specific characteristic of the targeted individual, for example: — Race — Gender identity — Religion or belief — Sexual orientation — Disability — Age
Bullying and victimisation	— Repeated (more than once) unreasonable behaviours which can present a risk to health, safety, and well-being at work; behaviours can be overt or covert, for example: — Social or physical isolation — Assigning meaningless or unfavourable tasks — Name-calling, insults, and intimidation — Undermining behaviour — Undue public criticism — Withholding information or resources critical for one's job — Malicious rumours or gossiping — Assigning impossible deadlines

Source: British Standards Institution. *Occupational health and safety management – Psychological health and safety at work – Guidelines for managing psychosocial risks*, BSI ISO 45003, 2021. BSI 2021.

More generally, ISO 45003 does not take into account the fact that various categories of workers' behaviour can have a detrimental effect on other workers' well-being and wellness. For the purposes of this book, these categories are referred to as 'prohibited behaviours' and, in addition to discrimination and victimisation, the categories are as follows.

Table 5.4 Work environment, equipment, and hazardous tasks

Examples	
Work environment, equipment, and hazardous tasks	— Inadequate equipment availability, suitability, reliability, maintenance, or repair
	— Poor workplace conditions, such as lack of space, poor lighting, and excessive noise
	— Lack of the necessary tools, equipment, or other resources to complete work tasks
	— Working in extreme conditions or situations, such as very high or low temperatures, or at height
	— Working in unstable environments such as conflict zones

Source: British Standards Institution. *Occupational health and safety management – Psychological health and safety at work – Guidelines for managing psychosocial risks*, BSI ISO 45003, 2021. BSI 2021.

Illegal activities. These include theft, fraud, bribery, and damaging property.

Activities that breach contractual arrangements. These include poor timekeeping, taking unauthorised leave, not following reasonable instructions, and disclosure of confidential information.

Nonconformity with an organisation's procedures and work instructions.

These prohibited behaviours have their detrimental effects in two main ways.

Effects arising from the behaviour itself. For example, loss of personal property as a result of theft, having to work harder because of a colleague taking unauthorised leave, and not being able to follow the organisation's procedure because of a colleague's nonconformity.

Effects arising from the knowledge of colleagues' behaviour. The detrimental effects arise when a decision has to be made about whether or not to report the prohibited behaviour. These effects can be severe if the prohibited behaviour is such that the worker may face criminal charges and/or be dismissed from the organisation as a result of the report.

Similarly, ISO 45003 does not take into account the effects of the absence of various categories of workers' behaviour that can have a detrimental effect on other workers' well-being and, for the purposes of this book, these are referred to as 'required behaviours'. Many required behaviours are the obverse of prohibited behaviours, for example, organisations can require conformity with procedures and work instructions, rather than prohibit nonconformity. However, organisations can specify required behaviours, for example, certain styles of leadership and respectful behaviour towards colleagues.

For the purposes of this book, the following terminology is used.

Hazards of a psychosocial nature – the psychosocial hazards listed in the three tables in ISO 45003.

Psychosocial hazards – hazards of a psychosocial nature, prohibited behaviours and absence of required behaviours taken together.

Risk sources

Introduction to risk sources

Individuals are used to the idea that a hazard such as a sharp knife creates a risk of injury when it is being used, and that the level of risk depends on things like what type of knife it is, who is using it, and what they are using it for. However, opportunities associated with the hazards are not normally taken into account. For example, a surgeon injures people nearly every working day using a scalpel and other tools. In these circumstances, the cuts inflicted are not considered injuries in health and safety risk management terms, because the risk is outweighed by the opportunity for an improved lifestyle for the patient.

In psychosocial risk management, hazards have to be dealt with in a more detailed way, and the next subsection of this chapter explains why this is so. Being made redundant is used as the psychosocial hazard since redundancy is a concept likely to be familiar to most readers. For ease of description, only the effects of redundancy on well-being are dealt with – in the real world, there could also be effects on wellness.

Redundancy

The possibility of redundancy is one of the *hazards of a psychosocial nature* listed in Table 1 of ISO 45003. However, if 100 workers in a hypothetical organisation were made redundant, there are likely to be the following outcomes among the 100 workers concerned.

A proportion will experience a significant reduction in their well-being for one or more of the following reasons:

They like their job and see no opportunity of getting a job they will like as much.
Their job is well paid because they have worked for the organisation for a long time, and they will not be able to match this pay in another organisation.
Their work colleagues are their main source of social interaction, and they do not want to have to make a new set of social contacts.
They think it is unlikely that they will get another job of any sort.

A proportion will experience no effect on their well-being because they are not particularly committed to their job and think they can easily get an equivalent job in another organisation.
A proportion will experience a significant increase in their well-being for one or more of the following reasons:

They do not like their job and redundancy gives them a good reason for trying to find a job they like more – or to try being self-employed.

They think they are under-paid and can see an opportunity to get a better-paid job.

They do not particularly like their colleagues and see redundancy as a way of changing to new colleagues.

They are approaching retirement, and being made redundant is, in effect, early retirement with the financial bonus of a redundancy payment.

That individuals can benefit from redundancy is clearly shown by the fact that some organisations that have offered voluntary redundancy have had more volunteers than they need. The volunteers are typically the workers nearing retirement who see the redundancy offer as early retirement with a financial bonus described in the last bullet point of the previous paragraph.

You can see from this description that for some of the workers, redundancy is a threat, for others it is an opportunity, and for others it is neither. With hazards of a psychosocial nature, the effect on specific workers has to be taken into account, not the effect on workers as a homogenous group. This is not the case with injury and ill health hazards – everyone gets cut if they come in contact with a sharp knife, and it is difficult to think of any good outcomes of coming into contact with rats' urine!

Another important feature of hazards of a psychosocial nature is the roles the organisation plays in creating them, and the redundancy example will continue to be used to illustrate these roles. There are three main groups of the organisation's personnel involved in redundancies:

The personnel, usually top management, or management at a high level, who decide that redundancies are necessary, and which workers will be made redundant.

The personnel, usually HR personnel, who work out the practicalities of making people redundant and ensure that any legal requirements are met.

The personnel, usually the line manager of the person being made redundant who informs him or her that this is about to happen.

A complexity arises because the well-being of these three groups is likely to be affected by the redundancy process and, as with being made redundant, making people redundant will have different effects on different people. Some of the possibilities are listed below.

Top management. Assuming that the redundancies are necessary for sound economic reasons, top management may experience

An increase in well-being because the redundancies enable the rest of the organisation to continue functioning.

A reduction in well-being because

They see having to make people redundant as a failure of their management.

They are losing people who are valuable to the organisation.

They know that some of the people being made redundant will suffer emotional and financial hardship.

HR personnel. HR personnel may experience

An increase in well-being because fewer workers mean a lighter workload.
A decrease in well-being because they see one of their roles as protecting the interests of workers, not making them redundant.

Line managers. Line managers are likely to have a sense of relief that they themselves are not being made redundant. However, the effect on their well-being of having to tell people that they are being made redundant will vary according to the manager's views of the people concerned. For example,

There will be a detrimental effect on the manager's well-being if they like the person and/or see them as a valued worker and/or believe that the person will suffer emotional or financial hardship.
There will be beneficial effects on the manager's well-being if the person they are making redundant is someone they want to dismiss for other reasons, or they think the person will be able to move to a better job.

The previous discussion was intended to show that psychosocial hazards are more complex in their effects than injury and ill health hazards. The next section discusses the implications of this complexity for psychosocial risk management and describes a framework for psychosocial hazard creation and the effects of such hazards.

Implications and framework

If the full implications of what are referred to as psychosocial hazards are to be taken into account, then the hazard terminology has to be dropped and risk sources used instead. However, this may not be an option in some organisations where it will be seen as a step too far and be put on the 'too difficult' pile.

When this is the case, and the organisation wishes to start implementing psychosocial risk management, it can follow the ISO 45003 guidance, which treats hazards as purely threats and has only a limited amount to say about opportunities.

The rest of this book deals with both approaches, usually beginning with versions of traditional health and safety risk management modified to deal with psychosocial hazards, and moving on to full-blown psychosocial risk management that deals with psychosocial risk sources.

The framework to be used for the rest of this book to describe how psychosocial risk sources are created and have their effects is given in Figure 5.2.

Figure 5.2 shows that psychosocial risk sources are created by perpetrators and that these psychosocial risk sources can create threats and opportunities. Note the following points about Figure 5.2.

There are direct perpetrators who create the psychosocial risk sources for the individual, for example, the line manager who tells you that you are going to be made redundant.

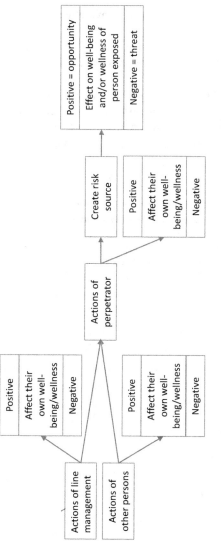

Figure 5.2 Framework of risk source creation and effect.

There are indirect perpetrators in the management line of control whose actions affect the perpetrator, for example, the top management who decides that redundancies are necessary.

There are other indirect perpetrators whose actions also affect the perpetrator, for example, the HR personnel who decides on the terms and conditions for the redundancies.

The actions of all of these perpetrators may have effects on their own well-being and wellness.

Psychosocial risk sources can create opportunities for individuals and increase their well-being and/or wellness, and these individuals will be referred to as 'beneficiaries'.

Psychosocial risk sources can create threats for individuals and reduce their well-being and/or wellness, and these individuals will be referred to as 'victims'.

When a psychosocial risk source has no effect on an individual's well-being or wellness, these individuals will be referred to as 'immune'.

References

1   British Standards Institution. *Occupational health and safety management – Psychological health and safety at work – Guidelines for managing psychosocial risks*, BSI ISO 45003, 2021. BSI 2021.

2   British Standards Institution. *Occupational health and safety management systems – Requirements with guidance for use*, BSI ISO 45001, 2018. BSI 2018.

6   The elimination and control

Crash course

This chapter deals with those psychosocial risk sources that you want to eliminate
or control because they are creating threats, that is, you want to treat them as psychosocial hazards. As was seen in Chapter 5, it is not always the case that a psychosocial risk source should be eliminated, and what to do in these circumstances
is dealt with in Chapter 23 'Psychosocial threat and opportunity assessment' and
Chapter 24 'Psychosocial threat and opportunity management'. However, there are
good reasons for elimination being the preferred option for certain categories of
psychosocial risk source, and for the purposes of this chapter, they will be referred
to as psychosocial hazards.

The majority of psychosocial hazards that it is desirable to eliminate are created
by the behaviour of workers. This means that elimination of these hazards will
require changes in the behaviour of the workers who are creating these hazards.

Irrespective of the methods of elimination, there will have to be arrangements
for dealing with possible recurrence.

Where elimination is not possible, there are various options.

Reducing the dose by decreasing the severity of the hazard, or shortening the
   period of exposure.
Selecting people who have natural immunity to the hazard – for example, introverts
   for lone working and extraverts for dealing with customers.
Increasing immunity by, for example, facilitating adaptation to a psychosocial
   hazard.
Providing coping strategies that enable those exposed to the psychosocial hazard to
   manage its detrimental effects.

Introduction

This chapter deals with those psychosocial risk sources that you want to eliminate
or control because they are creating threats, that is, you want to treat them as psychosocial hazards. As was seen in Chapter 5, it is not always the case that a psychosocial risk source should be eliminated, and what to do in these circumstances

DOI: 10.4324/9781003490555-7

is dealt with in Chapter 23 'Psychosocial threat and opportunity assessment' and Chapter 24 'Psychosocial threat and opportunity management'. However, there are good reasons for elimination being the preferred option for certain categories of psychosocial risk source, and for the purposes of this chapter, they will be referred to as psychosocial hazards.

Traditional health and safety uses hierarchies of elimination and control to rank the preferred methods of dealing with hazards and the hierarchy in ISO 45001[1] is

a) eliminate the hazard;
b) substitute with less hazardous processes, operations, materials or equipment;
c) use engineering controls and reorganization of work;
d) use administrative controls, including training;
e) use adequate personal protective equipment.

ISO 45003[2] does not use a hierarchy, instead, it provides extensive suggestions on how to control each of the three categories of hazards of a psychosocial nature: *work organization, social factors*, and *work environment, equipment, and hazardous tasks.*

Neither of these approaches is entirely satisfactory for psychosocial risk management, and what has been done in this chapter is to describe general principles to apply when deciding on psychosocial risk controls. These general principles are based on medical terminology because what the psychosocial risk controls are trying to achieve is prevention of sub-clinical medical conditions: impaired well-being and wellness. The general principles are dealt with under the following headings:

Eliminating the hazard
Reducing the dose
Selecting for natural immunity
Increasing immunity
Providing coping strategies
'Irrational' controls
Re-emergence of eliminated hazards
Health and safety risk control measures

Eliminating the hazard

There are good reasons for treating some categories of psychosocial risk sources as psychosocial hazards, and these reasons are discussed in this section. However, it is necessary to take into account the possibility that the elimination strategy will fail and that further action will be required. For example, even when bullying has been eliminated in an organisation, there must be arrangements for dealing with any recurrence. These arrangements are dealt with later in this chapter.

The following reasons for elimination are discussed in separate subsections:

Illegality
Duty of care
Effect on the bottom line

There is then a subsection outlining the main methods for eliminating psychosocial hazards.

Illegality

As was seen in Chapter 5, some illegal behaviours create psychosocial hazards and theft, fraud, bribery, and damaging property were given as examples. Since what is legal and not legal varies from place to place, you should have lists of illegal behaviours that you consider should be eliminated from the workplace. You may also have lists of illegal behaviours that would preclude a worker continuing to work in your organisation.

Some organisations already have such lists, although they are not usually comprehensive enough for psychosocial risk management purposes. However, they can provide a useful starting point. Similarly, there may also be arrangements for dealing with workers who behave illegally, but these arrangements are also unlikely to be comprehensive enough for psychosocial risk management purposes – for example, they rarely deal with actions with regard to the victims of the illegal behaviour.

Duty of care

All workers have a duty of care to their fellow workers and the people they come into contact with in the course of their work,[i] and in psychosocial risk management, this duty of care extends to care for the well-being and wellness of others. Discharging this duty of care requires workers to behave in certain ways – the required behaviours described in Chapter 5 – and avoid behaving in certain ways – the prohibited behaviours described in Chapter 5.

Elimination of psychosocial hazards on the basis of workers' duty of care would include the following psychosocial hazards – hazards of a psychosocial nature are in italic font

Prohibited behaviours
Discrimination of any sort

Violence at work
incidents involving an explicit or implicit challenge to health, safety or wellbeing at work; violence can be internal, external or client initiated, e.g.:
abuse
threats

assault (physical, verbal or sexual)
gender-based violence

Harassment
unwanted, offensive, intimidating behaviours (sexual or non-sexual in nature)
which relate to one or more specific characteristic of the targeted indi-
vidual, e.g.:
race
gender identity
religion or belief
sexual orientation
disability
age

Bullying and victimization
repeated (more than once) unreasonable behaviours which can present a risk to
health, safety and well-being at work; behaviours can be overt or covert, e.g.:
social or physical isolation
assigning meaningless or unfavourable tasks
name-calling, insults and intimidation
undermining behaviour
undue public criticism
withholding information or resources critical for one's job
malicious rumours or gossiping
assigning impossible deadlines
harassment, bullying, victimization (including using electronic tools such as
email and social media), third-party violence

Required behaviours
Civility and respect
lack of trust, honesty, respect, civility and fairness
lack of respect and consideration in interactions among workers, as well
as with customers, clients and the public

In addition, managerial workers have additional duties of care to the workers
whose activities they control. These additional duties of care cover the avoidance
of the following hazards of a psychosocial nature.

scenarios where workers do not have clear guidelines on the tasks they are
expected to do (and not do)

Leadership
lack of clear vision and objectives
management style unsuited to the nature of the work and its demand

failing to listen or only casually listening to complaints and suggestions
withholding information
providing inadequate communication and support
lack of accountability
lack of fairness
inconsistent and poor decision-making practices
abuse or misuse of power

Supervision
  lack of support from supervisors
  lack of constructive performance feedback and evaluation processes
  lack of encouragement/acknowledgement
  lack of communication
  lack of shared organizational vision and clear objectives
  lack of support and/or resources to facilitate improvements in performance
  lack of fairness
  misuse of digital surveillance

Effect on bottom line

The psychosocial hazards described in this section are ones that should be eliminated because, in addition to the detrimental effect they have on well-being and wellness, they also have a detrimental effect on the organisation's bottom line. The hazards of a psychosocial nature that are included in this category are listed below:

work underload
performing work of little value or purpose
fragmented or meaningless work – in the *Job demands* section of ISO 45003 Table 1
fragmented work or work that is not meaningful – in the *Working hours and schedule* section of ISO 45003 Table 1
lack of the necessary tools, equipment or other resources to complete work tasks

Methods of elimination

The majority of psychosocial hazards that it is desirable to eliminate are created by the behaviour of workers. This means that elimination of these hazards will require changes in the behaviour of the workers who are creating these hazards. Effective behavioural change will require the following:

Accurate identification of the causes of the unwanted behaviour. For example, if a worker is creating a psychosocial hazard because of pressure from their line manager, sending them on a behavioural change training course will have no effect when they get back to the workplace. Creating a psychosocial hazard is a nonconformity in the psychosocial management system, and dealing with such nonconformities is discussed in Chapter 26 'Psychosocial monitoring, auditing, and corrective action'.

Acceptable behavioural alternatives to the unwanted behaviour must be available. For example, if a worker's behaviour is creating a psychosocial hazard, but there is no other way of achieving the current objective, a behavioural change training course will be ineffective. What can be done in these circumstances is discussed in Chapter 24 'Psychosocial threat and opportunity management'.

There must be organisational commitment to eliminating the psychosocial hazard, and this may not be easy to achieve. The topic of organisational commitment is dealt with in Chapter 28 'The role of top management'.

Although an organisation may aim to eliminate the psychosocial hazards dealt with in this section, it may be necessary in the short term to reduce the dose. All of the psychosocial hazards just discussed can be the subject of dose reduction as an interim stage towards elimination, and dose reduction is dealt with in the next section.

Reducing the dose

This section deals with the psychosocial hazards that cannot be eliminated, for example, because they are essential to a role. What has to be done instead of elimination is to minimise the negative effects these hazards have on the well-being and wellness of workers and interested parties.

As was seen in Chapter 5, the hazard dose has two elements: the intensity of the hazard and the duration of the exposure to the hazard. Dose reductions of almost all psychosocial hazards are achievable by reducing either or both of these elements.

Intensity of hazard

The methods of reducing psychosocial hazard intensity can be obvious from the description of the psychosocial hazard. This is illustrated below using a selection of the hazards of a psychosocial nature from the ISO 45003 Tables 1 and 2.

Table 1 — Aspects of how work is organized

role ambiguity – make the role less ambiguous
lack of control over workload – enable more control over workload
limited opportunity to participate in decision-making – increase opportunities to participate in decision-making
underuse of skills – make better use of workers' skills

Table 2 — Social factors at work

poor communication, including poor information sharing – improve communication and information sharing

withholding information – provide more information
lack of access to support services – provide better access to support services

There are circumstances where reduction in intensity is not possible, or will be difficult to achieve, and the main reasons for this are:

The psychosocial hazard is an integral part of the role. For example, there are roles that involve the following hazards of a psychosocial nature:

duty of care for other people (nurses, care home workers)
exposure to events or situations that can cause trauma (police, members of the armed forces)
working with aggressive or distressed people (police, counsellors)
working in private homes (gas boiler engineers)
shift work (paramedics, service workers)
working in extreme conditions or situations, such as very high or low temperatures, or at height (some construction work)
working in *unstable environments such as conflict zones* (members of the armed forces, aid workers).

For these types of psychosocial hazard, the controls are selecting for immunity and increasing immunity, and these topics are dealt with in a later section.
Reducing the intensity of the psychosocial hazard requires behavioural changes in individuals over whom the organisation has no, or little, control, for example, the *customers, clients, and the public* referred to in ISO 45003.
The actions required to reduce the intensity of the psychosocial hazard are difficult to define or difficult to agree. For example, the following hazards of a psycho-social nature are rather nebulous:

imbalance between workers' effort and formal and informal recognition and reward
lack of appropriate acknowledgement and appreciation of workers' efforts in a fair and timely manner
unrealistic expectations of a worker's competence or responsibilities
poor relationships between managers, supervisors, co-workers, and clients or others that workers interact with
lack of support from supervisors and co-workers
unequal power relationships between dominant and non-dominant groups of workers.

However, there are various methods of reducing intensity, and these are listed below, together with examples of the types of hazards of a psychosocial nature they can be used to control.

Increasing the competence of particular categories of worker. For example, redu-cing the intensity of the following hazards of a psychosocial nature will require increasing the competence of the workers exposed to the hazard:

continual work exposure to interaction with people (e.g. the public, customers, students, patients)
career stagnation and uncertainty, under-promotion or over- promotion, lack of opportunity for skill development
lack of information/training to support work performance.

Increasing specific competences. For example:

Applying high levels of competence in change management will reduce the intensity of the following hazards of a psychosocial nature:

frequent changes to tasks and work standards
lack of practical support provided to assist workers during transition periods
prolonged or recurring restructuring
lack of consultation and communication about workplace changes, or consultation and communication which is of poor quality, untimely, or not meaningful

Applying high levels of competence in task management will reduce the intensity of the following hazards of a psychosocial nature:

uncertainty about tasks and work standards
conflicting demands and deadlines
working in locations that are far from home, family, friends and usual support networks (e.g. isolated working or 'fly-in-fly-out' work arrangements)
working alone in non-remote locations without social/human interaction at work (e.g. working at home).

Providing additional resources even if this will have a negative effect on the organisation's bottom line. These resources can be used to reduce the intensity of the following hazards of a psychosocial nature:

expectations within a role that undermine one another (e.g. being expected to provide good customer service, but also to not spend a long time with customers)
having too much to do within a certain time or with a set number of workers
work overload
high levels of time pressure
continually subject to deadlines
inflexible work schedules
unpredictable hours
long or unsociable hours
continual requirements to complete work at short notice
work tasks, roles, schedules or expectations that cause workers to continue working in their own time
work that impacts the workers' ability to recover.

Provide job security and remove roles that involve precarious work. This may not be possible in some cases, for example, in organisations that are close to insolvency, but profitable organisations can choose to reduce the intensity of the following hazards of a psychosocial nature:

uncertainty regarding work availability, including work without set hours
possibility of redundancy or temporary loss of work with reduced pay
low-paid or insecure employment, including non-standard employment.

Good-practice psychosocial risk control is to reduce the intensity of the psychosocial hazard, where possible, and how this might be done is discussed in detail in in Chapter 24 'Psychosocial threat and opportunity management'.

Duration of exposure

Reducing the duration of exposure to the hazard is used as a traditional health and safety risk control. For example:

Having four people work for two hours each in a very noisy environment, rather than having one person work in that environment for eight hours, thus reducing the likelihood of damage to hearing.
Using job rotation to avoid people having to do the same repetitious task for a whole shift, thus reducing the likelihood of repetitive strain injury and boredom.
Using job sharing with, for example, two part-time workers covering a full shift, rather than one full-time worker.

These techniques can be used for psychosocial hazards such as *duty of care for other people* and *working with aggressive or distressed people* where the intensity of the hazard cannot be reduced.
Other psychosocial hazards where these techniques can be used to reduce the duration of exposure include

lack of task variety or performing highly repetitive tasks
requirements for excessive periods of alertness and concentration
machine pacing
high level of repetitive work
lack of variety of work.

Selecting for natural immunity

The Oxford Dictionary of English (ODE)[3] defines immune as *totally or partially resistant to a particular infectious disease or pathogen.* For the purposes of psychosocial risk control, this definition can be changed to *totally or partially resistant to a particular psychosocial hazard.*

Selecting for natural immunity is not a technique used in health and safety. This is because although there appears to be some natural immunity to some non-psychosocial hazards – for example, not everyone exposed to asbestos develops mesothelioma – there is no way to predict who has the natural immunity. This is not the case with some psychosocial hazards because you can find out about individuals' natural immunity, and techniques for doing this are described later in this chapter. This can be illustrated by examples of hazards of a psychosocial nature.

Social or physical isolation. Some individuals do not have any significant impairment of their well-being or wellness as a result of social or physical isolation. These individuals prefer being alone at work and would, for example, rather be writing than training. Similarly, their preferred hobbies are solitary pursuits such as gardening and reading.

Shift work. Immunity to shift work largely depends on what is known as the diurnal cycle. This is how an individual feels at various points during the day and, in particular, how sleepy they feel. A typical diurnal cycle is to feel alert during the day with decreasing alertness after about 15 hours when increasing sleepiness takes over and the individual sleeps for around 8 hours. However, as with most things associated with human beings, there is a wide variety of diurnal cycles and of particular relevance to shift work is the varying strength of the diurnal cycle from individual to individual. Some individuals have a very strong diurnal cycle, which means that when they have to do night work, it seriously reduced their well-being (lack of alertness and irritability) and wellness (digestive problems). However, individuals with very weak diurnal cycles suffer very little, if any, detrimental effects to their well-being or wellness and have a natural immunity to shift work.

Lack of task variety or performing highly repetitive tasks. For some people all of the time, and for most people some of the time, performing a single highly repetitive task can be a way of maintaining well-being or wellness. For example, for individuals with a cognitive impairment, a single repetitive task may be their only route to employment. Similarly, people with highly stressful lives may need to spend time doing a single repetitive task as a way of 'winding down' – for example, weeding in the garden.

Working in unstable environments such as conflict zones. It is known from news coverage of conflict zones that there are people who voluntarily enter these zones either to take part in the conflict or to provide humanitarian aid. It seems very likely that these people have a natural immunity to this particular psychosocial hazard.

Effective use of selecting for natural immunity as a psychosocial risk control measure depends on being able to identify accurately the psychosocial hazards associated with a particular role, and having a way of measuring existing levels of immunity.

Identifying the psychosocial hazards associated with a role is usually straightforward. Health and safety practitioners are used to identifying the traditional health and safety hazards associated with roles, and the same techniques of observation and interview can be used to identify the psychosocial hazards. The use of these techniques in psychosocial hazard identification and risk assessment is dealt with in Chapter 23 'Psychosocial threat and opportunity assessment'.

Measuring existing levels of immunity is less straightforward, but there are two techniques that are generally useful.

Interviews. A competent interviewer should be able to identify accurately an interviewee's feelings about any given psychosocial hazard and the likely effects of exposure to that hazard on the interviewee's well-being and wellness. However, a high level of interviewee competence may be required in those circumstances where an interviewee's answers to questions about psychosocial hazards will influence whether or not they are appointed to a particular role. In these circumstances, the interviewer will, if possible, give answers that they think will get them appointed, not answers that describe what they actually think and feel. Unskilled interviewers may lack the competence to identify these sorts of answers and, even if they do recognise them, the unskilled interviewers will be unable to ask appropriate questions to 'get to the truth'. The interview skills for this type of interviewing are dealt with in Chapter 20 'Competences' and Chapter 27 'Psychosocial investigation'.

Past behaviour. It is generally the case that the best predictor of a person's future behaviour is their past behaviour. Accurately identifying an individual's past performance of behaviours relevant to a particular role is a technique frequently used in job selection. The behaviours checked during selection rarely include those of importance in immunity to psychosocial hazards, but the technique can readily be adapted to enable identification of existing immunity. Past behaviours are usually identified using detailed *curricula vitae* (CVs) and/or interviews of the type described in the previous bullet point.

Although these two techniques produce qualitative measures of immunity to psychosocial hazards, they can be used as screening techniques when appointing people to roles with significant psychosocial hazards.

In addition to these generally useful techniques, it is possible in appropriate circumstances to use a personality test, preferably one specifically designed for use in occupational settings. For example, the SHL *Occupational Personality Questionnaire* measures relationships with people, thinking style, and feelings and emotions across 32 different dimensions. Examples of how this type of test might be used to check for immunity to psychosocial hazards are given below.

Continual work exposure to interaction with people (e.g., the public, customers, students, patients). One of the scales commonly used in occupational personality questionnaires is Introversion–Extraversion. Introversion is *the quality of being shy and reticent* (ODE), and extraversion is *the quality of being outgoing and socially confident* (ODE).[ii] It is likely that *continual work exposure to interaction with people* will have a detrimental effect on the well-being and wellness of introverts.

Working alone in non-remote locations without social/human interaction at work. This also uses the Introversion–Extraversion scale, but in this case, it is extraverts who would suffer detrimental effects to their well-being and wellness were they to be exposed to this psychosocial hazard.

Uncertainty about, or frequent changes to, tasks and work standards. Occupational personality questionnaires use adaptability scales, and adaptability is *the quality of being able to adjust to new conditions* (ODE). A person who scored high or very high on the adaptability scale is likely to have a high or very high level of immunity to *uncertainty about, or frequent changes to, tasks and work standards*, while a person who scored low or very low would suffer detrimental effects to their well-being and wellness were they to be exposed to *uncertainty* or *frequent changes*.

A wide range of occupational personality tests is available, and a review of the personality dimensions they measure will identify ways of measuring immunity to more psychosocial hazards. However, this is a specialist area, and it is recommended that you consult a relevant expert if you wish to make use of these personality tests. How personality affects individual differences is dealt with in more detail in Chapter 9 'The psychology'.

Increasing immunity

There is a saying that human beings 'can get used to anything' and this is true of many psychosocial hazards. The 'getting used to' may be simply due to the passage of time, as with bereavement, for example, or it may be a more complex adaptation process. Sensory adaptation can be relevant in traditional health and safety, for example:

The eyes adapt to changes in light level, and most people are familiar with the way they are temporarily blinded when they move from the dark into the light, and how it is a little while before they can see properly when they move from the light to the dark.

If there is a smell in a room, people cease to notice it after a while, but if they leave the room for a time and come back to it they will notice the smell on their return.

Sensory adaptation is not usually relevant for psychosocial hazards, but two other types of adaptation are relevant: psychological adaptation and social adaptation.

The American Psychological Association[4] defines psychological adaptation as

modification to suit different or changing circumstances. In this sense, the term often refers to behavior that enables an individual to adjust to the environment effectively and function optimally in various domains, such as coping with daily stressors.

For our purposes, *stressors* can include hazards of a psychosocial nature such as

low levels of influence and independence (e.g. not being able to influence the speed, order or schedule of work tasks and workload)
low levels of support for problem-solving and personal development
lack of definition of, or agreement on, organizational objectives
inconsistent and untimely application of policies and procedures, unfair decision-making
conflicting demands of work and home.

Where there are good reasons to suppose that exposure to a psychosocial hazard will not cause severe or permanent impairment to a person's well-being and wellness, and the person involved gives their informed consent, psychological adaptation is a possible risk control measure. However, careful monitoring and agreed non-punitive withdrawal arrangements should be in place.

The American Psychological Association defines social adaptation as

adjustments to the demands, restrictions, and mores[iii] of society, including the ability to live and work harmoniously with others and to engage in satisfying social interactions and relationships.

Social adaptation can be used in the same way as psychological adaptation for hazards of a psychosocial nature such as

working in situations that are not properly covered or protected by labour law or social protection
interpersonal conflict
lack of social support.

The use of social adaptation as a psychosocial risk control measure is subject to the same caveats as the use of psychological adaptation.

When using adaptation in this way, you have to distinguish between individuals who are working despite suffering impairment of their well-being and wellness as a result of psychosocial hazards and individuals who have developed an immunity to the psychosocial hazards to which they are exposed. The individuals involved may hide the impairment they are suffering in order to retain their role, and careful monitoring by competent personnel is required to detect and deal with these circumstances.

Providing coping strategies

According to the ODE, to cope is to *deal effectively with something difficult* and, for our purposes, the *something difficult* is exposure to a psychosocial hazard. As was described earlier in this chapter, there are some roles that, by their very nature, include exposure to psychosocial hazards. In general, these roles will be filled by individuals who naturally have, or have developed, a high level of immunity to the psychosocial hazards involved. However, for people new to these roles, and for circumstances when the intensity of the psychosocial hazard is above routine levels, coping strategies can be used as a psychosocial risk control measure. The purpose of these coping strategies is to restore levels of impaired well-being and wellness, and they are dealt with in detail in Chapter 8 'The improvers'.

'Irrational' controls

There is an old joke as follows:

> A man was stopped by the police for throwing a white powder onto the pavement at Piccadilly Circus. When questioned the man claimed that it was 'anti-elephant powder' that scared off elephants, and he had to use it because he was afraid of elephants. The policeman told him that there were no elephants at Piccadilly Circus to which the man replied 'You see, it works!'.[iv]

So far as the man was concerned, the use of the anti-elephant powder was a psycho-social risk control measure for his elephant phobia – irrespective of how irrational his belief was. Phobias are defined as *an extreme or irrational fear of or aversion to something* (ODE), and they can have a significant impact at work. Two examples are as follows:

An individual had very strong acrophobia (fear of height) that made them avoid a whole range of tasks that involved work at height. On the few occasions they could not avoid this sort of task, their favoured control measure was 'three points of contact' – even when they were just in an office inspecting the fasteners on an open fifth-floor window.

A gas engineer who was terrified of spiders (arachnophobia) and who had to get someone to open the gas meter boxes for him in case there was a large spider inside. He said that sometimes this caused a delay in the work, but he knew of other engineers who had left the job because of strong arachnophobia.

Phobias are only one cause of people adopting irrational psychosocial risk control measures – others include superstitions and beliefs.

Superstition is defined as *a widely held but irrational belief in supernatural influences, especially as leading to good or bad luck, or a practice based on such a belief* (ODE), and belief is *an acceptance that something exists or is true, especially one without proof* (ODE). Superstitions and beliefs can also have an effect on work, for example:

A senior secretary had a first-floor office but had to make frequent visits to the ground floor using the stairs. Her strong superstition or belief was that crossing someone on the stairs would bring her bad luck, so she always waited until the stairs were clear before she set off. If she was climbing the stairs and someone started to come down them, she backtracked and waited for the stairs to be clear. Similarly, if she was going down the stairs and someone started to climb them, she went back up and waited on the landing until the stairs were clear. Because of the need for frequent trips, and the fact that she sometimes had to wait for the stairs to be clear, she lost a lot of working time each day.

Some people refuse to go to work on Friday the thirteenth because they believe that if they leave their home, something bad will happen to them.

Many workers, even those working on construction sites, will make considerable detours to avoid walking under a ladder.

People with strong religious beliefs may refuse to work on certain days of the week or on certain days of the year.

While some superstitions and beliefs have innocuous controls – for example, knocking on wood and carrying a lucky charm – control associated with other beliefs, such as making 'the sign of the cross' in the workplace to bring luck, or ward off evil, may have disturbing effects for other workers.

For the purposes of psychosocial risk management, organisations should have arrangements for dealing with these irrational controls. Suggestions on the nature of these arrangements are given in Chapter 24 'Psychosocial threat and opportunity management'.

Re-emergence of eliminated hazards

In traditional health and safety, elimination of hazards is usually completely effective but, for example,

Workers have been known to obtain and use personal supplies of forbidden chemicals because they believe these chemicals are more effective, or make their work easier – which may be true.

Workers may continue to indulge in behaviours that have been prohibited on safety grounds by continuing to take 'shortcuts' when not supervised.

The elimination of psychosocial hazards is more problematic. For example, bullying may have been eliminated for the current workforce and with the prevailing conditions in the organisation. However, new personnel or new pressures, such as a sharp reduction in profitability, can result in new instances of bullying. What is required to deal with re-emergence of psychosocial hazards is effective checking procedures, and these are dealt with in Chapter 26 'Psychosocial monitoring, auditing, and corrective action'.

Health and safety risk control measures

Although traditional health and safety risk control measures are intended to pre-vent injury and physical ill health, they can have an important role in maintaining workers' well-being and wellness. This is because these controls can make workers feel safe, and feeling safe is an important element of well-being. This is the case even if the control is an irrational one, and organisations should take this possibility into account when deciding on their arrangements for irrational controls.

Notes

i   In the UK, this duty of care is a legal requirement for health and safety. The Health and Safety at Work etc. Act, 1974 includes the following: *It shall be the duty of every employee while at work – a to take reasonable care for the health and safety of himself and of other persons who may be affected by his acts or omissions at work* (Section 7).

ii   There are technical definitions of introversion and extraversion used by psychologists and other specialists; however, these are not necessary for the present purposes.

iii Mores – pronounced more-ease – are *the essential or characteristic customs and conventions of a society or community* (ODE).

iv   Fear of elephants is a recognised mental condition – pachydermophobia. Pachyderm means thick skin and other pachyderms are rhinoceros and hippopotami.

References

1   British Standards Institution. *Occupational health and safety management systems – Requirements with guidance for use,* BSI ISO 45001, 2018. BSI 2018.
2   British Standards Institution. *Occupational health and safety management – Psychological health and safety at work – Guidelines for managing psychosocial risks,* BSI ISO 45003, 2021. BSI 2021.
3   MobiSystems, Inc. *Oxford Dictionary*, version 15.8. Last accessed 17 January 2024.
4   American Psychological Association. https://dictionary.apa.org/adaptation. Last accessed 22 February 2024.

7   The triggers

Crash course

A wide range of events outside work can impair well-being and wellness, including the following:

Alcohol, drugs, medicines, smoking, and vaping
Relationships, for example, bereavement, divorce or separation, and experiencing discrimination or racism outside work
Money worries (financial difficulties)
Lifestyle, for example, poor diet and lack of exercise, fresh air or sunlight
Life changes

Each of these events is a trigger because it is *an event that is the cause of a particular action, process, or situation* (ODE). In the present case, the process caused by the trigger is impairing well-being or wellness. In this chapter, the triggers described are those that occur as part of an individual's private life. Triggers that are associated with work life were dealt with in Chapter 5, where they are referred to as psychosocial hazards or risk sources. Some events such as bullying and racism can be both triggers and hazards depending on where they take place, but they are treated separately because of the differences in what organisations have to do to deal with them. Although organisations do not, in general, have an obligation to manage triggers, they may choose to take action because of the effects of reduced well-being and wellness on productivity and worker turnover. The triggers described in this chapter are, therefore, 'work-relevant' – they do not occur at work, so they are not 'work-related', but they do have an effect on work.

Introduction

Reduced well-being and wellness can be caused by a wide range of events, for example, bereavement or financial difficulties. This chapter describes the various categories of event that can have these adverse effects and gives examples of each category. The categories dealt with are

DOI: 10.4324/9781003490555-8

Alcohol, drugs, medicines, smoking, and vaping
Relationships
Money worries (financial difficulties)
Lifestyle
Life changes

An event in these categories is referred to as a trigger because it is *an event that is the cause of a particular action, process, or situation* (ODE).[1] In the present case, the process caused by the trigger is impairing well-being or wellness. In this chapter, the triggers described are those that occur as part of an individual's private life. Triggers that are associated with work life were dealt with in Chapter 5, where they are referred to as psychosocial hazards or risk sources. Some events such as bullying and racism can be both triggers and hazards depending on where they take place, but they are treated separately because of the differences in what organisations have to do to deal with them. Although organisations do not, in general, have an obligation to manage triggers, they may choose to take action because of the effects of reduced well-being and wellness on productivity and worker turnover. The triggers described in this chapter are, therefore, 'work-relevant' – they do not occur at work, so they are not 'work-related', but they do have an effect on work.

Note that some conditions such as depression and anxiety can occur without any external trigger or hazard. These triggers are known as internal or endogenous triggers, and they are discussed in Chapter 9 'The psychology'.

Alcohol, drugs, medicines, smoking, and vaping

Alcohol, drugs, medicines, smoking, and vaping are grouped together because they all involve introducing chemical substances into the body. For the purposes of this book, the following ODE definitions are used

a drug is *a substance taken for its narcotic or stimulant effects, typically illegally*

a medicine is *a drug or other preparation for the treatment or prevention of disease.*

This means that certain substances, such as cannabis, can be a drug or a medicine depending on how they are being used.

As was seen in Chapter 4, some medicines are important ways of improving a person's mental or physical state and are, therefore, improvers rather than triggers. These and other improvers are discussed in Chapter 8. However, some medicines can have side effects that reduce well-being or wellness and these side effects make these medicines triggers.

Appropriate levels of alcohol and drug use may also have beneficial effects on well-being and wellness; however, there is much argument about what would be appropriate levels. The problem with alcohol and drugs is that the body builds up a tolerance to them so that over time more of the substance is required to have the same effect. This leads to people taking quantities of the substance that are physically harmful or even fatal. Because of this, any level of alcohol or drug use should be treated as a potential trigger.

Smoking and vaping are methods for getting a particular drug – nicotine – into the body, and this is a highly addictive substance. For those addicted to nicotine, a continuing supply is necessary to maintain their well-being, and lack of supply can be a powerful trigger.

Relationships

A number of triggers are associated with relationships. The main ones are

Bereavement
Divorce or separation
Deteriorating relationship with a partner
Family difficulties
Being abused, bullied, harassed, or victimised outside work
Experiencing discrimination or racism outside work

Relationship triggers, like psychosocial hazards, vary on two dimensions – intensity and duration – and as was seen in Chapter 5, the combination of the two is the trigger's 'dose'. The concept of dose is used in traditional health and safety, but dose measurement for triggers is more complicated for a number of reasons.

It is difficult to measure the strength of the trigger – you can only measure the strength of its effects on an individual. For example, it is possible to say that bereavement, in general, is a powerful trigger, but this does not mean that all bereavements have a powerful negative effect. There are cases where a bereavement has a positive effect on the bereaved individual's well-being and wellness.
Bereavement, divorce, or separation have no duration, although the events an individual experiences during the time leading up to these events may be triggers in themselves. It is a common observation that well-being and wellness are at their lowest immediately after the event and gradually recover in the absence of other triggers.
It is difficult to assess the effect of duration of exposure. Human beings are very adaptable organisms and can adapt to a variety of adverse circumstances. For example, deteriorating relationship with a partner, or family difficulties, may initially cause impaired well-being and wellness, but the individual concerned 'learns to live with it' and the impairments to well-being and wellness do not get worse or deteriorate into mental or physical ill health. This is the equivalent of the acquired immunity to psychosocial hazards discussed in Chapter 6.
It is difficult to predict the effect any given dose of a trigger will have on an individual. It is possible to establish a clear relationship between noise dose and the extent of the adverse effect on a healthy human ear. This is because there is a high degree of similarity between one human ear and another. There is no such

similarity in the psychology of individuals, so that it is not possible to predict, at the individual level, the effect of a given dose of a trigger.

What can be measured, however, is the strength of the effects on well-being and wellness of a trigger's dose. This can be done using the types of measurement techniques described in earlier chapters.

Money worries (financial difficulties)

There are two ways in which money and well-being interact.

Not having sufficient income to meet required, or desired, expenditure, leading to impaired well-being or wellness.

Impaired well-being or wellness leading to an individual mismanaging their finances, for example, by ignoring debts or taking on debts to buy things that make them feel better.

Not having sufficient income to meet required expenditure can result in depression, anxiety, and panic attacks, and worrying about money is a common cause of sleep disorders. All of these, in their milder forms, are impairments to well-being. In addition, not having sufficient income to buy healthy food or to heat a home properly can directly impair wellness.

Not having sufficient income to meet desired expenditure can also impair well-being and wellness. For example, not being able to afford to travel to meet friends can lead to feelings of loneliness and isolation that impair well-being, and not being able to afford entertainments can lead to depression.

An individual mismanaging their finances can result in them not having sufficient income to meet required or desired expenditure, which results in impaired well-being and wellness. This can result in a vicious circle developing where increasing impairment of well-being and wellness causes increasing mismanagement of finances. This type of vicious circle can quickly result in severe mental or physical ill health.

Lifestyle

Many aspects of an individual's lifestyle can have a negative impact on their well-being and wellness. The following lifestyle triggers are dealt with in this section:

Poor diet
Lack of exercise, fresh air, and sunlight
Physical ill health and pain
Loneliness and isolation
Fatigue and lack of sleep
Housing problems

Poor diet

A poor diet is one that does not provide the things that an individual needs to stay healthy, including energy, vitamins, and minerals, or provides more energy than an individual needs.

In the short term, a poor diet is a well-being trigger because it can result in fatigue and stress. However, having a poor diet over a long period of time is primarily a wellness trigger because of the adverse effects it has on health. These include the following:

Being overweight or underweight
High blood pressure
High cholesterol
High blood sugar
Some cancers such as bowel cancer

What constitutes a good diet is dealt with in Chapter 8 'The improvers'.

Lack of exercise, fresh air, and sunlight

Lack of exercise over the long term creates the following:

Weight gain as a result of using too little energy
Loss of muscle strength due to lack of use
Loss of strength in bones due to lack of use
Deterioration of the digestive system

In the short term, lack of exercise may be a well-being trigger – especially for individuals who are normally very physically active.

Lack of fresh air usually results from spending too high a proportion of the day in poorly ventilated buildings, but in some cities, it can be as a result of outdoor air pollution.

The well-being impairments created by lack of fresh air include tiredness and difficulty concentrating. However, there is a much wider range of wellness impairments, including the following:

Headaches
Nasal problems such as a blocked nose or runny nose
Skin problems such as dry skin, itchy skin, or rashes
Eye problems such as sore eyes or dry eyes
Respiratory problems such as coughing or wheezing

These impairments can occur even with short periods of time without adequate fresh air.

Lack of sunlight has two principal effects: insufficient vitamin D and seasonal affective disorder (SAD).

Vitamin D is one of the vitamins essential for maintaining health, and the body produces vitamin D when the skin is exposed to sunlight. This is a self-regulating process, so that the body stops producing vitamin D when it has enough, even if the exposure to sunlight continues.

Vitamin D plays a role in moderating an individual's mood, which means that lack of vitamin D can be a well-being trigger leading to anxiety and depression. Vitamin D also plays a role in preventing certain diseases, which means that lack of vitamin D is also a wellness trigger leading to such things as heart disease and obesity.

The UK National Health Service website provides the following information on SAD[2]:

Seasonal affective disorder (SAD) is a type of depression that comes and goes in a seasonal pattern.

SAD is sometimes known as 'winter depression' because the symptoms are usually more apparent and more severe during the winter.

Some people with SAD may have symptoms during the summer and feel better during the winter.

Symptoms of SAD

Symptoms of SAD can include:

- *a persistent low mood*
- *a loss of pleasure or interest in normal everyday activities*
- *irritability*
- *feelings of despair, guilt and worthlessness*
- *feeling lethargic (lacking in energy) and sleepy during the day*
- *sleeping for longer than normal and finding it hard to get up in the morning*
- *craving carbohydrates and gaining weight*
- *difficulty concentrating*
- *decreased sex drive*

For some people, these symptoms can be severe and have a significant impact on their day-to-day activities.

Typically, SAD occurs in winter, but there are other patterns of mood disorders, for example, 6A80.4 in the ICD-11[3] classification, that is, *Seasonal pattern of mood episode onset.*

Physical ill health and pain

All forms of physical ill health can be triggers for well-being; this includes dental, oral, and sexual health. In addition, pain is a trigger for well-being.

Loneliness and isolation

The ODE has two relevant definitions of loneliness:

sadness because one has no friends or company
the fact of being without companions; solitariness.

It is the first definition that describes the trigger effect of loneliness. However, *the fact of being without companions* or *solitariness* does not necessarily lead to *sadness*. There are many individuals who, as the saying goes, are quite happy with their own company. For these individuals, *the fact of being without companions* or *solitariness* is not a trigger. In addition, being with people does not necessarily prevent loneliness – there has to be appropriate interaction with the *companions*. A single person on a cruise ship, otherwise occupied by couples, can feel intensely lonely despite being in close proximity with other people for most of the time.

Isolation, sometimes referred to as social isolation, is lack of social contacts and having few people with whom to interact. As with loneliness, isolation is a trigger only for some people. There are individuals who prefer to be isolated, and for these individuals, being in company is a trigger.

Responses to loneliness and isolation depend, to some extent, on personality, with introverts less likely to be negatively affected than extraverts. The role of personality in the response to triggers is dealt with in Chapter 9 'The psychology'.

Fatigue and lack of sleep

As was described in Chapter 4, fatigue is often discussed in health and safety because it is a causal factor in errors and accidents. However, fatigue is also a well-being and wellness trigger and typical effects are as follows:

Well-being – difficulty sleeping, difficulty in starting even simple tasks, loss of sex drive (libido), increased impatience and irritability, being over-emotional.
Wellness – loss of strength (or imagined loss of strength), feeling breathless, dizziness.

Lack of sleep is one of the causes of fatigue, and it can produce any of the effects of fatigue just described. In addition, lack of sleep can result in daytime sleepiness and excessive yawning.

Housing problems

Housing problems are many and various and include the following:

Increases in rent or mortgage payments resulting in financial difficulties.
Disputes with landlords or neighbours.
Requirements for expensive maintenance or repair resulting in financial difficulties.

Threats of eviction.

Living in unsafe accommodation, for example, apartments with inadequate fire safety provision.

Living in inadequate accommodation – for example, accommodation that is poorly maintained, overcrowded, or unsuitably located.

All of these housing problems are triggers. Typically, they initially produce reduced well-being via anxiety and panic attacks, but continuing exposure can result in depression and adverse effects on wellness. An extreme case in the UK occurred in 2020 when a child died from a respiratory condition as a result of prolonged exposure to mould in an inadequately ventilated rented apartment. In the two years prior to the child's death, he and his parents had suffered increasing detrimental effects on their well-being and wellness.

Life changes

It is an obvious fact that there are two sorts of changes – changes for better and changes for worse. However, whether any given change is for better or worse depends on the nature of the change and who is experiencing the change – 'one man's meat is another man's poison'. Some examples of common life changes are given below, together with notes on their complexities:

Moving home. Moving home can be a trigger if, for example, it is being enforced by a landlord, is due to financial difficulties that mean the individual cannot afford to live in their current home, or it is necessary to move to a location the individual does not like, for example, to look after an elderly relative. Moving home can have beneficial effects on well-being if, for example, it is moving to better accommodation or a better location.

Physical illness. As was seen in Chapter 3 'The harms', physical illness can be a trigger for both well-being and wellness. The typical effect on well-being is depression, but there can be anxiety and panic attacks if, for example, the physical illness is reducing the person's earning capacity. The negative effects on wellness typically arise from lack of physical activity, for example, loss of muscle strength and weight gain. However, some physical illnesses suppress the appetite and the effect of these illnesses on wellness is excessive weight loss.

Physical activity. There are two changes to consider – physically active people who become physically inactive and physically inactive people who become physically active. Typically, the negative effects on well-being and wellness are confined to physically active people who become physically inactive. These people can become depressed and put on weight. Physically inactive people who become physically active typically benefit from the change since physical activity is one of the improvers, which is discussed in Chapter 8.

Pregnancy. Pregnancy can be a trigger if, for example, it is unwanted or the mother does not have adequate access to financial and other resources. However, even when neither of these is the case mothers can suffer from 'baby blues', a condition that results in temporary impairment of well-being. Occasionally, there is postnatal depression where the symptoms are much more serious and may require medical intervention.

Just lots of changes. It can be the case that too many changes over a period of time have a detrimental effect on a person's well-being. Most animals prefer stability in their life and humans are no exception. Lots of changes threaten this stability and as a result impair well-being.

References

1   MobiSystems, Inc. *Oxford Dictionary*, version 15.8. Last accessed 17 January 2024.
2   National Health Service. www.nhs.uk/mental-health/conditions/seasonal-affective-disorder-sad/overview. Last accessed 22 February 2024.
3   World Health Organization. *International statistical classification of diseases and related health problems, 10th revision,* 2019. WHO 2019. ICD-10 Accessed online at https://icd.who.int/browse10/2019/en#/ on 5 November 2023.

8 The improvers

Crash course

One of the most important parts of psychosocial risk management is maintaining workers' and interested parties' awareness of the actions they can take to maintain and improve their well-being and wellness. For the purposes of this book, these actions are referred to as improvers and they are

The actions that individuals can take to improve their own well-being or wellness. These include connecting with other people, learning, giving their time, taking notice, being physically active, and having a healthy diet.

The resources that individuals can access to improve their well-being and wellness, these include the following:

Guidance and support for specific triggers, such as financial difficulties, housing problems, and relationship difficulties.

Guidance and support for specific well-being and wellness conditions, such as anxiety, depression, and being overweight.

Tutors who pass on competences, such as active listening, mindfulness, yoga, and Pilates

Counsellors and therapists

Self-help resources, such as books, websites, devices, and apps.

In general, the improvers are effective irrespective of the trigger that is making them necessary. There are a few trigger-specific improvers, for example, seeking financial advice when the trigger is financial difficulties, but, in general, it is possible to use a single improver to deal with one or more triggers, and to use multiple improvers to deal with one or more triggers.

Introduction

One of the most important parts of psychosocial risk management is maintaining workers' and interested parties' awareness of the actions they can take to maintain

DOI: 10.4324/9781003490555-9

and improve their well-being and wellness. For the purposes of this book, these actions are referred to as improvers and they are as follows:

The actions that individuals can take to improve their own well-being or wellness. The resources that individuals can access to improve their well-being and wellness.

In general, the improvers are effective irrespective of the trigger that is making them necessary. There are a few trigger-specific improvers, for example, seeking financial advice when the trigger is financial difficulties, but in general, it is possible to use a single improver to deal with one or more triggers, and to use multiple improvers to deal with one or more triggers.

Actions individuals can take and the resources they can access are dealt with in separate sections, and the chapter ends with a section dealing with the treatment of impairments to well-being and wellness.

Actions

Although there is no definitive list of the actions individuals can take to improve their own well-being or wellness, there is general agreement that following actions should be included in the list:

Connect with other people
Learn
Give your time
Take notice
Be physically active
Have a healthy diet

The first four of the actions are principally for improving well-being, the last two are principally concerned with improving wellness.

Connect with other people

Good relationships are important for well-being because they

Help individuals build a sense of belonging and self-worth.
Give individuals an opportunity to share positive experiences.
Provide emotional support and allow individuals to support each other.

A search of the internet will provide many lists of the things people can do to help connect with other people and build stronger and closer relationships. The subsections below describe the more mainstream items on these lists with the emphasis on relationships at work.

Active listening

There are various definitions of active listening, but the key elements are as follows:

Paying close attention to what is being said. In a typical conversation, the listener 'takes in' only a fraction of what is being said because, for example, they are thinking about what they are going to say next.

Not interrupting. Even when you want to ask a question, you should wait until the speaker reaches a natural break.

Making sure you understand what the speaker is saying by, for example, para-phrasing what they have just said.

Trying to obtain additional detail by, for example, asking follow-up questions.

Watching the speaker's body language to assess, for example, how forthcoming the speaker is being.

Active listening is a key element of competent interviewing, and it is discussed in more detail in Chapter 20 'Competences' and Chapter 27 'Psychosocial investigation'.

Make time for others

Individuals have things to do, and things to think about. For many individuals there are too many things to do, which means that they spend all their time doing them and neglect their relationships with others. Similarly, people with too much to think about do not form relationships, even when they are in the company of other people. They are too busy with their own concerns to take notice of other people's concerns.

Making time for other people can be as simple as taking a short tea break with them and talking about something of mutual interest – and using active listening during the conversation. When starting to improve the way you make time for others, it is best to start with simple action, rather than embark on an ambitious programme that will become too onerous, and fail.

Do what you say you would do

One of the ways of undermining your relationships with other people is to 'let them down'. Repeatedly saying 'we must meet up for a tea break and have a chat' but never making the time to do it will make it extremely difficult to connect with the people to whom you are making promises. Not keeping promises about more serious activities than tea breaks will have even stronger detrimental effects.

Show gratitude

Be alert to things people do for you, and make sure you express your gratitude in appropriate ways. In this context, appropriate means the degree of the response, and ensuring that the response is recognised by the person you are thanking. Your thank-you should not be gushing – that is *effusive or exaggeratedly enthusiastic* (ODE)[1] – and you should not give it begrudgingly – that is *give reluctantly or resentfully* (ODE). In addition, you should use suitable ways of sending your thank-you and checking that the person has received your thank-you.

Avoid gossip

The ODE defines gossip *as casual or unconstrained conversation or reports about other people, typically involving details that are not confirmed as being true*. The detrimental effects of gossip on connecting with other people arise from the *unconstrained* and *not confirmed as being true* parts of this definition. If you have a reputation as a gossip, no one will want to provide you with information about themselves, especially the sort of personal information that helps form relationships. In extreme cases, gossips may end up connecting only with other gossips, and this is not a psychologically healthy situation.

Know what you need and what they need

What do you talk about during a tea break? One person may want to talk about sport, another about cooking, and another about their favourite hobby. Do you talk about their preferred topic, or about a topic you prefer? This is a trivial example, but it illustrates the importance of knowing what you need and what other people need. You are unlikely to connect over tea breaks with someone who is only interested in football when you would rather watch paint dry than watch a football match.

There are obviously more important aspects of life than tea breaks where knowing what you need and what other people need are important. These include help with aspects of work, the need to discuss current personal concerns or personal triumphs, and the need to discuss perceived failings in the organisation and its management.

Set boundaries

Most people have experienced the problems that arise when someone is 'too friendly' – they take up too much of our time and force us to do things that are of low, or no, priority for our own well-being. Managing people like this can be difficult, but it has to be done if you are to avoid the negative effects it has on your well-being. You also have to make sure that you are not becoming one of these people yourself, keep asking yourself whether the ways you are using to connect with other people, and the extent of your connecting with other people, are acceptable to the people with whom you are trying to connect, or with whom you are trying to maintain a connection.

Other actions

Although the actions listed earlier have focused on relationships at work, relationships outside work – with family and friends for example – are equally important to an individual's well-being and wellness. There are additional actions for improving these personal relationships, and these can be found using an internet search.

Learn

Learning improves individuals' well-being because it

Makes them feel better about themselves.
Gives them a purpose in life.
Provides opportunities to connect with people.

Individuals should learn more about things they already know something about and also learn about things that are new to them. It is difficult to provide specific guidance on what to learn because of the vast range of things that people already know and the diversity of topics they might want to know about. In addition, people differ in their preferred learning style with, for example, some people preferring to go on training courses with other students, while others prefer online learning options such as webinars.

Give your time

Giving your time to help other people improves your well-being because, like learning, it

Makes you feel better about yourself.
Gives you a purpose in life.
Provides opportunities to connect with people.

This is an extension of the 'making time for others', described earlier in this chapter. However, it is extended to actions specifically intended to benefit the people with whom you are connecting.

This can begin with small acts of kindness towards other people and gradually extend to more significant activities, such as volunteering for charity work or work to help people with a disadvantage.

Take notice

Taking notice of what is happening around you, often called mindfulness, improves your well-being because it

Helps to reaffirm your life priorities.
Enhances your self-understanding.
Allows you to make positive choices based on your own values and motivations.

Mindfulness is, in effect, taking time for yourself and using it to enjoy the moment and the environment around you. There is a variety of types of mindfulness and a correspondingly wide variety of books, websites, and training courses dealing with them. Similarly, there is a wide variety of uses for mindfulness techniques. There are some individuals who make mindfulness a core element of their life, but many more simply use specific mindfulness techniques to deal with the difficulties of everyday life. However, there appears to be a general agreement that taking time for yourself to 'be in the moment', even if done infrequently, will help improve well-being.

Be physically active

Being active improves individuals' wellness, but it also makes an important contribution to individuals' well-being because it

Makes them feel better about themselves.
Enables them to set and achieve activity and fitness goals.
Causes chemical changes in their brains that reduce anxiety and depression.

The UK's National Health Service (NHS) website provides extensive guidance on physical activity[2], and what follows is a summary of the key points from this guidance of relevance to adults, with the authors' supplementary notes explaining the terms used on the website.

Adults should aim to:

- *do strengthening activities that work all the major muscle groups (legs, hips, back, abdomen, chest, shoulders and arms) on at least 2 days a week*
- *do at least 150 minutes of moderate intensity activity a week or 75 minutes of vigorous intensity activity a week*
- *spread exercise evenly over 4 to 5 days a week, or every day*
- *reduce time spent sitting or lying down and break up long periods of not moving with some activity*

Strengthening activities include the following:

- *carrying heavy shopping bags*
- *yoga*
- *Pilates*
- *tai chi*

- *lifting weights*
- *working with resistance bands*
- *doing exercises that use your own body weight, such as push-ups and sit-ups*
- *heavy gardening, such as digging and shovelling*

In addition to muscle-strengthening activities, you need to do aerobic activities, that is, activities that increase your heart rate and depth of breathing. Aerobic activities are also known as cardiovascular conditioning or simply cardio. There are various uses of the term aerobic – see, for example, the use of 'water aerobics' and 'aerobics' in the lists of examples given below. However, for our purposes, the definition just given is adequate. The aerobic activities can be of moderate intensity or vigorous intensity and the NHS website gives the following examples of the two levels of intensity.

Examples of moderate intensity activities include:

- *brisk walking*
- *water aerobics*
- *riding a bike*
- *dancing*
- *doubles tennis*
- *pushing a lawn mower*
- *hiking*
- *rollerblading*

Examples of vigorous activities include:

- *running*
- *swimming*
- *riding a bike fast or on hills*
- *walking up the stairs*
- *sports, like football, rugby, netball and hockey*
- *skipping*
- *aerobics*
- *gymnastics*
- *martial arts*

There are additional well-being benefits if physical activities take place in the open air, especially in green spaces. However, physical activity in highly polluted atmospheres, such as city centres, can impair wellness.

Have a healthy diet

The UK's NHS website also provides extensive guidance on what constitutes a healthy diet.[3]

This guidance begins with a general statement: *The key to a healthy diet is to eat the right amount of calories for how active you are so you balance the energy you consume with the energy you use* and then states that it is *recommended that men have around 2,500 calories a day (10,500 kilojoules). Women should have around 2,000 calories a day (8,400 kilojoules).* There are then eight tips for healthy eating with detailed notes on each of the tips. The eight tips are as follows:

1. *Base your meals on higher fibre starchy carbohydrates*
2. *Eat lots of fruit and veg*
3. *Eat more fish, including a portion of oily fish*
4. *Cut down on saturated fat and sugar*
5. *Eat less salt: no more than 6g a day for adults*
6. *Get active and be a healthy weight*
7. *Do not get thirsty*
8. *Do not skip breakfast*

Having a healthy diet is a major contributor to maintaining wellness, but it also contributes to well-being because people on a healthy diet tend to 'feel better about themselves'.

Resources

This section deals with the resources that individuals can access to improve their well-being and wellness. However, no details have been given on how these resources can be obtained since the mechanisms for this differ widely. In particular, there is a wide variety of availability of the resources from place to place, and differences in how much individuals have to pay for accessing the resources. The main types of resources are listed below.

Guidance and support with specific triggers. There are numerous organisations that specialise in triggers such as financial difficulties, housing problems, and relationship difficulties.

Guidance and support for specific well-being and wellness conditions. There are organisations that specialise in specific well-being and wellness conditions, such as anxiety, depression, and being overweight. There are also organisations that provide more holistic support and guidance, particularly for well-being conditions.

Tutors. Tutors are people who pass on competences. In the context of well-being, relevant tutors include those who teach such things as active listening and mindfulness, and in the context of wellness, they include those who teach such things as yoga, Pilates, and tai chi.

Counsellors and therapists. There is no definitive description of the difference between counsellors and therapists but, broadly speaking, counsellors provide support and guidance on a specific trigger such as bereavement or financial difficulties while therapists focus on broader well-being issues such as depression and anxiety. However, there is a broad overlap.

Self-help resources. There is a staggering range of self-help books, websites, devices, and apps devoted to well-being and wellness issues. Books on well-being and wellness can be found in the relevant section of most book shops, and they are also available online from bookseller and general sales websites. Some websites devoted to well-being and wellness may be of doubtful value, but the extensive self-help resources provided by authoritative organisations, such as the UK NHS, are very useful. The purchase price of some well-being and wellness devices may put them out of the reach of some people who would benefit from using them, but devices such as those for monitoring physical activity levels and cardiac functions can be literally life-saving. There is also an increasingly wide range of well-being and wellness apps, and some mobile device manufacturers provide them whether you want them or not!

All of the resources listed above can be accessed by individuals without the involvement of the organisation for which they work. However, organisations may choose to help their workers by, for example, identifying relevant local resources and providing workers with details of how they can be accessed, or providing selected resources such as free counselling for their workers.

Treatments

For the purposes of this book, treatments are interventions by competent professionals intended to restore impaired well-being or wellness. The competent professionals would typically be counsellors and therapists, but in cases of extreme impairment medical interventions might be required.

In traditional health and safety risk management, treatments have the following characteristics:

Organisations allocate responsibility for treating severe injury and severe mental and physical ill health to specialist medical personnel, almost always outside the organisation. There is rarely allocation of responsibility for treatment of impaired well-being or wellness.

Organisations provide treatments for minor injury and physical ill health, usually in the form of 'first aid' materials and/or personnel. There is rarely an equivalent provision of treatment for impaired well-being or wellness.

Increasingly, organisations are also providing mental health first aid in the form of personnel trained to recognise symptoms and make initial interventions. This is an important first step in dealing with workers' well-being, but it is focused on mental ill health, not impaired well-being which can be a precursor to mental and physical ill health.

All treatments are restorative, that is, they are intended to put things back to where they were before something went wrong – for example, an injury or an infection. There are no treatments that focus on prevention of impairment to, or improvement of, well-being and wellness.

This traditional approach to treatments is a necessary part of psychosocial risk management in order to deal with individuals whose well-being or wellness has deteriorated to such an extent that they have clinical-level symptoms. However, traditional treatment has to be extended in a number of ways for psychosocial risk management. These ways are as follows:

Taking into account the effects that injury and physical and mental ill health have on well-being and wellness.

Seeing impaired well-being and wellness as harms requiring treatment, just as injury and mental and physical ill health are harms requiring treatment.

Having arrangements in place for restorative well-being and wellness treatments that are available to workers who wish to restore their well-being and/or wellness following exposure to a psychosocial hazard or a trigger.

Ideally, also having arrangements for assisting workers to maintain and improve their well-being and wellness irrespective of their exposure to psychosocial hazards or triggers.

The types of treatment that will be required are those described in the earlier sections on *Actions* and *Resources* and organisations have a range of options for providing treatments. The most basic arrangements involve providing workers with information on the actions they can take to restore their well-being and wellness, and the local resources that are available to provide workers with help in restoring their well-being and wellness. The 'gold standard' arrangements would be treatment programmes customised for individual workers by relevant competent personnel, such as therapists, and funded by the organisation.

References

1   MobiSystems, Inc. *Oxford Dictionary*, version 15.8. Last accessed 17 January 2024.
2   www.nhs.uk/live-well/exercise/exercise-guidelines/physical-activity-guidelines-for-adults-aged-19-to-64/. Last accessed 28 January 2024.
3   www.nhs.uk/live-well/eat-well/how-to-eat-a-balanced-diet/eight-tips-for-healthy-eating/. Last accessed 28 January 2024.

9   The psychology

Crash course

There are aspects of human psychology that are important in psychosocial risk management but rarely have an impact on traditional health and safety, and you will have to be able to explain these aspects to your workers and interested parties. The aspects are

Individual differences. These are the differences between individuals caused by their nature, nurture, and current circumstances. These differences mean, among other things, that the same psychosocial risk source can have different effects on different individuals.

Personality. Personality affects immunity to psychosocial hazards, for example, introverts tend to enjoy working alone, while extraverts tend to hate it.

Self-selecting populations. Individuals do not usually apply for jobs that include psychosocial hazards that would have a negative impact on their well-being, for example, they do not apply to be a nurse if *duty of care* was a psychosocial threat for them. Similarly, individuals tend to leave jobs that are having a negative impact on their well-being or wellness. These factors mean that individuals in stable work settings tend to be ones with some immunity to the psychosocial threats associated with the role.

The power of the mind. Individuals can have feelings such as depression or anxiety without any external reason for these feelings that are known as endogenous depression and endogenous anxiety. Our minds can also generate illnesses, known as psychosomatic illnesses, that have no external cause. The power of the mind means that individuals may not always be able to identify an external cause of impaired well-being or wellness.

Introduction

This chapter deals with those aspects of human psychology that are important in psychosocial risk management but rarely have an impact on traditional health and safety. These aspects are

DOI: 10.4324/9781003490555-10

Individual differences, that is, the differences between individuals caused by their
nature, nurture, and current circumstances.
Personality and its role in immunity to psychosocial threats.
Self-selecting populations.
The power of the mind.

Individual differences

Individual differences are important in psychosocial risk management because of
the way they influence individuals' responses to psychosocial threats and triggers.
This was illustrated in Chapter 6 'The elimination and control', with differences
in personality and their effect on immunity to psychosocial threats. However,
there are many more individual differences that can affect immunity and these
are described in this section. The section begins with an overview of individual
differences, followed by a discussion of the causes of individual differences. The
section ends with a description of the role of personality in immunity to psychosocial hazards and triggers.

Overview

It is useful to divide individual differences into four categories as follows:

Physical differences. These include the differences that can be seen – for example,
height, hair colour, and weight – and those that cannot be seen – for example,
muscular strength, cardiovascular condition, and reaction time.
Physiological differences. These are differences that are caused primarily by the
chemical activities in the body. These can be short term – for example, the build-
up and dispersion of lactic acid in muscles that causes them to feel fatigued
and then recover – or long term – for example, the lack of insulin suffered by
diabetics.
Psychological differences. These are the differences that are primarily a function
of the activity in the brain. They include emotions, personality, motivation, and
intelligence. It is these differences that are the main focus in psychosocial risk
management.
Situational differences. These are differences external to the individual that
affect, or could affect, any or all of the three types of individual differences
just described. Situational differences include personal relationships, need
for financial and other resources, and opportunities for social contact and
learning.

Because of these differences, individuals behave, think, and feel differently
even if their circumstances are the same. In the context of psychosocial risk management, these differences mean that it may not be possible to predict a particular
individual's response to a specific psychosocial threat or trigger.

For each of these types of individual difference, there are two categories of relevance to psychosocial risk management.

Inter-individual differences. These are the differences between individuals. All of the examples of differences given in the previous paragraph create inter-individual differences. Some of these, such as height and weight, are visible, but the majority of physiological and psychological differences require special measurement techniques. For example, you can say that a person looks fit, or looks intelligent, but this has to be backed up with, for example, cardiovascular tests and intelligence tests, if it is to be more than a guess.

Intra-individual differences. These are the differences that occur within individuals over time. As with inter-individual differences, all of the examples of differences given in the previous paragraph also create intra-individual differences. Muscular fatigue is an obvious physiological example, and most people are familiar with the variations in their stress levels. Other examples include variations in individuals' ability to process information arising from fatigue, ill health, stress or alcohol consumption, and changes in their personal relationships affecting their emotions. There are also major intra-individual differences associated with ageing.

In the context of psychosocial risk management, intra-individual differences mean that it cannot be assumed, for example, because an individual currently has a high level of immunity to a specific psychosocial threat or trigger that this level of immunity will still be in place in a week, a month, or a year's time.

For the vast majority of health and safety hazards, for example, falling objects, electricity, and harmful chemicals, there is no need to consider differences between individuals – the harm will result irrespective of who comes into contact with the hazard. This means that it is possible to estimate the risk arising from a health and safety hazard without having to take into account inter- or intra-individual differences.[i]

Similarly, the outputs from health and safety risk assessment, that is, the recommendations for eliminating hazards and/or implementing risk control measures, rarely need to take into account inter- or intra-individual differences. The obvious exception is training as a risk control measure, which is a way of creating an intra-individual difference by increasing an individual's competence, but this is one of very few outputs of health and safety risk assessment that involves individual differences.

The picture is very different for psychosocial risk assessment. Here, the role of the individual is crucial both for estimating the risk and for deciding on risk control measures. These topics are discussed in Chapter 23 'Psychosocial threat and opportunity assessment' and Chapter 24 'Psychosocial threat and opportunity management'.

Causes of individual differences

There are three main causes of individual differences: nature, nurture, and current circumstances. Each of these is dealt with in separate subsections below.

Nature

The relevant ODE[1] definition of nature is the *inborn or hereditary characteristics as an influence on or determinant of personality.* The ODE also points out that nature is *Often contrasted with nurture,* and the nature–nurture debate will be discussed at the end of the subsection below on *Nurture.*

Many individual differences are determined by our genetic make-up. These include physical differences such as height and hair colour, physiological differences such as hormone secretion levels, for example, testosterone and insulin, and psychological differences such as personality and motivation. The key point about these genetically determined individual differences is that they are not subject to change, for example:

If your genetically determined height is two metres, then you will not grow beyond two metres. You may, however, not reach two metres if your nutrition during childhood is inadequate.

If your genetically determined hair colour is black, it will stay black until at a genetically determined time it starts to go grey. You can die your hair, but this will be a temporary effect.

If your genetically determined testosterone level is too high or too low, the adverse effects can be treated with medication and lifestyle changes, and similar actions can be taken for low levels of insulin.

If your genetically determined personality is introvert, you are never going to enjoy parties and other social events, although you may put up with them to obtain other benefits, or to carry out perceived duties.

If your genetically determined motivation is to support your family, you will avoid non-family-related activities and making decisions that might have a negative impact on your family, even if they would benefit you personally.

The evidence that there are genetically determined physical and physiological individual differences is very strong, but there is still debate about the evidence for genetically determined psychological differences. This is discussed at the end of the next subsection.

Nurture

Nurture is what an individual experiences while they are growing up. It covers all aspects of their upbringing, including their education, the environment they lived in, and the cultural influences of the people who brought them up, and to whom they were exposed.

Nurture has a role in determining many individual differences and some examples are given below.

Physical. Environment and nutrition affect physical differences such as muscle mass and body weight. Even when an individual difference is genetically determined, lack of adequate nutrition can mean that this genetically determined potential is not reached.

Physiological. Inadequate nutrition also affects physiological differences, particularly if the diet is deficient in the necessary minerals, such as zinc or iron, or in any of the required vitamins.

Psychological. The cultural environment in which an individual grows up determines a wide range of psychological individual differences, including preferences for food and drink, appropriate ways of behaving towards various groups of people, particularly towards members of the opposite sex, and the sorts of phobias, superstitions, and beliefs that were discussed in Chapter 6 'The elimination and control'.

Psychologists have expended a great deal of effort over the years debating whether nature or nurture is the more important in determining individual differences – the so-called nature–nurture debate. However, the most likely explanation is that nature determines potential and nurture determines achievement. It was noted earlier that an individual might have a genetic height of two metres but not reach this height because of inadequate nutrition. Other examples of potential versus achievement include

Intelligence – an individual might have an above-average potential intelligence quotient (IQ) of 120 but only reach the average 100 because of poor nutrition.

Motivation – an individual might be motivated by learning and self-development but be unable to use this motivation because of the educational and cultural circumstances in which they grow up.

Immune system – an individual might have an inbuilt immunity to a range of diseases but be unable to use this immunity because their immune system has been compromised by the lack of relevant vitamins and minerals in their childhood diet.

Although psychosocial risk professionals need to be aware of the wide range of individual differences and their effect on the requirements for psychosocial risk management, the source of these individual differences does not matter in practice. They have to be taken into account whether they are caused by genes or upbringing. In addition, they may be caused by neither – they may be caused by current circumstances, as described in the next subsection.

Current circumstances

Individuals can be thought of as having a characteristic physical, physiological, and psychological profile determined by their nature and nurture, and this profile is steady over time, apart from changes due to ageing. However, current circumstances can result in situational differences between individuals because the circumstances have different effects on different people, and these effects vary in nature and strength. Some examples of current circumstances and their various effects are given below.

A small improvement in financial circumstances due to, for example, a small lottery win or a small inheritance. Some individuals may 'blow the whole lot' on a new car or a holiday, providing a temporary boost to well-being, while others may open a savings account to provide a more-or-less permanent, but lower level, support for their well-being.

A very large improvement in financial circumstances due to, for example, a very large lottery win or a very large inheritance. This will result in some individuals changing to a lifestyle that creates high levels of well-being and wellness, others will embark on a programme of significant charitable donations that incidentally increases their own well-being, and some individuals will change to a lifestyle that destroys their well-being and wellness.

A physical illness. Some individuals are able to deal with physical illness in ways that result in minimal negative impacts on their well-being and wellness, while others go into a vicious cycle whereby their illness causes a decrease in well-being that, in turn, exacerbates their illness. This is discussed in more detail in the later section of this chapter that deals with the power of the mind.

In general, any change in an individual's circumstances has the potential to affect their well-being and/or wellness, either for better or for worse. However, as the earlier illustrations show, there is not usually a way of predicting the effect of a given change on well-being and wellness for a particular individual. This is important in psychosocial risk management because changes in current circumstances can have a major effect on an individual's immunity to psychosocial threats and triggers. Taking current circumstances into account is dealt with in more detail in Chapter 23 'Psychosocial threat and opportunity assessment'.

Personality and immunity

As was seen in Chapter 6 'The elimination and control', different types of personality have different levels of immunity to psychosocial threats and the Introversion--Extraversion scale and the Adaptability scale were used to illustrate this. The role of personality in individual differences is dealt with in more detail in the present section.

There are very many personality tests available, and they range from the 'jokey' tests, only done for fun, to 'serious' tests used by competent professionals, for example, in medicine to diagnose personality disorders and in HR during selection for particular roles. It is these 'serious' tests that are the subject of this section.

Personality tests measure individuals' personality on a number of scales, and the Introversion--Extraversion and Adaptability scales have already been mentioned. However, typical personality tests have more scales, and one well-known personality test has 16 scales. This is Cattell's 16 personality factor test (16 pf), and the factors used in this test and the personality characteristics associated with each factor are summarised in Table 9.1. Note that the 16 pf test has been revised many times since it was first published in the 1940s, hence the nonsequential lettering in Table 9.1.

Table 9.1 Cattell's 16 personality factors

Factor	Low-score characteristics	High-score characteristics
A – Warmth	Reserved, detached, critical	Outgoing, warm-hearted
B – Reasoning	Less intelligent, concrete thinking	More intelligent, abstract thinking
C – Emotional stability	Affected by feelings, easily upset	Emotionally stable, faces reality
E – Dominance	Humble, mild, accommodating	Assertive, aggressive, stubborn
F – Liveliness	Sober, prudent, serious	Happy-go-lucky, impulsive, lively
G – Rule consciousness	Expedient, disregards rules	Conscientious, persevering
H – Social boldness	Shy, restrained, timid	Venturesome, socially bold
I – Sensitivity	Tough-minded, self-reliant	Tender-minded, clinging
L – Vigilance	Trusting, adaptable	Suspicious, self-opinionated
M – Abstractedness	Practical, careful	Imaginative
N – Privateness	Forthright, natural	Shrewd, calculating
O – Apprehension	Self-assured, confident	Apprehensive, self-reproaching
Q1 – Openness to change	Conservative	Experimenting, liberal
Q2 – Self-reliance	Group-dependent	Self-sufficient
Q3 – Perfectionism	Undisciplined, self-conflict	Controlled, socially precise
Q4 – Tension	Relaxed, tranquil	Tense, frustrated

Source: Adapted from a range of internet sources by Tony Boyle for the purposes of this book.

Individuals will have different scores on each of the personality factors, and the pattern of these scores is their 'personality profile'. These personality profiles can be used in a number of ways, including selecting people for particular roles. This is done as follows:

A number of people who are known to be good at the role take the 16 pf, and the recruiters try to identify any common personality profiles.

Where one or more common personality profiles are identified, the recruiters work on the assumption that this personality profile at least contributes to success at the role.

Candidates for the role take the 16 pf, and only candidates with personality profiles similar to those who are already good at the role are recruited.

This 16 pf could be used in psychosocial risk management to recruit individuals who had personality profiles similar to individuals already in a role, and showing high immunity to the psychosocial threats associated with that role. However, one of the personality tests focused on personality profiles of particular relevance to occupational settings would probably be a better instrument for this purpose than general personality tests such as the 16 pf. One such test is the SHL *Occupational Personality Questionnaire* introduced in Chapter 6, and the full list of traits making up an SHL occupational personality profile is given in Table 9.2, together with the high score characteristics of each trait.

Table 9.2 Occupational personality questionnaire traits

Trait name	High-score characteristics
Persuasive (RP1)	Enjoys selling, comfortable using negotiation, likes to change other people's views
Controlling (RP2)	Likes to be in charge, takes the lead, tells others what to do, takes control
Outspoken (RP3)	Freely expresses opinions, makes disagreement clear, prepared to criticise others
Independent minded (RP4)	Prefers to follow own approach, prepared to disregard majority decisions
Outgoing (RP5)	Lively and animated in groups, talkative, enjoys attention
Affiliative (RP6)	Enjoys others' company, likes to be around people, can miss the company of others
Socially confident (RP7)	Feels comfortable when first meeting people, at ease in formal situations
Modest (RP8)	Dislikes discussing achievements, keeps quiet about personal success
Democratic (RP9)	Consults widely, involves others in decision-making, less likely to make decisions alone
Caring (RP10)	Sympathetic and considerate towards others, helpful and supportive, gets involved in others' problems
Data rational (TS1)	Likes working with numbers, enjoys analysing statistical information, bases decisions on facts and figures
Evaluative (TS2)	Critically evaluates information, looks for potential limitations, focuses on errors
Behavioural (TS3)	Tries to understand motives and behaviour, enjoys analysing people
Conventional (TS4)	Prefers well-established methods, favours a more conventional approach
Conceptual (TS5)	Interested in theories, enjoys discussing abstract concepts
Innovative (TS6)	Generates new ideas, enjoys being creative, thinks of original solutions
Variety seeking (TS7)	Prefers variety, tries out new things, likes changes to regular routine, can become bored by repetitive work
Adaptable (TS8)	Changes behaviour to suit the situation, adapts approach to different people
Forward thinking (TS9)	Takes a long-term view, sets goals for the future, more likely to take a strategic perspective
Detail conscious (TS10)	Focuses on detail, likes to be methodical, organised and systematic, may become preoccupied with detail
Conscientious (TS11)	Focuses on getting things finished, persists until the job is done
Rule following (TS12)	Follows rules and regulations, prefers clear guidelines, finds it difficult to break rules
Relaxed (FE1)	Finds it easy to relax, rarely feels tense
Worrying (FE2)	Feels nervous before important occasions, worries about things going wrong
Tough-minded (FE3)	Not easily offended, can ignore insults, may be insensitive to personal criticism

(*Continued*)

Table 9.2 (Continued)

Trait name	High-score characteristics
Optimistic (FE4)	Expects things will turn out well, looks to the positive aspects of a situation, has an optimistic view of the future
Trusting (FE5)	Trusts people, sees others as reliable and honest, believes what others say
Emotionally controlled (FE6)	Can conceal feelings from others, rarely displays emotion
Vigorous (FE7)	Thrives on activity, likes to be busy, enjoys having a lot to do
Competitive (FE8)	Has a need to win, enjoys competitive activities, dislikes losing
Achieving (FE9)	Ambitious and career-centred, likes to work to demanding goals and targets
Decisive (FE10)	Makes fast decisions, reaches conclusions quickly, less cautious

Source: Adapted from a range of internet sources by Tony Boyle for the purposes of this book.

It can be seen from Table 9.2 that many of the trait characteristics can readily be linked with psychosocial threats and triggers, and what tends to happen is that individuals self-select. That is, individuals whose personality profile does not provide immunity to the psychosocial threats associated with a role will either not apply for the role or leave after a brief exposure to the psychosocial threats. The next section deals with this topic in more detail.

Self-selecting populations

The concept of self-selecting populations is an important one in psychosocial risk management. This section describes what is meant by self-selecting populations, and how they influence psychosocial risk assessment and psychosocial risk control.

Tony Boyle first came across self-selecting populations in the early 1970s when he was working on job satisfaction measurement for factory workers – there were lots of people working in factories in those days. When his team looked at job satisfaction among shift workers, they found that it was extremely high. They did not expect this, probably because of their own dissatisfaction at having to work during the night to do the interviews. They also found that a large proportion of nightshift workers liked these shifts, and this was the case whether they were on permanent nights or alternating between night shifts and day shifts. Being thorough researchers, they wanted to know the cause of this satisfaction, so they adopted the radical approach of asking the workers – and their response was quite clear. People who do not like working night shifts move to other jobs in the factory, or jobs in another factory, where they do not have to work night shifts.

This, simple as it is, is the fundamental principle underlying self-selecting populations. Where, over a period of time, a group of workers is

Engaged in similar activities
In a stable environment
With opportunities for worker turnover

Then the majority of the workers will be the ones who are there because they like the job – or at least find it tolerable.

Self-selection can also take place before individuals take jobs. Most individuals know that there are types of jobs for which they would never apply because the work involved, or the conditions of work, would not suit their personal preferences.

The job satisfaction study just described predated the idea of psychosocial threats by a long way, but the principle holds. Put into up-to-date terminology, the following apply.

All roles have psychosocial threats associated with them. The psychosocial threats vary in nature and severity, but no job is completely free from psychosocial threats.

Where a number of workers are carrying out the same role, there will be a range of effects on their well-being and wellness due to individual differences.

Over a period of time, workers whose well-being or wellness is being impaired by the psychosocial threats, that is, workers who are victims of the threats, will tend to leave.

Replacement workers will stay if they are not affected, or affected very little, by the psychosocial threats.

Replacement workers will leave if they, in turn, become victims of the psychosocial threats.

The occurrence of self-selecting populations means that the existence of a psychosocial threat in particular circumstances does not necessarily mean that there are victims of that psychosocial threat. It can be the case that the population exposed to the psychosocial threat has self-selected to such an extent that all victims have left. Where this is the case, resources expended on removing the psychosocial threat, or reducing the psychosocial risk, would probably be better used elsewhere. The implications of self-selecting populations for psychosocial threat and opportunity assessment and management are discussed in Chapter 23 'Psychosocial threat and opportunity assessment' and Chapter 24 'Psychosocial threat and opportunity management'.

The power of the mind

Earlier chapters have dealt with the effects of psychosocial threats and triggers on the well-being and wellness of individuals. In psychological terminology these effects on well-being and wellness are exogenous – that is, they are *attributable to an agent or organism outside the body* (ODE). Thus, exposure to psychosocial threats at work can result in, for example, exogenous depression.

However, there are also cases of endogenous depression – that is depression that is *not attributable to any external or environmental factor* (ODE). Depression has been used as an example, but all aspects of well-being and wellness can alter endogenously. Most individuals have times when they feel 'low' or mildly anxious for no apparent reason, and at other times they feel unaccountably happy or content. For most individuals, most of the time, these endogenous effects are mild and transient, but for some individuals they can be extremely serious.

When it is primarily wellness that is being affected endogenously, it is usually referred to as psychosomatic illness. Somatic means *relating to the body, especially as distinct from the mind* (ODE), and a psychosomatic illness is one that is being created by the individual's mind, rather than by an identifiable external cause. There is a wide range of psychosomatic illness, but the ones of particular relevance to psychosocial risk management include the following:

Feeling tired and/or being unable to sleep.
Various aches and pains, for example, muscle pain, headaches, and migraines.
Heart problems such as high blood pressure and arrythmia (irregular heart beat).
Respiratory problems such as shortness of breath.
Gastric problems such as indigestion and stomach ulcers.
Skin problems such as acne, rashes, and shingles.

This brief note on psychosomatic illness is an oversimplification but, in the context of psychosocial risk management, it is important to maintain awareness of the fact that 'our minds have minds of their own', and individuals are not always in complete control of how they think, feel, and act. While it may always be necessary to try to identify the psychosocial threat or trigger that is causing impaired well-being or wellness in a particular individual, you have to bear in mind that the impairment may be endogenous. Where this is the case, treatment is usually the only effective option.

Note

i There are, however, some exceptions to this, for example, taking into account the needs of particular groups such as young people, new and expectant mothers, and people with particular disabilities.

Reference

1   MobiSystems, Inc. *Oxford Dictionary*, version 15.8. Last accessed 17 January 2024.

10 The people

Crash course

Psychosocial risk management has to take into account the fact that there are perpetrators of psychosocial risk sources, and that the presence of a psychosocial risk source does not necessarily mean that it is having a negative effect (creating victims). It may be having a positive effect on some individuals (creating beneficiaries) or having no effect at all (because, for example, those exposed are immune). A psychosocial management system should have processes for dealing with these categories of people, who may be workers or interested parties.

Introduction

As was seen in Chapter 5, the presence of a psychosocial risk source does not necessarily mean that it is having a negative effect (creating victims). Indeed, it may be having a positive effect on some individuals (creating beneficiaries) or having no effect because the individuals exposed are immune. It was also seen in Chapter 5 that many psychosocial risk sources are created by the behaviour of individuals, and these individuals were described as perpetrators. The present chapter deals with each of these categories of individual, who can be workers or interested parties.

This chapter has the following sections

Perpetrators
Victims
Beneficiaries
The immune
Interested parties

Perpetrators

Perpetrators are individuals whose behaviour creates psychosocial risk sources. Perpetrators' behaviour may involve carrying out an action (bullying and discrimination, for example), failing to carry out an action (not setting objectives or not

DOI: 10.4324/9781003490555-11

giving praise, for example), or carrying out an action inadequately (issuing unclear instructions or setting impractical objectives, for example). For the purposes of this chapter, perpetrator behaviour that creates a psychosocial hazard will be referred to as 'unacceptable behaviour'.

There are various aspects of unacceptable behaviour that need to be taken into account in psychosocial risk management, and the following aspects are dealt with in separate subsections below:

Lack of awareness or competence
Motivation
Punishment
Re-education
Relocation

The practicalities of dealing with perpetrators are described in Chapter 23 'Psychosocial threat and opportunity assessment' and Chapter 27 'Psychosocial investigation'.

Lack of awareness or competence

Many instances of unacceptable behaviour are due to the perpetrator simply not being aware that they are creating a psychosocial risk source. For example, bullies who see their unacceptable behaviour as 'robust management', managerial workers who set vague objectives because they think they are encouraging 'initiative' in their team, and some workers who think racist or sexist remarks are simply 'friendly banter'.

Similarly, lack of competence can result in the creation of psychosocial risk sources. For example, managerial workers who lack managerial and leadership skills can create a whole range of psychosocial risk sources for their team, workers lacking in interpersonal skills can create psychosocial risk sources for their co-workers, and top management can create the organisation-wide risk source of a psychosocial nature *lack of clear vision and objectives*.

Motivation

It is important to establish the motivation for a perpetrator's unacceptable behaviour since their motivation will determine the type of action required to remedy the situation, that is, to remove the psychosocial risk source. Examples of perpetrator motivation are discussed next.

Being ordered to do it. Most perpetrators have line managers, and these line managers can order them to indulge in unacceptable behaviour. For example,

A perpetrator may have a line manager who is a bully and who insists that their team members behave in the same way.

A perpetrator may have a line manager who refuses to set clear objectives to avoid accountability, and this means the perpetrator cannot, in turn, set clear objectives.

A perpetrator may have a line manager who thinks racist or sexist remarks are simply 'friendly banter' that increases team spirit, and expects his or her team to join in.

Having to do it through force of circumstances. The most extreme circumstances are those that occur in an emergency, but various psychosocial risk sources can be created by circumstances outside the perpetrator's control. For example, *having too much to do within a certain time or with a set number of workers* may be a circumstance that creates the need for unacceptable behaviours among the workers involved. These circumstances can be transient – a sudden but short increase in workload, for example – or it may be a deliberate feature of the way the organisation is set up – for example, some aspects of the gig economy.

Having to do it because of peer pressure. Peer pressure can be a very powerful force, and if the group norm is to indulge in unacceptable behaviours, then workers will conform to this norm – even if they disapprove of it. Peer pressure plays an important role in maintaining systemic psychosocial risk sources, that is, psychosocial risk sources that are a characteristic of an organisation's culture. Systemic psychosocial hazards are dealt with in detail in Chapter 23 'Psychosocial threat and opportunity assessment'.

Doing it to maintain their own well-being and wellness. It is unfortunately the case that some individuals have to indulge in unacceptable behaviours in order to maintain their own well-being and wellness. For example,

Some individuals are bullies because they need to be dominant and they like the feeling of power over other people that bullying gives them.

Some individuals believe that the nation, or race or religion to which they belong is so superior to other nations, races, or religions that they need to make demeaning remarks about other nations, races, or religions to justify this belief.

Some men believe that women are inferior to men and talk about women, and behave towards women, in ways that reflect this belief.

Determining perpetrators' motivation requires appropriate investigations, and the nature of these investigations is discussed in Chapter 27 'Psychosocial investigation'.

Punishment

For the purposes of this book, punishment is the action an organisation takes in retribution for a perpetrator's unacceptable behaviour. Punishments vary in severity from a mild reprimand from a line manager to summary dismissal for unacceptable behaviours such as theft and violence. Perpetrators may be subject to other punishments, for example, fines and imprisonment, for the more egregious unacceptable behaviours, but these types of punishment are outside the scope of the psychosocial management system.

Most organisations have a procedure in place that sets out types of unacceptable behaviour and the nature of the punishment that will be meted out for each type of unacceptable behaviour. Typically, this procedure is referred to as the *Disciplinary procedure* or, in organisations with outdated management systems, the *Disciplinary policy.* This procedure or policy may be supplemented by other procedures or policies dealing in more detail with specific types of behaviour that will result in disciplinary action, or setting out required behaviours that will result in disciplinary action if they are not carried out. However, for the purposes of a psychosocial risk management system, these procedures and policies have the following limitations:

They deal only with the more severe forms of unacceptable behaviour. There is nothing in the procedures about the day-to-day disciplinary action required to deal with low levels of unacceptable behaviour, for example, the mild reprimands from a line manager referred to in the first paragraph of this subsection.

They deal only with a subset of psychosocial risk sources. Typically, these procedures or policies are set up and operated by HR personnel, and their primary purpose is to meet legal requirements and protect the organisation from any actions of workers that would harm the organisation. This means that whole categories of psychosocial risk source, some of which may be essential to the operation of the organisation or benefit it financially, are not included in the lists of unacceptable behaviours.

They deal only with punishment, and not with causation. Typically, there is a one-to-one relationship between the severity of the unacceptable behaviour, and the severity of the punishment with little, if any, account being taken of the reasons why the perpetrator indulged in the unacceptable behaviour. As was seen in the previous section on motivation, in psychosocial risk management causes of unacceptable behaviour should be taken into account.

There are no alternatives to punishment, only different punishments and different degrees of severity of punishment. This may be an adequate approach when the unacceptable behaviours are all related to legal requirements, but when the unacceptable behaviours cover the full range of psychosocial risk sources alternatives to punishment are required. Two of these alternatives, re-education and relocation, are considered in the next two subsections.

Resolving the issues associated with the punishment of perpetrators is dealt with in Chapter 24 'Psychosocial threat and opportunity management'.

Re-education

As was seen earlier in the chapter, the creation of psychosocial hazards can be due to a lack of awareness or a lack of competence. Both of these can be remedied by appropriate re-education followed by monitoring to check that the re-education has been effective. In this context, the re-education could involve one or more of the following:

Written or verbal instruction on unacceptable behaviours and how to replace them with acceptable behaviours.
Guidance on means of self-help with attitude and behaviour modification.
Training courses to provide relevant awareness and competence.
Counselling for workers who, for example, are creating psychosocial hazards because of their personal circumstances.
Mentoring by co-workers or external mentors.

For those perpetrators who are creating a psychosocial risk source in order to maintain their own well-being and wellness, education in methods of restoring their well-being and wellness may also be required.

The use of re-education is dealt with in more detail in Chapter 24 'Psychosocial threat and opportunity management'.

Relocation

It can be the case that a perpetrator is not a suitable case for re-education, or the re-education is not effective. In these circumstances an alternative is to relocate the perpetrator to another location or another role where their unacceptable behaviour will not create a psychosocial risk source for others. This may involve financial loss for the perpetrator if, for example, they are moved from a managerial role to a non-managerial role due to failure to achieve the managerial competences necessary to avoid creating psychosocial risk sources. However, this financial loss may be preferable to dismissal from the organisation, which would be the only other option. Similarly, relocation might cause inconvenience, for example, having to work at a location further from home in order to be with co-workers who are immune to the psychosocial risk source the perpetrator is creating. However, inconvenience is usually better than dismissal.

Victims

Victims are the individuals who suffer impairment to their well-being or wellness as a result of exposure to a psychosocial risk source.

The nature and severity of the harm caused by a psychosocial risk source will vary from individual to individual due to inter-individual differences, and from time to time in the same individual due to intra-individual differences. The term 'vulnerability' will be used to describe the individual's state at the time of exposure, and for the purposes of this book, vulnerability has the following characteristics:

Vulnerability is risk source specific – an individual can be highly vulnerable to some psychosocial risk sources and not vulnerable at all to other psychosocial risk sources.

Vulnerability is individual specific – the same psychosocial risk source, at the same
    dose will affect different individuals to different degrees.
Vulnerability is equivalent to lack of immunity – as immunity to a psychosocial
    risk source increases, vulnerability to that risk source decreases.

Figure 10.1 illustrates the relationship between risk source dose and the victim's
vulnerability.
Note the following points about Figure 10.1.

Even very low doses of a psychosocial risk source can cause clinical symptoms in
    highly vulnerable individuals.
Low levels of vulnerability (high immunity) can be effective protection against
    even quite high psychosocial risk source doses.

In conventional health and safety risk assessments, practitioners only measure
the hazard. For example, they do a noise survey, or they get an occupational health
specialist to measure airborne contaminants. This is an effective approach because
the practitioners know that the victims of these health and safety hazards are all
equally vulnerable. There may be a few individuals who require special attention,
for example, those with existing hearing loss or respiratory problems, but in general, there will be a homogeneous population with regard to vulnerability to the
hazard. This is not the case with psychosocial hazards, and in some cases, there
are individuals for whom the psychosocial hazard is actually a psychosocial
opportunity from which they benefit. These beneficiaries are dealt with in the next
section.

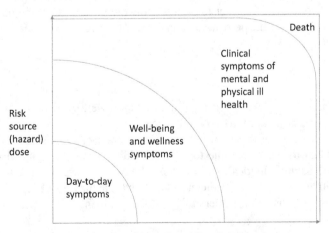

Figure 10.1 Risk source (hazard) dose and victim vulnerability.

In an ideal world, there would be no victims – either because psychosocial risk sources that had adverse effects on individuals had been eliminated, or because only individuals with the relevant immunity to the psychosocial risk sources were exposed to them. One aim of psychosocial risk management is to achieve this ideal state, and the techniques required are discussed in Chapter 24 'Psychosocial threat and opportunity management'. However, in the meantime, there will be victims, and this section discusses the following aspects of dealing with victims:

Identification
Treatment
Compensation

Identification

There are two problems associated with the identification of victims: not being able to identify them and identifying individuals who are falsely claiming to be victims.

There are various reasons why victims of psychosocial risk sources may not come forward:

The stigma associated with mental ill health may prevent some victims from reporting their impaired well-being.
The fear of losing their job if they complain.
There may be no suitable means of reporting psychosocial hazards, such as a bullying line manager or an aggressive co-worker.
Not wanting to appear 'weak' in front of their co-workers.

All of these reasons should be taken into account in a psychosocial risk management system, and the relevant issues are dealt with in Chapter 21 'Awareness and communication' and Chapter 26 'Psychosocial monitoring, auditing, and corrective action'.

The other problem with the identification of victims – identifying individuals who are falsely claiming to be victims – is more difficult to deal with, particularly when the victim is claiming harm to their well-being. Because impaired well-being is self-reported, and there are no effective ways of objectively verifying it,[i] impaired well-being can become a 'malingerer's charter' in the same way that unverifiable back pain can be a malingerer's charter in traditional health and safety. The usual way of identifying individuals who are falsely claiming impaired well-being is with an interview conducted by an interviewer with the relevant competences. These competences are discussed in Chapter 20 'Competences' and Chapter 27 'Psychosocial investigation'.

Treatment

Treatment of impaired well-being and wellness was discussed in Chapter 8 'The improvers', where treatment was defined as *interventions by competent professionals intended to restore impaired well-being or wellness*, and it was noted that *the competent professionals would typically be counsellors and therapists, but in cases of extreme impairment, medical interventions might be required.*

In traditional health and safety risk management systems, the only treatment in the scope of the management system is treatment of minor injuries, usually referred to as first-aid treatment – treatment of other injuries and ill health is not part of the system. However, in a psychosocial risk management system, it will be necessary to include the management of treatment for victims even if the treatment itself is provided by an external supplier.

Compensation

In traditional health and safety, financial compensation may be paid for work-related injuries and ill health. The amount of compensation is usually linked to the severity of the harm sustained and may be determined by a court. However, the degree of harm sustained usually has to be high before the payment of compensation is considered. There are usually no small financial payments for minor injuries, for example.

Using a similar model for exposure to psychosocial hazards would suggest the following structure for compensation for well-being and wellness impairment.

Minor and transient impairments would not be considered for compensation.
Serious and long-term impairments would require compensation.
There would be a 'sliding scale' of compensation between the two extremes listed above.

The rationale for this approach is that years of impaired well-being, for example, as a result of a bullying manager, even if only at a moderate level, warrants compensation.

Beneficiaries

Beneficiaries are the individuals for whom exposure to a psychosocial hazard improves their well-being or wellness. However, the relationship between dose level and benefits is not necessarily straightforward, and this is discussed next, beginning with a traditional health and safety example.

Many hazardous substances are actually beneficial in small doses. This is true of substances such as arsenic and a whole range of medicines. For example, widely used painkillers (analgesics) such as paracetamol produce huge benefits for the population, but the sale of paracetamol is usually restricted because it can be fatal in large doses.

There are psychosocial risk sources that behave in a similar manner. For example, the hazard of a psychosocial nature *performing highly repetitive tasks* is a benefit when it is an appropriate element of a job role. Authors who are struggling with a section of writing often seek out a repetitive task as a break. They still doing

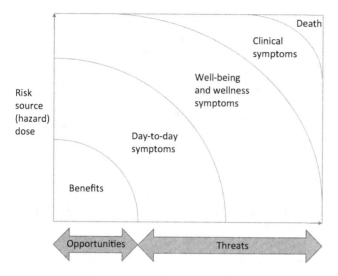

Figure 10.2 Risk source (hazard) dose and opportunities and threats.

something necessary and useful but their brain stops hurting! This is illustrated in Figure 10.2 that also shows that as the amount of repetitive work increases, the opportunities associated with the psychosocial risk source change to threats.

Note the following about Figure 10.2.

The opportunities are shown as taking up around one third of the horizontal axis, but this is an arbitrary amount for illustrative purposes. In practice, it will depend on individual differences. Inter-individual differences, such as level of cognitive ability, and intra-individual differences, such as level of negative emotion, will affect the extent to which the psychosocial risk source is an opportunity. Individuals with reduced cognitive ability will see the availability of repetitive tasks as a significant opportunity with very little threat, as will people temporarily suffering from severe negative emotions.

To be a true reflection of what happens in practice, there have to be individuals who are suitable to be beneficiaries. For example, Figure 10.2 would not work for individuals who would not tolerate repetitive work under any circumstances. The suitability as a beneficiary will be referred to as 'receptivity', and the terminology and phraseology for victims and beneficiaries will be as follows:

Victims have vulnerability, which means they are vulnerable, and as a result, when they are exposed to a psychosocial threat, they suffer symptoms.

Beneficiaries have receptivity, which means they are receptive, and as a result, when they are exposed to psychosocial risk sources, they obtain benefits.

Figure 10.2 clearly illustrates why, in psychosocial risk management, it is more appropriate to refer to psychosocial risk sources, rather than psychosocial hazards.

The immune

The immune are individuals whose well-being and wellness are not affected by a particular psychosocial risk source – for these individuals, the risk source is neither a threat nor an opportunity.

Because these individuals are unaffected, treatment and compensation are irrelevant, but it can be useful to determine why the individuals have their immunity. The techniques for doing this are discussed in Chapter 20 'Competences'.

Interested parties

An interested party is defined in ISO 45001[1] as

> *person or organization that can affect, be affected by, or perceive itself to be affected by a decision or activity.*

From the point of view of psychosocial risk management, interested parties are

Individuals who can be perpetrators, victims, or immune.
Organisations that create psychosocial hazards for your organisation's workers.

Typical interested parties are a

Provider or supplier – defined in ISO 9000[2] as an *organization that provides a product or a service.*[ii]
Customer – defined in ISO 9000 a *person or organization that could or does receive a product or a service that is intended for or required by this person or organization.*
Member of the public.

Part of the work required to set up a psychosocial management system is identifying possible interested parties and deciding which ones are within the scope of the management system. This is dealt with in Chapter 16 'Needs and expectations'.

The practical difficulty with interested parties is the lack of control an organisation has over their behaviours. How this can be dealt with is discussed in Chapter 24 'Psychosocial threat and opportunity management'.

Notes

i In theory, impaired well-being should produce chemical changes in the body – referred to as the physiological concomitants of impaired well-being. There is some evidence that this is the case, but there is not sufficient evidence to construct a physiological test for impaired well-being.
ii A product is an *output of an organization that can be produced without any transaction taking place between the organization and the customer* (ISO 9000), and a service is an

output of an organization with at least one activity necessarily performed between the organization and the customer (ISO 9000).

References

1   British Standards Institution. *Occupational health and safety management systems – Requirements with guidance for use,* BSI ISO 45001, 2018. BSI 2018.
2   British Standards Institution. *Quality management systems – Fundamentals and vocabulary,* BSI ISO 9000, 2015. BSI 2015.

11 The psychosocial management system terminology

Crash course

This is a very nerdy chapter, dealing with differences in definitions, and why some definitions need to be changed for use in the psychosocial management system described in this book. If this is not the sort of thing that interests you, you can skip this chapter if you are willing to accept that the following definitions are needed for Part II of this book.

Psychosocial objective

> Objective which, if achieved, will maintain or improve worker well-being and/ or wellness.

Psychosocial risk

> Effect of uncertainty on psychosocial objectives.

Psychosocial opportunity

> Circumstance or set of circumstances that can lead to improvement of worker well-being and/or wellness.

Psychosocial threat

> Circumstance or set of circumstances that can lead to reduction in worker well-being and/or wellness.

Psychosocial risk source

> Element which, alone or in combination, has the potential to give rise to psychosocial risk.

Psychosocial risk control

> Measure that maintains and/or modifies psychosocial risk.

DOI: 10.4324/9781003490555-12

Introduction

ISO 45003[1] provides guidelines for managing psychosocial risk but is not a stand-alone management system. Its *Introduction* begins as follows.

> *This document provides guidance on the management of psychosocial risks and promoting well-being at work, as part of an occupational health and safety (OH&S) management system.*

> *This document is intended to be used together with ISO 45001, which contains requirements and guidance on planning, implementing, reviewing, evaluating and improving an OH&S management system.*

This means that it is ISO 45001[2] that forms the basis for the ISO 45003, *management of psychosocial risk*, and it is also the basis for the psychosocial management system described in this book.

However, ISO 45001 is, in turn, based on the harmonised structure for management systems given in Annex SL of the Consolidated ISO Supplement to the ISO/IEC Directives.[3] All ISO management systems must include the identical core text, common terms, and core definitions, and this requirement explains some of the problems with ISO 45001 – for example, having two types of risk.

In addition, ISO 45001 and ISO 45003 are primarily about preventing injury and ill health and the terminology used in these documents reflects this. For example, the use of the term 'psychosocial hazards' implies that these hazards can only result in harm, not opportunities. ISO 45002[4] provides further guidance on opportunities but not in sufficient detail for the purposes of the psychosocial management system described in this book.

In contrast, the risk management described in ISO 31000:2018 *Risk management – guidelines*[5] deals with risks that can have positive effects – referred to as opportunities – as well as negative effects – referred to as threats. For this reason, general risk management terminology has been used in this book. The terminology is taken from ISO 31000 *Risk management – guidelines*, ISO 31010 *Risk management – risk assessment techniques*,[6] and Guide 73 *Risk management – vocabulary*,[7] and it is needed to allow for positive outcomes of risk.

This chapter describes how the contents of the six documents just described have been interpreted and it has the following sections.

Definitions related to risk. As was mentioned in the introduction, risk in ISO 45001 and ISO 45003 has purely negative effects. Since the psychosocial management system described in this book includes ways of improving well-being and wellness, risk definitions that allow for this are needed. This section describes the terms to be used and the reasons for using them.

Definitions related to organisations. Despite there being six documents contributing to the psychosocial risk management system, many of the terms used are not defined. This section deals with terms of relevance to organisations, and it sets out how these terms will be used.

Definitions related to *occupational* and *at work*. These terms are used in ISO 45001, ISO 45002, and ISO 45003, but they appear to be synonymous. This section is a description of how these terms, and related terms such as job and employment, will be used.

Definitions related to *work*. The term work is used in a variety of ways in ISO 45003 and the usages are not always consistent. This section is a description of how *work* and related terms will be used in the rest of this book.

Definitions related to risk

There is a problem with the use of the term 'risk' because it has two different meanings.

Risk as a cause of negative and positive effects. This usage occurs in Annex SL, which defines risk as *the effect of uncertainty*, and in note 1 to the definition states *An effect is a deviation from the expected – positive or negative.* All ISO management systems have to include the Annex SL definitions and text, so they are reproduced in ISO 45001.

Risk as a cause of only negative effects. This usage also occurs in Annex SL in the phrase *risks and opportunities*, where *risks* appear to be negative and *opportunities* (a term not defined) appear to be positive. Because the phrase *risks and opportunities* is used in Annex SL, it is also used in ISO 45001.

It appears that Annex SL is saying that risk gives rise to risks and opportunities – which does not make much sense.

ISO 45001 had an opportunity to clarify the matter when it attempted to bypass the Annex SL definition of risk by creating *occupational health and safety risk (OH&S risk)* defined as

> *combination of the likelihood of occurrence of a work-related hazardous event(s) or exposure(s) and the severity of injury and ill health that can be caused by the event(s) or exposure(s).*

In practice, ISO 45001 sees OH&S risk as purely negative, and the positive aspect of Annex SL risk takes the form of *OH&S opportunities*, defined as

> *circumstance or set of circumstances that can lead to improvement of OH&S performance.*

ISO 45003 defines psychosocial risk as the

> *combination of the likelihood of occurrence of exposure to work-related hazard(s) of a psychosocial nature and the severity of injury and ill-health that can be caused by these hazards.*

This definition suffers from the same problems as the ISO 45001 definition, with the added problem from the point of view of this book that there is no mention of well-being or wellness.

Annex SL states that *further information* on risk is available in ISO 31000, and ISO 45001 includes ISO 31000 in the *Bibliography*, although it does not refer to it in the text.

As described earlier, ISO 31000 is *Risk management – guidelines*, and there are two other documents that support ISO 31000: ISO 31010 *Risk management – risk assessment techniques* and Guide 73 *Risk management – vocabulary*. These documents allow for risk to have positive outcomes as well as negative outcomes, and the relevant definitions are described next.

In ISO 31000, the definition of risk is *effect of uncertainty on objectives* and Note 1 is

An effect is a deviation from the expected. It can be positive, negative or both, and can address, create or result in opportunities and threats.

This means that in ISO 31000, risk gives rise to opportunities and threats – which makes sense – rather than the Annex SL risk, which gives rise to risks and opportunities – which, as was said earlier, does not make much sense.

There is also further explanation of the term *uncertainty* and a definition of *objective*.

Uncertainty is the state, even partial, of deficiency of information related to, understanding or knowledge of, an event, its consequence, or likelihood.
(Notes to entry in Annex SL, Guide 73 and ISO 45001)

An objective is a *result to be achieved*
(Annex SL and ISO 45001)

Based on the information above, the following terms and definitions have been used for the purposes of the psychosocial risk management system.

Psychosocial objective

Objective which, if achieved, will maintain or improve worker well-being and/or wellness.

Psychosocial risk

Effect of uncertainty on psychosocial objectives.

It is worth emphasising that uncertainty has effects that can be

positive, resulting in opportunities for gain and/or improvement and/or negative, resulting in threats of loss and/or deterioration.

In ISO 31010, both opportunity and threat are defined terms and the relevant text is

opportunity
combination of circumstances expected to be favourable to objectives

Note 1 to entry: An opportunity is a positive situation in which gain is likely and over which one has a fair level of control.

Note 2 to entry: An opportunity to one party may pose a threat to another.

Note 3 to entry: Taking or not taking an opportunity are both sources of risk.

The notes to this entry are of particular relevance to psychosocial risk management. For example, as will be seen in later chapters, an opportunity to improve one group of individuals' well-being may result in harm to other individuals' well-being.

threat
potential source of danger, harm, or other undesirable outcome

Note 1 to entry: A threat is a negative situation in which loss is likely and over which one has relatively little control.

Note 2 to entry: A threat to one party may pose an opportunity to another.

The linking of level of control with opportunities and threats is not helpful in the context of psychosocial risk management. There are opportunities over which individuals have no control – lottery wins, for example – and threats which they can control effectively – with exercise and diet, for example.
The following definitions have been used in this book.

Psychosocial opportunity

Circumstance or set of circumstances that can lead to improvement of well-being and/or wellness.

Psychosocial threat

Circumstance or set of circumstances that can lead to reduction in well-being and/or wellness.

In ISO 31000, note 3 to the definition of risk is

Risk is usually expressed in terms of risk sources, potential events, their consequences and their likelihood.

Risk source, event, consequence, and likelihood are defined terms in ISO 31000 as follows:

risk source
element which alone or in combination has the potential to give rise to risk

event
occurrence or change of a particular set of circumstances

Note 1 to entry: An event can have one or more occurrences, and can have several causes and several consequences.

Note 2 to entry: An event can also be something that is expected which does not happen, or something that is not expected which does happen.

Note 3 to entry: An event can be a risk source.

consequence
outcome of an event affecting objectives

Note 1 to entry: A consequence can be certain or uncertain and can have positive or negative direct or indirect effects on objectives.

Note 2 to entry: Consequences can be expressed qualitatively or quantitatively.

Note 3 to entry: Any consequence can escalate through cascading and cumulative effects.

likelihood
chance of something happening

Note 1 to entry: In risk management terminology, the word 'likelihood' is used to refer to the chance of something happening, whether defined, measured or determined objectively or subjectively, qualitatively or quantitatively, and described using general terms or mathematically (such as a probability or a frequency over a given time period).

Note 2 to entry: The English term 'likelihood' does not have a direct equivalent in some languages; instead, the equivalent of the term 'probability' is often used. However, in English, 'probability' is often narrowly interpreted as a mathematical term. Therefore, in risk management terminology, 'likelihood' is used with the intent that it should have the same broad interpretation as the term 'probability' has in many languages other than English.

Probability is defined in ISO 31000 as a *measure of the chance of occurrence expressed as a number between 0 and 1, where 0 is impossibility and 1 is absolute certainty.* This is a widely accepted definition among statisticians who also allow for probability to be expressed as a percentage between 0% and 100%.

Amended versions of these terms and definitions have been used for the purposes of this book, and these amended terms and definitions are set out below, together with the reasons for any changes.

Psychosocial risk source

Element which, alone or in combination, has the potential to give rise to psychosocial risk.

Psychosocial event

Occurrence or change of a particular set of circumstances affecting psycho-social result(s).

Note 1 to entry: A psychosocial event can have one or more occurrences and can have several causes and several results.

Note 2 to entry: A psychosocial event can also be something that is expected which does not happen, or something that is not expected which does happen.

Note 3 to entry: A psychosocial event can be a psychosocial risk source.

Psychosocial result

Outcome of an event affecting psychosocial objectives.

Note 1 to entry: A psychosocial result can be certain or uncertain and can have positive or negative direct or indirect effects on psychosocial objectives.

Note 2 to entry: Psychosocial results can be expressed qualitatively or quantitatively.

Note 3 to entry: Any psychosocial result can escalate through cascading and cumulative effects.

Note 4 to entry. The equivalent term in ISO 31000 and Guide 73 is 'conse-quence'. However, since this has negative connotations, the term 'result' is used in psychosocial risk management.

Note 5 to entry. The equivalent term in ISO 45001 and ISO 45003 is 'severity'. However, since this allows only for negative outcomes, the term 'result' is used in psychosocial risk management.

Likelihood

Chance of something happening.

Note 1 to entry: In the context of psychosocial risk management, the 'some-thing' can be the occurrence of

A specified psychosocial risk source
A specified psychosocial event
A psychosocial result of a specified nature and extent

Definitions related to organisations

Organisation is defined in Annex SL and ISO 45001 as

person or group of people that has its own functions with responsibilities, authorities and relationships to achieve its objectives.

Both documents have the following *Note 1 to entry*:

The concept of organization includes, but is not limited to sole-trader, company, corporation, firm, enterprise, authority, partnership, charity or institution, or part or combination thereof, whether incorporated or not, public or private.

Neither document defines *functions, responsibilities, authorities, or relationships*, but how these terms will be used in this book is described later in this section.
Note that, according to this definition, a self-employed person or a single volunteer can be an organisation.

Top management

Top management is defined in Annex SL and ISO 45001 as

person or group of people who directs and controls an organization at the highest level

and there are two notes to the entry that are relevant here.

*Note 1 to entry: Top management has the power to delegate authority and provide resources within the organization, **provided ultimate responsibility for the OH&S management system is retained.***

(The authors' emphasis, the text in bold is only in
ISO 45001, not in Annex SL)

Note 2 to entry: If the scope of the management system covers only part of an organization, then top management refers to those who direct and control that part of the organization.

The terms *direct* and *control* are not defined in Annex SL or ISO 45001, and dictionary definitions are not very helpful. For example, the ODE[8] definitions are

Direct – *control the operations of; manage or govern*
Control – *determine the behaviour or supervise the running of.*

For the purposes of this book, direct is used to mean

Deciding what the organisation will do, and how it will do it.

and control is used to mean

Ensuring that these decisions are implemented.

Functions

Annex SL, ISO 45001, and ISO 45003 all use the phrase *levels and functions* with regard to organisations, but none of the documents provides a definition of functions.

Organisations consist of various functions, usually shown from left to right on an organisation chart (organogram). These functions vary according to the nature of the organisation, but typical functions are:

Production and/or Operations – the part of the organisation that produces its products and/or services.

Finance – the part of the organisation that controls expenditure and ensures income is collected.

Sales and marketing – the part of the organisation that identifies potential customers and persuades them to purchase the organisation's products and/or services.

Human resources – *The HR function aims to help an organisation deliver its corporate strategy and objectives by effectively managing people and performance* (Chartered Institute of Personnel and Development).

Health and safety – the part of the organisation that provides advice on the identification and control of health and safety risks.

According to the definition of *organisation*, each function has *responsibilities, authorities, and relationships to achieve its objectives*. However, for the purposes of this book, it is more useful to deal with *responsibilities, authorities, and relationships* as they relate to the individuals who make up the function, rather than to the function itself. These individual *responsibilities, authorities, and relationships* are described in later sections.

The ODE defines function as

an activity that is natural to the purpose of a person or thing

and a modified version of this will be used as the definition of function for the purposes of this book. The modified version is

an activity that is natural to the purpose of an organisation.

Organisations do not normally use the term *function* – department, directorate, or team are more commonly used. However, for the purposes of this book, the term function will be used, except when quoting a source that uses another term to describe functions.

Levels

Each function in an organisation has one or more levels, usually shown from the top to the bottom of an organisation chart (organogram). Level is defined in the ODE as *a position in a hierarchy*, and the hierarchy in organisations consists of different levels of *worker*, and these levels are described in the next section.

Worker

Worker is defined in ISO 45001 as

a person performing work or work-related activities that are under the control of the organization

and there are three notes to the entry

Note 1 to entry: Persons perform work or work-related activities under various arrangements, paid or unpaid, such as regularly or temporarily, intermittently or seasonally, casually or on a part-time basis.

Note 2 to entry: Workers include top management, managerial and non-managerial persons.

Note 3 to entry: The work or work-related activities performed under the control of the organization may be performed by workers employed by the organization, workers of external providers, contractors, individuals, agency workers, and by other persons to the extent the organization shares control over their work or work-related activities, according to the context of the organization.

Note 2 clearly identifies three levels of worker: *top management, managerial,* and *non-managerial.* As has been seen, top management is a defined term, but *managerial* is not defined in ISO 45001. The relevant ODE definitions are

managerial – *relating to management or managers,* and
management – *the process of dealing with or controlling things or people.*

A modified version of managerial will be used for the purposes of this book, and the definitions of managerial worker and non-managerial worker are as follows.

Managerial worker – a worker who controls other workers in the organisation.
Non-managerial worker – a worker who does not control other workers in the organisation.

Typical levels of managerial worker are top management and middle managers – who control other managerial workers – and first-line managers – who control non-managerial workers. In some organisations, first-line managers are not managerial workers so far as their conditions of employment are concerned, and they have role titles such as supervisor or team leader. For the purposes of this book, these roles are considered as managerial because they involve control of non-managerial workers. The terms supervisor or team leader are not used in this book except in quotations.

Roles and responsibilities

A phrase used in Annex SL, ISO 45001, and ISO 45003 is *roles and responsibilities*, but there are no definitions of either term.

The ODE defines role as *the function assumed or part played by a person or thing in a particular situation*, and the following revised version of this definition will be used:

the part played by a worker in a particular situation.

Each function in an organisation is discharged (defined in the ODE as *do all that is required to perform (a duty) or fulfil (a responsibility)* by workers having defined roles. For example, the roles in the Production function might include

Production director – a member of the top management team
Production managers (managerial workers)
Production operatives (non-managerial workers)
Maintenance engineers (non-managerial workers)

Organisations usually refer to these roles as *Job Titles* but, for the purposes of this book, *Role Title* will be used to describe the labels for individual roles in an organisation. This will make it possible to deal with Role Titles such as Volunteer, First Aider, and Fire Marshall that are not Job Titles in the usual sense. It will also enable a discussion of roles outside the organisation such as parent and partner that are relevant to psychosocial risk sources in some circumstances.

Each role in an organisation has associated with it one or more responsibilities, and there are various definitions of responsibility. One of the ODE definitions is *a thing which one is required to do as part of a job, role, or legal obligation*, and a thing is defined as *an action, event, thought or utterance.* For the purposes of this book, *a thing which one is required to do as part of a role* will be used as the definition of responsibility.

The responsibilities associated with a role can be described in either, or both, of the following ways.

As a list of tasks to be carried out. The ODE defines *task* as *a piece of work to be done or undertaken* and *work* as *activity involving mental or physical effort done in order to achieve a purpose or result.* There is a lot of overlap between the terms *task* and *work*, but for the purposes of this book, these modified ODE definitions will be used.

Task – *a piece of work to be done or undertaken as part of a role.*
Work – *tasks involving mental and/or physical effort done under the control of the organisation in order to achieve an outcome.*

As a list of outcomes or results to be achieved. The ODE defines outcome as *the way a thing turns out* and *result* as *a thing that is caused or produced by*

something else; a consequence or outcome. As with task and work, there is a lot of overlap between outcome and result, but for the purposes of this book, outcome will be defined as the way a thing turns out.

Objective would have been an alternative to outcome, but this has not been used because it is already used in two ways in ISO 45001. That is

Objective – *result to be achieved,* and
OH&S objective – *objective set by the organization to achieve specific results consistent with the OH&S policy.*

Result would also have been an alternative, but this has not been used to avoid misunderstandings arising from an alternative ODE definition of *result,* that is, *a favourable outcome of an undertaking or contest.*

Both of these methods of describing responsibilities can be elaborated in various ways. For example

There can be descriptions of how a particular task should be carried out. These descriptions have a variety of names, including Standard Operating Procedure and Method Statement. However, the term work instruction will be used in this book since this is a recognised management system term and is defined in ISO 10013[9] as a *detailed description of how to perform tasks.* ISO 10013 is dealt with in detail in Chapter 12.

Outcomes can be qualified and quantified. For example, the required quality of a product or service can be described, and the required number of units to be produced can be specified.

Authorities

The ODE has two definitions of relevance to authorities in a management system:

the power or right to give orders, make decisions, and enforce obedience, and *the right to act in a specified way, delegated from one person or organization to another.*

For the purpose of this book, two types of authority have been defined as follows:

Managerial authority – the right to give orders, make decisions, and enforce obedience.
Delegated authority – the right to act in a specified way, delegated from one worker to another.

The ODE defines delegate as *entrust (a task or responsibility) to another person, typically one who is less senior than oneself.* The following modified version will be used for the purposes of this book:

Entrust a task or responsibility to another worker, typically one who is less senior.

Relationships

The ODE has two definitions of relevance to relationships in a management system:

> *the way in which two or more people or things are connected, or the state of being connected,* and
> *the way in which two or more people or groups regard and behave towards each other*

The ODE defines connected as *associated or related in some respect* and regard as *consider or think of in a specified way.*

For the purpose of this book, four types of relationship have been defined as follows:

Role relationship – the way in which two or more roles are connected. For example, the relationship between a managerial worker and a non-managerial worker.

Function relationship – the way in which two or more functions are connected. For example, the way in which the HR function and Health and Safety function cooperate in psychosocial risk management.

Work relationship – the way in which two or more workers or groups of workers think of and behave towards each other. For example, the relationships that create psychosocial hazards such as bullying and discrimination.

Non-work relationship – the way in which a worker thinks of, and behaves towards, non-workers such as family and friends.

Relationship and relationships will be used as stand-alone terms in this book where the context makes it clear which type of relationship is being referred to.

Definitions related to *occupational* and *at work*

The title of ISO 45001 is *Occupational health and safety management systems – Requirements with guidance for use.* However, *occupational* is not defined.

The title of ISO 45003 is *Occupational health and safety management – Psychological health and safety at work – Guidelines for managing psychosocial risks.* ISO 45003 does not define *occupational* or *at work.*

In the text of ISO 45001, the phrase *at work* is not used,[i] and it has been assumed that this is because *occupational* implies *at work* in this Standard. Conversely, the word *occupational* in ISO 45003 is used only in the phrases *occupational health* and *occupational health and safety management systems.* It appears that *at work* is used in ISO 45003 where *occupational* is used in ISO 45001.

For example, the phrase *affect health, safety and well-being at work* (ISO 45003 clause 7.3.1 a) could be rephrased as *affect occupational health, safety and well-being* in ISO 45001.

The ODE defines *at work* as *engaged in work,* and an amended version of this definition will be used in this book. This amended definition is described in the next section.

The ODE definition of *occupational* is *relating to a job or profession. Job* is defined as *a paid position of regular employment* and *employment* is *the state of having paid work.* Profession is defined as *a paid occupation, especially one that involves prolonged training and a formal qualification.*

The complication in ISO 45003 is that, in addition to *at work* being synonymous with occupational work also has other meanings, for example, 'engaged in work' and 'at a place of work'. The following terms will be used to differentiate between these three usages:

Occupational will be used where *at work* is used in ISO 45003 as the equivalent of *occupational* in ISO 45001.

Working will be used where *at work* is used in ISO 45003 to mean engaged in work.

At a place of work will use this where *at work* is used in ISO 45003 to mean the location where work is carried out.

Job and employment

ISO 45001 does not use the term job[ii] but ISO 45003 does, but without a definition. Four of these usages

job satisfaction used in the *Introduction*
job description used in clause 6.1.2.1.3
job sharing used in clause 8.1.2.2
job security used in clause 8.1.4

could be justified on the grounds that they are 'common usage'. However, it has already been argued that the common usage 'job title' is not appropriate for this book, and a similar argument applies to the three common usages listed earlier.

Other uses of *job* in ISO 45003 are as follows:

Table 1 *Job control or autonomy*
Job demands
Job security and precarious work
Table 2 *withholding information or resources critical for one's job.*
6.1.2.1.3 g) The organization is expected to take into account the knowledge, expertise and competence of workers in relation to their jobs ...

Arguably, in all of these uses of *job*, 'work' could be substituted for 'job' without any loss of meaning.

The ODE defines job in various ways, including

a paid position of regular employment
a task or piece of work, especially one that is paid
a responsibility or duty.

It is possible that ISO 45003 is using *job security* to mean security of pay, and this is the interpretation that will be used in this book. As mentioned earlier, the term *job* will only be used in quotations.

As was pointed out earlier in this chapter, in ISO 45001, Note 3 to the definition of *worker* is

> *The work or work-related activities performed under the control of the organization may be performed by workers employed by the organization, workers of external providers, contractors, individuals, agency workers, and by other persons to the extent the organization shares control over their work or work-related activities, according to the context of the organization.*

This appears to make it clear that workers employed by the organisation are a separate category of workers, and that there are other categories. This is reinforced in clause 7.2: *Competence* where the note to the clause is

> *Applicable actions can include, for example, the provision of training to, the mentoring of, or the re-assignment of currently employed persons, or the hiring or contracting of competent persons.*

There is also a reference to *employment agreements* in Annex A, clause *A.6.1.3 Determination of legal requirements and other requirements.*

The ODE defines employment as *the state of having paid work*, and the implication in ISO 45001 appears to be that 'employed workers' could also be referred to as 'workers paid by the organisation'.

ISO 45003 uses the term *employment* in the following places:

Introduction
Psychosocial hazards can be present in all organizations and sectors, and from all kinds of work tasks, equipment and employment arrangements.

4.1.2 External issues
The organization should determine external issues relevant to achieving the intended outcomes of the OH&S management system in relation to psychosocial risk. External issues can include:

>   ...
>
>   *f) the nature of work contracts, remuneration, employment conditions and industrial relations;*

Table 1
low-paid or insecure employment, including non- standard employment

8.1.3 Management of change
Organizational and work-related changes can influence psychosocial risks or create additional psychosocial risks. The organization should establish,

implement and maintain a process(es) for communication and control of changes that can impact health, safety and well-being at work, including:

a) *changes to the organization's objectives, activities, work processes and leadership, (e.g. workplace locations and surroundings; equipment and resources; workforce and terms of employment);*

It has been assumed for the purposes of this book that *employment* in ISO 45003 is used in the same way as it is in ISO 45001. That is, employment is an arrangement between an organisation and its workers that involves pay for discharging a role.

Definitions related to *work*

As was seen earlier in the chapter, both ISO 45001 and ISO 45003 use the term work, but neither Standard defines the term. However, for the present purposes, work can be defined as *tasks involving mental and/or physical effort done under the control of the organisation in order to achieve an outcome.*

ISO 45001 also uses the terms *workplace* and *work-related activities*, and this section is a discussion of these terms, beginning with workplace.

Workplace

Workplace is defined as a *place under the control of the organization where a person needs to be or to go for work purposes.*

The *or to go* appears to be redundant. However, the main problem with this definition is the fact that many types of work are carried out in places not controlled by the organisation, for example, in customers' homes (maintenance and repair of domestic appliances, for example) and in the open air (maintenance and repair of overhead and underground gas, electricity, and water supplies, for example). A term is needed for the place where these types of work are carried out and worksite will be used for this purpose, defined as a

place not under the control of the organisation where a person needs to be for work purposes.

In addition, to avoid having to say 'workplaces and worksites', a term has been defined for the two taken together, that is, 'place of work' defined as a

place where a person needs to be for work purposes – irrespective of who controls that place.

Work-related activities

The ODE defines activity as *a thing that a person or group does or has done*, and this is the definition used in this book.

ISO 45001 does not define *work-related activities* but for the purposes of this book it is 1 assumed that they include, but are not restricted to, the following three categories of activity:

Activities involving mental and/or physical effort done under the control of the organisation order to achieve an outcome not directly related to a role. For example, travel that is not part of a role that requires travel such as delivery driver, performance assessment interviews, and team meetings.

Activities sanctioned[iii] by the organisation that are not part of a role. For example, worker parties away from the workplace, staying in hotels (alone or with other workers), eating in restaurants (alone or with other workers).

Activities carried out at a place of work that are not part of a role. For example, moving around a place of work, eating in an organisation-controlled canteen, using organisation-controlled car parks, sanitary facilities or gymnasia, and socialising at a place of work.

Notes

i   It is used once in Annex A in the phrase *The objective of a management of change process is to enhance occupational health and safety at work* (clause A.8.1.3 *Management of change.* However, it is assumed that this is an editorial lapse.

ii   It does occur in Annex A at A.6.1.1 in the phrase *b) job hazard analysis (job safety analysis) and task-related assessments;* but nowhere else in the Annex.

iii Sanction – *official permission or approval for an action* (ODE).

References

1 British Standards Institution. *Occupational health and safety management – Psychological health and safety at work – Guidelines for managing psychosocial risks,* BSI ISO 45003, 2021. BSI 2021.

2 British Standards Institution. *Occupational health and safety management systems – Requirements with guidance for use,* BSI ISO 45001, 2018. BSI 2018.

3 *ISO/IEC Directives, Part 1 Consolidated ISO Supplement – Procedure for the technical work – Procedures specific to ISO (Thirteenth edition, 2022). Annex SL (normative) harmonised approach for management system standards. Appendix 2 (normative) Harmonized structure for MSS with guidance for use.*

4 British Standards Institution. *Occupational health and safety management systems – General guidelines for the implementation of ISO 45001:2018,* BSI ISO 45002, 2023. BSI 2023.

5 British Standards Institution. *Risk management – guidelines,* BS ISO 31000, 2018. BSI 2018.

6 British Standards Institution. *Risk management – Risk assessment techniques,* BS EN IEC 31010, 2019. BSI 2019.

7 British Standards Institution. *Guide 73: Risk management – Vocabulary,* BS EN Guide 73, 2009. BSI 2009.

8 MobiSystems, Inc, *Oxford Dictionary,* version 15.8. Last accessed 17 January 2024.

9 British Standards Institution. *Quality management systems — Guidance for documented information,* BSI ISO 10013, 2021. BSI 2021.

12 The documented information

Crash course

ISO 10013 gives guidance on quality management system documented information, and this guidance can be applied to psychosocial management system documented information.

Key documented information requirements are

A *Psychosocial management system manual* that includes a *Description* of the psychosocial management system and references, as necessary,

procedures for carrying out psychosocial management system processes
work instructions for completing psychosocial management system tasks and roles, including

forms and checklists for recording that these tasks and roles were carried out and their results.

Other considerations are

The media to be used – modern mobile devices create a number of options.
The structure to be used – an amorphous mass of documented information that no one can navigate has to be avoided.

Introduction

Both ISO 45001[1] and ISO 45003[2] require 'documented information', and ISO 45002[3] provides a list of the minimum requirements for documented information. However, there is no guidance on how to prepare the documented information. For this reason, when preparing documented information for a management system, it is best to follow the guidance in ISO 10013[4], the latest version of which was published in 2021 with the title *Quality management systems – Guidance for documented information.*

This chapter begins by describing the ISO 10013 guidance on quality management system documented information, and how this guidance applies to

DOI: 10.4324/9781003490555-13

psychosocial management system documented information. The following types of documented information are then described.

Management system manual
Procedures
Work instructions
Forms and checklists
Other documented information

The chapter ends with a discussion of two other topics.

The media to be used for documented information. The traditional medium of printed copies is still useful, but there are more convenient electronic options now available.

The structure to be used for the documented information. A fully documented psychosocial management system can require a large number of separate documents, and a structure is needed that makes individual documents easy to identify and locate.

ISO 10013

Although ISO 10013 is intended for quality management systems, the *Scope* clause states

This document can also be used to support other management systems, e.g. environmental or occupational health and safety management systems.

References to 'quality' in the quotations from ISO 10013 that follow should, therefore, be substituted with 'psychosocial' for the purposes of this chapter.

ISO 10013 deals with three categories of documented information.

Documented information to be maintained to meet the requirements of the relevant Standard – in the present case ISO 45001. The scope, policy, and psychosocial objectives dealt with in Chapter 15 are examples of this type of documented information. The full list of documented information required by ISO 45001 is given in Chapter 32.

Documented information to be maintained that *the organization determined necessary to support the operation of the quality management system and its processes.* Examples in this category of particular relevance to this book are the *Psychosocial management system manual*, procedures, work instructions, forms, and checklists. All of these types of documented information are dealt with in this chapter.

Documented information to be retained (i.e. records) for providing evidence of results achieved. Records of relevance to the psychosocial management system will also be dealt with in this chapter.

In order to meet the requirements for documented information, ISO 10013 suggests using the following types of documented information:

A management system manual. This is an overarching document that contains, or refers to, all of the management system documented information. However, its main section is a description of the management system that sets out how the organisation will meet the requirements of the relevant Standard.

Procedures. These describe *inter alia* who will do what and when in order to ensure that a particular process is carried out in the way the organisation wants it to be carried out.

Work instructions. These describe how a particular activity should be carried out. This might be a role, for example, a top management psychosocial work instruction, or a task, for example, psychosocial threat and opportunity assessment.

Forms and checklists. These are the types of documented information used to record that activities have been carried out, and the results of these activities. A completed form or checklist is a record.

Other types of documented information. ISO 10013 described various other types of documented information. Types that might be of relevance in a psychosocial management system include specifications, plans, and schedules.

What follows is a summary of the ISO 10013 guidance of particular relevance to the types of documented information listed above.

Management system manual

ISO 10013 suggests that a management system manual is one way of maintaining an organisation's documented information, and it is the authors' preferred approach to preparing management system documented information.

The principal contents of a Psychosocial management system manual are

An introduction describing what the manual is for and how it is to be used.

The organisation's purpose, intended outcomes, scope, policy, and psychosocial objectives as described in Chapter 15. ISO 10013 suggests that *Information about the organization, such as name, location, context and means of communication including relevant specific terms and definitions, should be included in the quality manual. Additional information such as its line of business, a brief description of its background, history and size may also be included.*

A description of the psychosocial management system. According to ISO 10013, *The quality manual can provide a description of the quality management system and its implementation in the organization. Descriptions of the processes and their interactions or a reference to them should be included in the manual.* ISO 10013 also suggests that *Cross-referencing between the selected standard and the processes of the organization can be useful*, and this is the authors' preferred approach to writing a description.

A suggested structure and possible content for a manual are discussed in Chapter 17 'The Psychosocial management system manual'.

Procedures

ISO 45001 adopts the ISO 9000[5] definition of a procedure which is the

specified way to carry out an activity or a process.

A process is defined in the current version of Annex SL[6] as

set of interrelated or interacting activities that uses or transforms inputs to deliver a result.

ISO 45001 uses the definition of a process from an earlier edition of Annex SL, that is,

set of interrelated or interacting activities which transforms inputs into outputs.

What this means in practice is that, although there are many ways to carry out a process such as psychosocial threat and opportunity assessment, when an organisation decides on which way it will carry out psychosocial threat and opportunity assessment and documents the results of its decision, the documented information is its psychosocial threat and opportunity assessment procedure.

ISO 10013 suggests that the *structure and format of documented procedures should be defined by the organization* and points out that a *procedure generally answers questions such as who, what, when, where and with what resources.* However, ISO 10013:2021 does not include the suggested structure for a procedure that was included in previous versions of ISO 10013. The authors have found this structure helpful in the past, and it is reproduced below as a suggested starting point for preparing the *structure and format* for your procedures. A *Psychosocial threat and opportunity assessment procedure* has been used to illustrate the possible content of each section.

Title. This should clearly describe the nature of the procedure and include a unique identifier. The title can also include a version number and date, although these can be included elsewhere, for example, in the *Identification of changes* section.

P02 *Psychosocial threat and opportunity assessment procedure* – Version 1 May 2023

Purpose. This should be a succinct and accurate statement of what the procedure is intended to achieve. Where a procedure has more than one purpose, the heading should be changed to *Purposes* and each purpose described separately.

The purpose of this procedure is to ensure that psychosocial threat and opportunity assessments are carried out when necessary, and in a consistent manner.

Scope. This section is used to describe what the procedure covers, and to list any exceptions.

This procedure covers all psychosocial threat and opportunity assessments, with the exception of psychosocial threat and opportunity assessments required for workers suffering from mental or physical ill health.

Responsibility and authority. This is an optional section. Where it is used, it should list all of the individuals with responsibility for an activity or activities in the procedure – usually in the form of their role titles. There should also be a general statement such as *individuals' authority within this procedure are commensurate with their organisational role* or details of any restrictions on, or extensions to, the authority of particular individuals should be given. The authors' preference is not to include this section and to put any necessary information on responsibility and authority in the *Activities* section, which is described next.

Activities. This section is the one that describes the *who, what, when, where, and with what resources.* There is no generally applicable way of describing the activities required by a procedure because there is such a wide variety of procedures. However, the best way to start is with an attempt to describe the activities in chronological order, and only use another format if this does not work. The list of subheadings below illustrates some of the topics to be covered in a psychosocial threat and opportunity assessment procedure. Full details of a psychosocial threat and opportunity assessment procedure are given in Chapter 23 'Psychosocial threat and opportunity assessment'.

Competence provision
Periodic assessment
Identifying need for additional assessment
Conducting an assessment

Records. This section should describe the forms and/or checklists to be used to record the activities undertaken and the results of these activities. Where necessary, instructions on how to fill in the forms and checklists should be given in the *Activities* section. The *Records* section should also describe what should be done with completed forms and checklists. Forms and checklists are discussed in the next section of this chapter.

Appendices. This is another optional section that the authors rarely use. Typically, appendices contain detailed information that may be helpful but is not essential to the understanding of the procedure. For example, a useful appendix to a Psychosocial threat and opportunity assessment procedure might be a list of the hazards of a psychosocial nature given in the three tables in ISO 45003 and a list of the other psychosocial risk sources to be taken into account.

Review, approval, and revision. Most organisations have existing arrangements for review, approval, and revision, and the best approach is to use these existing arrangements. Setting up arrangements for review, approval, and revision from scratch is outwith the scope of the present book.

Identification of changes. As with review, approval, and revision, most organisations have existing arrangements for identification of changes that can be followed. Where these arrangements do not exist, a word processor Track Changes facility can be used for this purpose.

When preparing a procedure, it is necessary to keep in mind the target audiences for the document. This is the case with any documents but is particularly important for procedures because there are three target audiences.

The top management, or the level of management that has to agree that the procedure is correct for the organisation and allocate the resources for its implementation and maintenance.

Auditors who will check whether the procedure is being carried out as described.

Individuals with responsibility for one or more activities in the procedure. This target audience is the one that usually creates a difficulty. If the procedure is used to describe how activities are carried out, it can end up being a very large document, and workers will have to read a lot of information they do not need to know. For example, including descriptions of how to carry out a psychosocial threat and opportunity assessment in the *Activities* section of the procedure is not good practice because it is only needed by assessors and not by others with responsibilities within the procedure. To avoid this problem, use work instructions instead, and these are described next.

Work instructions

A work instruction is defined in ISO 10013 as a *detailed description of how to perform tasks*, and ISO 10013 points out that *Documented procedures generally describe activities that can cross different functions, while work instructions generally apply to tasks within one function.*

In addition, as was mentioned earlier, a work instruction can be used to describe the psychosocial activities required by a particular role such as top management.

For example, a psychosocial threat and opportunity assessment procedure may include tasks to be carried out by HR personnel, health and safety personnel, and well-being and wellness counsellors. The procedure will describe **what** these people have to do and the interactions between their various tasks. There will then be a separate work instruction for each category setting out **how** they carry out the required task, for example, a *Psychosocial threat and opportunity assessment work instruction* describing how to carry out a psychosocial threat and opportunity assessment, and a *Psychosocial counselling work instruction* setting out how the organisation wants these counselling sessions to be conducted.

Because there is such a wide variety of tasks and roles that might require a work instruction, there is no general format for written work instructions. However, the procedure format described in the previous section can be used as a starting point, and in the majority of cases the only headings required are *Title, Purpose, Activities* and *Records*. Various examples of work instructions are given in relevant chapters in Part II of this book.

Forms and checklists

A form is defined in ISO 10013 as

documented information to be maintained and used to record data required by the quality management system.

Note 1 to entry: A form becomes documented information to be retained (i.e. a record) when data are entered.

There is no formal definition of checklist in ISO 10013, but there is the following description.

Checklists are a special kind of form that are developed and maintained to have confidence that the processes are being carried out as planned and to provide a consistent means of recording results of activities. They should be referenced in any associated documented information.

ISO 10013 also explains that

Forms and checklists can be considered documented information to be maintained, while completed forms and checklists can be considered documented information to be retained.

As with procedures and work instructions, forms and checklists should have a title that clearly describes the nature of the form or checklist and includes a unique identifier. Examples of forms and checklists relevant to a psychosocial management system are provided in various chapters in Part II of this book.

Other documented information

As was mentioned earlier in this chapter, ISO 10013 describes various other types of documented information. Types that are of relevance in a psychosocial management system and are used in Part II of this book are as follows:

Specifications. These are lists of requirements for a product or service. For example, an organisation might specify the requirements for a blood pressure monitor or the delivery of well-being support services.

Plans. These are statements about what an organisation, or part of an organisation, is going to do, usually to achieve some objective. Chapter 30 'Psychosocial planning and continual improvement' deals with the planning processes within a psychosocial management system and Chapter 32 'The psychosocial management system development plan' deals with the planning required to set up a psychosocial management system.

Schedules. There are various types of schedule, but the most common ones are lists of things to be done, and when they are to be done. Schedules can be included in procedures or work instructions or provided as stand-alone documents. Examples of schedules are given in relevant chapters in Part II.

Media

The traditional medium for documented information has been paper, and printed copies of manuals, procedures, and work instructions are still used. However, printed copies have a number of limitations, and some organisations are moving to 'screen-only' documented information.[i] This has a number of advantages including the following.

The master copy can be changed without having to reissue printed copies.

There is less chance of out-of-date documents being used in error. People can be prevented from printing copies of the document, or printed copies can be clearly marked *Uncontrolled when printed.*

Hyperlinking can be used to move around within large documents.

Hyperlinks can be provided to other documents, websites, email addresses, and so on.

By providing versions that can be used on mobile devices, workers can have easy access to large quantities of information at their place of work.

If you intend to go down the route of screen-only documented information, you should consider using e-book software rather than a straightforward word processor. Depending on the version you are using, this type of software enables such things as checklists, videos, and questionnaires to be embedded in the book to provide highly interactive documented information.

Now that it is much easier to take photographs using phones and tablets, using photographs to illustrate written documents is becoming more common and can result in significant increases in the usefulness of these documents.

These mobile devices are also being used to provide videos that replace work instructions. These videos are often easier to understand than their written equivalent and can sometimes take less time to prepare. They are particularly useful when the target audience has a wide range of literacy competence. Examples of these videos include how to use a blood pressure monitor correctly and how to exercise safely, and many such videos are freely available.

The increasing use of mobile devices has also led to organisations purchasing or developing their own 'apps' to facilitate management system tasks. For example, there is a range of monitoring and auditing apps on the market, and these have two main functions – they remind auditors what they have to check, and they provide a convenient means of recording the results of these checks.

Structure

As was mentioned in the introduction, a psychosocial management system documented information may include many procedures, work instructions, and forms, including forms that are checklists. For this reason, it is good practice to have a structure for the documented information and a unique identifier on each document that shows where it fits in the overall structure. What follows is a description of the simple structure that the authors have used in the past to meet the criteria just described.

Description and procedures

The structure used begins with the *Description* section of the *Psychosocial management system manual*. This is a description of how the organisation will deal with each of the ISO 45003 clauses, and most clauses will require a procedure. There are two options for documenting these procedures.

Include it in the *Description*. This can be appropriate when the required procedure is short and simple. For example, the requirement for Health and well-being policy review could be dealt with in the *Description* with a simple statement that *Top management will review the Health and well-being policy as part of their annual management review.* However, having detailed procedures in the *Description* is poor practice because each required change to a procedure will require a revised version of the *Description*.

Have a separate procedure. This is the preferred approach for any procedure that requires more than a few lines of written explanation. This approach has a major advantage early in the drafting of your *Description* in that you can identify the need for a procedure, record its title, and move on to the next clause. This enables you to have a complete *Description* for discussion without having to consider individual procedures in detail. In the long term, it also avoids the need to alter your *Description* every time a procedure is changed.

As the need for each procedure is identified, it is given it a title in the following format

P[rocedure][number] Title

For example

P02 *Psychosocial threat and opportunity assessment procedure*
P05 *Psychosocial awareness procedure*
P09 *Psychosocial audit procedure*

The numbers and titles used in the examples above are for illustration only. The numbering and titles of your procedures will depend on how many are included in the *Description*, rather than prepared as separate procedures. A suggested list of psychosocial procedures is given in Chapter 32.

Work instructions

It is not good practice to include work instructions in a *Description* because of the number required, their level of detail, and their susceptibility to change. It is much better to use one of the following options.

Reference the work instruction in the *Description*. For example, if the *Health and well-being policy review* procedure is in the *Description*, as described earlier, the *Top management will review the Health and well-being policy as part of their annual management review* can be followed by 'This review will be carried out in accordance with WI51 *Top management psychosocial work instruction*. This work instruction can then be used to record all of the activities required of top management with regard to the psychosocial management system'.

Reference the work instruction in the relevant procedure. For example, in P02 *Psychosocial threat and opportunity assessment procedure*, there is likely to be the need for the following work instructions. WI02A *Psychosocial threat and opportunity assessment work instruction* and WI53 *First line manager psychosocial work instruction*.

Note the following points about the nature and numbering of work instructions.

There are two types of work instruction. Work instructions for a task, for example, psychosocial threat and opportunity assessment, and work instructions for a category of workers, for example, first-line management.

When a work instruction is for a task, it takes the number of the procedure in which it is referenced, and a capital letter. For example, WI02A is the first work instruction referenced in procedure 02. When more than one task-based work instruction is referenced in a procedure, they are identified as WI02B, WI02C, and so on. This means that you can readily identify where a task-based work instruction fits in to the overall structure of the psychosocial management system's documented information.

When work instructions are for a category of worker, it is convenient to number them starting from 51 – usually with WI51 *Top management psychosocial work instruction*. This ensures that the numbering of these work instructions does not clash with the numbering of the work instructions linked to procedures. The authors have never had to write a management system that had more than 50 procedures!

The ideal set of work instructions is one that

includes all activities where, in the words of ISO 10013, *the expected outcomes of the activity would be adversely affected by lack of such instructions*, and has a work instruction for each role in the psychosocial management system such that all of the required psychosocial activities for a particular role are dealt with in a single document.

A suggested set of procedures and work instructions is given in Chapter 32 'The psychosocial management system development plan'.

Forms and checklists

Most people are used to completing forms and checklists, but experience of creating these types of documented information is much rarer. What is described below is what the authors do with regard to the identification of the need for forms and checklists, and guidance on preparing specific forms and checklists is given at relevant points in Part II.

For the purposes of identification, checklists are treated as a type of form. All forms should be accompanied by instructions for their completion, and each field of the form should have an explanation of what should be entered in that field. This may sound like overkill, but the authors have seen many examples of misrecording because of lack of instructions. A particularly egregious example was an *Accident reporting form* that had, *inter alia*, fields for *Name* and *Time*. In the Name field, some people recorded the name of the person reporting, while others recorded the name of the person injured, and in the Time field, some people recorded the time of the accident, while others recorded the time the report was made.

The best place for the instructions on how to complete a form is in the form itself, and this can readily be done for forms that are to be completed electronically. For paper-based forms, particularly if they require extensive instructions, the relevant work instruction should include these instructions. For example, the instructions for completing a psychosocial threat and opportunity assessment form should be in the *Psychosocial threat and opportunity assessment work instruction*, and the identifier in the title of the form should be used to show this by using the identifier from the relevant work instruction and a lower-case letter to identify the form. The titles of the partial documented information for psychosocial threat and opportunity assessment would include the following:

P02 *Psychosocial threat and opportunity assessment procedure*

WI02A *Psychosocial threat and opportunity assessment work instruction*

F02Aa *Psychosocial threat and opportunity assessment form*

Where there is more than one form associated with a work instruction, they are also identified with lower-case letters. For example, if there was a separate form for psychosocial risk assessors to use to record required psychosocial risk controls, this would be

F02Ab *Psychosocial risk control form.*

There can be circumstances that require elaborations of these arrangements – for example, when more than one role is involved in completing a form – but these are dealt with as necessary in Part II.

Overview of structure

The complete structure of the psychosocial management system documented information is illustrated in the following overview.

The top-level document is the *Psychosocial management system manual*, the main section of which is a
Description of the psychosocial management system.
The *Description* contains

details of procedures that can be described succinctly, and
references to procedures that require more detailed descriptions – these procedures are numbered sequentially as P01, P02, to Pnn, – with Pnn being the last procedure referenced in the *Description*
references to work instructions – these work instructions are either

task-based and associated with a procedure in which case they are identified using the procedure number and a capital letter, for example, if there were two work instructions associated with P01, they would be WI01A and WI01B, or
associated with an organisational role using a number beginning at 51, for example, WI51 *Top management psychosocial work instruction.*

Work instructions include instructions on how to complete any forms required by that work instruction, and the forms are identified using the work instruction identifier and a lower-case letter, for example, if there were two forms associated with WI01A, they would be F01Aa and F01Ab. Forms associated with organisational roles are identified in a similar way, for example, if there were two forms associated with WI51 *Top management psychosocial work instruction*, they would be F51a and F51b.

This overall structure, if followed, ensures that the identifier of any item of documented information identifies what type of documented information it is, and its place in the psychosocial management system. What it looks like in practice can be seen in Chapter 17 'The psychosocial management system manual'.

Note

i The use of paper copies also has environmental implications, and some organisations include restrictions on printing as part of their environmental management system.

References

1   British Standards Institution. *Occupational health and safety management systems – Requirements with guidance for use*, BSI ISO 45001, 2018. BSI 2018.
2   British Standards Institution. *Occupational health and safety management – Psychological health and safety at work – Guidelines for managing psychosocial risks*, BSI ISO 45003, 2021. BSI 2021.
3   British Standards Institution. *Occupational health and safety management systems – General guidelines for the implementation of ISO 45001:2018*, BSI ISO 45002, 2023. BSI 2023.
4   British Standards Institution. *Quality management systems – Guidance for documented information*, BSI ISO 10013, 2021. BSI 2021.
5   British Standards Institution. *Quality management systems – Fundamentals and vocabulary*, BSI ISO 9000, 2015. BSI 2015.
6   *ISO/IEC Directives, Part 1 Consolidated ISO Supplement – Procedure for the technical work – Procedures specific to ISO (Thirteenth edition, 2022). Annex SL (normative) harmonised approach for management system standards. Appendix 2 (normative) Harmonized structure for MSS with guidance for use.*

Part II
The practicalities

13 Part II overview

This part of the book is about the practicalities of setting up and running a psycho-social management system. When you set up a management system, you have to go through the following steps.

You begin by doing the work that is needed before you can begin to prepare the documented information for your psychosocial management system, for example, finding out what is already in place and agreeing the scope of your system. This work is dealt with in the first three chapters in Part II as follows.

14 What is already in place?

Most organisations have arrangements for dealing with some psychosocial risk sources – typically bullying and harassment. In addition, some organisations have arrangements for promoting wellness – for example, annual medical checks and free gym membership – and dealing with impaired well-being – for example, free access to counsellors. There is no point in 'reinventing the wheel', so you need to find out what is already available.

15 Purpose, intended outcomes, scope, and psychosocial objectives

Clause 4.1 of ISO 45001[1] is

The organization shall determine external and internal issues that are relevant to its purpose and that affect its ability to achieve the intended outcome(s) of its OH&S management system.

These requirements also apply to a psychosocial management system, so you need to agree a statement of your organisation's purpose and the intended outcomes of your proposed psychosocial management system. You will also have to have an agreed scope for your psychosocial management system and the psychosocial objectives it is intended to achieve.

16 Needs and expectations

You have to decide whose needs and expectations will be taken into account in your psychosocial management system. That is, which categories of workers will be included and whether any interested parties will be included, for

DOI: 10.4324/9781003490555-15

example, workers' family members and your organisation's suppliers. You then have to agree which needs and expectation of these individuals will be taken into account in your psychosocial management system.

It is then possible to draft a manual for the management system, and how to do this is described in Chapter 17.

17 The psychosocial management system manual

Both ISO 45001 and ISO 45003[2] require *documented information*. However, neither ISO 45001 nor ISO 45003 provides guidance on how to prepare the required documented information. The authors' favoured approach is to prepare a *Psychosocial management system manual* with three main sections.

Introduction. An explanation of what the manual is for.

Preliminaries. The agreed purpose, intended outcomes, scope, and psychosocial objectives, as described in Chapter 15.

Description. A brief description of what the organisation intends to do about each of the clauses in ISO 45001 and ISO 45003. The details of how it will do things are set out in separate procedures and work instructions, and suggested content for the required procedures and work instructions is given in Chapters 18–31 as listed below.

18 SWOT analysis
19 Consultation and participation
20 Competences
21 Awareness and communication
22 Psychosocial risk sources
23 Psychosocial threat and opportunity assessment
24 Psychosocial threat and opportunity management
25 Psychosocial measurement, analysis, and evaluation
26 Psychosocial monitoring, auditing, and corrective action
27 Psychosocial investigation
28 The role of top management
29 Management review
30 Psychosocial planning and continual improvement
31 Change, procurement, and emergencies

When the management system manual has been agreed, you can draw up and agree a development plan, and the final chapter of the book, Chapter 32, deals with this development plan.

There are three broad strategic approaches to implementing a psychosocial management system.

Have a stand-alone psychosocial management system that operates independently of other management systems in your organisation.

Extend an existing management system, such as ISO 45001 or BS 76000,[3] to cover your psychosocial objectives.

Use a hybrid approach where some ISO 45003 clauses are dealt with using stand-alone processes and other clauses are dealt with by an existing management system. For example, you could amend your ISO 45001 OH&S policy to cover well-being and wellness and use an existing HR measurement system for ill health data to protect worker confidentiality.

However, irrespective of your final strategy, it is best to begin by assuming that you will use a stand-alone psychosocial management system since this enables you to decide what you want do with regard to each of the ISO 45003 clauses. The chapters in Part II include the information you need for a stand-alone psychosocial management system, and there are suggestions, where appropriate, for integrating a psychosocial management system with other management systems.

References

1   British Standards Institution. *Occupational health and safety management systems – Requirements with guidance for use*, BSI ISO 45001, 2018. BSI 2018.
2   British Standards Institution. *Occupational health and safety management – Psychological health and safety at work – Guidelines for managing psychosocial risks*, BSI ISO 45003, 2021. BSI 2021.
3   British Standards Institution. BS 76000:2015 *Human resource – Valuing people – Management system – Requirements and guidance*, BSI 76000, 2015. BSI 2015.

14 What is already in place?

Introduction

Most organisations have arrangements for dealing with some psychosocial risk sources. However, these arrangements do not usually enable organisations to follow the guidance set out in ISO 45003.[1] This chapter describes the sorts of arrangements that may be in place in your organisation, their likely weaknesses in the context of the type of psychosocial management system described in this book, and how these weaknesses can be addressed.

Health and safety hazard identification and risk assessment

The ISO 45003 *Work environment, equipment and hazardous tasks* category of hazards of a psychosocial nature is illustrated by the following examples.

Work environment, equipment and hazardous tasks
Inadequate equipment availability, suitability, reliability, maintenance or repair
Poor workplace conditions such as lack of space, poor lighting and excessive noise
Lack of the necessary tools, equipment or other resources to complete work tasks
Working in extreme conditions or situations, such as very high or low temperatures, or at height
Working in unstable environments such as conflict zones

All of these are routinely dealt with in traditional health and safety hazard identification and risk assessment. However, it is rare that their possible effects on well-being and wellness are considered during these risk assessments. The harms taken into account during these assessments are typically confined to injury and physical ill health.

Some of the other ISO 45003 hazards of a psychosocial nature are also taken into account in health and safety risk assessments, including the following.

Remote and isolated work
Workload and work pace
Working hours and schedule

DOI: 10.4324/9781003490555-16

However, as with the *Work environment, equipment and hazardous tasks* category, assessment of these hazards is confined to injury and physical ill health.

Nevertheless, it is worth reviewing what is done by way of health and safety risk assessment to look at the differences between the work of different risk assessors. Because risk assessment is a subjective activity, it is strongly influenced by the assessor's mental and emotional state. In particular, assessors will differ in their level of empathy, that is, their ability to understand and share the feeling of those exposed to a health and safety hazard. Assessors with a high level of empathy in your organisation may already be identifying well-being and wellness issues associated with the health and safety hazards they are assessing. However, it is typically the case that the health and safety risk assessment process is not designed to deal with these issues, so they go unrecorded.

Highly empathetic risk assessors may also be picking up well-being and wellness issues arising from psychosocial hazards that are not typically included in health and safety risk assessments. That is, the empathetic assessors identify that workers are suffering reduced well-being or reduced wellness and consider that this is due to a psychosocial hazard not covered in their health and safety risk assessment process. Again, this means that the occurrences of reduced well-being or reduced wellness, and the psychosocial risk source causing them, go unrecorded.

Chapter 23 'Psychosocial threat and opportunity assessment' deals with the ways in which existing health and safety hazard identification and risk assessment processes can be extended to take into account psychosocial hazards and their effects. Chapter 20 'Competences' deals with the competences required for psychosocial threat and opportunity assessment, including the competences required to emulate the work of existing empathetic health and safety risk assessors.

Health and safety incident investigation

The authors' experience is that all organisations investigate their health and safety incidents but, in general, the quality of these investigations is poor. The reason for this is that health and safety investigators are not provided with the relevant competences, in particular:

Interview competence. Health and safety incident investigators are very good at having conversations with the people involved in an incident but do not realise that a conversation is not the same as an interview. Health and safety incident investigators who are competent interviewers collect more information, and more relevant information, than health and safety incident investigators who are not competent interviewers.

Causal factors competence. Health and safety investigators are fairly good at finding out what happened but not so good at finding out why it happened. This could be remedied by providing health and safety incident investigators with competence in causal factors analysis techniques such as events and causal factors analysis (ECFA).

Recommendations competence. The usual stated purpose of health and safety investigations is to *prevent recurrence* (of the incident). However, effective prevention of recurrence requires that the causes of the incident have been accurately identified. If this has not been achieved, the recommendations will have little beneficial effect, and may even have detrimental effects. There are techniques for assessing the likely effects of recommendation, but these are rarely used.

All of the competences listed above are dealt with in Chapter 20 'Competences'.

As with health and safety risk assessment, there is a difference in performance between health and safety incident investigators. This arises from the individual differences in motivation, competence, and resources between these investigators. A review of the current health and safety incident processes, and how they are implemented by different health and safety investigators, may identify processes and individual investigator behaviours that can be of use in psychosocial investigation. The practicalities of these investigations are dealt with in Chapter 27 'Psychosocial investigation'.

Health and safety performance measurement

OH&S performance is defined in ISO 45001[2] as *performance* (separately defined as *measurable result*) *related to the effectiveness of the prevention of injury and ill health to workers and the provision of safe and healthy workplaces.* This definition can also be used for more general health and safety performance.

Typically, health and safety performance measurement has the following elements.

Number of injuries resulting from accidents at work, and the number of days injured workers are absent from their work.

Number of occurrences of specific types of physical ill health caused by work factors, and the number of days affected workers are absent from their work. The vast majority of physical ill health data are, however, held by HR departments, and these data are discussed in a later section.

Number of occurrences of stress caused by work factors, and the number of days affected workers are absent from their work. Data on other types of mental ill health are held by HR departments.

Very patchy measurement of how safe and healthy workplaces are. Some organisations have monitoring and/or audit processes that produce quantified measures of, for example, compliance with requirements to maintain health and safety risk control measures. However, consistent measurement of workplace health and safety conditions is rare.

If the psychosocial management system is to be effective, it has to have access to all of the physical and mental ill health data and be able to carry out appropriate analysis of these data. A review of how these data are currently collected and analysed should focus on what needs to be done, and by whom, to ensure the psychosocial management system requirements can be met without raising confidentiality issues.

The review should also try to identify whether there are any instances of well-being and wellness measurement – even if the measures used are qualitative.

With regard to measurements of workplace conditions, where there are any such measurements, the review should concentrate on identifying processes that could readily be extended to meet psychosocial risk management requirements. A typical example would be inspection checklists used to provide a health and safety workplace score that could be extended to include questions of relevance to psychosocial risk sources.

All of the issues discussed above are dealt with in detail in Chapter 25 'Psychosocial measurement, analysis, and evaluation'.

Other health and safety processes

You should review the rest of your current health and safety processes focussing on whether, and to what extent, they can be used to meet psychosocial management system requirements. Examples include:

Health and safety policy. Some organisations include in their *Health and safety policy* a commitment to improving (or at least maintaining) worker well-being and/or wellness. Where this is the case, the *Health and safety policy* can be adopted for use in the psychosocial management system.

Documented information processes. Some organisations have organisation-wide processes for creating, updating, and controlling documented information for health and safety, and where this is the case, the psychosocial management system can simply 'plug in' to these processes.

Awareness and communication processes. Where there are existing processes for maintaining worker awareness and communicating with workers on health and safety issues, these can be utilised as part of the psychosocial management system requirements for awareness and communication.

Management review processes. Where there is an effective management review process for health and safety management reviews, the inputs to these reviews could be extended to include psychosocial data, and the results of the analyses of these data could be extended to include decisions on well-being and wellness issues.

A good strategy is to work systematically through the ISO 45001 and ISO 45003 clauses and prepare a detailed clause-by-clause gap analysis. You can then use this as a basis for preparing your *Psychosocial management system manual* as described in Chapter 17 'The psychosocial management system manual'.

Current HR processes

The following HR processes are relevant to the psychosocial management system.

Data collection and analysis
Definition of prohibited and required behaviours
Investigation of noncompliance
Disciplinary procedures
Anonymous reporting
HR in general

Each of these processes is dealt with in a separate subsection below.

Data collection and analysis

As mentioned earlier in this chapter, HR departments typically collect and analyse data on the number of occurrences of injuries not related to work, and mental and physical ill health. The types of data usually collected are as follows.

Injury and ill health that result in absence from work. This category is usually recorded in terms of number of occurrences and the number of days of absence for each occurrence. The category may include the health and safety data, that is, the occurrences that result from accidents at work. However, it is typically the case that the number of occurrences and days of absence as a result of accidents at work are very small in comparison with the overall occurrence and absence figures.

Injury and ill health that do not result in absence from work. The recording of these data is more problematic. First, it relies on the person suffering the injury or ill health, or someone who is aware of the person's injury or ill health, reporting the occurrence to the HR department. Second, it can be extremely difficult to assess the effect the injury or ill health is having on the person's work performance – and hence the cost to the organisation. However, reduced well-being and reduced wellness are both conditions that can result in degraded work performance rather than absence from work. This can result in reduced productivity and other effects that have a negative impact on the organisation. It is important, therefore, to identify what, if anything, the HR department is doing about these data and what, if anything, the HR department could do about them.

The typical types of analysis of these data are as follows.

Number of occurrences and days of absence by type of injury. Usually, this consists of more or less systematic and comprehensive lists of types of injury (cut, burn, strain, etc.) and part of the body injured (head, left leg, right foot, etc.). Both the type of injury and part of the body injured lists require an 'other' option since comprehensive lists would be too long to be manageable. These lists enable 'tick box' classification of injury types, which facilitates analysis, but can hide subtleties in the data.

Number of occurrences and days of absence by type of ill health. As with injuries, there are usually lists of types of ill health that enable tick box classification. However, because there are so many causes of ill health, it is often the case that the 'other' category has the highest number of occurrences. Another common weakness is that the list of types of mental ill health is very limited – often to just 'stress' and 'other'.

These types of analysis enable HR departments to keep top management informed about the number of occurrences and days of absence as a result of injury and ill health and to give top management a rough idea of the nature of these occurrences. In some organisations, this is the only use to which these data are put, but other types of analyses are possible. The following are of particular relevance to psychosocial risk management.

More detailed lists of mental ill health. In particular, the inclusion of items such as depression and anxiety that are of relevance to well-being and wellness. A close examination of the 'other' category in the list of type of ill health may identify types of ill health that are occurring frequently in the organisation and should be put on the list for tick box analysis.

Analysis of causes of mental ill health. As was described in Part I, mental ill health can arise without an external cause, for example, endogenous depression, but there are many external factors that can have a detrimental effect on well-being and wellness. When data are collected on the external factors that are causing mental illness, it is possible to carry out analysis by cause. This sort of epidemiological or pattern analysis is the same as that used in health and safety to identify patterns in the causes of accidents.

Other uses of epidemiological analysis. This type of analysis can be used to identify such things as where in the organisation mental ill health is occurring, what types of people are suffering from mental ill health (age, gender, role, etc.), and whether there are seasonal variations.

There are difficulties with the collection and analysis of mental ill health data, and the same difficulties will occur when collecting and analysing data on well-being and wellness. For this reason, it is worth making an early start on clearly identifying what the problems will be and how they will be resolved. In particular:

How will data on the external factors causing reduced well-being and wellness be collected? A possible solution would be to add the recording of causes to whatever data collection and recording processes are currently used.

How will confidentiality be ensured? This can be done by restricting access to well-being and wellness data to HR personnel, or by giving one or more of the health and safety personnel a dual role as health and safety and HR, but solely for the purpose of well-being and wellness data handling.

How will competence be ensured? There are two main sets of competence required. First, competence in data collection, particularly collection of data on external causes of reduced well-being and wellness which may require high levels of interview skills. Second, competence in the types of epidemiological analysis described above. Both sets of competences can be supplied by providing HR personnel with the competences or having dual role health and safety personnel, as described in the previous subparagraph.

All of these issues are dealt with in Chapter 25 'Psychosocial measurement, analysis, and evaluation'.

Definition of prohibited and required behaviours

Prohibited and required behaviours occur in health and safety – for example, the prohibition on entry into confined spaces and the requirement to wear specified PPE when carrying out certain tasks. However, the range of prohibited and required behaviours dealt with by HR departments is usually much wider, and the majority of these behaviours can be psychosocial risk sources.

Typically prohibited and required behaviours fall into one of the following two categories.

Legal requirements. There is a wide range of legal requirements that result in particular behaviours being included in HR lists. For example, discrimination, theft, and bribery.

Organisation requirements. These are imposed to maintain the image the organisation wishes to project. They include prohibiting workers from wearing certain types of clothing and jewellery, and requiring certain styles of leadership and behaviour towards colleagues and interested parties.

As was described in Chapter 5 'The hazards and risk sources', the effect of these behaviours can be direct – someone is the victim of discrimination – or indirect – someone witnesses discrimination and this causes a reduction in their well-being. This means that all of the items on the HR lists can become psychosocial risk sources. For this reason, a detailed review of the lists is an important step in establishing what is already in place by way of psychosocial risk management.

The sorts of prohibited and required behaviours included in typical HR lists of such behaviours is discussed in Chapter 21 'Awareness and communication'.

It is also important to establish how the HR department deals with occurrences of prohibited behaviour and failure to carry out required behaviours. This is dealt with in the next two subsections.

Investigation of noncompliance

For the purposes of this section, a noncompliance is carrying out a prohibited behaviour or failing to carry out a required behaviour. These types of noncompliance become nonconformities when the requirements are included in the psychosocial management system.

Investigations of minor noncompliances are typically carried out by managerial workers one or two grades above the accused individual's grade, perhaps with some assistance from HR personnel. Serious noncompliances are typically investigated by a team consisting of senior managerial workers and HR personnel. Both types of investigation often suffer from the following weaknesses.

Failure to establish the causes of the noncompliance. For example, an investigation of bullying establishes the nature and extent of the bullying, but not why the bullying occurred. This limits the usefulness of the investigation as a source of ideas for prevention of recurrence.

Failure to look beyond the particular incident being investigated to establish whether it is an isolated incident or part of a more widespread problem. For example, investigating a racism incident without considering whether this is an example of institutionalised racism.

These weaknesses arise from the lack of competences described earlier for health and safety incident investigation, that is, lack of competence in interviewing, analysing causal factors, and making recommendations. Investigation of these types of nonconformity is dealt with in Chapter 27 'Psychosocial investigation'.

Disciplinary procedures

HR departments tend to use the term 'disciplinary procedure' to describe the processes used to deal with workers who are judged to have committed a noncompliance. Where the noncompliance is a psychosocial risk source, these workers are, in psychosocial risk management terminology, perpetrators.

The HR disciplinary procedures can form the basis for the psychosocial procedure for dealing with perpetrators, but it typically has to be extended in the following ways.

The investigation of the noncompliances has to be improved in the ways described in the previous section.

The relationship between the nature and severity of the noncompliance and the punishment imposed for the noncompliance has to be more flexible. HR disciplinary sanctions tend to be in the form 'if the perpetrator does "x" then the organisation will do "y"' – with no reference to extenuating circumstances or the effect on the victims. See Chapter 10 'The people' for a discussion of the role of perpetrators.

The need to deal sensitively with any victims of the noncompliance. HR disciplinary procedures 'do what they say on the tin' – they discipline individuals found guilty of a noncompliance. However, there is rarely a 'victim procedure' that sets out what the organisation will do by way of support and compensation for victims of noncompliances. This issue is also addressed in Chapter 10 'The people'.

Dealing with perpetrators and victims is dealt with in detail in Chapter 22 'Psychosocial risk sources'.

Anonymous reporting

For the purposes of this section, anonymous reporting is an individual passing information on noncompliances to the HR department without revealing their identity. Individuals can pass information to other organisations – for example, they can inform the police or regulatory authorities. External anonymous reporting is usually referred to as whistleblowing.

HR department anonymous reporting processes usually include the following elements.

The types of noncompliances that could be the subject of anonymous reporting.
Actions that should be taken before resorting to anonymous reporting, for example, discussions with a line manager.
Who to report to if the reporter is willing to be identified – this is usually someone in the HR department.
The mechanism for anonymous reporting within the organisation.
A warning not to resort to external whistleblowing until all internal options have failed. This is usually accompanied by details of the punishment for whistleblowing the organisation considers inappropriate.

An effective anonymous reporting process is an essential element of a psychosocial management system, and anonymous reporting is dealt with in Chapter 23 'Psychosocial threat and opportunity assessment'.

HR in general

HR procedures can form the basis for psychosocial management procedures. However, it should be remembered that the principal function of the HR department is to protect the organisation. The HR procedures based on legal requirements are designed to prevent the organisation being prosecuted, and the HR procedures based on organisational requirements are to prevent the organisation's reputation and image being damaged. In contrast, the principal function of psychosocial procedures is to protect the well-being and wellness of workers and interested parties. While there is common ground, the fundamental difference in function between the two sets of procedures may make it necessary to have separate procedures for some aspects of psychosocial risk management. For example, HR departments may not see the treatment of victims as part of their function.

Other relevant activities

Across organisations, there is a range of activities relevant to psychosocial risk management. These may be organised by the HR department or the Health and Safety department, but they can also be organised by *ad hoc* committees and groups of volunteers. There are the following broad categories of these activities.

Information collection. These are activities designed to find out about the state of well-being and wellness of workers and interested parties, and/or what these individuals would like to do, and have done, about their well-being and wellness. Typical activities of this type are worker surveys, focus groups, well-being and wellness suggestion schemes, and arrangements for reporting well-being and wellness issues.

Information provision. These are activities designed to provide workers and interested parties with information about things that will enable them to maintain and improve their well-being and wellness. These activities can be one-way communications with, for example, the provision of leaflets or videos, or they can be interactive, for example, with workshops and training courses.

Resource provision. This is the organisation providing workers and interested parties with resources that are known to be beneficial for well-being and wellness. Examples include the following.

Providing access to such things as gyms, and Pilates and yoga classes.

Providing access to such things as social events and entertainments.

Providing physical resources such as healthy options in canteens and food dispensing machines, and blood pressure monitors.

Providing access to help for people suffering from reduced well-being or wellness, for example, external and/or internal help lines and counsellors.

All of these activities are relevant in psychosocial risk management, and they are dealt with in the appropriate chapters later in Part II.

Using review results

Your review should identify

existing procedures that

are appropriate for a psychosocial management system and can be utilised in the system you are setting up

could be made appropriate for a psychosocial management system if the current 'owners' agreed to certain changes

required psychosocial management system procedures that are not currently implemented in your organisation.

This information can be used when preparing your psychosocial management system development plan as described in Chapter 32.

References

1   British Standards Institution. *Occupational health and safety management – Psychological health and safety at work – Guidelines for managing psychosocial risks,* BSI ISO 45003, 2021. BSI 2021.
2   British Standards Institution. *Occupational health and safety management systems – Requirements with guidance for use*, BS ISO 45001, 2018. BSI 2018.

15 Purpose, intended outcomes, scope, policy, and psychosocial objectives

Introduction

This chapter deals with the guidance in ISO 45003[1] that has to be dealt with before you can begin to draft a description of your psychosocial management system. The requirements are listed below together with the relevant ISO 45003 clause numbers.

The purpose of your organisation. You need this to complete clause 4.1.
The intended outcomes of your psychosocial management system. This is also required to complete clause 4.1.
The scope of your psychosocial management system. This is required to complete clause 4.3.
Your *Well-being and wellness policy*. This is required to complete clause 5.2.
Your psychosocial objectives. This is required to complete clause 6.2.

It is a good strategy to draft documented versions of how you will meet these requirements and agree these with relevant workers and interested parties, in particular top management. If you do not, you may begin developing psychosocial management system elements that will have no, or very little, support in your organisation.

Purpose

Neither ISO 45001[2] nor ISO 45003 has a requirement to identifying your organisation's purpose, but clause 4.1 of ISO 45001 is *The organization shall determine external and internal issues that are relevant to its purpose and that affect its ability to achieve the intended outcome(s) of its OH&S management system.*

The purpose of your organisation is probably recorded in some other document, for example, as part of another management system such as quality or environment. It may also be available in the form of a 'mission statement', 'vision statement', or description of the organisation's 'values'. Where possible, you should use an existing documented version of your organisation's purpose.

DOI: 10.4324/9781003490555-17

It is unlikely that you will be able to change the purpose of your organisation so what you need to do is tailor your psychosocial management system to suit this purpose. For example, the ISO 45003 hazard of a psychosocial nature *duty of care for other people* cannot be eliminated in the wide range of organisations providing medical, residential, and domiciliary care. This means that psychosocial risk control for these organisations has to adopt a risk mitigation approach, rather than a hazard elimination approach. There are many hazards of a psychosocial nature listed in ISO 45003 that, because of the purpose of your organisation, will require you to adopt this risk mitigation approach.

Intended outcomes

Rather confusingly, ISO 45001 has two versions of the intended outcomes of an OH&S management system. Section 1.2 of the *Introduction* to ISO 45001 includes the statement

The aim and intended outcomes of the OH&S management system are to prevent work-related injury and ill health to workers and to provide safe and healthy workplaces.

This version of the intended outcomes is repeated in Note 1 to the ISO 45001 definition of *OH&S management system* which is

The intended outcomes of the OH&S management system are to prevent injury and ill health to workers and to provide safe and healthy workplaces.

The second version of the intended outcomes of an OH&S management system occurs in paragraph 3 of the *Scope* clause of ISO 45001 as follows.

the intended outcomes of an OH&S management system include:

a) continual improvement of OH&S performance;
b) fulfilment of legal requirements and other requirements;
c) achievement of OH&S objectives.

However, since *OH&S performance* is defined in ISO 45001 as

performance related to the effectiveness of the prevention of injury and ill health to workers and the provision of safe and healthy workplaces

it appears that bullet point a) is equivalent to the first version of the intended outcomes and that bullet points b) and c) go beyond this first version.

Since the second version is more comprehensive, it is the one the authors use when developing OH&S management systems and the one the authors recommend you use as a basis for your psychosocial management system's intended outcomes.

There is more information on psychosocial management system intended outcomes later in this section.

In ISO 45003, *intended outcomes* appears only in clauses 4.1.2 and 4.1.3, both of which use the phrase

intended outcomes of the OH&S management system in relation to psychosocial risk,

but these *intended outcomes* are not mentioned again in ISO 45003.

In deciding upon the intended outcomes of your psychosocial management system, it is important to bear in mind the following points.

Psychosocial risk management is about improvement, not just prevention.
Psychosocial risk sources are not just psychosocial threats, they can create opportunities for improving well-being and wellness instead of, or as well as, being threats to well-being and wellness.

As was discussed in Chapter 11 'The psychosocial management system terminology', it is necessary to adopt different definitions in the psychosocial management system if these points are to be adequately taken into account. The intended outcomes below, which are an extension of the second version of the ISO 45001 requirements for intended outcomes, are the authors' suggestion for intended outcomes for a psychosocial management system. Text in square brackets in these suggestions indicates alternative or extended versions of the intended outcomes.

The intended outcomes of the psychosocial management system are to

maximise [optimise] the well-being and wellness of workers [and defined interested parties]
minimise [reduce] [eliminate] the adverse effect of work and workplaces on the well-being and wellness of workers [and defined interested parties]
maximise [optimise] [promote] the positive effect of work and workplaces on the well-being and wellness of workers [and defined interested parties]
ensure the fulfilment of psychosocial legal requirements and other psychosocial requirements
ensure the achievement of psychosocial objectives.

How the achievement of these intended outcomes can be measured is dealt with in Chapter 25 'Psychosocial measurement, analysis, and evaluation'.

Scope

The ISO 45001 requirements with regard to scope are set out below – text in square brackets is explanatory notes.

The organization shall determine the boundaries and applicability of the OH&S management system to establish its scope.

When determining this scope, the organization shall:

a) *consider the external and internal issues referred to in 4.1;* [That is *Understanding the organization and its context*]
b) *take into account the requirements referred to in 4.2;* [That is *Understanding the needs and expectations of workers and other interested parties*]
c) *take into account the planned or performed work-related activities.*

The OH&S management system shall include the activities, products and services within the organization's control or influence that can impact the organization's OH&S performance.

The scope shall be available as documented information.

The *external and internal issues referred to in 4.1* are dealt with in Chapter 18 'SWOT analysis' and the *requirements referred to in 4.2* are dealt with in Chapter 16 'Needs and expectations'. However, it is useful to do preliminary work on the scope of your psychosocial management system prior to collecting this information. This preliminary work is discussed next.

It is helpful to consider the following issues when documenting the scope of a management system.

The organisation's locations.
The organisation's activities.
The individuals who will be within scope.
The risk sources that will be within scope.

Each of these is dealt with in a separate subsection below.

Locations

This is straightforward when the organisation has only one location and all the organisation's activities take place within that location. However, this is rarely the case and typical complications include the following.

Working at home. This is increasingly common following the Covid pandemic, and you need to agree whether working at home will be within the scope of the psychosocial management system and, if it is, what, if any, exclusions there will be. For example, exposure to psychosocial risk sources happening during weekends and holidays, or more generally, outside normal working hours, might be excluded.

Working at customers' premises. Depending on the organisation, these premises could be other commercial premises, for example, machinery repair and maintenance organisations, or domestic premises, for example, domestic central heating repair and maintenance organisations. Since the organisation has no control over these premises, or very limited control, careful thought has to be given to what can realistically be included in the scope of the psychosocial management system.

Working at other locations. This category includes a wide range of locations including roadside repairs, installation of fibre-optic cables, and, more generally, work that is not done on premises such as driving vehicles on public roads.

Note that any of the above complications may be exacerbated if they involve lone working, and this possibility should be taken into account when considering the scope of your psychosocial management system.

Activities

As with locations, this can be straightforward when all of the organisation's activities take place at a location, or locations, that are within the scope of the psychosocial management system. However, the following complications can occur.

Non-work activities at in-scope locations. These activities include parking in the location car park, using the location welfare facilities, and social activities taking place at the in-scope location. The simplest option is to include all activities that take place at your locations, but there may be particular reasons why you need to exclude some of them.

Non-work activities at out-of-scope locations. This can get very complicated. For example, if working at home is within scope, what does this 'working' include? It was seen in the previous section that there can be exclusions on the basis of when the activity takes place – for example, outside working hours – and it is also possible to have exclusions based on the nature of the activity. Including all the activities that take place at out-of-scope locations is not usually an option, and an agreement will have to be reached as to what will be included and what will be excluded.

People

In ISO 45001, people are either *workers* or *interested parties*.
A worker is a

person performing work or work-related activities that are under the control of the organization.

The notes to this definition make it clear that the term *worker* covers a wide range of people.

Note 1 to entry: Persons perform work or work-related activities under various arrangements, paid or unpaid, such as regularly or temporarily, intermittently or seasonally, casually or on a part-time basis.

Note 2 to entry: Workers include top management, managerial and non-managerial persons.

Note 3 to entry: The work or work-related activities performed under the control of the organization may be performed by workers employed by the organization, workers of external providers, contractors, individuals, agency workers, and by other persons to the extent the organization shares control over their work or work-related activities, according to the context of the organization.

Where all workers are employees of the organisation, things are usually straight-forward since they should all be within the scope of the psychosocial management system. The complications arise when there are workers where your organisation *shares control over their work or work-related activities.* When this is the case, careful thought has to be given to whether, and in what ways, these workers will be included in the scope. Typical reasons for including these workers are that they are working at an in-scope premises, or that they are working almost completely under the organisation's control.

An *interested party* is a

person or organization that can affect, be affected by, or perceive itself to be affected by a decision or activity

which, again, is a very wide definition. ISO 45001 gives the following guidance on interested parties. Text in square brackets is comments on the guidance.

Interested parties, in addition to workers, can include:

a) legal and regulatory authorities (local, regional, state/provincial, national or international);
b) parent organizations;
c) suppliers, contractors and subcontractors; [ISO 45001 gets muddled with this terminology – contractors are suppliers of services and, if they are working under the control of the organisation, they are workers, not interested parties.]
d) workers' representatives;
e) workers' organizations (trade unions [sic – it should be trades union]*) and employers' organizations;*
f) owners, shareholders, clients, visitors, local community and neighbours of the organization and the general public;

g) *customers, medical and other community services, media, academia, business associations and non-governmental organizations (NGOs);*
h) *occupational health and safety organizations, occupational safety and health-care professionals.*

For the purposes of a psychosocial management system, the most important interested parties from the list above are *workers' representatives* and *medical and other community services.* Item (h) in the list could usefully be replaced with 'well-being and wellness organizations' and 'well-being and wellness care professionals'.

What is missing from the list in the context of a psychosocial management system are the individuals who provide psychosocial support for workers and interested parties, and the psychosocial dependents of workers and interested parties. Psychosocial support typically involves family and friends with, where necessary, interventions from well-being and wellness care professionals. Family members are the typical psychosocial dependents, although some individuals may take on the psychosocial support of others.

An important point to decide upon when setting the scope of your psychosocial management system is which interested parties, other than workers, will be within this scope.

Risk sources

In Chapter 5 'The hazards and risk sources', it was shown that there are large numbers of psychosocial hazards and risk sources – and that there are many ways of classifying them. As was seen earlier, ISO 45003 uses three categories:

Aspects of how work is organised
Social factors at work
Work environment, equipment, and hazardous tasks

This classification can be useful when deciding who will be responsible for managing particular psychosocial risk sources. For example, the work environment, equipment, and hazardous tasks category could be dealt with by extending the competence of the health and safety personnel, and the other categories could be dealt with by human resources personnel.

However, the focus in this section is the classification of risk sources in ways that facilitate the setting of priorities for action on these risk sources. There are so many psychosocial risk sources that starting to manage them all simultaneously is an impossible task. What is needed, therefore, is a strategy that enables the selection of a manageable number of psychosocial risk sources as a starting point. The various subsections that follow describe classifications that can be used to help you decide on your priorities for action.

ISO 45003

The obvious priority would be to tackle the hazards of a psychosocial nature listed in ISO 45003 since this would be a clear way to demonstrate conformity with this guidance. The problem with this is that the hazards of a psychosocial nature listed in ISO 45003 are so numerous and so varied that, for most organisations, tackling them all simultaneously would not be a realistic approach.

In addition, extensive as the ISO 45003 list of hazards of a psychosocial nature is, it does not include some of the risk sources relating to wellness, or the psychosocial harms arising from behaviours such as bribery, theft, and discrimination. It is likely, therefore, that you will want to consider psychosocial hazards not included in the ISO 45003 list. The other classifications described in this chapter enable alternative approaches to classification.

Legal compliance

Different countries have different legal requirements with regard to psychosocial risk sources. For organisations committed to compliance with local legislative requirements, prioritising psychosocial risk sources that are the subject of local legislation is a good strategy. For example, in Great Britain[ii] these legislative requirements include the following.

Equality Act 2010. This Act deals with discrimination against individuals because of, for example, their sex [*sic*], race, or marital status.

Bribery Act 2010. As its name suggests, this Act deals with bribery and related activities, including the duty of organisations to prevent bribery.

Employment Rights Act 1996. This Act is relevant because it covers so-called whistleblowing activities that can be important in identifying the occurrence of certain psychosocial risk sources.

Workplace (Health, Safety and Welfare) Regulations 1992. These Regulations set minimum standards in workplaces for issues that can affect wellness, for example, ventilation, lighting, and facilities for eating and changing clothes.

In Australia, there is an explicit duty to manage psychosocial risks, and there is a detailed approved code of practice under section 274 of the *Work Health and Safety Act*.

Unacceptable behaviours

As was seen in Chapter 14 'What is already in place?', organisations can mandate that certain behaviours are unacceptable in their organisation, and obvious candidates for such mandates are bullying, harassment, and violence – both physical and verbal. The prohibition of these behaviours can then be written into whichever documents the organisation uses to mandate worker behaviour, for example, employee handbooks and work instructions.

One strategy for an initial psychosocial management system is to focus on these prohibited behaviours, preferably in conjunction with the required behaviours discussed in the next subsection.

Required behaviours

Chapter 14 'What is already in place?' also dealt with the fact that the avoidance of some psychosocial hazards can only be ensured if people in an organisation behave in certain ways. For example, eliminating poor leadership or poor communication requires that the behaviour of leaders and communicators conforms with good practice behaviour for these activities. When an organisation considers that some behaviours should be a requirement of a particular role, they can mandate these behaviours and ensure they are recorded in similar ways to the unacceptable behaviours described in the previous subsection.

Improving efficiency

A number of psychosocial risk sources have a detrimental effect on the organisation's efficiency. Examples include the following.

Poor leadership and poor supervision are likely to lead to sub-optimal performance from those being led or supervised.
Lack of clarity over job roles and responsibilities can result in tasks being duplicated and some essential tasks being missed.
Performing work of little value or purpose is obviously inefficient.
Unrealistic expectations of workers' competence can result in tasks being carried out ineffectively, or not at all.

You will need to take soundings in your organisation to get a feel for which psychosocial risk sources are having a detrimental effect on your organisation's efficiency. However, this does not have to be a formal survey to be useful. It can be the case that major sources of inefficiency can be identified quite readily when you focus on the effects of psychosocial risk sources.

Self-interest and altruism

Self-interest and altruism have the same effect, but for the purposes of this section, they have different motivations. Put simply, altruism is doing good with no thought of reward, while self-interest is doing good in the hope that the doer receives some benefit from their action. Organisations using this method of classification typically 'cherry pick' the list of psychosocial risk sources and select the ones that they think will do the most good for workers (altruism) or the ones that will benefit both workers and the organisation (self-interest).

As might imagined, there is such a wide variation between organisations, and between the requirements of workers, that there is no single system for identifying psychosocial risk sources that are relevant to this type of classification. However, there are usually some psychosocial risk sources that can be removed, or mitigated, without any cost to the organisation and these can form a beginning for the use of this classification.

Workers and worker representatives

This option allows workers, and their representatives where these exist, to determine the priorities for managing psychosocial risk sources. Obviously, top management will have the ultimate say in which psychosocial risk sources are actually managed, but obtaining the views of workers and their representatives can give a very accurate picture of which psychosocial risk sources are important to the workers.

Real life

So far, a number of ways in which you can prioritise psychosocial risk sources for psychosocial management system purposes in your organisation have been described. However, because of the variety and complexity of real life in an organisation, you are unlikely to be able to use only one classification. What is important in practice is that you

find out what top management want
find out what other levels of worker in the various functions making up your organisation want
be clear about what you want.

Figure 15.1 summarises the descriptions and discussions contained in this section.

Policy

ISO 45003 does not require you to have a separate *Well-being and wellness policy.* Clause 5.2.1 states that *top management should … determine if there is a need for a separate policy about managing psychosocial risk.* This is reinforced in clause 5.2.2, which includes *The organization should consider if a specific policy to manage psychosocial risk is necessary.*

There is very little guidance in ISO 45003 on what should be in a *Well-being and wellness policy.* The relevant clauses are

Clause 5.2.1 – *ensure that commitments to preventing ill health and injuries related to psychosocial risk and promoting well-being at work are included in the OH&S policy.*

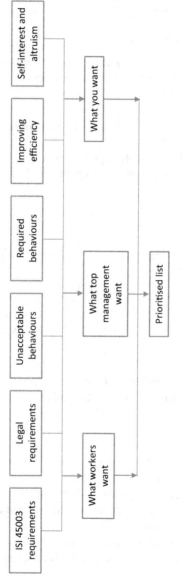

Figure 15.1 Prioritising psychosocial risk sources for a psychosocial management system.

Clause 5.2.2 – *include a commitment to fulfil legal requirements and other requirements related to health, safety and well-being at work, including a commitment to manage psychosocial risk.*

Both of these commitments could be easily added to most OH&S policies. However, clause 5.2.2 includes a more complex suggestion in that the policy should

promote and enhance a working environment consistent with the principles of dignity, mutual respect, confidentiality, cooperation and trust in the OH&S management system.

This may be more difficult to incorporate in an existing OH&S policy, but the following suggestions may help.

ISO 45001 requires that the OH&S policy includes a number of commitments, and a typical ISO 45001-compliant OH&S policy will include some version of the following list.

The organisation is committed to

providing safe and healthy working conditions for the prevention of work-related injury and ill health

fulfilling legal requirements and other requirements

eliminating hazards and reducing OH&S risks

continual improvement of the OH&S management system

consultation and participation of workers, and, where they exist, workers' representatives.

This could be easily modified to create a combined *OH&S, well-being and wellness policy* by using some version of the following.

The organisation is committed to

providing safe and healthy working conditions for promoting and enhancing worker well-being and wellness

promoting and enhancing a working environment consistent with the principles of dignity, mutual respect, confidentiality, cooperation, and trust in the OH&S management system

fulfilling legal requirements and other requirements

eliminating hazards, including psychosocial hazards and reducing OH&S risks, including psychosocial risks

continual improvement of the OH&S management system

consultation and participation of workers, and, where they exist, workers' representatives.

If your existing OH&S policy cannot be adapted to cover psychosocial requirements, or there is going to be a separate psychosocial management system, you will have to have a separate *Well-being and wellness policy*. However, this can readily be adapted from any existing OH&S policy that meets the ISO 45001 policy requirements. A 'bare bones' version of such a *Well-being and wellness policy* is given in Box 15.1 as a starting point.

Box 15.1 Well-being and wellness policy

The top management is committed to ensuring working conditions throughout the organisation that protect and promote worker well-being and wellness.

To this end, the top management maintains and continually improves a psychosocial management system that evaluates

the effectiveness of well-being and wellness management activities, and well-being and wellness performance.

The top management is also committed to

fulfilling psychosocial legal requirements and other psychosocial requirements
minimising the threats from psychosocial risk sources
optimising the opportunities from psychosocial risk sources
continual improvement of the psychosocial management system
consultation and participation of workers, and, where they exist, workers' representatives.

The top management ensures that the resources necessary to maintain and continually improve the psychosocial management system are made available.

You may have noticed that there is no equivalent in this outline *Well-being and wellness policy* of the ISO 45003 guidance

promoting and enhancing a working environment consistent with the principles of dignity, mutual respect, confidentiality, cooperation and trust in the OH&S management system.

The reason this is omitted from the *Well-being and wellness policy* is because of the difficulty of measuring conformity with the guidance, and the authors are always hesitant about committing to achieving anything that they are not going to be able to measure.

Because of the overlaps between the psychosocial management system work and the work of HR, it is worthwhile checking for compatibility between your

Well-being and wellness policy and any HR policies. ISO 45003 suggests more general checks as follows: *consider how other policies (e.g. human resources, corporate social responsibility) support and are consistent with the OH&S policy to achieve common objectives.*

Finally, clause 5.2.2 also states that the policy should *provide a framework for setting and reviewing, evaluating and revising objectives for the management of psychosocial risk.* These psychosocial objectives are discussed in the next section.

Psychosocial objectives

In ISO 45001, an objective is *a result to be achieved* and an OH&S objective is an *objective set by the organization to achieve specific results consistent with the OH&S policy.* This is rather confusing since substituting the definition of objective in the definition of OH&S objective gives you *result to be achieved set by the organization to achieve specific results consistent with the OH&S policy.*

This is one of the reasons why general risk management terminology is adopted for certain aspects of psychosocial risk management and, as was set out in Chapter 11 'The psychosocial management system terminology', a psychosocial objective was defined as an *objective which, if achieved, will maintain or improve worker well-being and/or wellness.* The application of this definition will be dealt with after a description of the ISO 45003 guidance on, and the ISO 45001 requirements for, objectives.

The ISO 45003 guidance on objectives is set out in clause 6.2 *Objectives to address psychosocial risk,* and it is very succinct.

The organization should:

a) establish measurable objectives consistent with the policy;
b) develop and implement plans to ensure that these objectives can be achieved.

The ISO 45001 requirements with regard to OH&S objectives are more extensive and they are set out in clause 6.2.1.

The organization shall establish OH&S objectives at relevant functions and levels in order to maintain and continually improve the OH&S management system and OH&S performance.

This ISO 45001 clause is carried over from Annex SL,[3] but for our present purposes, there is no need to discriminate between the two categories of objectives mentioned in this clause.

What is needed for the present purposes is to recognise that there are two types of psychosocial objective.

Project objectives. These are objectives that have a natural end point, for example, draft a procedure, train a group of workers, or install a psychosocial risk control measure.

System objectives. These are objectives that have no natural end point and are used for things that have to be kept going indefinitely. For example, maintain an up-to-date procedure, maintain the competence of a group of workers, or maintain a psychosocial risk control measure.

The authors have argued for a long time that one of the main weaknesses in OH&S management is the use of project objectives when system objectives were needed. This results in undesirable circumstances, such as out-of-date procedures, because there is no requirement to review them, workers lacking competences because there is no requirement for refresher training, and degradation of risk controls because responsibility for maintaining them has not been allocated.

When you are setting up your psychosocial management system, it may be appropriate to set project objectives such as 'prepare a first draft of the Well-being and wellness policy' or 'reach agreement with HR on the definition of prohibited behaviours'. However, what is of interest in this section are the system objectives that will set out what you intend your psychosocial management system to continue to achieve.

You should already have the intended outcomes of your psychosocial management system, and the example given earlier in this chapter was

maximise [optimise] the well-being and wellness of workers [and defined interested parties]

minimise [reduce] [eliminate] the adverse effect of work and the workplaces on the well-being and wellness of workers [and defined interested parties]

maximise [optimise] [promote] the positive effect of work and the workplaces on the well-being and wellness of workers [and defined interested parties]

the fulfilment of psychosocial legal requirements and other psychosocial requirements

the achievement of psychosocial objectives.

The first three bullet points can be considered as very broad objectives, and more specific psychosocial objectives can be set as stepping stones to the achievement of these broad objectives. For example, specific psychosocial objectives for *maximise [optimise] the well-being and wellness of workers [and defined interested parties]* could include

establish and maintain procedures for

measuring workers' well-being
measuring workers' wellness
measuring defined interested parties' well-being
measuring defined interested parties' wellness

establish and maintain a procedure for keeping the list of defined interested parties up-to-date

establish and maintain a procedure for psychosocial threat and opportunity assessment

establish and maintain a procedure for prioritising psychosocial threat control measure implementation and maintenance.

Identifying 'stepping stone' objectives will enable you to plan the implementation of your psychosocial management system more easily. For example, you may restrict the initial implementation to worker wellness, but you will also have identified what else you need to do to achieve your intended outcomes. Planning the implementation of your psychosocial management system is dealt with in Chapter 32 'The psychosocial management system development plan'. Note however, that you will also need processes for planning to achieve objectives as part of your ongoing psychosocial management system. This type of planning is dealt with in Chapter 30 'Psychosocial planning and continual improvement'.

Iteration

Iteration is the repetition of a process and, in the context of this chapter, it is the repeated consideration of each of the topics dealt with in the chapter as events occur in the real world. It is said that no plan survives first contact with the enemy, and it could also be said that no draft of a *Well-being and wellness policy* will survive first contact with top management and/or the trades union and/or the HR department and/or the Health and Safety department and/or anyone else you choose to ask about its content.

You are likely to have similar experiences with your drafts of intended outcomes, scope, and psychosocial objectives and iteration is the answer. Keep revising and discussing until you have versions that are agreed by top management and are not too violently opposed by other workers and interested parties.

Notes

i   This is the Scope of ISO 45001, not the scope of your psychosocial management system, which is dealt with in the next section of this chapter.

ii   The legislation listed as applying to Great Britain has various extensions to Northern Ireland and restrictions within Great Britain. However, these details are not relevant for the purposes of this book.

References

1   British Standards Institution. *Occupational health and safety management – Psychological health and safety at work – Guidelines for managing psychosocial risks*, BSI ISO 45003, 2021. BSI 2021.

2 British Standards Institution. *Occupational health and safety management systems – Requirements with guidance for use*, BSI ISO 45001, 2018. BSI 2018.

3 *ISO/IEC Directives, Part 1 Consolidated ISO Supplement – Procedure for the technical work – Procedures specific to ISO (Thirteenth edition, 2022). Annex SL (normative) Harmonised approach for management system standards. Appendix 2 (normative) Harmonized structure for MSS with guidance for use.*

16 Needs and expectations

Introduction

The chapter deals with the concepts of needs and expectations, and it has the following sections.

Needs and expectations in practice
The ISO 45001[1] requirements and the ISO 45003[2] guidance with regard to needs and expectations
Establishing the needs and expectations to be taken into account
Needs and expectations documented information

Needs and expectations in practice

ISO 45001 defines requirement as a

need or expectation that is stated, generally implied or obligatory.

However, there are no definitions for need or expectation. The relevant ODE[3] definitions are

need – *a thing that is wanted or required*
expectation – *a strong belief that something will happen or be the case.*

This means that, in the context of a psychosocial management system, needs and expectations can be treated in the same way. That is, in practice, it does not matter whether a worker requirement is a need or an expectation, because it has to be dealt with irrespective of its origin. Dealing with these requirements is discussed next.

Individuals have various requirements, for example, food, rest, and social contact, and for each requirement, there will be a range of ways in which an organisation can meet that requirement. For example, in the case of workers:

Most workers will require food at some time during their work shift. However, these requirements will vary from worker to worker with, at one extreme,

DOI: 10.4324/9781003490555-18

some workers requiring a full, cooked meal, and at the other extreme, some workers requiring an apple or snack food, or no food at all. The extent to which organisations meet their workers' requirements for food also varies with some organisations providing high quality, heavily subsidised canteens or restaurants, while others provide no facilities at all. In a stable, self-selecting population, workers' requirements will match the organisation's provision. For example, no one with a strong requirement for a cooked midday meal will stay with an organisation which does not provide such a meal, and is in a location where such a meal cannot be obtained nearby. More generally, in stable populations, workers' requirements will match the organisation's provision – be it restaurant or canteen, food preparation and eating areas, snack and drink dispensing machines, or no facilities at all.

Workers will require suitable rest breaks during their work shift and, as with food, the workers' requirements will vary. Variations in requirements can be created by individual differences – some workers are fitter than others, for example – role differences – some roles are more strenuous than others – and external factors such as temperature and time of day. Provision of rest facilities also differs; some organisations provide no facilities for rest – workers simply stop working for a while. However, other organisations provide rest areas, or 'quiet rooms', or outside seating areas for use during clement weather. As with food, populations of workers will be self-selecting and, in general, workers' requirements with regard to rest breaks will match the organisation's provisions for such breaks.

Many workers require social contact and for some, their place of work is their main source of social contact. However, some workers do not require social contact, and for others, social contact at work is detrimental to their well-being. Typically, organisations do not have formal arrangements for social contact in the way that they do for food and rest. In some circumstances, this is because social contact is detrimental to productivity. However, workers usually make their own arrangements for social contact. For example, those who require opportunities for social contact during the working day meet up during food and rest breaks, and those who want to avoid social contact sit in their car in the car park, or go for a walk during food and rest breaks.

While worker requirements have to be taken into account to some extent in OH&S, they are vitally important in psychosocial risk management. Not meeting a workers' requirements for food, rest, or social contact may have only a small effect on the organisation's OH&S performance or the organisation's productivity and worker turnover, but it will have a significant effect on most workers' well-being and wellness. This means it is important to look at what these requirements might be.

In general, all psychosocial risk sources imply a worker requirement, for example, role ambiguity is a threat for those workers who require clarity of their role. If all, or a large majority of workers have a requirement for role clarity, the organisation can voluntarily adopt an organisational requirement to clearly define all roles. Further illustrations of this are given in Table 16.1, using examples from Tables 1 and 2 of the ISO 45003 tables of hazards of a psychosocial nature.

　Table 16.1 raises a number of important points.

It shows that it is easy to identify relevant worker requirements, but it may be extremely difficult to establish how these requirements can be met in practice. For example, there is probably general agreement that workers should be treated with *trust, honesty, respect, civility, and fairness*, but how to ensure that workers are treated with *trust, honesty, respect, civility, and fairness* could be the subject of endless debate.

At various points, it is necessary to use qualifiers, for example, **essential** *part of the role,* **acceptable** *frequency,* and **suitable** *levels of influence and independence.* All of these qualifiers imply that definitions and criteria will have to be agreed before judgements can be made on whether the relevant requirement is being met.

There are many terms such as *trust, respect, consideration,* and *civility* where there will have to be agreement about what they look like in practice.

The *Table 2 Supervision* entry shows that there may be the need for extensive competence provision, competence assessment, and additional monitoring of performance. It is no longer sufficient for supervisors to 'get the job done' – they must also ensure that getting the job done does not have a negative impact on their team's well-being or wellness.

The *Table 2 Civility and respect* entry shows that some requirements can only be met if the organisation takes action to influence the behaviour of individuals other than workers. Notices posted in places such as shops and medical practices warning customers and service users that abuse of workers will not be tolerated are, sadly, becoming more common. This is an example of organisations taking action to influence the behaviour of individuals other than their workers.

　In a mature psychosocial management system, there will have been analysis of the requirements associated with all of the ISO 45003 hazards of a psychosocial nature and all of the other psychosocial risk sources discussed in Chapter 5 'The hazards and risk sources'. However, when you are starting out, you can restrict your analysis to those psychosocial risk sources that are within the scope of your initial psychosocial management system.

ISO 45001 and ISO 45003

To avoid confusion, in this section, 'workers' needs and expectations' has been used rather than 'workers' requirements' to avoid phrases such as 'the ISO 45001 requirements with regard to requirements of workers'.

Table 16.1 Worker psychosocial requirements

Category	Hazard of a psychosocial nature	Worker requirement	Organisation requirement
Table 1 Roles and expectations	role ambiguity role conflict	clarity of role role that is free from conflict	Organisation will clearly define all roles Organisation will eliminate conflict from all roles
	duty of care for other people	no duty of care that is not an essential part of the role	Organisation will eliminate non-essential duty of care from all roles
	scenarios where workers do not have clear guidelines on the tasks they are expected to do (and not do)	clear guidelines on the tasks to be done	Organisation will ensure that clear guidelines are given on the tasks to be done
	expectations within a role that undermine one another (e.g., being expected to provide good customer service, but also to not spend a long time with customers)	no undermining expectations within role	Organisation will eliminate undermining expectations from all roles
	uncertainty about, or frequent changes to, tasks and work standards	clarity of tasks and work standards changes to tasks and work standards at an acceptable frequency	Organisation will clearly define tasks and work standards Organisation will only make changes to tasks and work standards at an acceptable frequency
	performing work of little value or purpose	all required work will have a value or purpose	Organisation will not require work with no value or purpose
Table 1 Job control or autonomy	limited opportunity to participate in decision-making	opportunities to participate in decision-making	Organisation will provide opportunities to participate in decision-making
	lack of control over workload	control over workload	Organisation will provide suitable means of control over workload

(*Continued*)

Table 16.1 (Continued)

Category	Hazard of a psychosocial nature	Worker requirement	Organisation requirement
	low levels of influence and independence (e.g., not being able to influence the speed, order, or schedule of work tasks and workload)	suitable levels of influence and independence	Organisation will provide suitable levels of influence and independence
Table 2 Supervision	lack of constructive performance feedback and evaluation processes lack of encouragement /acknowledgement	constructive performance feedback and evaluation processes encouragement and acknowledgement	Organisation will ensure all those with a supervisory role - Have the relevant competences to meet worker requirements - Are monitored to check that competences are being used effectively - Are subject to corrective action when competences are not being used effectively
	lack of communication lack of shared organisational vision and clear objectives lack of support and/or resources to facilitate improvements in performance	suitable communication shared organisational vision and clear objectives support and resources to facilitate improvements in performance	
	lack of fairness misuse of digital surveillance	fairness no misuse of digital surveillance	Organisation will ensure that there is no misuse of digital surveillance by supervisors
Table 2 Civility and respect	lack of trust, honesty, respect, civility, and fairness	trust, honesty, respect, civility, and fairness	Organisation will ensure that workers are treated with trust, honesty, respect, civility, and fairness
	lack of respect and consideration in interactions among workers, as well as with customers, clients, and the public	respect and consideration in interactions among workers, as well as with customers, clients, and the public	Organisation will ensure respect and consideration in interactions among workers, as well as with customers, clients, and the public

Source: Prepared by Tony Boyle for this book.

ISO 45001

Needs and expectations are dealt with in ISO 45001 clause 4.2 *Understanding the needs and expectations of workers and other interested parties.*

The organization shall determine:

a) *the other interested parties, in addition to workers, that are relevant to the OH&S management system;*
b) *the relevant needs and expectations (i.e. requirements) of workers and other interested parties;*
c) *which of these needs and expectations are, or could become, legal requirements and other requirements.*

Deciding which interested parties will be within the scope of your initial psychosocial management system was discussed in Chapter 15, and the needs and expectations of these individuals were discussed in the previous section. All that is necessary now is look at *legal requirements and other requirements.*

In the earlier description of needs and expectations food, rest breaks and social contact were used as examples of needs. They will also be used to illustrate legal requirements and other requirements.

In the context of OH&S, there is no general legal requirements for UK organisations to provide workers with food, or opportunities for social contact. However, there are legal requirements with regard to rest breaks. Your organisation should already be dealing with these legal requirements via the OH&S management system or the HR management system, but if responsibility is to be transferred to the psychosocial management system, you need to:

Accurately identify the legal requirements, and how they apply to the workers and interested parties within the scope of your psychosocial management system.
Establish how the legal requirements are currently being met and the effect the current arrangements are having on the well-being and wellness of the affected workers and interested parties.
Establish the views of affected workers and interested parties with regard to how the legal requirements might best be met.

Further work would then be needed if changes were an option, but this additional work is discussed in Chapter 23 'Psychosocial threat and opportunity assessment' and Chapter 31 'Change, procurement, and emergencies'.

Where there is no legal requirement to meet workers' needs and expectations, as is the case with food or opportunities for social contact, there are two options for the organisation:

Ignore the need or expectation

Voluntarily decide to take action with regard to the need or expectation so that it becomes an *other requirement* – what was referred to as *Organisation requirement* in Table 16.1.

When organisations do decide to take action, the additional work discussed in Chapter 23 'Psychosocial threat and opportunity assessment' and Chapter 31 'Change, procurement, and emergencies' will be required.

ISO 45003

Rather confusingly, ISO 45003 deals with needs and expectations in both clause 4.1 *Understanding the organization and its context* and clause 4.2 *Understanding the needs and expectations of workers and other interested parties.*

Clause 4.1.1 *General* includes the following.

> *In relation to managing psychosocial risk, the organization should:*
> ...
>
> b) *understand the needs and expectations of workers and other relevant interested parties;*
> c) *consider which of these needs and expectations are, or could become, legal requirements and other requirements;*

Subparagraph (c) is identical to the equivalent paragraph in clause 4.2 of ISO 45001, but subparagraph (b) is different from its ISO 45001 equivalent which is as follows:

> *The organization shall determine:*
> ...
>
> *the relevant needs and expectations (i.e. requirements) of workers and other interested parties;*

Note that ISO 45001

only requires you to *determine* needs and expectations, while ISO 45003 requires you to *understand* needs and expectations

explains that needs and expectations are requirements

restricts requirements to *relevant needs and expectations*, but the *relevant* is dropped from ISO 45003.

To disentangle these issues, it is necessary to go back to clause 4.2 of Annex SL[4] because this is the source of the problems. Although the title of clause 4.2 is *Understanding the needs and expectations of interested parties*, there is no mention of *understanding, needs,* or *expectations* in clause 4.2 of Annex SL. The full text of this clause is

The organization shall determine

- *the interested parties that are relevant to the XXX management system, and*
- *the relevant requirements of these interested parties;*
- *which of these requirements will be addressed through the XXX management system.*

Since the definition of a requirement is a *need or expectation that is stated, generally implied, or obligatory,* the use of *needs and expectations* in the title of clause 4.2 is not inconsistent. However, there is nothing in the text of clause 4.2 that justifies the use of *understanding* in the title.

As was mentioned earlier, ISO 45003 also deals with needs and expectations in clause 4.2 *Understanding the needs and expectations of workers and other interested parties,* which includes the following.

In relation to managing psychosocial risk, the organization should understand and determine the needs and expectations of workers and other interested parties.

Workers and other interested parties have a range of needs and expectations that can be influenced by psychosocial risks at work. These needs and expectations can include:

— *financial security;*
— *social interaction and support;*
— *inclusion, recognition, reward and accomplishment;*
— *personal development and growth;*
— *equal opportunity and fair treatment at work.*

Needs and expectations can be included in legal requirements (e.g. OH&S and human rights legislation), collective agreements, and voluntary agreements and other requirements to which the organization subscribes or adheres.

It seems odd that organisations should *understand and determine* – determine and understand would seem a more sensible sequence. However, taking into account all of the anomalies in ISO 45001 and ISO 45003, mostly arising from Annex SL, the following approach to needs and expectations is suggested:

Avoid fruitless discussions about what is a need and what is an expectation by referring only to requirements.
By all means adopt universal worker requirements – for example, 'all workers require to be free from role ambiguity' – but remember that this is being done

as a matter of organisation policy, and that some workers may prefer ambiguity in their role.

Universal worker requirements that are already being dealt with effectively – as might be the case with bullying and discrimination – can be excluded from your psychosocial management system by tailoring its scope.

While a lot of the work you have to do on needs and expectations can be done as a 'desk exercise', in consultation with HR personnel when appropriate, accurate identification of needs and expectations will require information from the individuals who have the needs and expectations.

Needs and expectations vary over time. There is a change over the years reflecting the general changes in the population's needs and expectations – for example, 50 years ago smoking at work and alcohol with lunch were considered normal. In another 50 years it may be illegal to drive a motorised vehicle on public roads – you may have to travel in one driven by a computer.

There can be temporary needs and expectations. Events in the outside world or within the organisation can affect an individual's needs and expectations. This can be very localised, for example, a worker suffering a bereavement, or worldwide, for example, coronavirus disease (COVID-19), or steep rises in the price of food or bank interest rates.

All of the points listed above are addressed in the *Needs and expectations documented information* section of this chapter.

Establishing needs and expectations

You have to take into account the needs and expectations of the individuals within the scope of your psychosocial management system. Who these individuals might be was discussed in Chapter 15, and the two main categories were workers and interested parties. What you need to do about each of these categories is discussed next.

Workers

Workers are not a homogenous group, and it is the case that different subgroups of workers will have different needs and expectations. Typical subgroups of workers include the following.

Levels. ISO 45001 describes *top management, managerial and non-managerial persons*. However, it is useful to divide *managerial persons* into middle managers and first-line managers, with first-line managers being equivalent to the *supervisors* referred to in ISO 45003.

Functions. The different types of work done by the various functions in the organisation may mean that the workers in different functions have different needs and expectations.

Geographical areas. Factors such as climate and culture are different in different parts of a country, and in different countries. Some of these differences are likely to affect the needs and expectations of workers and interested parties.

Other subgroups. Depending on circumstances, the gender, race, and religious beliefs of groups of workers may have to be taken into account.

To avoid repetition, it is preferable to list those needs and expectations that apply to all workers irrespective of their level, function, geographical area, gender, race, or religious beliefs. You can then review the various subgroups and, where necessary, make a list of any additional needs and expectations for each subgroup.

The practicalities of preparing these lists are dealt with in a later section of this chapter *Needs and expectations documented information.*

Interested parties

As might be expected from the list of interested parties included in ISO 45001, and reproduced in Chapter 15, identifying which interested parties will be within the scope of your psychosocial management system is not a trivial task. However, you have to keep your list of interested parties up to date, and these updates provide an opportunity for identifying interested parties that were not included in your original list. This means that it is possible to begin drafting your *Psychosocial management system manual* even if you have only a partial list of interested parties.

Needs and expectations documented information

The following documented information is needed.

A brief statement in the *Description of the psychosocial management system* to the effect that the Head of well-being and wellness will maintain up-to-date lists of the needs and expectations of workers and interested parties.

Statements in the work instructions for the Head of well-being and wellness and the Head of HR describing what they have to do. For example, the statement for the Head of well-being and wellness could be

Maintain an up-to date list of the types of workers in the organisation, their requirements (needs and expectations), and which requirements are, or could become, legal requirements and/or other requirements. Update the Category of worker section of the *Worker and interested party requirements form* as necessary.

Maintain an up-to-date list of the organisation's interested parties, their requirements (needs and expectations), and which requirements are, or could become, legal requirements and/or other requirements. Update the Interested party section of the *Worker and interested party requirements form* as necessary.

Table 16.2 A worker and interested party requirements form

	Category of worker	Requirements	LO
W1	Top management		
W2	Middle management		
W3	First-line management		
W4	Non-managerial workers		
W5			
W6	Well-being and wellness professionals		
W7	OH&S professionals		
W8	HR professionals		
W9			
W10			
	Interested party	Requirements	LO
IP1	OH&S consultants		
IP2	Well-being consultants		
IP3	Wellness consultants		
IP4	Well-being counsellors		
IP5	Wellness counsellors		
IP6	Workers' representatives		
IP7			

Source: Prepared by Tony Boyle for this book.

A *Worker and interested party requirements form.* This form should have fields for recording when and by whom the form was updated, and sections for recording details of types of workers and interested parties. A simple version of the workers and interested parties sections is given in Table 16.2 and instructions for completing these sections are given below.

Instructions for completing Table 16.2

The columns headed **LO** should be completed as follows.

Record an L if the requirement is, or could become, a legal requirement.
Record an O if the requirement is, or could become, an 'other requirement'.

References

1 British Standards Institution. *Occupational health and safety management systems – Requirements with guidance for use,* BSI ISO 45001, 2018. BSI 2018.
2 British Standards Institution. *Occupational health and safety management – Psychological health and safety at work – Guidelines for managing psychosocial risks,* BSI ISO 45003, 2021. BSI 2021.
3 MobiSystems, Inc, *Oxford Dictionary,* version 15.8. Last accessed 17 January 2024.
4 *ISO/IEC Directives, Part 1 Consolidated ISO Supplement – Procedure for the technical work – Procedures specific to ISO (Thirteenth edition, 2022). Annex SL (normative) Harmonised approach for management system standards. Appendix 2 (normative) Harmonized structure for MSS with guidance for use.*

17 The psychosocial management system manual

Introduction

In the past, when the authors have helped organisations set up a management system, they have drafted a management system manual that included the relevant policy and objectives – for example, the OH&S policy and OH&S objectives – and a description of how the management system would meet the requirement of the relevant Standard – for example, ISO 45001.[1]

Preparing a management system manual has a number of advantages.

Having to write down what you propose to do encourages clarity of thought.

The early drafts are discussion documents for agreement among interested parties, in particular the top management who will be providing the necessary resources.

You can use a format that allows you to say what you will do – for example, psychosocial threat and opportunity assessment – but leave the details of how you will do it for later consideration – for example, by referring in the manual to a separate *Psychosocial threat and opportunity assessment procedure.*

The manual forms the basis for a psychosocial management system development plan.

When preparing these manuals, you should follow the guidance in ISO 10013,[2] which was introduced in Chapter 12 'The documented information'.

The present chapter begins by describing the ISO 10013 guidance on quality management system manuals, and how this guidance applies to a psychosocial management system manual. There are then sections dealing with the following contents of a *Psychosocial management system manual.*

Introduction
Preliminaries
Description

DOI: 10.4324/9781003490555-19

ISO 10013

As was described in Chapter 12, ISO 10013 suggests that a management system manual is one way of maintaining an organisation's documented information, and it provides guidance on the content of such a manual.

Following this guidance, the principal contents of a *Psychosocial management system manual* should be:

An *introduction* describing what the manual is for and how it is to be used.

A *Preliminaries* section containing, as a minimum, the organisation's purpose, the intended outcomes of the psychosocial management system, the scope of the psychosocial management system, the Well-being and wellness policy, and the psychosocial objectives, as described in Chapter 15. However, this section could also contain general information about the organisation, its specific terms and definitions, and any other information considered relevant.

A *Description* section setting out the details of the psychosocial management system and referencing relevant psychosocial management system documented information such as procedures and work instructions.

The following sections give an outline of the content of the type of management system manual the authors would prepare for a psychosocial management system.

Psychosocial management system manual

The first three subsections below deal with the main contents of a *Psychosocial management system manual*, that is, *Introduction, Preliminaries*, and *Description*. There is then a brief subsection dealing with the format of the *Psychosocial management system manual*. However, the following assumptions have been used throughout the discussion of the draft manual.

There will be a person with overall responsibility for the day-to-day running of the psychosocial management system. This person is referred to as the Head of well-being and wellness, but alternative titles could be Well-being and wellness director or Well-being and wellness manager.

The Head of well-being and wellness will not be responsible for all of the processes required by a psychosocial management system – for example, the analysis of worker ill health data and the disciplinary process. It is assumed that these other processes will be the responsibility of the Head of HR – or the HR director or HR manager.

Time periods such as annually, six monthly, and quarterly have been used to indicate that processes must be continual. You may need to change these time periods in your manual.

Introduction to the manual

As was mentioned earlier, the *Introduction* to the manual should describe what the manual is for, and how it is to be used. It is preferable to begin with a formal statement of the basis for the psychosocial management system, for example:

This manual contains the documented information for <the Organisation's> psychosocial management system. The psychosocial management system is based on ISO 45001:2018 *Occupational health and safety management systems – Requirements with guidance for use* (ISO 45001), ISO 45002:2023 *Occupational health and safety management systems – General guidelines for the implementation of ISO 45001:2018* (ISO 45002), and ISO 45003:2021 *Occupational health and safety management – Psychological health and safety at work – Guidelines for managing psychosocial risks* (ISO 45003).

This manual has been prepared following the guidance in ISO 10013:2021 *Quality management systems – Guidance for documented information* (ISO 10013).

What the manual is for and how it is to be used differ from organisation to organisation, but the two extremes are as follows:

The manual contains all of the psychosocial management system documented information, and everyone with a role in the psychosocial management system is given access to the manual.

The manual is a brief outline of the psychosocial management system and references, rather than contains, the other documented information. This type of manual is primarily used by the Head of well-being and wellness who ensures that individuals with roles in the psychosocial management system are provided with the documented information they require, for example, role and task work instructions.

The authors' preference is for a manual that is needed only by the owners of the psychosocial management system and psychosocial management system auditors. Other individuals with roles in the psychosocial management system should be provided with the specific documented information they need, usually via work instructions, although anyone who shows an interest should be given access to the complete psychosocial management system manual.

Preliminaries

The *Preliminaries* section of the manual contains the following documented information.

The purpose of the organisation.
The intended outcomes of the psychosocial management system.

The scope of the psychosocial management system.
The Well-being and wellness policy.
The psychosocial objectives.

  This documented information is put in a *Preliminaries* section because it is difficult to begin work on the description of the psychosocial management system until
agreement has been reached on the content of each of these items of documented
information. All of these items were dealt with in Chapter 15.

Description

The description of the psychosocial management system makes up the majority of
the *Psychosocial management system manual*, and the authors' preferred approach
is to have a separate section for each clause in ISO 45001, ISO 45002,[3] and ISO
45003.[4] What follows are suggestions for the contents for each of these sections,
presented in text boxes and preceded by explanatory notes.

4 Context of the organisation

The authors' preferred method of dealing with clause 4 is to use periodic SWOT
analyses to meet all of the ISO 45001 requirements and ISO 45003 guidance.
Details are given in Chapter 18 'SWOT analysis'. Suggested text for clause 4 is
given in Box 17.1.

Box 17.1 Clause 4 Context of the organisation

Twice each year, the Head of well-being and wellness and the Head of HR
review and revise, as necessary, the records of the organisation's

strengths, weaknesses, opportunities, and threats (clause 4.1 *Understanding
  the organization and its context*)
categories of workers in the organisation and their requirements (clause 4.2
  *Understanding the needs and expectations of workers and other interested
  parties*)
interested parties and their requirements (clause 4.2 *Understanding the needs
  and expectations of workers and other interested parties*)
scope of the psychosocial management system (clause 4.3 *Determining the
  scope of the OH&S management system*).

  These tasks are carried out during SWOT analyses in accordance with the
relevant sections of

WI54 *Head of well-being and wellness work instruction*, and
WI55 *Head of HR well-being and wellness work instruction.*

The two work instructions listed above also cover actions to maintain and continually improve the psychosocial management system (clause 4.4 *OH&S management system*) – see section 10 *Improvement* for details.

5 Leadership and worker participation

The *Leadership and worker participation* section has four clauses, and each of these is dealt with separately below.

5.1 LEADERSHIP AND COMMITMENT

The suggested text for this clause is given in Box 17.2. It assumes that there will be a well-being and wellness work instruction for top management. However, alternative approaches are discussed in Chapter 28 'The role of top management'.

Box 17.2 Clause 5.1 Leadership and commitment

The organisation's top management demonstrate leadership and commitment with respect to the psychosocial management system by carrying out the activities allocated to them in WI51 *Top management well-being and wellness work instruction.*

5.2 OH&S POLICY

The heading for this clause in both ISO 45001 and ISO 45003 is *OH&S policy*, but the suggested text in Box 17.3 assumes that there will be a stand-alone *Well-being and wellness policy.* The *Top management well-being and wellness work instruction* need only state that the top management will review the Well-being and wellness policy during each management review, and revise it if necessary.

Box 17.3 Clause 5.2 Well-being and wellness policy

The organisation's top management deals with the ISO 45003 Policy guidance in accordance with WI51 *Top management well-being and wellness work instruction.*

5.3 ORGANIZATIONAL ROLES, RESPONSIBILITIES, AND AUTHORITIES

The suggested text for this clause is given in Box 17.4. It is based on the following assumptions.

There will be a well-being and wellness work instruction for each specific role in the psychosocial management system.

General worker well-being and wellness responsibilities will be set out in a *Well-being and wellness handbook* – see Chapter 21 'Awareness and communication' for details.

There will be a Well-being and wellness committee with specified well-being and wellness responsibilities. If there are other committees that might be of relevance to the psychosocial management system, for example, a Health and safety committee, details of their expected contribution should be inserted here, or at another relevant point in the *Description*.

Box 17.4 Clause 5.3 Organizational roles, responsibilities, and authorities

Responsibilities associated with the roles of relevance to the psychosocial management system are described in the following work instructions.

WI51 *Top management well-being and wellness work instruction*
WI52 *Middle management well-being and wellness work instruction*
WI53 *First-line management well-being and wellness work instruction*
WI54 *Head of well-being and wellness work instruction*
WI55 *Head of HR well-being and wellness work instruction*

Well-being and wellness responsibilities of all workers are set out in the *Well-being and wellness handbook*.

Members of the Well-being and wellness committee also have responsibilities in the psychosocial management system, and their activities are set out in the *Terms of reference for the Well-being and wellness committee*.

Authorities associated with these roles are commensurate with the role holder's authorities as an organisation worker.

The organisation's top management has assigned the Head of well-being and wellness responsibility for monitoring the need for additional roles of relevance to the psychosocial management system and, when necessary, specifying the responsibilities and authorities for these roles. The Head of well-being and wellness carries out these tasks in accordance with WI54 *Head of well-being and wellness work instruction*.

The organisation's top management has assigned the Head of well-being and wellness responsibility and authority for

---

ensuring that the psychosocial management system conforms to the requirements of ISO 45001 and the guidance in ISO 45002 and ISO 45003, and reporting to them on the performance of the psychosocial management system.

The Head of well-being and wellness carries out these tasks in accordance with WI54 *Head of well-being and wellness work instruction.*

5.4 CONSULTATION AND PARTICIPATION OF WORKERS

The suggested text for this clause is given in Box 17.5. It is based on the assumption that there is a Well-being and wellness committee that has oversight of well-being and wellness consultation and participation. Alternative approaches to well-being and wellness consultation and participation are discussed in Chapter 19 'Consultation and participation'.

Box 17.5 Clause 5.4 Consultation and participation of workers

Consultation with, and participation of, workers is overseen by the Well-being and wellness committee in accordance with the relevant sections of the *Terms of reference for the Well-being and wellness committee.*

The Head of well-being and wellness and the Head of HR identify opportunities for consultation with, and participation of, workers and, where appropriate, ensure that these opportunities are taken. These activities are carried out in accordance with the well-being and wellness work instructions for these two roles.

All other aspects of well-being and wellness consultation and participation are carried out in accordance with P01 *Well-being and wellness consultation and participation procedure.*

---

6 *Planning*

Section 6 of ISO 45001 and ISO 45003 has two main clauses: 6.1 *Actions to address risks and opportunities* and 6.2 *Psychosocial objectives and planning to achieve them.* However, as discussed in other chapters, the content of both these clauses is rather muddled, particularly with regard to risks and opportunities.

The suggested text for the *Planning* section is given in Box 17.6. It is based on the revised versions of these clauses described in other chapters. In particular:

'Risk source' is used instead of hazard.
'Threats and opportunities' is used instead of 'risks and opportunities'.
The need to plan for the general risks and opportunities is reinstated.

'Psychosocial objectives' is used instead of the ISO 45003 term *Objectives to address psychosocial risk.*

In addition, it is assumed that there is a *Psychosocial planning and continual improvement procedure* that deals with all aspects of the psychosocial management system planning, including planning for continual improvement.

Box 17.6 Clause 6.1 Actions to address threats and opportunities

6.1.1 General

The psychosocial threats and opportunities that need to be addressed to

give assurance that the psychosocial management system can achieve its intended outcomes
prevent, or reduce, undesired effects, and
achieve continual improvement

are determined and recorded during the SWOT analyses described in Section 4.

6.1.2 Risk source identification and assessment of threats and opportunities

All aspects of the identification of psychosocial risk sources and the assessment of psychosocial threats and opportunities are carried out in accordance with P02 *Psychosocial threat and opportunity assessment procedure.*

6.1.3 Determination of legal requirements and other requirements

The Head of well-being and wellness identifies legal requirements arising from health and safety legislation, and the Head of HR identifies legal requirements arising from HR legislation, and they maintain a *Psychosocial legal register* in accordance with their respective well-being and wellness work instructions.

6.1.4 Planning action

The Head of well-being and wellness and the Head of HR maintain plans for action on the psychosocial issues that fall within their responsibility and authority. These plans are updated following each of the SWOT analyses described in Section 4. All this psychosocial planning work is carried out in accordance with their respective well-being and wellness work instructions, and P03 *Psychosocial planning and continual improvement procedure.*

6.2 Psychosocial objectives and planning to achieve them

6.2.1 Psychosocial objectives

Prior to each SWOT analysis, the Head of well-being and wellness and the Head of HR review progress on the current psychosocial objectives and initiate correction and corrective action as necessary.

At the end of each SWOT analysis, the Head of well-being and wellness and the Head of HR prepare, if necessary, a revised list of psychosocial objectives and agree the list, or an amended version of it, with the organisation's top management.

The two Heads of Department carry out these actions in accordance with their respective work instructions.

6.2.2 Planning to achieve psychosocial objectives

When psychosocial objectives have been agreed, the Head of well-being and wellness and the Head of HR allocate responsibility for planning to achieve the objective in accordance with their respective work instructions, and P03 *Psychosocial planning and continual improvement procedure.*

7 Support

The *Support* section is a wide-ranging one consisting of five clauses, each of which is dealt with separately.

7.1 RESOURCES

The suggested text for this clause is given in Box 17.7. It is based on the assumption that the Head of well-being and wellness determines resource requirements, and the top management ensures that the resources are made available.

Box 17.7 Clause 7.1 Resources

The Head of well-being and wellness, in accordance with *WI54 Head of well-being and wellness work instruction*, determines the resources required to maintain and continually improve the psychosocial management system.

The organisation's top management, in accordance with *WI51 Top management well-being and wellness work instruction*, ensures that the resources they consider necessary are made available in a timely manner.

7.2 COMPETENCE

The provision and maintenance of psychosocial competences are complex activities. The minimum requirement is ensuring that individuals with a role in the psychosocial management system maintain the relevant competences. However, the need to ensure the psychosocial competences of workers and interested parties means that a psychosocial competence procedure will usually be required – identified as P04 *Psychosocial competence procedure* in Box 17.8 *7.2 Competence*.

Box 17.8 Clause 7.2 Competence

The Head of well-being and wellness and the Head of HR carry out the following tasks for the psychosocial responsibilities of each of the roles listed in Section 5.3.

Identify the competences required to meet the described responsibilities.
Determine the most effective methods for delivering the required competences.
Ensure that the required competences are delivered by the most effective methods and in a timely manner.
Check at appropriate intervals that the required competences are being maintained.
Where appropriate, retain relevant documented information as evidence of competence.

The Heads of Department carry out these tasks in accordance with their respective work instructions.
More general psychosocial competence requirements for workers are dealt with in accordance with P04 *Psychosocial competence procedure*.

7.3 AWARENESS

As with psychosocial competences, maintaining psychosocial awareness is a complex activity that usually requires its own procedure. The suggested entry for the Description is given in Box 17.9.

Box 17.9 Clause 7.3 Awareness

The Head of well-being and wellness and the Head of HR ensure that

the *Well-being and wellness policy* and the psychosocial objectives are promulgated throughout the organisation, and the *Well-being and wellness policy* is brought to the attention of all interested parties.

All other aspects of awareness are dealt with in accordance with P05 *Psychosocial awareness procedure*.

7.4 COMMUNICATION

Organisations vary widely in their requirements for communication and their arrangements for meeting these requirements, and these should be set out in an organisation-specific procedure. The suggested entry for this section of the Description is given in Box 17.10.

Box 17.10 Clause 7.4 Communication

7.4.1 General

General requirements for communication are set out in P06 *Psychosocial communication procedure*, which deals with, *inter alia*,

the topics of communication and their timing
the target audiences for the communication and the methods to be used for these audiences
responsibility for responding to communications on the psychosocial management system.

7.4.2 Internal communication

Those with roles in the psychosocial management system deal with psychosocial management system internal communication in accordance with P06 *Psychosocial communication procedure* and their respective work instructions or, in the case of Well-being and wellness committee members, that committee's terms of reference.

7.4.3 External communication

Communication between the psychosocial management system personnel and interested parties is dealt with in accordance with P06 *Psychosocial communication procedure*.

7.5 DOCUMENTED INFORMATION

The suggested text for this clause is given in Box 17.11. It is based on the assumption that the organisation has arrangements for creating, updating, and controlling documented information, and that the psychosocial management system documented information can be included in these arrangements.

Box 17.11   Clause 7.5 Documented information

7.5.1 General

The documented information as listed in Table 12 of ISO 45002 is contained in, or referenced in, this *Description* which also includes or references the documented information the organisation considers necessary for the effectiveness of the psychosocial management system.

The Head of well-being and wellness keeps the need for documented information under review in accordance with WI54 *Head of well-being and wellness work instruction.*

7.5.2 Creating and updating

The Head of well-being and wellness ensures that the psychosocial management system documented information is created and updated in accordance with the guidance in ISO 10013:2021 *Quality management systems – Guidance for documented information.*

7.5.3 Control of documented information

General control of psychosocial management system documented information is included in the arrangements for controlling the organisation's other documented information.

The arrangements for the control of specific items of psychosocial management system documented information are set out in the relevant sections of work instructions.

---

8 Operation

The *Operation* section has three main clauses: 8.1 *Operational planning and control,* 8.2 *Emergency preparedness and response,* and 8.3 *Rehabilitation and return to work,* and each of these is discussed below.

8.1 OPERATIONAL PLANNING AND CONTROL

Operational planning and control covers the following topics:

The processes needed to meet requirements of the psychosocial management
system.
Eliminating hazards, reducing OH&S risks, and promoting well-being at work.
The management of change.
Procurement, contracting, and outsourcing.

All four topics are dealt with in Box 17.12 8.1 Operational planning and control.

Box 17.12   Clause 8.1 Operational planning and control

8.1.1 General

The processes making up the organisation's psychosocial management
system have been described or referenced in this *Description*. Ongoing activities with regard to general operational planning and control are set out in
P03 *Psychosocial planning and continual improvement procedure.*

Where necessary, the Head of well-being and wellness plans cooperation on well-being and wellness issues between the organisation and other
employers on multi-employer sites.

*8.1.2 Eliminating hazards, reducing OH&S risks, and promoting well-being
at work*

All aspects of eliminating psychosocial risk sources and reducing psychosocial threats are dealt with in P02 *Psychosocial threat and opportunity
assessment procedure.*

Promoting well-being and wellness at work is dealt with in P03
Psychosocial planning and continual improvement procedure.

8.1.3 Management of change

As part of the SWOT analyses described in Section 4, planned temporary
and permanent changes with implications for well-being and wellness are
identified.

When a SWOT analysis identifies a relevant change, the Head of well-
being and wellness, with the support of the organisation's top management, as necessary, allocates responsibility for ensuring that a procedure, or
procedures, for the monitoring and control of well-being and wellness during
the change is established.

The Head of well-being and wellness carries out these actions in accordance
with WI54 *Head of well-being and wellness work instruction.*

When an unintended change with implications for well-being and wellness is reported, the Head of well-being and wellness ensures the following:

The consequences of the change on well-being and wellness of workers and interested parties are reviewed.

If necessary, action is taken to mitigate any psychosocial threats and exploit any psychosocial opportunities.

The Head of well-being and wellness carries out these actions in accordance with WI54 *Head of well-being and wellness work instruction.*

8.1.4 Procurement, contracting, and outsourcing

The procurement of products and services is carried out in accordance with the P07 *Psychosocial procurement procedure*, and this procedure also deals with contracting and outsourcing.

8.2 EMERGENCY PREPAREDNESS AND RESPONSE

The description for this clause is based on the assumption that there is already a fully functional emergency plan to which the health and safety personnel are willing to add the psychosocial aspects of emergency planning. The suggested text is given in Box 17.13 8.2 *Emergency preparedness and response.*

Box 17.13 Clause 8.2 Emergency preparedness and response

The Head of well-being and wellness in consultation with the Head of health and safety ensures that psychosocial issues are included in all emergency preparedness and response procedures and work instructions.

The Head of well-being and wellness carries out these actions in accordance with WI54 *Head of well-being and wellness work instruction.*

8.3 REHABILITATION AND RETURN TO WORK

Since the psychosocial management system described in this book is principally concerned with impaired well-being and wellness that typically does not lead to absence from work, the return to work part of this ISO 45003 clause is not relevant. The rehabilitation part of the clause would be relevant if rehabilitation was interpreted as restoring impaired well-being and wellness, but this is not a typical interpretation, and the terms treatment and improvement have been used rather than rehabilitation.

In any event, it is unlikely that dealing with return to work and rehabilitation would be the responsibility of the psychosocial risk management team – return to work is more likely to be an HR function, and rehabilitation is a specialist medical function.

9 Performance evaluation

The three clauses making up the *Performance evaluation* section are dealt with in Box 17.14.

Box 17.14 Clauses 9.1 Monitoring, measurement, analysis, and performance evaluation and 9.1.2 Evaluation of compliance

All aspects of psychosocial monitoring, measurement, analysis, and performance evaluation are dealt with in accordance with P08 *Psychosocial monitoring, measurement, analysis and evaluation procedure*. This procedure also deals with evaluation of compliance with psychosocial legal requirements.

9.2 Internal audit

All aspects of psychosocial internal audit are dealt with in accordance with P09 *Psychosocial audit procedure* that also deals with external audit.

9.3 Management review

Each year, the top management reviews the psychosocial management system to ensure its continuing suitability, adequacy, and effectiveness. This review is carried out in accordance with WI51 *Top management well-being and wellness work instruction*.

---

10 Improvement

There are two clauses in this section: clauses 10.1 and 10.3, that deal with improvement, and the suggested text for these clauses is given in Box 17.15. This box also deals with clause 10.2 *Incident, nonconformity and corrective action.*

Box 17.15 Clauses 10.1 General and 10.3 Continual improvement

Opportunities for improvement are determined and recorded during the SWOT analyses described in Section 4, and during the management reviews which are described in Section 9.3.

The Head of well-being and wellness and the Head of HR ensure that the actions needed to achieve the intended outcomes of the psychosocial management system are implemented.

The top management and the Heads of Well-being and wellness and HR carry out these tasks in accordance with their respective work instructions.

Other aspects of continual improvement are dealt with in P03 *Psychosocial planning and continual improvement procedure.*

10.2 Incident, nonconformity, and corrective action

All aspects of psychosocial incidents, nonconformities, and corrective actions are dealt with in accordance with P10 *Psychosocial nonconformity and corrective action procedure.*

Format of the manual

Because the *Psychosocial management system manual* is such a wide-ranging document, it is inevitably the case that revisions are required fairly frequently. For this reason, each of the main sections of the manual should have its own review and changes information. This can be done quite easily using the relevant facilities in your word processor.

References

1   British Standards Institution. *Occupational health and safety management systems – Requirements with guidance for use*, BSI ISO 45001, 2018. BSI 2018.
2   British Standards Institution. *Quality management systems – Guidance for documented information*, BSI ISO 10013, 2021. BSI 2021.
3   British Standards Institution. *Occupational health and safety management systems – General guidelines for the implementation of ISO 45001:2018*, BSI ISO 45002, 2023. BSI 2023.
4   British Standards Institution. *Occupational health and safety management – Psychological health and safety at work – Guidelines for managing psychosocial risks*, BSI ISO 45003, 2021. BSI 2021.

18 SWOT analysis

Introduction

Strengths, weaknesses, opportunities, and threats (SWOT) analysis is one of a number of analytical techniques that organisations use to support their planning processes. SWOT is often used by top management to inform their decision-making, and various functions such as HR and marketing use it to analyse their function's performance and identify changes that might be required. In the context of the management systems the authors help organisations implement it is their preferred technique for analysis during the planning process.

This chapter begins with an overview of SWOT analysis and then there are sections dealing in more detail with

the SWOT analysis team
the SWOT analysis process
outputs from SWOT analysis
potential weaknesses of SWOT analysis.

The chapter ends with a brief description of some of the other analytical techniques that can be used in support of, or instead of, SWOT analysis.

Note that the description of the SWOT analysis in this chapter refers to analysis of issues relevant to the psychosocial management system – they should not be read as descriptions of more general SWOT analysis.

SWOT analysis overview

SWOT analysis is not a one-off process. There is an initial SWOT analysis that you carry out when you are setting up your psychosocial management system and then there are periodic SWOT analyses as part of the planning process. The role of these periodic analyses is discussed in Chapter 30 'Psychosocial planning and continual improvement'.

DOI: 10.4324/9781003490555-20

The main stages in a SWOT analysis are as follows.

Select a SWOT analysis team. You need to select team members who have access to the relevant psychosocial data and information, and other team members who represent relevant workers and interested parties.

Get each team member to review the purpose, intended outcomes, scope, *Well-being and wellness policy*, and psychosocial objectives. The team members should come to the SWOT analysis meeting with any suggestions they might have for changes to these documents.

Get the team members to collect any relevant data and information to which they have access. The data and information are usually quite limited for your first SWOT analysis, but they become a richer source with each subsequent SWOT analysis.

Conduct the SWOT meeting. This has the following main stages:

Reviewing and agreeing the purpose, intended outcomes, scope, *Well-being and wellness policy*, and psychosocial objectives.

Providing the available data and information to all the team members and dealing with any queries about the data and information.

Brainstorming strengths, weaknesses, opportunities, and threats.

Identifying which strengths, weaknesses, opportunities, and threats require further analysis and/or action.

Drafting an action plan and allocating responsibilities for completing the agreed actions.

Selecting the SWOT analysis team is dealt with in the next section of this chapter. There is then a section on the SWOT analysis process, and a separate section on the outputs from SWOT analysis.

The SWOT analysis team

SWOT analysis is, in essence, a brainstorming exercise and the ideal team size is, therefore, between four and seven people. This is usually adequate for the initial SWOT analysis for a management system, but larger groups are required as the management system matures. How to deal with these larger groups is discussed later in this section.

The SWOT analysis team should include people with knowledge of

past performance of relevance to psychosocial issues, for example, days lost through mental and physical ill health, and the effectiveness or otherwise of particular controls for psychosocial threats

changes of relevance to psychosocial issues, for example, planned organisational changes or changes to the organisation's products and/or services

the needs and expectations (requirements) of relevant categories of workers and interested parties.

The team will have to have a team leader, and for the purposes of this discussion, it is assumed that the Head of well-being and wellness will be the SWOT team leader.

A suitable group for the initial SWOT analysis could be made up as follows.

The Heads of well-being and wellness, health and safety, and HR to provide information on past performance.

A relevant member of top management to provide information on future performance. Ideally this would be the Chief Executive (although the job title varies from organisation to organisation) or someone acting on his or her behalf.

A worker representative to provide information on worker needs and expectations (requirements). Ideally this would be a well-being and wellness representative, but if such an individual is not in place, a health and safety representative, a Trade Union representative, or a general Worker representative could take on this role.

This 'core' group should be able to complete the initial rounds of SWOT analyses without further input from additional team members, but, as the psychosocial management system matures, additional inputs are likely to be required. There are two categories of further inputs.

More detailed information on the organisation's functions, and any changes in these functions, that can affect worker well-being and wellness. Relevant functions include procurement, finance, marketing, sales, production, and transport.

More detailed information on the needs and expectations (requirements) of categories of workers and interested parties. For example, representatives of various categories of managerial worker, and representatives of workers' partners, relatives, and dependants.

It is also possible to include any other persons you consider might make a useful contribution to a particular SWOT analysis. For example

a medic to provide an expert view on the health, well-being, and wellness data, and the way these data are being analysed

an external well-being and wellness consultant to provide a fresh eye on your whole psychosocial SWOT analysis arrangements and their results

providers of well-being and wellness services who may be able to suggest alternative, or additional, approaches to improving the well-being and wellness of your workers and interested parties.

Your psychosocial SWOT analysis process should allow for a rolling programme of meetings that enables different people to join the team from time to time while maintaining the ideal number of fewer than eight people in the team.

The SWOT analysis process

The SWOT analysis process consists of the following main steps:

Pre-meeting actions
Reviewing documents
Reviewing data and information
Brainstorming
Analysing results of brainstorming
Preparing an action plan.

Each of these steps is dealt with in a separate subsection below.

Pre-meeting actions

Pre-meeting actions include practical issues such as agreeing the date, time, and venue, but this discussion of the pre-meeting actions has been restricted to those actions of particular relevance to psychosocial SWOT analysis.

The Head of well-being and wellness should carry out the following actions prior to each SWOT analysis meeting.

Brief any team members who are unfamiliar with SWOT analysis on the whole SWOT analysis process, and their role in the process.

Send out documents to be reviewed prior to the SWOT analysis meeting. These documents are usually sent to SWOT team members, but they may also be sent to other people. For example, you may ask health and safety representatives to review the current psychosocial objectives. Reviewing documents during the SWOT analysis meeting is discussed in detail in the next subsection.

Send out the data and information that will be required as inputs to the SWOT analysis. As with documents for review, the data and information are usually sent to SWOT team members but may also be sent to other people. For example, you may ask managerial workers for information on the effectiveness of particular psychosocial risk controls for their direct reports. Using data and information during the SWOT analysis meeting is discussed in detail in a later subsection.

Collate the comments on reviewed documents in a format that will facilitate discussion and, where necessary, organise the data and information in ways that will make them more useful to the SWOT analysis team members. Suggestions for collation of comments and organisation of data and information are given in the next two subsections.

SWOT analysis meetings can be quite hard work and may be protracted. They can be easier and shorter if the pre-meeting actions outlined earlier are carried out effectively. It is also important that team members 'do their homework'. One team member who holds up the meeting because they have not read the documents to be reviewed, or who has not delivered the required data until the last minute, can spoil the whole meeting. Brainstorming involves team members volunteering information – if they are annoyed by the poor performance of another team member, they are likely to 'clam up' in the hope that the meeting finishes quickly. Heads of well-being and wellness will need good 'people skills' if they are to manage these sorts of occurrence.

Reviewing documents

The following documents should be reviewed at all SWOT analysis meetings.

The purpose of your organisation.
The intended outcomes of your psychosocial management system.
The scope of your psychosocial management system.
The *Well-being and wellness policy*.
The psychosocial objectives.

Typically, none of the reviewers suggests changes to the documents, but if they do, these changes should be discussed. The important issue for the SWOT analysis is whether the proposed change has implications for the strengths, weaknesses, opportunities, and threats that have to be taken into account during the analysis. This might be the case if, for example, the change was to the scope of the psychosocial management system or to the psychosocial objectives. In these circumstances, it might be necessary to suspend the SWOT analysis and undertake a psychosocial change threat and opportunity assessment instead. Change assessment in a psychosocial context is dealt with in Chapter 31 'Change, procurement, and emergencies'.

The documents listed earlier are likely to be the only ones for review at the initial SWOT analysis meeting but, as the psychosocial management system matures, individual procedures, work instruction, or forms may be included in the review. Typically, this is because the document in question is considered unfit for purpose and is, therefore, a weakness that has to be addressed. However, in the long term it is worth considering a rolling programme of documented information review as a means of keeping documents and records up-to-date and relevant.

Reviewing data and information

Data and information are not defined terms in ISO 45001[1] or ISO 45003,[2] but they are defined in ISO 9000.[3] It is necessary, therefore, to make a slight digression and look at the ISO 9000 definitions.

Data are defined in ISO 9000 as *facts about an object*, and an object is defined as an *entity, item,* or *anything perceivable or conceivable*. ISO 9000 gives the following examples of objects *Product, service, process, person, organization, system, resource*. So, an object can be pretty well anything.

Information is defined in ISO 9000 as *meaningful data.*

The distinction between data and information is an important one, and the sickness absence data will be used to illustrate the sorts of conversions that are required.

If the HR department provides the numbers of days lost as a result of ill health, these are data and they are not very useful. Even if the HR department provides breakdowns of such things as type of ill health and category of worker, these are still only data. In order to make these data *meaningful*, they need to be put into a context, for example:

Time – are the numbers of days lost as a result of ill health increasing or decreasing? This is the information needed to find out, for example, whether particular psychosocial initiatives are effective in practice.

Number of days worked – what is the number of days lost as a percentage of the number of days worked by the organisation's workers? This is the information needed to find out, for example, whether particular functions in the organisation or particular locations in the organisation have a worse ill health performance than other functions or locations. It is also the information needed to compare the organisation's ill health performance with the ill health performance of other organisations.

Accuracy of diagnosis – how many of the days lost are reported as physical ill health to avoid the real or imagined stigma associated with mental ill health? This is a difficult area but one that has to be addressed since without this information there can be no accurate picture of the magnitude of the effects of degradation in well-being and wellness. The interview skills discussed in Chapter 27 'Psychosocial investigation' can help with diagnosis.

A key skill for the Head of well-being and wellness is being able to convert data into information. In the context of SWOT analysis, it is particularly important to deal with information rather than data. Where this is not the case, the meetings deteriorate into a discussion of what the data mean, rather than being able to consider the implications of information for the organisation's psychosocial strengths, weaknesses, opportunities, and threats.

Data and information of relevance to the psychosocial management system are dealt with in Chapter 25 'Psychosocial measurement, analysis, and evaluation'.

There may not be many data to analyse or much information to review for the initial SWOT meeting, but initial information on the needs and expectations (requirements) of workers and interested parties should be available and should be reviewed prior to all SWOT analysis meetings.

Brainstorming

There are various brainstorming techniques and, if you have not done so already, you can experiment with them and decide which ones suit you and your team best. Guidance on brainstorming techniques is readily available online, so none is given in this book.

Irrespective of the technique used, the aim of brainstorming in the context of a psychosocial management system is to identify the following:

Organisational strengths that can be exploited to improve the well-being and/or wellness of workers and/or interested parties. These organisational strengths include the competences of individuals in the organisation, and resources that can be used on behalf of the organisation – for example, workers volunteering to be well-being or wellness champions.

Organisational weaknesses that have to be addressed or they will have a detrimental effect on the well-being and/or wellness of workers and/or interested parties. These organisational weaknesses include lack of individual competences, such as poor leadership skills.

Opportunities to

improve the well-being and/or wellness of workers and/or interested parties
improve the effectiveness and/or efficiency of the psychosocial management system.[i]

Threats to

the well-being and/or wellness of workers and/or interested parties
the effectiveness and/or efficiency of the psychosocial management system.

There are two key roles in the SWOT analysis team during brainstorming:

The team leader. This person's tasks are to ensure that the brainstorming part of the meeting does not deteriorate into analysis, and that there is full coverage of the strengths, weaknesses, opportunities, and threats.

The recorder. This person's task is to ensure that all of the suggestions with regard to strengths, weaknesses, opportunities, and threats are accurately recorded during the brainstorming. Traditionally, the recorder used one or more sheets of flip-chart paper and felt-tip pens during the brainstorming. However, the authors' preference is to use a computer and a data projector since this provide an easy way of giving all team members a copy of the brainstorming results at the end of the meeting. The computer and a data projector have other uses during the SWOT analysis meeting, and these are discussed in the next subsection.

Usually, the team leader and the recorder take part in the brainstorming, but it is possible to have a team leader who is there because they have good facilitation skills, and a recorder who is there because they have good keyboard skills. In these circumstances, the team leader and recorder are supernumerary and do not contribute ideas during the brainstorming.

Analysing results of brainstorming

As was indicated in the previous subsection, brainstorming and analysis are two separate processes and in a SWOT analysis meeting they should be sequential – complete the brainstorming and then analyse the results.

Analysis of the brainstorming results involves considering each item carefully and putting it into one of the following categories.

Items that should be ignored. By its very nature, brainstorming produces ideas that are fanciful, irrelevant, or impractical. These items can be marked as such and dropped from the analysis.

Items that are outside the scope of psychosocial management system but warrant consideration by other functions in the organisation. Typically, this is the largest category since the psychosocial management system does not have control of many of the functions that can affect the well-being and wellness of workers and interested parties. These items should be marked for the attention of the relevant function.

Items that are within the scope of psychosocial management system and warrant further action. Dealing with these items forms the major part of the action plan described in the next subsection.

It is during the analysis stage of the SWOT analysis meeting that a computer and a data projector are particularly useful because they enable the following.

Notes to be added against each of the items recorded during the brainstorming. These notes should summarise what action, if any, is to be taken with regard to that item. The recorded notes should be agreed by all the SWOT analysis team members or, if necessary, details of disagreements should be recorded.

Access to the organisation's intranet. This can be extremely useful during analysis where, for example, further information is required before a decision can be made about a particular item. It is also useful for obtaining contact details when requests for action on particular items are being referred to functions outside the psychosocial management system.

Access to the internet. Search engines can be used to obtain information on a vast array of topics, including many topics of relevance to well-being and wellness. When it has been decided that action is required on a particular issue, it is often useful to conduct searches of relevance to the topic. This can produce ideas that would not otherwise be considered by the SWOT analysis team members.

When all of the items suggested during the brainstorming have been analysed, and a decision reached on what to do about each one, you can move on to preparing the action plan as described in the next subsection.

Action plan

Action plans arising from SWOT analyses are only one of the types of action plan required in a psychosocial management system that meets the requirements of ISO 45001 and the guidance in ISO 45003. Other required action plans include those for achieving the psychosocial objectives and action plans for dealing with psychosocial threats and opportunities. Chapter 30 'Psychosocial planning and continual improvement' describes a psychosocial management system planning process that covers all of the ISO 45001 and ISO 45003 planning requirements and includes action plans created as an output from SWOT analysis meetings. It is important to keep track of why actions have been included in a mixed source action plan, and methods of doing this are described in Chapter 30.

Outputs from SWOT analysis

In summary, the outputs from a SWOT analysis should be the following:

A list of the documents that have been reviewed and notes on any recommendations for changes.

A list of the data and information that were discussed by the SWOT analysis team and any relevant results from these discussions.

Separate lists of the strengths, weaknesses, opportunities, and threats identified during the SWOT brainstorming session and, for each item on each list, the decision reached about the item and the action, if any, that has been taken or will be taken with regard to that item.

An action plan for those actions that are within the scope of the psychosocial management system.

Ideally, all of the items in the list above will be recorded and agreed during the SWOT analysis meeting, and there are notes on documented information for SWOT analysis meetings in the last section of this chapter. Where items are not agreed, or there are items that require further work before a decision can be made, it is the SWOT analysis team leader's responsibility to ensure that these items are 'closed out' and the records updated.

Potential weaknesses of SWOT analysis

Used properly, SWOT analysis is a very powerful tool, but its usefulness can be reduced by any of the following.

Seeing SWOT analysis as a one-off or intermittent activity. To be really effective, SWOT analyses should be central to the psychosocial management system planning processes and take place at least twice per year. In addition, SWOT analyses should be carried out when significant changes have occurred or are being planned.

Misjudging the amount of data and information to be used as inputs to the SWOT analyses. Using too little can oversimplify matters and lead to poor decisions, and using too much can lead to 'paralysis by analysis'. Getting the correct amount of data and information is a trial-and-error process, but, initially, it is better to err on the side of too much rather than too little.

Not having access to internal data and information because they are confidential or commercially sensitive. There are usually ways round this, for example, using anonymised medical data for confidential health information, and having a SWOT analysis team member who has access to the commercially sensitive information and can contribute to the analysis on the basis of their knowledge without divulging this knowledge to the other team members.

Not being clear about any assumptions being made about, for example, the causes of past events or the likelihood of future events. This is important because assumptions can prove to be incorrect and, if they are, actions based on them may not have the intended beneficial effect and may have a negative effect. The more you know about what incorrect assumptions have been made in the past, and why they were made, the more chance you have of avoiding incorrect assumptions in the future.

Failure to take adequate account of external issues in brainstorming of opportunities and threats. This can be countered by using PESTLE analysis as described in the next section.

One way of countering the first four of the potential weaknesses of SWOT analyses is to supplement their results with results for other analytical techniques, and some of these techniques are discussed in the next section.

Other analytical techniques

This section describes four analytical techniques you can use to supplement SWOT analyses. Two of them, SOAR and NOISE analyses, are variants on SWOT, while the other two, PESTLE and Lewin's force field analysis, adopt different frameworks. Guidance on how to use these techniques is readily available online, and all that has been done in this section is to give an overview of each of the analytical techniques.

SOAR analysis

SOAR uses strengths and opportunities in the same way as SWOT, but it replaces weaknesses and threats with aspirations and results, which are as follows.

Aspirations. These are the elements that make up your vision for the future. In the context of a psychosocial management system, this would include what you wanted to achieve with regard to worker well-being and wellness, and the differences you could make to the way your organisation dealt with well-being and wellness.

Results. This is a description of what success would look like, preferably in numerical terms, so that you can track your results and measure progress. This can be particularly useful in a psychosocial management system where measuring well-being and wellness may be a contentious issue.

NOISE analysis

NOISE analysis also uses strengths and opportunities in the same way as SWOT, but it replaces weaknesses and threats with needs, improvements, and exceptions.

Needs. What does the organisation need to achieve what it wants to achieve? For example, in a psychosocial management system, what resources, organisational and individual, will be required to achieve the psychosocial objectives.

Improvements. What changes in the organisation will be required if the needs are to be met and opportunities taken?

Exceptions. This is a list of needs, opportunities, improvements, and strengths that are already in place even if they are not currently having the desired effect.

PESTLE analysis

PESTLE analysis examines the effect of political, economic, social, technological, legal, and environmental factors. In the context of a psychosocial management system, the analysis is used to determine whether, and in what ways, each factor is affecting well-being and wellness.

Political. The extent to which the government is involved in well-being and wellness in your organisation and the extent to which government policy influences this well-being and wellness. For example, local government policies on health care and policing.

Economic. The economic factors that are influencing well-being and wellness, for example, interest rates, the gig economy, threats of unemployment, and inflation.

Social. The demographic changes or changes in social factors that are affecting well-being and wellness in your organisation, for example, labour turnover or an ageing workforce.

Technological. The effect that technological innovation is having on well-being and wellness in your organisation, for example, the effects of automation or the adoption of artificial intelligence.

Legal. Possible changes in legislation that may affect well-being and wellness in your organisation.

Environmental. The effect that the surrounding environment and ecological impact is having on well-being and wellness in your organisation, for example, air pollution or having plants in the office.[ii]

Occasional use of PESTLE analysis can be a valuable addition to regular SWOT analysis since it is a different structured brainstorming exercise.

Lewin's force field analysis

Lewin's force field analysis is focused on achieving changes within an organisation and can be particularly useful in the early stages of implementing a psychosocial management system. Lewin argued that there were forces that would lead to change – driving forces – and forces that resisted change – restraining forces – and whether or not a particular change occurred would depend on the relative strengths of these two forces. For a change to occur, the driving forces have to be stronger than the restraining forces. The main stages in a force field analysis are as follows.

Define your change.

Brainstorm the driving forces.

Brainstorm the restraining forces.

Evaluate the driving and restraining forces. This can be done by giving a numerical rating to each force, for example, from 1 = weak to 5 = strong and calculating the totals for driving and restraining forces. However, the evaluations can also be done qualitatively without using numbers.

Review the forces. Decide which of the forces can be changed or influenced.

Strategise. Create a strategy to strengthen the driving forces and/or weaken the restraining forces.

Prioritise action steps. Choose action steps that will be most effective and efficient.

Lewin's force field analysis can also be used to analyse why intended changes have not happened.

Documented information for SWOT analyses

It is possible to have a documented SWOT analysis procedure, but if the SWOT analysis team leader is the Head of well-being and wellness, then all that is required is a SWOT analysis section in the *Head of well-being and wellness work instruction*. A suggested entry is given in the Box 18.1 *Clause 4 Context of the organization*.

Box 18.1 Clause 4 Context of the organization

In <month > and <month> each year lead a SWOT analysis to determine the threats and opportunities that need to be addressed to

give assurance that the psychosocial management system can achieve its intended outcomes

prevent, or reduce, undesired effects

achieve continual improvement.

Convene a group to carry out the SWOT analysis that includes

a representative of top management

the Head of HR

and, as appropriate to circumstances at the time,

---

representatives of managerial workers
representatives of non-managerial workers
representatives of interested parties
relevant competent persons, for example, well-being counsellors
such other persons as you consider necessary for a particular SWOT
analysis.

Include in the inputs to your SWOT analysis

the contents of the *External and internal issues form*
the contents of the *Needs and expectations form*
the psychosocial management system scope
the psychosocial objectives
the list of legal and other requirements of relevance to the psychosocial management system
the results of previous SWOT analysis
such other data and/or information as you consider necessary for a particular
SWOT analysis.

During the SWOT analysis review and revise as appropriate

Strengths, Weaknesses, Opportunities and Threats form
Psychosocial threats and opportunities register and Actions table.

Ensure the outputs of the SWOT analysis are

actions, and allocations of responsibility for ensuring these actions are
completed, recorded in the *Actions table*
such other decisions as you and the SWOT analysis team agree are appropriate, given the results of a particular SWOT analysis.

Where there are aspects of the SWOT analysis that cannot be carried out by the
Head of well-being and wellness, for example, reviewing medical data and information, the required actions should be included in the work instruction for the relevant role. For example, the *Head of HR well-being and wellness work instruction*
could include the following.

In <month > and <month> each year take part in a SWOT analysis convened by
the Head of well-being and wellness. Prior to each meeting carry out any data
reviews and information preparation requested by the Head of well-being and
wellness.

Remember that the Head of well-being and wellness and the Head of HR will be
competent persons and this, in accordance with ISO 10013,[4] reduces the need for

detailed work instructions. In effect, the work instructions for the Head of well-being and wellness and the Head of HR will be providing an *aide memoire* rather than detailed instructions on how to carry out a SWOT analysis meeting.

Notes

i   Effectiveness and efficiency are both defined terms. Effectiveness is defined in ISO 45001 as the *extent to which planned activities are realized and planned results achieved.* Efficiency is not used in ISO 45001 and used only once in ISO 45003. Efficiency is defined in ISO 9000 as the *relationship between the result achieved and the resources used.* When dealing with these terms informally, it is convenient to say that effectiveness means *did it work?* and efficiency means *was it worth it?.*

ii There is increasing use of so-called 'biophilic design' that includes the use of plants in work environments. This is done because research has shown that appropriate arrangement of plants can have beneficial effects on the well-being of workers.

References

1   British Standards Institution. *Occupational health and safety management systems – Requirements with guidance for use*, BSI ISO 45001, 2018. BSI 2018.
2   British Standards Institution. *Occupational health and safety management – Psychological health and safety at work – Guidelines for managing psychosocial risks*, BSI ISO 45003, 2021. BSI 2021.
3   British Standards Institution. *Quality management systems – Fundamentals and vocabulary*, BSI ISO 9000, 2015. BSI 2015.
4   British Standards Institution. *Quality management systems – Guidance for documented information*, BSI ISO 10013, 2021. BSI 2021.

19 Consultation and participation

Introduction

Consultation and participation are important in traditional health and safety, and ISO 45001[1] has an extensive list of requirements with regard to consultation and participation. It is necessary to meet these requirements in a psychosocial management system, but not sufficient. There are additional needs for consultation and participation that have to be met in a psychosocial management system. For example, you do not need to consult workers about whether electricity and asbestos are hazards, but you should consult them about the effects of psychosocial risk sources such as redundancy. As will be seen later in this chapter, some of these additional needs for consultation and participation are included in the ISO 45003[2] guidance.

Both ISO 45001 and ISO 45003 deal with the role of workers' representatives and committees in consultation and participation, and these topics are included in this chapter.

The chapter is set out in the following sections.

Terms and definitions
Consultation
Participation
Workers' representatives
Committees
Consultation and participation documented information

Terms and definitions

It is necessary to be clear about the definition of

consultation and participation
engagement
decisions

and these definitions are discussed in the next three subsections.

DOI: 10.4324/9781003490555-21

Consultation and participation

Consultation and participation are defined in ISO 45001 as follows:

consultation – *seeking views before making a decision*
participation – *involvement in decision-making*

It is important to remember that ISO 45001 restricts the scope of consultation and participation to decision-making because, in the context of a psychosocial management system, consultation and participation should have a much wider scope. ISO 45001 also restricts consultation and participation to workers, with the emphasis on non-managerial workers, but ISO 45003 extends consultation and participation to include interested parties. This is dealt with in more detail later in this chapter.

The ODE[3] definition of consultation is *the action or process of formally consulting or discussing*, and consult is defined as *have discussions with (someone), typically before undertaking a course of action.* These more general definitions suggest that consultation can be much wider than just decision-making. For example, workers could be consulted about their needs and expectations (requirements).

The ODE definition of participation is *the action of taking part in something*, and workers can participate in things other than decision-making, for example, they can participate in well-being and wellness initiatives.

Where consultation and participation are used in this book, it is the more general definitions that are being used – *consultation on decision-making* and *participation in decision-making* will be used when referring to the ISO 45001 definitions of consultation and participation.

Engagement

The definitions of both consultation and participation in ISO 45001 have a note that refers to *engaging health and safety committees and workers' representatives*, but there is no definition of engaging and no use of the term in the text of ISO 45001. ISO 45003 does not define engagement either but uses the term at various points, for example,

5.1   j) *actively engage workers in a continual dialogue on the management of psychosocial risk;*

5.4   b) *encourage participation and engagement, e.g. in health and safety committees or peer-to-peer support networks if appropriate to the size and context of the organization.*

5.4   [last paragraph] *Organizations should also support ongoing consultation, participation and engagement, and get input at all stages of planning and implementation.*

It is obvious from these examples that the ISO 45003 authors see engagement as a separate process from consultation and participation, but they do not make it clear in what way it differs. The ODE has several definitions of engagement, but the only relevant one for the present purposes is *the action of engaging or being engaged* – which is not terribly helpful. Engaging has no relevant definition in the ODE, but the following definitions are relevant.

Engage in – *participate or become involved in*
Engage with – *establish a meaningful contact or connection with.*

One interpretation of the ISO 45003 use of engagement is that it is a way of overcoming the ISO 45001 restriction of consultation and participation to decision-making. That is, engagement is consultation and participation related to matters other than decision-making. Since it has already been stated that more general definitions of consultation and participation will be used, there is no need, for the purposes of this book, to use the term engagement.

Note that there is another good reason for avoiding the term engagement. This is because the terms *worker engagement* and *employee engagement* are used to describe a psychological state of workers or employees. There are innumerable definitions of these terms, but an engaged employee is, in general, one who makes an effort at work, shows enthusiasm for, and pride in, their work and gets engrossed in what they are doing at work. The theory is that engaged workers are more productive than workers who are not engaged so that it is in an organisation's interests to engage its workers. Worker engagement can be relevant to worker well-being and wellness, and any worker engagement programmes should be considered for inclusion in your psychosocial management system. However, dealing with worker engagement as a separate concept is not covered in this book.

Decisions

As was noted earlier in this chapter, the ISO 45001 definitions of consultation and participation are restricted to decision-making. However, clause 5.4 *Consultation and participation of workers* does not mention decisions or decision-making. Instead, it provides a list of issues on which non-managerial workers should be consulted, and a separate list of issues in which non-managerial workers should participate. There is no obvious rationale for the allocation of issues to one list or the other.

What is clear from the lists is that the issues included in ISO 45001 are all within the scope of the OH&S management system and that the primary concern is with non-managerial workers. ISO 45003 extends the ISO 45001 requirements to cover issues such as feedback from workers on the effectiveness of psychosocial risk controls, and, as was mentioned earlier, the inclusion of interested parties. The ISO 45003 clause 5.4 includes the following:

Active and meaningful involvement of relevant interested parties is an important factor for the management of psychosocial risks in any organization.

In the context of a psychosocial management system, it is necessary to broaden the range of decisions to be taken into account. This is because decisions are almost always about change – and change is a major psychosocial risk source. Even when the decision is to maintain the *status quo*, this will be a psychosocial threat for the people who wanted the change.

There are two broad categories of decisions that should be taken into account.

Psychosocial management system decisions. These are decisions that are within the scope of the psychosocial management system, and they are similar to those listed in clause 5.4 of ISO 45001. That is, decisions on, for example, the psychosocial objectives, how to measure well-being and wellness, and how to control psychosocial threats. This type of decision is dealt with in the *Consultation* and *Participation* sections later in this chapter.

Business decisions. This term is used to describe decisions on matters outside the scope of the psychosocial management system. They include

Decisions made by top management about the purpose of the organisation and how this purpose will be achieved.

Decisions made by functions of the organisation on how the functions will be fulfilled.

Decisions made with regard to the procurement of goods and services.

Business decisions should be subject to business risk assessment – to identify any downsides to the proposed change – and they may be subject to health and safety risk assessment. In an ideal world, they would also be subject to psychosocial risk assessment, and the psychosocial risk assessment of business decisions is dealt with in Chapter 31 'Change, procurement, and emergencies'.

Consultation

So far as the psychosocial management system is concerned, consultation is seeking information from people. It has already been seen that widespread consultation is advisable when setting up a psychosocial management system, but continual consultation is an essential element of a functioning psychosocial management system. It is this continual consultation that is the subject of this section.

In ISO 45001, there is a general requirement for consultation

The organization shall establish, implement and maintain a process(es) for consultation and participation of workers at all applicable levels and functions, and, where they exist, workers' representatives, in the development, planning, implementation, performance evaluation and actions for improvement of the OH&S management system.

There is also a requirement to *emphasize the consultation of non-managerial workers* in a subset of OH&S management system elements. However, for a psychosocial management system to be effective, there has to be a much wider range of consultation. For example, because of the psychological issues discussed in Chapter 9, it is not usually possible to predict the effects of a particular action on well-being and wellness, and consultation may help with this problem.

In addition to the sorts of consultation required by ISO 45001 and suggested by ISO 45003, consultation focused on well-being and wellness must also be carried out. This can be in the form of general enquiries such as the following:

What can the organisation do to improve your well-being?
What can the organisation do to improve your wellness?

It is also possible to ask what, if anything, the organisation is doing to harm well-being and wellness, but focusing on improvement usually has better results.

These are the sorts of questions that would be asked in a general consultation process, either specifically about well-being and wellness or as part of a more general consultation such as a worker survey.

However, consultation on well-being and wellness must be built into all relevant processes, and well-being and wellness work instructions for managerial workers must include requirements for consultation such as the following:

This is what we propose to do, how will this affect your well-being and wellness?
This is what we need to achieve, how can we do this without detrimental effects on your well-being and wellness?
This is the problem, how can we solve this in ways that improve your well-being and wellness?
how can we solve it without detrimental effects on your well-being and wellness?

Finally, although ISO 45001 emphasises consultation with non-managerial workers, in a psychosocial management system, consultation at all levels is required. If top management do not consult middle management on well-being and wellness issues, and middle management do not consult first-line management on well-being and wellness issues, it will be difficult to build and sustain a well-being and wellness culture. Similarly, consultation with interested parties should take into account well-being and wellness issues.

Participation

So far as the psychosocial management system is concerned, participation is getting people to do things of relevance to well-being and wellness – either their own or other people's. As with consultation, participation is necessary when setting up a psychosocial management system, but continual participation is also necessary. It is this continual participation that is the subject of this section.

As was seen in the previous section, ISO 45001 has a general requirement for participation. There is also a requirement to *emphasize the participation of non-managerial workers* in a subset of OH&S management system elements. However, for a psychosocial management system to be effective, there has to be a much wider range of participation. For example, if workers do not participate in well-being and wellness initiatives, then, obviously, these initiatives will not have the desired effect.

Participation can require significant time and effort from those involved, and this means that careful management is required if it is to be successful. For example, key points for participation in initiatives to improve worker well-being and wellness are as follows.

Consult prior to setting up participation initiatives. There is little point in setting up a well-being and wellness initiative when the people you want to take part, or a representative sample of them, say that this is not what they want, and that they will not take part. It may be the case that people say they will participate in a particular initiative and then do not – but this is a chance that may have to be taken.

Remove barriers to participation. ISO 45001 has a requirement to *determine and remove obstacles or barriers to participation and minimize those that cannot be removed* and provides the following note:

> *Obstacles and barriers can include failure to respond to worker inputs or suggestions, language or literacy barriers, reprisals or threats of reprisals and policies or practices that discourage or penalize worker participation.*

Maximise incentives to participate. For example, initiatives that take place during work hours are more likely to be successful than initiatives that have to take place outside work hours. Similarly, initiatives that have a financial benefit, such as free gym or swimming pool membership, are likely to have a higher take-up.

Although setting up initiatives to improve worker well-being and wellness was used as an example, similar issues apply when you want people to participate in other aspects of the psychosocial management system, for example, psychosocial threat and opportunity assessment and psychosocial threat control. In these cases, lack of competence may be a barrier, and free training in work time may be needed to overcome this barrier.

Finally, although ISO 45001 emphasises participation of non-managerial workers, in a psychosocial management system, participation at all levels is required and interested parties should also be involved. This is recognised in ISO 45003 which, as was described earlier, states *Active and meaningful involvement of relevant interested parties is an important factor for the management of psychosocial risks in any organization.*

Representatives

In traditional health and safety, there is often a 'Health and safety representative' or 'Safety representative' role within the scope of the health and safety management system. ISO 45001, in the third note to the definition of legal requirements and other requirements, points out that

> *Legal requirements and other requirements include those that determine the persons who are workers' representatives in accordance with laws, regulations, collective agreements and practices.*

One such set of legal requirements is contained in the *Safety Representatives and Safety Committees Regulations 1977* (SI 500:1977), and the list of functions of a safety representative includes the following:

(a) *to investigate potential hazards and dangerous occurrences at the workplace (whether or not they are drawn to his attention by the employees he represents) and to examine the causes of accidents at the workplace;*

(b) *to investigate complaints by any employee he represents relating to that employee's health, safety or welfare at work;*

(c) *to make representations to the employer on matters arising out of sub-paragraphs (a) and (b) above;*

(d) *to make representations to the employer on general matters affecting the health, safety or welfare at work of the employees at the workplace;*

In these Regulations, 'welfare' is restricted to welfare requirements covered by health and safety at work legislation, but some of these requirements are relevant to worker well-being and wellness. However, for the purposes of a psychosocial management system, welfare could be extended to include all factors affecting well-being and wellness. It is likely that safety representatives who accept this expanded role will require additional competences and these are described in Chapter 20 'Competences'.

In addition to safety representatives, organisations may have trade union representatives who will have their own list of functions agreed with the employer and recorded as, for example, *collective agreements*. There may also be worker representatives, sometimes referred to as employee representatives, who are not appointed by a trade union but serve a similar function to trade union representatives.

In traditional health and safety, there is rarely a role in the health and safety management system for representatives other than safety representatives, but this is not the case in a psychosocial management system. Because of the broad range of psychosocial hazards, many of which are not normally taken into account in traditional health and safety, all types of workers' representatives must be included in a psychosocial management system. There is also a case to be made for having well-being and wellness representatives with one or more of the following functions.

Acting as a confidential source of advice and guidance.
Acting as a confidential route for reporting well-being and wellness issues.
Monitoring the well-being and wellness of other workers.
Taking on the role of a Mental health first aider.
Identifying psychosocial risk sources and assisting with dealing with the associated
threats and opportunities.
Raising well-being and wellness issues with appropriate levels of management.
Taking part in the work of the Well-being and wellness committee.

When well-being and wellness representatives are being used, they should be
provided with a *well-being and wellness representatives work instruction* setting
out what they are expected to do, and how they are expected to do it. Similarly,
when you are asking other types of worker representative to extend their role to
include aspects of well-being and wellness, you should provide them with relevant
work instructions. These work instructions can, if appropriate, be relevant subsets
of the *Well-being and wellness representatives work instruction*.

Committees

The *Safety Representatives and Safety Committees Regulations 1977* mentioned
in the previous section, as the title suggests, also allow for the setting up of safety
committees. However, the Regulations make no mention of what these committees
should do. In the authors' experience, the Safety committees, or Health and
safety committees, in different organisations do different things, but there are two
extremes:

Health and safety committees that effectively run most aspects of the health and
safety management system and are really an extension of the Health and safety
department.
Health and safety committees that are only 'talking shops' with meetings taking
place just to enable the appropriate box to be ticked.

What these disparate Health and safety committees have in common is the fact
that they do not usually include worker well-being or wellness in their terms of reference. However, there may be other committees in an organisation that do include
some aspects of worker well-being and wellness. These committees have a range of
titles, including Worker committee, Works committee, or Staff association.
Irrespective of the name of the committee, or its terms of reference, its work
should be taken into account in the psychosocial management system and, where
possible, its terms of reference should be extended to include relevant aspects of
well-being and wellness. Consideration should also be given to setting up a Well-
being and wellness committee with the following functions.

To monitor the performance of the psychosocial management system and identify
opportunities for improvement.

To review information on psychosocial performance and make recommendations on psychosocial objectives and required investigations and audits.

To liaise with other committees, for example, the Staff association and the Health and safety committee.

To benchmark the organisation's psychosocial performance and psychosocial management practices against other organisations.

More detail on these functions is given in the *Well-being and wellness committee terms of reference* section later in this chapter.

Consultation and participation documented information

Arrangements for consultation and participation vary widely from organisation to organisation, so it is not possible to produce a one-size-fits-all set of documented information for these topics. What follows is a suggested framework for the consultation and participation documented information and outline content for each of the documents in the framework.

The following documented information will be required.

Section 5.4 of the *Description* in the *Psychosocial management system manual.*

A *Well-being and wellness consultation and participation procedure.*

Sections in the work instructions of those who have to carry out consultation and participation activities describing what these activities are and how they should be carried out.

A section or sections in the *Well-being and wellness handbook* describing the organisation's arrangements for consultation and participation.

Terms of reference for the Well-being and wellness committee.

Addenda to the terms of reference of other relevant committees.

Each of these types of documented information is dealt with in a separate section below.

Description

The main options for Section 5.4 *Consultation and participation of workers* in the *Description* are:

A brief outline of the arrangements for well-being and wellness consultation and participation. This option would be appropriate if the arrangements were simple, as might be the case when you first set up your psychosocial management system, or you are going to extend existing health and safety and/or HR arrangements for consultation and participation to include well-being and wellness.

A statement such as 'All aspects of well-being and wellness consultation and participation are carried out in accordance with the *Well-being and wellness consultation and participation procedure'*. This would be the appropriate option for a mature stand-alone psychosocial management system with its own psycho-social consultation and participation procedure.

Procedure

The *Well-being and wellness consultation and participation procedure* should follow the structure described in Chapter 12 and have sections describing the pur-pose, scope, and activities to be carried out. Suggested outline text for these three sections is given in Box 19.1.

Box 19.1 Outline text for consultation and participation procedure

Purpose

The purpose of the procedure is to ensure effective consultation on and par-ticipation in issues that affect the well-being and wellness of workers and interested parties.

Scope

This procedure covers all consultation and participation with regard to well-being and wellness for all workers and interested parties within the scope of the psychosocial management system.

In this procedure, 'consultation' means 'consultation on issues that affect the well-being and wellness of workers and interested parties', and 'par-ticipation' means 'participation in activities that affect the well-being and wellness of workers and interested parties'.

Activities

Since the nature and extent of well-being and wellness activities will vary widely from organisation to organisation and will also depend on the maturity of the psychosocial management system, it is not appropriate to provide written descriptions. Instead, what is provided is a list of activities that might be included in this section.

Consultation

Consultation by survey. This subsection should describe any arrangements for worker and interested party surveys of relevance to well-being or wellness. For example, well-being and wellness surveys conducted by

---

external organisations, well-being and wellness items in more general surveys such as job satisfaction surveys, and focussed surveys to collect information about specific psychosocial risk sources. As necessary, this section should reference work instructions for carrying out specific types of survey, and the role work instructions for role titles with responsibilities associated with surveys.

Consultation by committee. This subsection should describe any arrangements for a Well-being and wellness committee, and the role to be played in well-being and wellness consultation by other committees. As appropriate, this subsection should reference the relevant committee terms of reference and the role work instructions for role titles with responsibilities associated with ensuring the committees are effective.

Consultation by managerial workers. This subsection should outline the consultation that the organisation expects managerial workers to carry out as part of their day-to-day managerial activities. These were described in the earlier section on *Consultation.* The subsection should reference the material in the *Well-being and wellness handbook* that describes managerial workers' responsibilities with regard to their teams' well-being and wellness. See Chapter 21 'Awareness and communication' for details.

Other forms of consultation. This subsection should describe any forms of well-being and wellness consultation not dealt with in the previous subsections, and any links with consultation on other issues such as health and safety and HR.

Participation

Participation in decision-making. This subsection should describe the arrangements for dealing with the ISO 45001 requirements and the ISO 45003 guidance for participation in decision-making on well-being and wellness issues. As necessary, the subsection should reference the role work instructions for role titles with responsibilities for ensuring effective participation.

Participation in well-being and wellness initiatives. Since there may be an extensive and fluid list of well-being and wellness initiatives, it may be preferable to restrict this subsection to references to other documented information that sets out responsibility for managing well-being and wellness initiatives and creating new well-being and wellness initiatives.

Other forms of participation. This subsection should describe any forms of well-being and wellness participation not dealt with in the previous subsections, and any links with participation on other issues such as health and safety and HR.

Work instructions

All role work instructions should include a section covering the required consultation and participation activities for that role. Each section should describe what these activities are and, if necessary, how they should be carried out. Remember that ISO 10013[4] states that *The level of detail can vary depending on the ... levels of competency of people*. This means that it is unnecessary to describe in detail how to carry out activities when it is known that these activities will always be carried out by a person with the relevant competences.

Activity work instructions may be required for activities such as conducting surveys or running focus groups.

Well-being and wellness handbook

The *Well-being and wellness handbook* has a crucial role to play in promoting well-being and wellness consultation and participation because it includes details of the organisation's requirements with regard to these topics and sets out the organisation's arrangements for supporting well-being and wellness consultation and participation. The content of the *Well-being and wellness handbook* is discussed in detail in Chapter 21 'Awareness and communication'.

Terms of reference

A committee's terms of reference should include a number of administrative issues such as membership, frequency of meetings, and who does what with minutes of the meetings. However, this section deals only with matters of direct relevance to well-being and wellness.

Well-being and wellness committee

The Well-being and wellness committee has four main activities: monitoring, reviewing, liaising, and benchmarking. Suggested content for these sections of the committee's terms of reference are given in Box 19.2.

Box 19.2 Suggested contentment for committee terms of reference

Monitoring

On the basis of information available to them, the committee members monitor the extent to which the psychosocial management system is achieving its intended outcomes. As appropriate, the committee members identify, and agree,

---

corrections and corrective actions
opportunities for continual improvement.

The Head of well-being and wellness and/or the Head of HR take responsibility for ensuring implementation of agreed actions and the realisation of agreed opportunities in accordance with the *Psychosocial planning and continual improvement procedure.*

Review

The committee members review data, the results of their analyses, and information from across the organisation, and

initiate corrective action when the required data and/or analyses and/or information are not supplied
as appropriate, make recommendations on extending the range of data to be collected and/or the analyses to be carried out and/or the information to be supplied.

The data, analyses, and information the committee review are as follows.

Well-being and wellness data. These include the data needed to evaluate the status of the well-being and wellness of workers and interested parties, and the data needed for epidemiological analyses of well-being and wellness.
Significant psychosocial incidents, nonconformities, and changes. Significant psychosocial incidents are incidents resulting in significant alterations in the well-being or wellness of workers or interested parties. Significant nonconformities are nonconformities with the potential to cause significant alterations in the well-being or wellness of workers or interested parties. Significant changes are as follows:

Planned changes with the potential to cause significant alterations in the well-being or wellness of workers or interested parties.
Unintended changes that resulted in, or had the potential to result in, significant alterations in the well-being or wellness of workers or interested parties.

Performance evaluation information. This includes results from monitoring, measurement, and evaluation of compliance, internal audit results, and minutes of management reviews.
Continual improvement information. This includes progress on achieving psychosocial objectives, identified opportunities for improvement, and actions to continually improve the suitability, adequacy, and effectiveness of the psychosocial management system.

Where a review suggests it is necessary, the committee instigates investigations of well-being and wellness issues.

Where a review or investigation suggests it is necessary, the committee instigates audits of well-being and wellness issues.

Where a review, investigation, or audit suggests it is necessary, the committee makes recommendations for changes to, or additional, well-being and wellness requirements.

Liaison with other committees

Committee members liaise with the Health and safety committee and the HR committee and

ensure well-being and wellness best practices are identified and promulgated throughout the organisation
make recommendations on improving consultation on, and participation in, well-being and wellness matters.

Benchmarking

The aim of benchmarking is to identify ways in which all or parts of the organisation can improve the management of the well-being and wellness of workers and interested parties.

The committee members take benchmarking action of the following types:

Benchmarking between the organisation's functions.
Benchmarking between the organisation and its interested parties.
Benchmarking between the organisation's interested parties.
Benchmarking between the organisation and other organisations.

When a possible improvement is identified, the committee members agree the action required to ensure appropriate implementation and allocate responsibility for carrying out this action.

Other committees

It is worth reviewing the terms of reference for committees such as the Health and safety committee and the Works committee to see if there are already terms or reference of relevance to well-being and wellness. Where there are, reference to them can be incorporated in the psychosocial management system.

However, a more likely scenario is that there are terms of reference with the potential for dealing with psychosocial issues but that are, at present, restricted to other uses such as legal compliance. In these circumstances, it may be possible to get the committee's agreement to an addendum to their terms of reference that allows well-being and wellness issues to be taken into account. These addenda can then be incorporated in the psychosocial management system.

References

1   British Standards Institution. *Occupational health and safety management systems – Requirements with guidance for use*, BSI ISO 45001, 2018. BSI 2018.
2   British Standards Institution. *Occupational health and safety management – Psychological health and safety at work – Guidelines for managing psychosocial risks*, BSI ISO 45003, 2021. BSI 2021.
3   MobiSystems, Inc, *Oxford Dictionary*, version 15.8. Last accessed 17 January 2024.
4   British Standards Institution. *Quality management systems – Guidance for documented information*, BSI ISO 10013, 2021. BSI 2021.

20 Competences

Introduction

In traditional health and safety, there are two broad categories of required competences:

The competences required to work safely and without risks to health.
The competences required to maintain and improve a health and safety management system

This chapter assumes that these health and safety competences are in place and it deals only with the additional competences that are required to:

Work in ways that maintain or promote well-being and wellness.
Maintain and improve a psychosocial management system.

The chapter begins with a section dealing with behavioural objectives and their role in competence delivery and assessment. There are then sections on the following topics:

Workers' competences
Interested parties' competences
General psychosocial management system competences
Documented information for psychosocial management system competences

Note that this chapter focuses on the skills element of competence. The underpinning knowledge element of competence is dealt with in Chapter 21 'Awareness and communication'.

Behavioural objectives

'Behavioural objectives' is the phrase used to describe a method of specifying particular competences. It is a rather grandiose way of saying that you always specify

DOI: 10.4324/9781003490555-22

competences in terms of what people will be able to do. When you have a behavioural objective, it is then possible to specify

any necessary underpinning knowledge – that is, what individuals need to know if they are to achieve the competence.

any necessary standards – that is, what level of competence individuals have to achieve, and over what scope.

appropriate delivery methods – that is, how individuals will be taught the competence.

the assessment methods – that is, how to determine whether an individual has achieved the competence, and how the results of these assessments will be recorded.

For the purposes of this chapter, the emphasis is on setting out the required behavioural objectives. The additional tasks required to make sure that these behavioural objectives are delivered and assessed have not been dealt with. This is because there are so many possible methods for delivery and assessment of competences that is not practical to address them all in a single chapter. Other chapters in this book contain the underpinning knowledge and standards required for a range of competences and, where appropriate, suggest delivery and assessment methods.

Setting out what you want individuals to be able to do in order to support the psychosocial management system is an essential first step – and a significant task. However, note the following:

Change within or outside the organisation can mean that new competences are required and existing competences are redundant. Managing these issues is dealt with in Chapter 31 'Change, procurement, and emergencies'.

Many competences decay with time – bad habits and shortcuts creep in – and if the competence is not used, it can disappear completely. Effective assessment techniques are required to detect deteriorations in competence – preferably before the deterioration is so bad that it causes harm. These assessment methods are dealt with at relevant points in other chapters in Part II.

The fact that someone is able to do something is not a guarantee that they will do it when required. Effective monitoring is needed to check that psychosocial competences continue to be applied properly. The relevant monitoring is dealt with in Chapter 26 'Psychosocial monitoring, auditing, and corrective action'.

Workers' competences

This section deals first with the competences required of all workers, irrespective of their role in the organisation. There are then separate subsections dealing with the additional competence required for the following roles:

Head of well-being and wellness and Head of HR
Managerial workers

All workers

The following four subsections describe the main psychosocial competences required by all workers.

Measuring

All workers should be able to measure their own well-being and wellness, ideally using whatever measures the organisation has chosen as its preferred measures. However, all of the common measures of well-being and wellness are simple to learn, so that competence provision is rarely a problem.

Promoting own well-being and wellness

All workers should be able to behave in ways that promote their own well-being and wellness. This includes competence in

avoiding, or mitigating the effects of, psychosocial threats
maximising the value of psychosocial opportunities
techniques for maintaining and improving well-being and wellness

Promoting others' well-being and wellness

All workers should be able to behave in ways that promote the well-being and wellness of other workers and relevant interested parties. This includes competence in

social skills, also known as interpersonal skills or people skills, are skills that enhance others' well-being and wellness and avoid any detrimental effects on others' well-being and wellness
recognising deteriorating well-being or wellness in others and being able to take appropriate action

Reporting

All workers should be able to report

examples of good practice in well-being and wellness
detrimental effects of work on their well-being or wellness
detrimental effects of work on the well-being or wellness of other workers or interested parties
decreases in their well-being or wellness caused by factors outside work that are having an impact on their work
decreases in the well-being or wellness of others caused by factors outside work that are having an impact on their work

Ideally, there should be a range of reporting options, including

anonymous reporting
reporting verbally or in writing to HR, or via a well-being and wellness reporting
   procedure
reporting associated with a source of help on well-being or wellness problems, for
   example, reporting to a Well-being and wellness counsellor

Head of well-being and wellness and Head of HR

The Head of well-being and wellness and Head of HR will require a wide range
of competences, particularly good people skills. In practice, they will have to be
competent in all of the activities allocated to them in Part II of this book. The only
exceptions will be circumstances where the Head of well-being and wellness or
the Head of HR appoints a competent person to act on their behalf. For example,
the Head of well-being and wellness might employ a well-being and wellness consultant to carry out a particularly complex psychosocial threat and opportunity
assessment, and the Head of HR might employ a medical expert to assist a worker
with a severe well-being or wellness problem being experienced by a worker.

Information on the competence requirements for specific psychosocial activities
is given in the chapter that deals with the activity.

Managerial workers

Managerial workers will, in general, require the competences needed to ensure that
their behaviour

does not have detrimental effects on their team's well-being or wellness
where possible, promotes their team's well-being or wellness

More specific areas of competence are dealt with in the following subsections.

Roles, responsibilities, and authorities

Clause 5.3 *Organizational roles, responsibilities and authorities* of ISO 45003[1]
includes the following

> Top management is responsible for the functioning of the OH&S management
> system and should clarify roles, responsibilities and authorities for managing
> psychosocial risk in the workplace.

In practice, the need to *clarify roles, responsibilities and authorities for managing
psychosocial risk in the workplace* is present at all levels of management. However,
the relevant competences are rarely specified, delivered, or assessed. This will have
to be addressed if certain types of psychosocial risk sources are to be managed. For

example, *Table 1 Aspects of how work is organized* in ISO 45003 lists the following hazards of a psychosocial nature that can be created by lack of competence in defining roles, responsibilities, and authorities:

> *role ambiguity*
> *role conflict*
> *scenarios where workers do not have clear guidelines on the tasks they are expected to do (and not do)*
> *expectations within a role that undermine one another (e.g. being expected to provide good customer service, but also to not spend a long time with customers)*
> *performing work of little value or purpose.*

These hazards of a psychosocial nature can be addressed with the following behavioural objectives:

Able to prepare role descriptions that are without role ambiguity or role conflict and without expectations within a role that undermine one another.
Able to provide clear guidelines on the tasks to be performed.
Able to ensure that there is no work done that has little value or purpose.

When you decide that a psychosocial risk source is to be within the scope of your psychosocial management system, you should try to specify any behavioural objectives of relevance to the associated psychosocial threats and opportunities. This applies to all of competence requirements discussed in this chapter.

Leadership

Clause 5.1 *Leadership and commitment* of ISO 45001[2] and ISO 45003 have extensive lists of leadership requirements and guidance for top management. However, as with roles, responsibilities, and authorities, these leadership requirements and the detailed guidance have to be met at all levels of managerial worker if the psychosocial management system is to be effective. This is recognised in clause 5.1 of ISO 45003 that includes the following statement:

> *The successful management of psychosocial risk calls for a commitment throughout the organization. Top management should lead this, and managers and workers at all levels should assist in its implementation.*

Psychosocial leadership skills are essential if certain types of psychosocial risk sources are to be managed. For example, *Table 1 Aspects of how work is organized* in ISO 45003 lists the following hazards of a psychosocial nature that can be created by lack of competence in leadership skills:

lack of clear vision and objectives
management style unsuited to the nature of the work and its demand

failing to listen or only casually listening to complaints and suggestions
withholding information
providing inadequate communication and support
lack of accountability
lack of fairness
inconsistent and poor decision-making practices
abuse or misuse of power.

These hazards of a psychosocial nature can be addressed with the following behavioural objectives:

Able to provide a clear vision and objectives.
Able to adopt a management style suited to the nature of the work and its demands.
Able to listen properly to complaints and suggestions.
Able to provide all relevant information, communication, and support.
Able to accept accountability, act fairly, and not abuse or misuse their power.
Able to use appropriate decision-making practices.

It can be seen from the above list that some of these behavioural objectives require conventional management skills that might be included in existing managerial training courses. However, others require people skills that are unlikely to be an element of these training courses.

Interested parties' competence

As was seen in Chapter 16, an important activity in a psychosocial management system is the setting up and maintenance of a list of the interested parties that will be within the scope of the management system. It was also pointed out in Chapter 16 that it is important to specify accurately the role these interested parties are to play in the psychosocial management system. Typical categories of role include the following.

Interested parties that can affect the well-being and wellness of workers and be affected by the actions of workers, for example, customers, suppliers, and members of the public.
Interested parties who are in a relationship with a worker that has psychosocial implications, for example, partner, relative, dependant, or carer.
Interested parties who are competent in well-being and wellness interventions, for example, doctors, nurses, well-being and wellness counsellors, and well-being and wellness trainers.

Specifying the competence requirements for these, interested parties can be done in a similar way to that used for workers. However, competence provision and assessment can be much more difficult. For example:

It is easy to say that 'customers must be able to avoid behaving in ways that have a detrimental effect on workers' well-being and wellness', but what can you do to ensure the competence is in place?

How do you know that interested parties providing professional services actually have the competences they claim? They may be able to demonstrate their qualifications by showing you relevant certificates – but qualifications are not proof of competence.

Despite these sorts of difficulties, specifying behavioural objectives for interested parties is an important first step in managing their role in the psychosocial management system. At least you have a clear view of what you want them to be able to do, even if it is going to be difficult to ensure that they are able and willing to do it.

General psychosocial management system competences

Specific psychosocial management system competences are dealt with in the various chapters in Part II of this book. For example, psychosocial threat and opportunity assessment is dealt with in Chapter 23 and psychosocial investigation is dealt with in Chapter 27. However, there are certain general competences that are required across a range of specific psychosocial management system competences. For example, competence in interviewing is required for effective psychosocial threat and opportunity assessment, psychosocial investigation, and psychosocial auditing.

This section deals with the following general psychosocial management system competences:

Interviewing
Causal analysis
Mental health first aid
Counselling
Treatment
Documented information preparation

Interviewing

Interviewing is obviously a competence that is required for traditional health and safety management system procedures, but, in the authors' experience, the level of competence can be poor. This is because, as was noted in Chapter 14, people are competent in holding conversations and are unaware that there is a huge difference between a conversation and an interview. It is rarely the case that a health and safety professional has been on an interview training course, and the ones who have, are usually ex-police officers. Poor interview technique (and poor causal analysis, which is dealt with in the next subsection) results in less than optimum incident investigation.

The detail on this weakness in interviewing has been emphasised because psychosocial interviewing requires an even higher level of competence than health and safety interviewing. This is because psychosocial interviewing has to go into sensitive areas that would not be relevant in health and safety interviewing. For example, you may have to explore people's opinions on, and feelings about, a whole range of personal issues. Poor interview technique can have a range of detrimental effects – from interviewees telling you what they think you want to hear, rather than what they really think, to not telling you anything at all.

It is essential that you become a competent interviewer if you are to be effective in psychosocial risk management, and this competence should preferably be in the context of psychosocial issues. Many aspects of competence in interviewing apply to all types of interview, so that training in, for example, accident investigation or candidate selection interviewing would be useful. However, training focused on interviewing people about their well-being and wellness will be of the most value. Psychosocial interviewing is dealt with in more detail in Chapter 27 'Psychosocial investigation'.

Causal analysis

Causal analysis techniques such as events and causal factors analysis (ECFA) are used in traditional health and safety, most often to analyse the causal factors associated with health and safety incidents. These techniques can also be used for psychosocial investigation, and this use is discussed in Chapter 27 'Psychosocial investigation'. However, ECFA can also be used to analyse the results of psychosocial threat and opportunity assessments and as a predictive tool when comparing the likely effects of different proposed psychosocial threat control measures.

You have to take care when determining psychosocial events and causal factors – for example, a single occurrence of bullying is an event, but bullying that carries on for a period of time is a causal factor. However, an ECFA chart almost always gives a better picture of what is being analysed than an equivalent written or spoken description.

Training in ECFA is widely available in the context of accident investigation, but ECFA training in the context of psychosocial issues is less common.

Mental health first aid

Mental health first aid is the psychosocial equivalent of health and safety first aid. Various commercial and charitable organisations provide training in mental health first aid, and although there are differences in course content, these courses have much in common. The Saint John Ambulance version of the course is typical, and its course description states that mental health first aiders will *be able to recognise the signs and symptoms of common workplace mental health issues and know how to effectively guide a person towards the right mental health support.*

Mental health first aiders, like health and safety first aiders, have an important role to play in their own right. However, the mental health first aider competences are useful for others with a role in the psychosocial management system. For example, psychosocial threat and opportunity assessors may encounter workers who are in need of mental health first aid and, for this reason, all psychosocial risk assessors should preferably be competent mental health first aiders. In general, any role in the psychosocial management system that might involve contact with vulnerable workers or vulnerable interested parties should have mental health first aid competences as part of the competence requirements for the role.

However, care should be taken to ensure that workers have access to a mental health first aider who is an independent source of advice. For example, managerial workers should not be the sole source of mental health first aid for the workers under their control.

Counselling

As was pointed out in Chapter 8, counsellors provide support and guidance on specific causes of impairment to well-being and wellness, such as bereavement or financial difficulties. However, there is a large overlap between counselling and treatment, and treatment is dealt with in the next subsection.

The competences required for effective counselling are extensive, and details can be found on the websites of the professional organisations that oversee the work of various types of counsellor, or the websites of universities and other organisations that provide training and qualifications in counselling.

Treatment

Treatment for impaired well-being and wellness is provided by therapists who focus on well-being issues such as depression and anxiety or wellness issues such as obesity. As with counselling, the competences required for effective treatment are extensive, but details can be found from the professional bodies and teaching organisations mentioned in the previous subsection.

Documented information preparation

The Head of well-being and wellness must have, or have access to, the skills necessary to prepare and maintain all of the documented information required by the psychosocial management system, and a suggested list of required documented information is given in Chapter 32 'The psychosocial management system development plan'.

Key competences are as follows:

Able to draft documents that meet the relevant psychosocial management system requirements and are suitable for their intended audience.
Able to select and use the media that are most appropriate for the subject covered by the document and its target audience.

Able to design forms and checklists for recording required data and information, and able to specify criteria for the use and retention of forms.

Guidance on preparing documented information was given in Chapter 12 'The documented information'.

Documented information for psychosocial competences

The main types of documented information associated with psychosocial competences are as follows.

Specifications of competences. Behavioural objectives were described earlier in the chapter as the preferred method for recording competence specifications. However, in some circumstances, it is better to use videos of the competent behaviour.

Specifications of underpinning knowledge. This can be done in a variety of ways, including written documents such as the *Well-being and wellness handbook*, training course material, podcasts and videos, and apps.

Assessment tools. These range from written examinations to test underpinning knowledge, to *aides-memoire* for assessors to use during observation of the required behaviour. Irrespective of the nature of the assessment tool, it should be accompanied by a method for recording the results of its use. For example, the *aides-memoire* just mentioned could also be a checklist for recording the results of the assessor's observations.

Typically, there will be a need for a *Psychosocial competence procedure* to draw together the need for, and use of, the various activities described in this chapter.

References

1   British Standards Institution. *Occupational health and safety management – Psychological health and safety at work – Guidelines for managing psychosocial risks*, BSI ISO 45003, 2021. BSI 2021.
2   British Standards Institution. *Occupational health and safety management systems – Requirements with guidance for use*, BSI ISO 45001, 2018. BSI 2018.

21 Awareness and communication

Introduction

This chapter deals with the related topics of awareness and communication, with a separate section on each topic.

Awareness

Introduction to awareness

Both ISO 45001[1] and ISO 45003[2] have lists of things that workers should be made aware of, for example, the OH&S policy and the OH&S objectives. ISO 45003 extends these requirements to *relevant interested parties* and gives an extensive list of things to be taken into account *when developing awareness of psychosocial risk*. However, if a psychosocial management system is to be effective, awareness among workers and interested parties must be much broader than the items listed in ISO 45001 and ISO 45003. In addition, the awareness must be

tailored to the scope and nature of the psychosocial risk management system – for example, with clear descriptions of what your organisation means by well-being and wellness
written using appropriate terminology – the terminology used in this book is not usually appropriate for communicating with non-specialists.

What is recommended for general awareness is a single document that contains all of the well-being and wellness information you want to make workers and interested parties aware of, and that is written in language that all of these people will understand. In this book, this document is referred to as a *Well-being and wellness handbook*, and this handbook is the subject of the first part of this section.

This section also deals with other topics of relevance to awareness, and the documented information required for awareness.

DOI: 10.4324/9781003490555-23

Handbook

Your *Well-being and wellness handbook* should be a succinct account of what your organisation means by well-being and wellness, and what your organisation is doing to maintain and improve the well-being and wellness of its workers and interested parties. The first subsection below deals with the contents of a *Well-being and wellness handbook*, and the second subsection deals with the medium, or media, to be used to ensure effective communication of these contents.

Handbook content

The detailed content of your handbook will obviously depend on the scope and nature of your intended psychosocial risk management activities, but it is possible to suggest a general outline. The suggested content for a handbook has the following sections:

Introduction
Measuring and improving your well-being
Measuring and improving your wellness
Other people's well-being and wellness
What the organisation will do
Reporting well-being and wellness issues

Each of these sections is discussed below with sample text given in boxes.

INTRODUCTION

The introduction should tell readers what the handbook is for and what it contains. An example *Introduction* is given in Box 21.1.

Box 21.1 Introduction

Using this handbook will help you improve your well-being and wellness, and the well-being and wellness of others.
   It describes

what is meant by well-being and wellness
how you can measure your own well-being and wellness
self-help activities for improving your well-being and wellness
what to do, and what not to do, to promote other people's well-being and wellness
what the organisation is doing about well-being and wellness
how to report well-being and wellness issues.

MEASURING AND IMPROVING YOUR WELL-BEING

This section should contain the following information.

Your organisation's agreed description of what is meant by well-being.
A copy of, or means of accessing, your organisation's agreed means of measuring well-being with instructions for their use.
Your organisation's agreed list of self-help activities for improving well-being.
Your organisation's agreed list of other sources of information on well-being.

Box 21.2 gives sample text for the *Measuring and improving your well-being* section. For illustrative purposes

the chosen method of measuring well-being is the WHO 5 Well-being index as described in Chapter 3
it is assumed the organisation has a well-being counselling service
the well-being self-help measures are those widely recommended by experts in the field.

Box 21.2 Measuring and improving your well-being

Your well-being is your mental condition at any given time, for example, happy or sad, relaxed or anxious, and interested or bored.

Measuring your well-being

You can measure your well-being in various ways, but we suggest you use the World Health Organisation's WHO 5 Well-being index.

<A copy of the Index or a hyperlink to it should be inserted here by your organisation>

You get your total score on the WHO 5 Well-being index by adding up your scores for the five separate items.
Your total score will vary from day to day but, in general, a total score of more than 13 means your well-being is at an acceptable level. However, you might want to improve your well-being, and ways of improving well-being are described later.
If your total score is 13 or less, you should take action to improve your well-being. You can do this in one or more of the following ways.

Self-help. Use the ways of improving well-being described later in this handbook.

Make an appointment to have a confidential meeting with a Well-being and wellness counsellor – <your organisation to insert phone number, email address, URL>.

Make an appointment with your own doctor.

You should also take one or more of the three actions listed above if you score 0 or 1 on any of the five items on the WHO 5 Well-being index.

Improving your well-being

Although there are five separate well-being items in the WHO Index they are linked. For example, if you do not wake up fresh and rested, you are less likely to be active and vigorous. This means that the things you can do to improve your well-being often improve more than one of the items in the WHO Index. The recommended activities for improving your well-being are described next.

Connect with other people

Good relationships are important for your well-being because they

help you to build a sense of belonging and self-worth
give you an opportunity to share positive experiences
provide emotional support and allow you to support others.

You should find things that you could do to help you build stronger and closer relationships.

The organisation does the following to help you with this:

< your organisation to insert details of any relevant organisation initiatives>

Be physically active

Being active improves your physical health, but it also improves your well-being because it

makes you feel better about yourself
lets you set and achieve activity and fitness goals
causes chemical changes in your brain that reduce anxiety and depression.

You should find physical activities you enjoy and do them as often as you can.

Learn

Learning improves your well-being because it

makes you feel better about yourself
gives you a purpose in life
provides opportunities to connect with people.

You should learn more about the things you already know something about, and learn about things that are new to you.

<your organisation to insert details of any relevant organisation initiatives>

Give your time

Giving your time to help other people improves your well-being because, like learning, it

makes you feel better about yourself
gives you a purpose in life
provides opportunities to connect with people.

You should begin with small acts of kindness towards other people and gradually add larger ones like volunteering in your local community.

<your organisation to insert details of any relevant organisation initiatives>

Take notice

Taking notice of what is happening around you, often called mindfulness, improves your well-being because it

helps to reaffirm your life priorities
enhances your self-understanding
allows you to make positive choices based on your own values and
    motivations.

You should take time to enjoy the moment and the environment around you.

<your organisation to insert details of any relevant organisation initiatives>

Other sources of information

More information on improving your well-being is available at

<your organisation to insert details of any recommended sources of information including freely available sources such as

www.nhs.uk/mental-health/self-help/guides-tools-and-activities/five-steps-to-mental-wellbeing/ and
www.mind.org.uk/workplace/mental-health-at-work/taking-care-of-yourself/five-ways-to-wellbeing/
and any sources paid for by the organisation>

MEASURING AND IMPROVING YOUR WELLNESS

This section should contain the following information.

Your organisation's agreed description of what is meant by wellness.
Your organisation's agreed list of self-help activities for measuring and improving wellness.
Your organisation's agreed list of other sources of information on wellness.

Sample text is given in Box 21.3.

Box 21.3 Measuring and improving your wellness

Your wellness is your physical condition at any given time, for example, your weight, blood pressure, and cholesterol level.

The organisation suggests that you check your wellness in the ways described below. There is also guidance on how you can improve your wellness.

Waist size

The British Heart Foundation has the following information on waist circumference as a measure of wellness.

The recommended waist measurements are:

* *below 37 inches (94cm) for men*
* *below 31.5 inches (80cm) for women.*

People with waist sizes bigger than these are more likely to develop certain health problems, such as type 2 diabetes, high blood pressure, heart disease and stroke.

Adults from certain ethnic backgrounds, including South Asian, Chinese, other Asian, Middle Eastern, Black African or African-Caribbean, with waist sizes higher than 90cm for men and 80cm for women are at greater risk of developing ... health problems.

The main ways to reduce your waist size are:

Aerobic exercise, for example, brisk walking, swimming, running, or cycling. Do at least 30 minutes of moderate-intensity activity five or more days per week. Ideally, do 45–60 minutes every day.

Resistance training, for example, exercising with weights, bands, or machines, or doing push-ups. Do two to three sessions per week.

Improved diet. Eat foods that contain complex carbohydrates and have a high-fibre content, for example, bread, pasta, rice, and beans. Avoid sugary foods and drinks, especially those containing fructose, because fructose can trigger cravings and cause overeating.

Sleep. You should get seven to nine hours of sleep each night. Too little sleep and too much sleep can both cause an increase in waist size.

Reduce stress. Stress that goes on for a long time raises the sugar level in your blood, which stimulates the formation of abdominal fat. Make time every day for activities that help with well-being, particularly relaxation.

The organisation does the following to help you with reducing your waist size.

<Your organisation to insert details of organisation initiatives and facilities, for example,

Opportunities for aerobic exercise – individual and group
Resistance training
  Free equipment – weights, bands
  Gym membership

Improved diet – no easy access to 'poor diet' options, and easy access to 'good diet' options>

Body mass index

Your body mass index (BMI) is a number calculated using your weight and height. This can be done using a BMI chart but these charts do not take into account individual differences such as gender, age, and ethnicity. You can get a more accurate measure of your BMI by using an online BMI calculator, such as www.nhs.uk/live-well/healthy-weight/bmi-calculator/. This calculator also provides guidance on what constitutes a healthy BMI for you and gives advice on what to do to maintain your healthy BMI.

The things you do to reduce your waist size also reduce your BMI.

Heart rate

A healthy resting heart rate, or pulse rate, for an adult is between 60 and 100 per minute.

If your heart rate is too slow or too fast either

make an appointment to have a confidential meeting with a Well-being and wellness counsellor – <your organisation to insert phone number, email address, URL> or
make an appointment with your own doctor.

Blood pressure

There are two measures of blood pressure

Systolic blood pressure. This is the pressure when your heart beats and pushes blood through your arteries.
Diastolic blood pressure. This is the pressure when your heart rests between beats.

You need a blood pressure monitoring machine to measure your blood pressure. These are readily available and not expensive. The instructions for using the monitor will also give guidance on what constitutes healthy measures of blood pressure.

<The organisation provides free access to blood pressure monitoring devices – contact a Well-being and wellness counsellor for details – <your organisation to insert phone number, email address, URL>

If your blood pressure is too low or too high either

make an appointment to have a confidential meeting with a Well-being and wellness counsellor – your organisation to insert phone number, email address, URL> or
make an appointment with your own doctor.

Blood oxygen level

Oxygen in your bloodstream is essential for life, and reduced levels of oxygen in your bloodstream impair your wellness. You can measure the oxygen in your bloodstream using an oximeter. These are small devices that clip over the end of your finger and measure the oxygen level in your blood and also give your heart rate. These devices are readily available and not expensive. The instructions for using them will give guidance on what constitutes a healthy level of blood oxygen.

<The organisation provides free access to blood oxygen monitoring machines – contact a Well-being and wellness counsellor for details – <your organisation to insert phone number, email address, URL>

If your blood oxygen is too low either

make an appointment to have a confidential meeting with a Well-being and wellness counsellor – your organisation to insert phone number, email address, URL> or

make an appointment with your own doctor.

Lung function

An important job the lungs do is to get oxygen into your bloodstream, and one of the causes of low blood oxygen level is poor lung function. There are various ways of measuring lung function, but the simplest is how strongly you can breathe out. This is known as the 'peak flow', and there are simple devices for measuring this, known as spirometers. You blow into these as hard as you can and they measure the strength of your breathing out (exhalation). The instructions for using them will also give guidance on what constitutes a healthy measure of peak flow.

If your peak flow is too low, you should do one or more of the following.

Use a breathing exerciser machine to improve your lung function.

Make an appointment to have a confidential meeting with a Well-being and wellness counsellor – <your organisation to insert phone number, email address, URL>.

Make an appointment with your own doctor.

<The organisation provides free access to spirometers and breathing exercise machines – contact a Well-being and wellness counsellor for details – your organisation to insert phone number, email address, URL>

Blood sugar level

Too high a sugar level in your blood, or too low a level, will reduce your wellness, and for people with diseases such as diabetes, it can be a life-threatening condition.

Common symptoms of high blood sugar levels include

feeling very thirsty
urinating a lot
feeling weak or tired
blurred vision
losing weight.

Common symptoms of low blood sugar levels include

sweating
feeling tired
dizziness
feeling hungry
tingling lips
feeling shaky or trembling
a fast or pounding heartbeat (palpitations)
becoming easily irritated, tearful, anxious, or moody
turning pale.

There are two methods you can use to measure your blood sugar level. The first involves pricking your finger to produce a drop of blood for testing, the second, less accurate, method is a meter you hold next to your skin.

The equipment for both methods can be purchased online, but the meter can be an expensive option.

If you are having symptoms of too high or too low blood sugar level, or a self-test shows you have too high or too low blood sugar level,

make an appointment to have a confidential meeting with a Well-being and wellness counsellor – <your organisation to insert phone number, email address, URL> or
make an appointment with your own doctor.

More information on wellness

More information on improving your wellness is available at
    <your organisation to insert details of any recommended sources of information, including freely available sources such as
    www.nhs.uk/live-well/eat-well/
    www.nhs.uk/live-well/exercise/
    www.nhs.uk/conditions/high-cholesterol/how-to-lower-your-cholesterol/
and any sources paid for by the organisation>

OTHER PEOPLE'S WELL-BEING AND WELLNESS

This section is based on the assumption that your organisation has an agreed list of things that workers have to do to protect and promote the well-being and wellness of others – required behaviours – and another list of things they must not do because they can harm the well-being and wellness of others – prohibited behaviours. Most organisations have a list of prohibited behaviours, but usually because they are illegal, rather than because they are psychosocial risk sources.

Few organisations have a list or required behaviours of relevance to psycho-social risk sources. However, as was discussed in Chapter 5, lists of required and prohibited behaviours will be needed as part of the psychosocial management system documented information.

Box 21.4 gives suggested text for this section, and it assumes that relevant training courses will be available, and that there is a *Disciplinary procedure* for behavioural transgressions.

Box 21.4 Other people's well-being and wellness

The way you behave can have a strong effect on other people's well-being and wellness. The effect can be good – for example, if you are friendly and supportive – or bad – for example, if you insult people or bully them.

This section describes behaviours that affect well-being, and there are two types.

Required behaviours. These are behaviours that maintain and improve the well-being and wellness of your colleagues and other people your behaviour might affect, for example, members of the public. The organisation requires you to behave in these ways when necessary.

Prohibited behaviours. These are behaviours that have a negative effect on the well-being and wellness of your colleagues and other people your behaviour might affect. The organisation prohibits you from behaving in these ways.

Required behaviours

Everyone is required to behave with respect for other people, and leaders have additional required behaviours. Respect and leadership are the next two sections.

Respect

Respecting someone is having due regard for their feelings, wishes, and rights. Behaving respectfully towards someone shows that you care about their well-being and wellness, and that you consider them a person of worth.

Important behaviours that help you show respect include the following.

Active listening. Make the effort to really hear and understand what people are saying to you.

Finding things you have in common. It is easier to respect someone who, for example, shares your views on some matter, likes some of the things you like, or is interested in some of the things that interest you.

Show empathy when there are differences. No two people can have everything in common, but if you respect someone, you will make an effort to understand and share their feelings.

Help and support people. Watch out for opportunities to help and support people – even in simple ways – and help and support them when you can.

Show gratitude. Obviously, you thank people who help you directly, but you should also show gratitude for other things, such as being treated with respect.

Apologise when you are wrong. Most people find it difficult to say sorry, but if you are in the wrong, the respectful thing to do is to apologise to the individuals involved.

Be polite. This is an important way of showing respect, and there is never an excuse for not being polite.

Celebrate people's achievements. Not just achievement of work objectives but other achievements at work, and in their life outside work.

Find something good to say. The old saying is 'if you can't find something good to say, don't say anything', but you should make the effort to find something good to say.

Do what you say you will do. If you do not, you lose people's trust, and trust is essential for a respectful relationship.

And finally, take care of yourself. If you have low levels of well-being and wellness, you will not be in a position to carry out effectively all the behaviours listed above.

The organisation provides *Behaving with respect* training courses – contact a Well-being and wellness counsellor – <your organisation to insert phone number, email address, URL> – for details.

If you fail to treat people with respect, it will be dealt with in accordance with the *Disciplinary procedure*.

If you are not being treated with respect, you should report it – how to report lack of respect is described at the end of this handbook.

Leadership required behaviours

The main behaviours for leadership for well-being and wellness are

consulting on psychosocial issues
encouraging participation in psychosocial decision-making and psychosocial
   initiatives
reducing uncertainty
eliminating wasted effort
giving constructive feedback
giving praise
reinforcing the organisation's well-being and wellness messages.

The organisation provides *Leadership for well-being and wellness* training courses – contact a Well-being and wellness counsellor – <your organisation to insert phone number, email address, URL> – for details.

If you fail to lead for well-being and wellness, it will be dealt with in accordance with the *Disciplinary procedure.*

If you are not being led with due regard for your well-being and wellness, you should report it – how to report lack of well-being and wellness leadership is described at the end of this handbook.

Prohibited behaviours

The organisation has identified a range of prohibited behaviours, and they are dealt with in separate sections below.

Bullying and harassment

Bullying and harassment are unwanted behaviours towards another person that

violates that person's dignity, or
creates an intimidating, hostile, degrading, humiliating, or offensive environment for them.

Bullying and harassment can

be a regular pattern of behaviour or a one-off incident
happen face-to-face, on social media, in emails, or during telephone calls
happen at work or in work-related situations.

Bullying and harassment may not always be obvious or noticed by others. Examples of bullying and harassment include

spreading malicious rumours
putting people down in meetings
putting humiliating, offensive, or threatening comments or photographs on social media
undermining your manager's authority
making unwanted physical contact
using aggressive or threatening language or behaviour
telling unwelcome jokes
indulging in unwelcome banter
using offensive or demeaning language
gossiping or telling lies about people

using unwanted nicknames

using obscene posters, graffiti, or gestures

making unwelcome sexual advances, or making threats when sexual advances
  are rejected

offering a reward, for example, promotion, for going along with sexual
  advances

isolating people or not cooperating with them

excluding people from work or social activities

intrusion by pestering, spying, or stalking.

You must not bully or harass people. If you are accused of bullying or harassment, it will be dealt with in accordance with the *Disciplinary procedure*.

If you are being bullied or harassed, you should report it – how to report
bullying and harassment is described at the end of this handbook.

Discrimination

Discrimination is treating a person less favourably because of their

age

disability

gender reassignment

marriage or civil partnership

race

religion or belief

gender

sexual orientation

pregnancy or maternity.

You must not discriminate against people. If you are accused of discrimination, it will be dealt with in accordance with the *Disciplinary procedure*.

If you are being discriminated against, you should report it – how to report
discrimination is described at the end of this handbook.

Victimisation

Victimisation is treating a person unfairly because they have made a complaint about bullying, harassment, or discrimination, or because they have
supported someone when they have made this type of complaint.

You must not victimise people. If you are accused of victimisation, it will
be dealt with in accordance with the *Disciplinary procedure*.

If you are being victimised, you should report it – how to report victimisation is described at the end of this handbook.

Misconduct

Your misconduct is relevant to the well-being and wellness of others because of the adverse effect it has on the people who witness it or are affected by it.
For example,

If you are late for work, or take unauthorised leave, your colleagues may have to do extra work and may suffer stress if they have to 'cover up' for you.

Not following required procedures may make your colleagues' work more difficult and make them worry about whether or not to report you.

The organisation considers the following behaviours as misconduct:

Persistent bad timekeeping
Unauthorised absence
Absences that are not genuine or not for the reason provided
Damage to the organisation's property
Failure to observe required procedures
Rude or abusive behaviour
Unreasonable refusal to follow a reasonable instruction issued by a manager
Data protection breaches and misuse of the organisation's information
Behaviour that is likely to bring the organisation into disrepute
Bribery
Making malicious or vexatious grievances

If you are accused of misconduct, it will be dealt with in accordance with the *Disciplinary procedure.*

If you are a witness to misconduct, you should report it – how to report misconduct is described at the end of this handbook.

Gross misconduct

Gross misconduct is misconduct that is so serious that it may result in your dismissal from the organisation. Gross misconduct can put a severe strain on the people who witness it because they know that if they report you, you may lose your job.

The organisation considers the following behaviours are gross misconduct:

Theft or fraud

Physical violence or threatening behaviour

Deliberate cover-up of deficiencies or falsification of records, reports, timesheets, or expense claims, whether or not for personal gain

Falsification of a qualification that is a stated requirement of employment or results in your financial gain

Deliberate unauthorised disclosure of confidential organisation information

Conviction of a criminal offence that is relevant to your employment

Misuse or abuse of social media in or outside work

Deliberately accessing pornographic, offensive, or obscene material at work

Conduct that brings the organisation's name into disrepute

Serious breach of the organisation's procedures

Attending work under the influence of alcohol or illegal substances

Deliberate damage to, or misuse of, property or systems belonging to the organisation, the public, suppliers, or colleagues

Serious insubordination

Negligence which causes severe loss, damage, or injury

Bringing prohibited items into work, for example, illegal drugs or offensive weapons

If you are accused of gross misconduct, it will be dealt with in accordance with the *Disciplinary procedure*.

If you are a witness to gross misconduct, you should report it – how to report gross misconduct is described at the end of this handbook.

WHAT THE ORGANISATION WILL DO

This section should set out what your organisation will do with regard to well-being and wellness that are additional to the ones already described. There is no text box for this section, but examples of additional things an organisation might do include the following.

Extending well-being and wellness facilities and counselling to worker's' families if they are not already included as interested parties.

Providing free access to medical services for the treatment of impaired well-being and wellness.

Arranging social events, volunteering opportunities, and learning opportunities.

REPORTING WELL-BEING AND WELLNESS ISSUES

There are usually long-standing arrangements for health and safety reporting and HR reporting, and it may be possible to adapt a combination of these to meet the requirements for well-being and wellness reporting. However, it is possible that the competences needed for effectively responding to well-being and wellness reports may not be in place among managers, and for this reason a reporting system that is run by Well-being and wellness counsellors may be a better option. This is the option used for illustrative purposes in Box 21.5 *Reporting well-being and wellness issues.*

Box 21.5 Reporting well-being and wellness issues

With well-being and wellness, it is important to report the good news as well as the bad.

Reporting the good news

If you think you have found something that will help improve the well-being or wellness of your colleagues, tell a Well-being and wellness counsellor – <your organisation to insert phone number, email address, URL> – and they will make sure your report is acted on.

Reporting the bad news

If there is something at work that is having a detrimental effect on your well-being or wellness, make an appointment with a Well-being and wellness counsellor – <your organisation to insert phone number, email address, URL>. These appointments, and what you discuss during them, will be confidential.

If there is something at work that is having, or could have, a detrimental effect on the well-being or wellness of one or more of your colleagues make an appointment with a Well-being and wellness counsellor – <your organisation to insert phone number, email address, URL>. These appointments, and what you discuss during them, will be confidential.

If you are having well-being or wellness issues outside work, you can also make an appointment with a Well-being and wellness counsellor – <your organisation to insert phone number, email address, URL> – for a confidential discussion of your issues.

Anonymous reporting

If you have a well-being or wellness issue to report and you would rather not be identified, you can make an anonymous report by

posting a written message to a Well-being and wellness counsellor
leaving a verbal message on a Well-being and wellness counsellor's voice-mail

Handbook media

The most appropriate medium for your handbook will depend on its content, its target audience, and the resources available to you for its creation and maintenance. However, the key point is to make it user friendly, and this may involve the extensive use of illustrations. These may be instructional or simply to break up the text. Unless you are competent in this type of work, you should seek expert help with the presentational issues associated with your handbook.

The main media options, in ascending order of resource requirements, are as follows.

A 'read-only' copy on your organisation's intranet. This has the major advantage that you can make changes easily, and workers always have access to an up-to-date copy. The disadvantage is that separate arrangements may have to be made for interested parties who do not have access to your intranet.

Printed copies. This is the preferred option where computer access is limited, but it can be expensive and the ways of updating it are limited.

E-books. E-book versions of *Well-being and wellness handbooks* are cheaper to produce than paper versions and are more convenient for many users. Depending on the software used to produce e-books, they may also allow for interactive content and the sorts of external links available when using read-only versions on your organisation's intranet.

Apps. A well-designed *Well-being and wellness handbook* app is probably the gold standard for handbooks, but they take some time and often require significant resources to produce and keep updated.

Other awareness topics

The *Well-being and wellness handbook* provides awareness of psychosocial issues that are relatively stable. However, you will need processes for making workers and interested parties aware of other, more transient, matters that may affect their well-being or wellness, for example, organisational change. Passing on these types of information requires effective communication, so they are dealt with in the *Communication* section of this chapter.

Documented information for awareness

In addition to the *Well-being and wellness handbook*, the following awareness documented information will be required.

A *Psychosocial awareness procedure* that, as a minimum, sets out the arrangements for maintaining and promulgating the *Well-being and wellness handbook* but should also cover any other awareness processes. Where existing health and safety awareness arrangements are being used for psychosocial awareness (see Chapter 14), the relevant health and safety procedure can be referenced.

Work instructions for those with psychosocial awareness responsibilities, for example, first-line managers who have to maintain their team's awareness of the content of the *Well-being and wellness handbook.*
Forms for recording activities intended to create or maintain psychosocial awareness.

Communication

Introduction to communication

When dealing with arrangements for communication in a management system, it is preferable to go back to the Annex SL[3] communication requirements because, in the authors' view, they are clear, succinct, and comprehensive. These requirements are

The organization shall determine the need for internal and external communications relevant to the XXX management system including

> *on what it will communicate*
> *when to communicate*
> *with whom to communicate*
> *how to communicate.*

ISO 45001 and ISO 45003 elaborate on these requirements in various ways, but these can mainly be considered as additional requirements (ISO 45001) or suggestions (ISO 45003) for dealing with the Annex SL requirements. When setting up a psychosocial management system, it is more useful to focus on the basic Annex SL requirements, rather than trying to deal with the individual communications issues identified in ISO 45001 and ISO 45003. There will be more on this point in the discussion of documented information for psychosocial communication later in this chapter.

There are, however, certain issues that you need to take into account with regard to psychosocial communication, and these are dealt with in the next three subsections.

Psychosocial threats and opportunities

An important aspect of communication in the context of a psychosocial management system is the fact that the content or delivery of the communication may be a psychosocial threat or opportunity. In traditional health and safety, it is not usually necessary to consider the effect a communication, or its method of delivery, will have on the well-being and wellness of the recipients. However, this is not the case in a psychosocial management system, and there should be arrangements for screening the content of psychosocial communications and checking that they are being delivered in appropriate ways.

In addition, as has been seen in earlier chapters, inappropriate communication and lack of communication are the basis of a number of psychosocial risk sources, and appropriate and timely communication can have positive effects on the well-being and wellness of workers and interested parties.

These factors mean that communication in a psychosocial management system is a more sensitive topic than in a traditional health and safety management system, and this also applies to the means and media for communication, which are discussed later in this section.

Specific topics and audiences

ISO 45001 and ISO 45003 list specific topics for awareness and communication including

the results of investigations
the results of audits
factors that

    affect well-being at work
    potentially create or increase stigma and/or discrimination
    reduce psychosocial risks.

However, as was seen in the discussion of the *Well-being and wellness handbook*, there are many other psychosocial topics that should be the subject of communication in a psychosocial management system.

ISO 45001 also identifies audiences for communication as contractors, visitors to the workplace, and other interested parties. However, as was seen in earlier chapters, the range of interested parties in a psychosocial management system is likely to be much wider than in a traditional health and safety management system.

Means and media

As with the content of communications, the means and media used for psychosocial communications can have an effect on well-being and wellness. For example, there have been various reports of the distress caused by informing workers by email, rather than face-to-face, that they have been made redundant. Where an organisation is committed to managing well-being and wellness effectively, it must have arrangements for assessing the immediate impact of potentially sensitive communications on the well-being and wellness of those who receive those communications.

The ideal means of delivery is face-to face delivery by a person competent in delivery methods and the methods for the assessment of the effects of their communications on well-being and wellness. This means should always be used for very sensitive communications.

Documented information for communication

The following communication documented information will be required.

A *psychosocial communication procedure* setting out, as a minimum, your organisation's responses to the basic Annex SL requirements described at the beginning of this section.

Work instructions for those with psychosocial communication responsibilities not covered by the *Well-being and wellness handbook.*

Forms, as necessary, for recording the content of verbal communications and for recording the results of communications.

References

1   British Standards Institution. *Occupational health and safety management systems – Requirements with guidance for use*, BSI ISO 45001, 2018. BSI 2018.
2   British Standards Institution. *Occupational health and safety management – Psychological health and safety at work – Guidelines for managing psychosocial risks*, BSI ISO 45003, 2021. BSI 2021.
3   *ISO/IEC Directives, Part 1 Consolidated ISO Supplement – Procedure for the technical work – Procedures specific to ISO (Thirteenth edition, 2022). Annex SL (normative) Harmonised approach for management system standards. Appendix 2 (normative) Harmonized structure for MSS with guidance for use.*

22　Psychosocial risk sources

Introduction

Traditional health and safety risk management focuses on the tasks workers carry out and the environment in which they carry out those tasks. As ISO 45001[1] puts it, the *intended outcomes of the OH&S management system are to prevent injury and ill health to workers and to provide safe and healthy workplaces.* This approach is necessary in psychosocial risk management, but it has to be extended in a number of ways, and the required activities are described in Chapter 23 'Psychosocial threat and opportunity assessment' and Chapter 24 'Psychosocial threat and opportunity management'.

The present chapter deals with the following broader issues associated with psychosocial risk sources

Psychosocial risk sources that must be eliminated
Psychosocial risk sources inherent in the organisation as a whole
Psychosocial risk sources inherent in functions
Exploiting psychosocial opportunities
The purpose of initiatives
Work-relevant improvers and triggers

Psychosocial risk sources that must be eliminated

As was seen in Chapter 14 'What is already in place?', most organisations have procedures for mandating prohibited behaviours, and many of these behaviours are psychosocial risk sources. There may also be procedures for mandating required behaviours the absence of which creates psychosocial risk sources.

The first step in dealing with psychosocial risk sources that must be eliminated is to draw up, and agree, clear statements of what these risk sources look like in practice. If this is not done, much effort can be wasted on 'Oh yes it is – Oh no it isn't' arguments to the detriment of the efforts to eliminate the psychosocial risk source. Where the risk source can be accurately specified in terms of prohibited and required behaviours, this can be relatively straightforward. However, many psychosocial risk sources require value judgements. For example, the risk sources

DOI: 10.4324/9781003490555-24

of a psychosocial nature – *poor communication, lack of fairness, social or physical isolation* and *limited opportunity to participate in decision-making* – all require value judgements. Where such risk sources are to be mandated for elimination, the criteria for the value judgements must also be agreed and recorded. For example, you will need to specify what good and poor communication look like, or at least provide examples of what they look like in your organisation.

When the descriptions and criteria have been agreed, you have then to identify the method, or methods, that will be used to eliminate the psychosocial risk source. There is little point in mandating elimination if you have no method of fulfilling the mandate. For the wide range of psychosocial risk sources involving prohibited and required behaviours, the two main options are providing the relevant competences or removing the person from the role, or that part of the role where the role holder's behaviour is creating a psychosocial risk source. For psychosocial risk sources such as *social or physical isolation*, the methods of elimination will involve changes to organisational arrangements, and these may be more difficult to implement.

For each of the mandated psychosocial risk sources, it is also necessary to agree and record how the well-being and wellness of the perpetrators, victims, and beneficiaries will be dealt with in your organisation.

As was described in Chapter 14, HR procedures focus on punishing perpetrators and do not usually deal with the perpetrator's well-being and wellness. It is arguably the case that organisations have a duty of care to perpetrators – for example, if a bully relies on their bullying behaviour to maintain their well-being, is the organisation required to provide support if it insists this behaviour stops? This can be a serious problem when the organisation has 'turned a blind eye' to the perpetrator's behaviour, perhaps over many years. It can also be a very serious problem if the bully is a member of your top management.

With regard to victims, there are two issues that have to be addressed: treatment for impaired well-being and wellness and compensation. Organisations will have to provide initiatives and/or access to improvers that ensure that victims' well-being and wellness are returned to an acceptable level. What constitutes acceptable levels of well-being and wellness should be agreed when setting up the psychosocial measuring systems, and this is dealt with in Chapter 25 'Psychosocial measurement, analysis, and evaluation'. There should also be arrangements for compensating victims, as discussed in Chapter 10 'The people'. As with support for perpetrators, treatment of, and compensation for, victims can be significant issues when the organisation has 'turned a blind eye' to the existence of a psychosocial risk source that has been creating victims, perhaps over many years.

You also have to have arrangements for dealing with beneficiaries of the psychosocial risk source that is to be eliminated. These arrangements will have to take into account the extent of the beneficial effects on the well-being and wellness of the individual(s) concerned and for how long these beneficial effects have been in place. In extreme cases, removing a psychosocial risk source that has beneficiaries may be seen as changing the beneficiaries' terms of employment, and in these circumstances, the change management techniques discussed in Chapter 31 'Change, procurement, and emergencies' may be required.

Because of these complexities, great care has to be taken before mandating psychosocial risk sources for elimination. It is tempting to say that you will eliminate particular behaviours or organisational arrangements, but if you do say this, and it does not happen, the whole psychosocial management system may be adversely affected. Where the elimination of a particular psychosocial risk source is desirable but is, for the time being, impracticable, then it is better to deal with occurrences of the psychosocial risk source on a case-by-case basis, rather than announce that its elimination has been mandated.

The following techniques can be used to identify occurrences of psychosocial risk sources that must be eliminated.

Ensure that workers and interested parties are aware of the nature of psychosocial risk sources and the need to report them. This was dealt with in Chapter 21 'Awareness and communication'.

Establish an effective reporting system. It should be easy for workers and interested parties to report occurrences of psychosocial risk sources, and reporting should have no adverse consequences for the reporter. Reporting systems for psychosocial hazards are discussed in detail in Chapter 25 'Psychosocial measurement, analysis, and evaluation'.

Establish an effective psychosocial threat and opportunity assessment procedure, either by extending the existing health and safety risk assessment procedure or by setting up a separate psychosocial threat and opportunity assessment procedure. These alternatives are dealt with in Chapter 23 'Psychosocial threat and opportunity assessment'.

Build the identification of psychosocial risk sources into existing health and safety monitoring and auditing, and into any other relevant checking activities such as those used by the HR department. Possible ways of doing this are discussed in Chapter 26 'Psychosocial monitoring, auditing, and corrective action'.

Psychosocial risk sources inherent in the organisation as a whole

An organisation's psychosocial risk management system should take into account the psychosocial risk sources inherent in the organisation and its activities. These psychosocial risk sources can have positive or negative effects, and these effects are discussed next.

Examples of organisational activities that typically have positive effects on well-being and wellness include activities that involve the following.

Helping animals, for example, animal rescue centres and veterinary practices.

Helping people, for example, health care organisations, organisations helping the homeless, and food banks.

Protecting the environment, for example, government agencies and environmental pressure groups.

Protecting flora and fauna, for example, government agencies and wildlife protection groups.

Examples of organisational activities that typically have negative effects on well-being and wellness include activities that involve the following.

Inflicting pain on animals or killing animals, for example, some cosmetic companies and abattoirs.

Manufacturing munitions and military equipment.

Damaging the environment, for example, some farmers and organisations that discharge sewage or chemicals into watercourses.

Harming or killing flora and fauna, for example, some farmers and major infrastructure projects.

Harming people, for example, tobacco and alcohol production.

However, there are two factors that complicate these typical findings: individual differences and the outcomes of the activities.

Individual differences. As has been seen in earlier chapters, individual differences are central to psychosocial risk management, and they also determine the effects of organisational activities on well-being and wellness. For example:

The majority of individuals are likely to be against inflicting pain on animals or killing them. However, there will be some who are indifferent, and a few who do it for enjoyment and as a sport, for example, fox hunters and hare coursers.

Individuals who enjoy tobacco or alcohol are unlikely to be strongly against the manufacturers of their chosen drug.

The majority of individuals are likely to be supportive of charitable activities such as providing shelter for the homeless and food banks for the hungry, but there is a minority who see the homeless and hungry as work-shy scroungers, and this minority disapproves of these charitable activities.

Outcomes of activities. The outcome of an organisational activity can determine whether it has a positive or negative effect on well-being and wellness. For example:

Individuals who, overall, disapprove of inflicting pain on animals or killing them may support these activities when they are part of research to find cures for fatal human diseases.

Individuals who, overall, disapprove of keeping animals in zoos may make exceptions for zoos that are primarily engaged in preserving endangered species.

Individuals who are against the manufacture of munitions and military equipment may change their mind when the munitions and military equipment are required for their defence, or the defence of a close ally.

These inherent psychosocial risk sources can have practical implications. For example, when the psychosocial risk source is creating threats, it may be difficult to recruit workers, whereas there may be a plentiful supply of applicants when the psychosocial risk source is creating opportunities. However, from the point of view of the psychosocial management system, it is the effects on well-being and wellness that are of concern, and decisions on a number of matters will have to be made and agreed. These matters are as follows.

Which, if any, of the psychosocial risk sources inherent in your organisation will be within the scope of your psychosocial management system. A case can be made for excluding them all on the grounds that these psychosocial risk sources are not likely to change. However, it is still worth documenting the psychosocial risk sources that may be having a significant effect on well-being and wellness so that they do not become 'elephants in the room'.

Which interested parties likely to be affected by the psychosocial risk source will be within the scope of your psychosocial management system. You will remember that ISO 45001 defines interested party as a *person or organization that can affect, be affected by, or perceive itself to be affected by a decision or activity.* Clearly, this definition would include the sorts of individuals referred to earlier in this section, for example, members of the public who have strong views on animal welfare or the protection of the environment. As with the psychosocial risk sources themselves, it is possible to exclude members of the public from the scope of your psychosocial management system, but you should record details of who you are excluding and why. This can conveniently be done as part of the work on needs and expectations (requirements) described in Chapter 16.

When one or more of the psychosocial risk sources inherent in your organisation will be within the scope of your psychosocial management system, responsibility for dealing with threats and exploiting opportunities must be allocated. The well-being and wellness function may be able to make suggestions on these matters, but it is unlikely to have the competences and resources necessary to implement and maintain the required actions.

The above discussion has assumed a homogenous organisation, and that it is the whole organisation that is creating the psychosocial risk sources. However, in larger organisations, it may be only part of the organisation that is having an effect, and in complex organisations, some parts may be creating psychosocial threats while other parts are creating psychosocial opportunities. Where different parts of the organisation are having different effects, these parts should be treated as separate functions for the purposes of the psychosocial management system. How to deal with risk sources inherent in functions is the subject of the next section.

Psychosocial risk sources inherent in functions

There are two reasons why an organisation's functions may have to be treated separately within the psychosocial management system. The first is because they are creating the sorts of psychosocial risk sources described in the previous section, and the second is because they are creating psychosocial risk sources that are affecting the well-being and wellness of workers in other functions. Examples of the second category include the following.

Actions by personnel in the HR department. How HR personnel deal with their fellow workers can have a major impact on these workers' well-being and wellness, and this impact can be positive or negative. You should review any existing documents describing how HR personnel should deal with their fellow workers from the point of view of psychosocial risk management and suggest changes where necessary. Where no such document exists, you should draft appropriate psychosocial requirements and agree them with the Head of HR.

Actions by personnel in the Finance department. The issues here are the same as those for the HR department personnel, and these issues should be dealt with in a similar way.

Actions by 'welfare' providers. Welfare has been used as shorthand for the whole range of facilities that can have an impact on the well-being and wellness of workers and interested parties. Examples include provision of carparking spaces, food and drink, washing and changing facilities, sanitary facilities, and a comfortable working temperature in buildings. Although some welfare facilities may be within the scope of a traditional health and safety management system, this is usually because it is a legal requirement, not because of its effect on worker well-being and wellness.

More generally, you must have arrangements for identifying and dealing with any psychosocial risk sources that arise due to conflict between functions. This can be an issue in traditional health and safety, and significant incidents have occurred because of, for example, conflict between shifts resulting in failure to transfer information needed for safe operation.

However, impairment of well-being and wellness due to conflict between functions is much more common.

Exploiting psychosocial opportunities

An early decision you need to make when setting up your psychosocial management system is whether taking psychosocial opportunities will be within scope from the beginning, or something that will be added when there are effective arrangements for dealing with threats.

Whenever you decide to implement arrangements for taking psychosocial opportunities, you will have to address the following issues.

Individual differences. Remember that what is a psychosocial opportunity for some individuals will be a psychosocial threat for others, and it may not be obvious which individuals fall into which category.

Fairness. If some workers or interested parties are to receive a benefit from the taking of a psychosocial opportunity, thought needs to be given to the possible reactions of workers and interested parties who are similarly circumstanced but who do not receive a benefit.

Extent. The potential for taking psychosocial opportunities is typically identified at a local level, but it can be the case that the psychosocial opportunities could also be taken elsewhere in the organisation, or even taken across the whole organisation. Where this is the case, consideration has to be given to resource and management issues to avoid workers and interested parties in some parts of the organisation receiving a benefit that is not available to workers and interested parties in other parts of the organisation.

Because of these issues, all proposed actions to take psychosocial opportunities should be treated as psychosocial changes and be subject to the change management processes described in Chapter 31 'Change, procurement, and emergencies'.

The purpose of initiatives

The purpose of initiatives in the context of a psychosocial management system is to improve the well-being and wellness of the workers and, if relevant, the interested parties who take part in the initiative. This may be a purely altruistic act on the part of your organisation, or it may be done in the hope that it will increase productivity and/or reduce worker turnover.

Initiatives offered across an organisation are subject to the vagaries of individual differences that effect most psychosocial issues – some individuals will see the initiative as a benefit but others may not. The category of individuals who do not benefit is likely to comprise individuals who are completely indifferent to the initiative, and others whose well-being or wellness is impaired by the initiative. The initiative of offering free gym membership can be used to illustrate the sorts of problems that may arise.

The purpose of offering free gym membership to workers and interested parties is to get these individuals to exercise in the hope that this will improve their well-being and wellness. Once the initiative has started, the following issues may arise.

Some individuals may take up the offer but not visit the gym, or visit the gym and not take any exercise.

The initiative may be seen as payment for exercising, and individuals who exercise in other ways, for example, using home gym equipment or outdoor running or cycling, may be aggrieved that they are not paid for this. This may reduce the well-being of these individuals.

Individuals who do not want to, or are unable to, exercise in the ways provided at a gym may also feel aggrieved that others are receiving a financial benefit from the initiative.

Although gym membership has been used as an example, these problems can arise with any initiative that provides resources that have, or can be perceived to have, financial or other benefits for those who take part in the initiative.

Even initiatives that do not involve financial benefits can run into problems because of the effects of individual differences. For example, the initiative of publishing details of local organisations that provide free advice and guidance on well-being and wellness issues would appear to be a fairly uncontentious initiative. However, if some of the local organisations are, for example, faith, religion, or race based, there may be a detrimental effect on the well-being of any workers and interested parties whose faith, religion, or race is not represented. In these circumstances, it may be necessary to state that this lack of representation was because no relevant local organisations were found, and that workers and interested parties should provide details of any that have been missed, so that these organisations can be added to the list.

Because of the potential problems with even apparently straightforward psychosocial initiatives, all of these initiatives should be treated as psychosocial changes and be subject to the change management processes described in Chapter 31 'Change, procurement, and emergencies'.

Work-relevant improvers and triggers

As was described in Part I, improvers are actions individuals can take to improve their well-being and wellness, and triggers are things that can impair an individual's well-being and wellness. Improvers and triggers are work-related when their effect on an individual's well-being or wellness has an impact on their performance at work.

Because improvers and triggers are, by definition, outside work, there is no requirement for an organisation to include them in the scope of its psychosocial management system. However, organisations appear to be increasingly aware of the effects on their bottom line of reduced productivity and increased worker turnover due to the impaired well-being and wellness of workers. This is one of the reasons organisations are implementing psychosocial management systems that take into account some improvers, typically those that require only limited resources for their effective implementation.

When setting up a psychosocial management system, you will have to consider which, if any, improvers and triggers will be within the initial scope. You can keep this aspect of your psychosocial management system's scope under review as part of the SWOT analyses described in Chapter 18.

Reference

1   British Standards Institution. *Occupational health and safety management systems – Requirements with guidance for use*, BSI ISO 45001, 2018. BSI 2018.

23 Psychosocial threat and opportunity assessment

Introduction

As has been pointed out in earlier chapters, there are individual differences in reactions to psychosocial risk sources. This means that, in practice, the only way you can assess the effect of a psychosocial risk source is to ask the individuals exposed to that risk source – and hope that they give you an honest answer.

Because of this, the risk assessment methodologies used in traditional health and safety, and in ISO 31000[1] based risk assessment, are not appropriate. This is why this book has only used the term risk assessment when referring to these methodologies. In the context of psychosocial risk management, the process is referred to as psychosocial threat and opportunity assessment.

What is needed in psychosocial risk management is a methodology centred around identifying the effects of existing psychosocial risk sources, rather than predicting the possible occurrence of various types and severity of injury and ill health. The first seven sections of this chapter outline such a methodology under the following headings.

Scope of the methodology
Identification of psychosocial risk sources
Establishing the causes of psychosocial risk sources
Establishing who is exposed to the psychosocial risk sources
Assessing the effects of psychosocial risk sources on individuals
Establishing the pattern of effects of psychosocial risk sources
Systemic psychosocial threats

The chapter ends with a discussion of a method that can be used to incorporate impairment of well-being and wellness into traditional health and safety risk assessment.

Scope of the methodology

The scope in the present context is what will be assessed, and you will have to make decisions on which psychosocial risk sources will be assessed, and which workers

DOI: 10.4324/9781003490555-25

and interested parties will take part in the assessments. For brevity, workers and interested parties will be referred to as individuals for the rest of this chapter.

The easy decision would be to include all psychosocial risk sources and all the individuals exposed to them, but this is rarely a practical option. What you need is a 'let's get started' approach that provides a manageable scope for the application of your psychosocial threat and opportunity assessment methodology.

The important issues to take into account when deciding on the scope of your methodology include the following.

What is already in place. There is no point in reinventing the wheel, and if there are already arrangements in place for dealing with a particular psychosocial risk source, even if the arrangements have to be 'tweaked' to make them suitable for use as a psychosocial procedure, then the psychosocial risk sources already being dealt with should be within the scope of the psychosocial management system.

Top management. Top management may have views on which psychosocial risk sources should be within the scope of the psychosocial management system. This may be for business reasons (see the next bullet point on what is causing problems), for personal reasons, or to influence the organisation's image. Irrespective of the reason, top management's wishes with regard to the inclusion of psychosocial risk sources should be sought and met.

What is causing problems. It is typically the case in organisations that there are psychosocial risk sources that are causing problems. This may be because they are systemic psychosocial risk sources, which are dealt with in the penultimate section of this chapter, or characteristic of particular parts of the organisation. Whichever is the case, psychosocial risk sources that are known to be causing problems should be within the scope of the psychosocial management system. If this is not done, it will create a poor impression since individuals will see a psychosocial management system that is failing to deal with what they know to be obvious problem areas. This poor impression can be reduced by ensuring that workers and interested parties are informed of the reasons for the exclusion of the relevant psychosocial risk source.

Resources. As with any procedure, the resources that will be available for implementing and maintaining it must be determined and taken into account when deciding on what the scope of the procedure will be. This is particularly important for those aspects of procedures that have to be carried out by individuals who are not under psychosocial management system control. For example, when specifying what managers will be required to do, you need to check that they will have the resources of time, motivation, and competence to meet the requirements you wish to specify.

HR. What HR is already doing to manage particular psychosocial risk sources must obviously be taken into account, but you need to reach agreement with HR about the list of psychosocial risk sources you propose to include in the scope of your initial psychosocial threat and opportunity assessment.

When you have an agreed list of the psychosocial risk sources to be included in the scope of your initial psychosocial threat and opportunity assessment procedure, you should make clear to the relevant individuals the reasons for any significant omissions. For example, there could be a section in the *Well-being and wellness handbook* that describes current limitations and, if appropriate, gives details of how and when these limitations will be remedied.

You may find it useful to carry out a round of identification of psychosocial threats and opportunities before finalising your first assessment scope, and methods for psychosocial risk source identification are discussed in the next section.

Identification of psychosocial risk sources

A variety of proactive and reactive techniques should be used for identifying psychosocial risk sources, as this will maximise the chances of identifying the ones that are having significant effects. Proactive techniques involve taking action to collect data and information – for example, using interviews and inspections – reactive techniques involve waiting for individuals to provide you with data and information – for example, by using reporting procedures.

Some of these techniques were introduced in Chapter 22, and the present chapter provides more detail. The main proactive and reactive techniques are discussed next.

Proactive psychosocial risk source identification

Proactive psychosocial risk source identification is carried out in two ways:

Worker-focused. This approach involves risk source identification by asking workers whether they are affected by psychosocial risk sources.

Risk source-focused. This approach involves identifying circumstances that are creating, or could create, psychosocial risk sources.

The next two subsections deal with possible arrangements for these two approaches.

Worker-focused

The most generally useful form of worker-focused proactive identification of psychosocial risk sources is a structured interview carried out by individuals who are competent in this type of interview. The relevant competences were described in Chapter 20.

This interview should begin with the usual courtesies and an explanation of the purpose of the interview. There should then be a review of the organisation's meaning of well-being and wellness, so that the interviewee is clear about what the interview is intended to achieve with regard to their well-being and wellness.

Ideally, this review will be a summary of the relevant material from the *Well-being and wellness handbook* described in Chapter 21 'Awareness and communication'.

The main part of the interview should be based on the following questions, which should be rephrased as necessary to suit local terminology.

Wellness

Is there anything at work that is having a negative effect on your wellness?

Is there anything at work that could be done to improve your wellness?

Do you know of anything at work that is having a negative effect on your colleagues' wellness?

Do you know of anything at work that is having a positive effect on your colleagues' wellness?

Well-being

Is there anything at work that is having a negative effect on your well-being?

Is there anything at work that could be done to improve your well-being?

Do you know of anything at work that is having a negative effect on your colleagues' well-being?

Do you know of anything at work that is having a positive effect on your colleagues' well-being?

The questions on wellness are asked first because interviewees are usually more willing to talk about physical effects than mental effects, and talking about wellness first helps build a rapport.

The questions about the wellness and well-being of colleagues are asked for two reasons.

Colleagues may genuinely be being affected, positively or negatively, by psychosocial risk sources, and the interviewee may have identified these effects and be willing to describe them.

This type of question is known as an attributional question, and attributional questions are asked because interviewees who are reluctant to describe the effects of psychosocial risk sources on themselves may be willing to attribute these feelings to their colleagues. For example, 'I don't think my boss is a bully, but some of my colleagues do'. However, they do not usually name the colleagues they say are affected. Attributional questions can be an extremely useful method of obtaining information on psychosocial risk sources.

The interviewer should also make an assessment of the forthcomingness of the interviewee. This will be a subjective judgement, but the ability to make such judgements is one of the competences required for this type of assessment. There is little point taking action on the results of interviews when the interviewer has no confidence in the accuracy or veracity of the answers given to the questions asked.

There are other methods for worker-focused proactive identification of psycho-social risk sources, but they are all attempting to find out what, if any, psychosocial risk sources are being identified by workers. The main differences between the techniques are as follows.

One-to-one or one-to-many. The interview method just described is a one-to-one approach – one interviewer and one interviewee. However, one-to-many approaches such as focus groups or team meetings led by competent interviewers can also be used. These methods have the advantage of making good use of the interviewer's time, but they may fail to collect the views of members of the group who are diffident, that is, *modest or shy because of a lack of self-confidence* (ODE)[1].

Written versus spoken. Written responses to questions are much easier to provide anonymously, and this can be useful for psychosocial risk sources involving interpersonal relationships. For example, a group being questioned about the effects of particular psychosocial risk sources can be given a questionnaire to complete and put into a 'ballot box'. In extremely sensitive cases, you can increase the chances of anonymity by ensuring the questionnaire requires only ticks or crosses (handwriting not identifiable) and issue everyone in the group with an identical pen or pencil. Alternatively, you can use software designed for this type of work, for example, Forms in Microsoft 365. This software has the advantage that it also collates the data collected to create information.

Worker led or well-being and wellness professional led. Depending on the maturity of the psychosocial management system, worker-led psychosocial threat and opportunity identification can be adopted. For example, well-being and wellness champions can be appointed, and well-being and wellness working parties set up, with one of their functions being the identification of psychosocial threats and opportunities.

Work-related only or work-related and work-relevant. The example interview questions, given earlier in this section, were about work-related psychosocial risk sources. However, they can be adapted to cover work-relevant psychosocial risk sources if required. For example:

Is there anything outside work that is having a negative effect on your wellness at work?

Is there anything that could be done, or that the organisation could do, about things outside work to improve your wellness at work?

Is there anything outside work that is having a negative effect on your well-being at work?

Is there anything that could be done, or that the organisation could do, about things outside work to improve your well-being at work?

The important thing to remember about all of these techniques for identification of psychosocial risk sources is that they are only a first step. Any action to be taken with regard to an identified psychosocial risk source will depend on the effect it is having. This is dealt with in the *Assessing effects of psychosocial risk sources* section later in this chapter.

Risk source-focused

There are various methods that can be used for risk source-focused identification of psychosocial risk sources. Brief details of the main options are given next.

Analysis of absence data. The analysis of absence data can be used to identify the possible role of psychosocial risk sources in the causes of absences. However, there may be confidentiality issues, and the analyses may have to be carried out by HR personnel with the relevant competences. The analysis of absence data is dealt with in more detail in Chapter 25 'Psychosocial measurement, analysis, and evaluation'.

Analysis of health and safety incident and nonconformity reports. The information contained in the initial reports of such things as accidents, near misses and health and safety hazards and nonconformities is unlikely to be sufficient for the identification of psychosocial risk sources. However, analysis of the detailed reports of investigations of health and safety incidents, hazards, and nonconformities can suggest the presence of psychosocial risk sources as causal factors. They are not usually labelled as psychosocial risk sources, but typical examples include such hazards of a psychosocial nature as *scenarios where workers do not have clear guidelines on the tasks they are expected to do (and not do), poor communication,* and *conflicting demands and deadlines.*

Analysis of work records. Personnel with the relevant competences can analyse records that describe the type of work done, and when and where it was done, and identify ways in which these factors could create psychosocial risk sources such as excessive hours worked and lone working.

Health and safety risk assessments. Health and safety risk assessments are principally concerned with injury and physical ill health. However, health and safety personnel with the relevant competences can extend their risk assessments to include mental ill health, well-being and wellness. They can do this in various ways, including the sorts of interviews described in the previous section, and extending their site inspections and job observations to include the observable hazards of a psychosocial nature such as *machine pacing.*

Document reviews. Personnel with the relevant competences can review documents that describe roles, responsibilities, and behaviours and identify psychosocial risk sources such as role ambiguity, conflicting responsibilities, and lack of variety in behaviours.

Workplace inspections. Some hazards of a psychosocial nature, for example, *poor workplace conditions such as lack of space, poor lighting and excessive noise* and *working in extreme conditions or situations, such as very high or low temperatures, or at height* can be identified during workplace inspections.

Job observation. Some hazards of a psychosocial nature, for example, *machine pacing* and a *high level of repetitive work* can be identified using job observation.

Extending existing checking activities to include the identification of psychosocial
  risk sources. These activities include HR activities, such as worker surveys and
  performance evaluation, and health and safety activities, such as internal audit,
  and monitoring by managerial workers. These checking activities are dealt with
  in Chapter 26 'Psychosocial monitoring, auditing, and corrective action'.

Proactive identification of psychosocial risk sources is the preferred approach,
but it must be backed up by reactive identification, and this is dealt with in the next
subsection.

Reactive psychosocial risk source identification

As was described earlier in this chapter, reactive techniques for psychosocial risk
source identification involve waiting for people, usually workers and interested
parties, although it could be others – members of the public, for example – to provide you with data and information on the existence of psychosocial risk sources.

The effectiveness of these techniques depends on individuals being aware of
what the organisation means by well-being and wellness, and the arrangements for
reporting factors that are affecting their well-being or wellness. One mechanism
for creating and maintaining the relevant awareness – the *Well-being and wellness
handbook* – was described in Chapter 21.

The following methods for the reactive identification of psychosocial risk
sources should be in place.

Direct reports to the worker's immediate line manager. This should be the first
  option used by workers, but it may be unavailable because, for example, the
  worker's immediate line manager is the perpetrator, or the worker's immediate
  line manager refuses to take action.
Direct reports to a more senior line manager. This option should be used by
  workers when they encounter the sorts of circumstances described in the previous bullet point.
Direct reports to human resources personnel. This option should be available in
  addition to, or as an alternative to, direct reports to a more senior line manager.
  Workers can use this option when, for example, they know, or believe, senior
  line managers are also perpetrators, or they know, or believe, that senior line
  managers will not take action.
Direct reports to a worker representative. Where worker representatives are present
  in the organisation, whether they are health and safety representatives or more
  general worker representatives, they should be incorporated in the arrangements
  for reporting effects on worker well-being and wellness. Since the actions taken
  by worker representatives when they are fulfilling their role as a representative
  are not under the control of the organisation, there will have to be discussion of,
  and agreement on, this aspect of the worker representatives' role.
Anonymous reports. Workers and interested parties should be able to report effects
  on their well-being and wellness anonymously by, for example,

placing a written message in a well-being and wellness reporting box

posting a written message to their local human resources personnel

leaving a verbal message on a dedicated voice mail.

Whistle-blowing. The ODE defines a whistle-blower as *a person who informs on a person or organization regarded as engaging in an unlawful or immoral activity.* As was seen in Chapter 5 'The hazards and risk sources', illegal activities such as theft, fraud, bribery, and damaging property can be psychosocial risk sources, and they would be activities of relevance to whistle-blowing. In addition, there can be quite a wide interpretation of *immoral activity* so that, for example, bullying might be considered to be within the scope of activities covered by whistle-blowing. To be effective, arrangements for whistle-blowing must be independent of your organisation, since it may be your organisation the whistle-blower is complaining about. What your organisation has to do is to ensure workers and interested parties remain aware of any local arrangements for whistle-blowing.

For all of the arrangements for reporting factors that affect well-being or wellness, you should ensure that those who may need to make a report and those who may need to respond to a report have the necessary competences.

Establishing the causes of psychosocial risk sources

The effective management of psychosocial risk sources requires accurate identification of the causes of these risk sources. For illustration, the first hazard of a psychosocial nature *role ambiguity* has been chosen as a 'worked example' in the present chapter on assessment of psychosocial threats and opportunities. It is also used in Chapter 24 to illustrate the management of these threats and opportunities.

The ODE defines ambiguity as *the quality of being open to more than one interpretation.* In the context of role ambiguity, the ambiguity could be about the purpose of the role, how the role should be carried out, the quality of the outputs from the role, or a whole range of more detailed aspects of the role. The first step in establishing the causes of role ambiguity is, therefore, to establish the nature and extent of the ambiguity.

Let us suppose for the purposes of illustration that the role ambiguity is ambiguity about how the tasks making up the role should be carried out. This ambiguity can have a variety of causes, including

there is no effective verbal instruction

there are no written work instructions

there are work instructions, but they are poorly written and contain ambiguities

there are work instructions, but they are not used because, for example, they are out of date or include impractical elements

there are work instructions, but they are not available where the work is to be carried out

the work instructions are simply ignored.

It can be seen from this list that without accurately establishing the causes of the ambiguity any action taken to remedy it will be effective only by chance. For example, redrafting ambiguous work instructions will not reduce ambiguity if the real cause of the ambiguity is that work instructions are simply ignored.

An important aspect of cause identification is establishing the involvement, if any, of perpetrators. For the list of possible causes of role ambiguity just given, the possible perpetrators are as follows:

No effective verbal instruction. The relevant first-line managers.
No written work instructions. The person responsible for ensuring work instructions are prepared.
Poorly written work instructions. The person who wrote the work instruction.
Work instructions out of date or include impractical elements. The person responsible for ensuring work instructions are appropriate and kept up to date.
Work instructions not available where the work is to be carried out. The person responsible for ensuring work instructions are available.
Work instructions are simply ignored. The relevant workers.

If necessary, further investigation will have to be carried out to determine the reasons for the perpetrators' behaviour. For example, no effective verbal instruction by first-line managers could be due to lack of awareness of the need for instructions, lack of competence in delivering instructions, or lack of motivation.

Establishing the causes of psychosocial risk sources, the relevant perpetrators, and the reasons for their behaviour, can sometimes be straightforward, but more often the psychosocial investigation techniques described in Chapter 27 'Psychosocial investigation' will be required.

Establishing who is exposed to the psychosocial risk source

Establishing who is exposed to a particular psychosocial risk source can also be straightforward. For example, if you have identified ambiguity in a specific role, then those exposed to this psychosocial risk source are the workers carrying out that role. However, things are rarely that simple and typical complications are as follows.

The workers exposed to the specific role ambiguity you are dealing with tell you about other, perhaps more important to them, psychosocial risk sources to which they are exposed.
You find that your specific role ambiguity is one of a number of other possible role ambiguities because of, for example, first-line managers' lack of competence in issuing instructions, or lack of competence in preparing work instructions, is widespread throughout the organisation.
Role ambiguity is only one of the psychosocial risk sources being created by the lack of competences, and other behaviours such as workers ignoring work instructions that your investigations have identified.

Getting individuals in addition to the workers exposed to the specific role ambiguity you are dealing with to talk about psychosocial risk sources can result in the identification of a wide variety of other psychosocial risk sources that are causing problems.

The authors call the phases of establishing the causes of psychosocial risk sources and identifying those exposed to these risks in the psychosocial threat and opportunity assessment process as the 'can of worms' phases. This is because, in their experience, once you start talking to individuals about the causes of psychosocial threats and opportunities, and who is being affected by these threats and opportunities, you never know what you are going to uncover, or where your interviews will take you. Consultants being paid by the hour find this ideal, but for their clients it is signing a blank cheque. The compromise to use as a general approach is to focus on dealing with the task in hand – for example, role ambiguity for a specific group of workers – but to record carefully details of all the additional issues that arise. These additional issues can then be brought to the attention of the relevant managerial workers in your organisation, and approaches to addressing these issues can be discussed and agreed.

Assessing the effects of psychosocial risk sources on individuals

It should be apparent by now that, apart from a few wellness issues such as being overweight, the only way to determine the effect a psychosocial risk source is having on an individual is to ask them – and hope they give you an honest answer.

Given that this is the case, the methods for assessing the effects of psychosocial risk sources follow naturally from the methods of identifying these risk sources described in the previous section. For example, if you are using an interview to identify the presence of psychosocial risk sources, you can use the same interview to ask the interviewee what effects any identified psychosocial risk sources are having on them. Because of this natural follow-on, the same framework has been used in this section for describing the assessment methods as was used for describing the identification methods.

However, as with most aspects of psychological measurement, you have to be very careful to ensure that you are clear what you want to measure, and that the individuals taking part in the measurement are clear about what you are trying to achieve. In the context of assessing the effects of psychosocial risk sources, interviewers and interviewees have to be clear about the following.

What is being measured is the effect of psychosocial risk sources to which the interviewee is exposed at work. With role ambiguity, there is unlikely to be any problem, but with more generally prevalent psychosocial risk sources such as misogyny or racism, you have to separate the contribution to reduced well-being and wellness that misogyny or racism experienced at work is having, from the contribution misogyny or racism experienced outside work is having.

What is being measured is the effect the psychosocial risk source has on well-being and wellness while the interviewee is at work. Among interviewees who are suffering impaired well-being from role ambiguity some will 'leave the impairment at work' while others will continue to suffer from the impairment outside work.

These restrictions must be made clear to interviewees, and more generally to individuals taking part in any measurement of their well-being or wellness. This can be done with suitable verbal or written guidance, which could be included in the *Well-being and wellness handbook* and repeated as an introduction to each measurement.

The restrictions on measurement just described are purely for practical reasons – in effect, the restrictions limit the scope of the psychosocial management system. As your psychosocial management system matures, you can consider measuring the effects of psychosocial risk sources experienced outside work and the effects psychosocial risk sources experienced at work are having on well-being and wellness outside work.

In the discussion of assessment which follows, it is assumed that

you are measuring the effect on individuals of psychosocial risk sources at work
you are measuring the effect on individuals' well-being and wellness while at work
appropriate guidance is used to ensure that individuals take these restrictions into
    account when taking part in assessments.

Proactive assessment

As with proactive psychosocial risk source identification, assessing the effects of psychosocial risk sources can be worker-focused or risk source-focused, and the next two subsections deal with possible arrangements for these two approaches.

Worker-focused

As was mentioned earlier, the structured interview carried out to identify psychosocial risk sources can be extended to assessing the effects of the identified psychosocial risk sources simply by asking the interviewee. However, a more structured approach is to be preferred and one such approach is described next.

The interviewer can take into the interview a form such as the one shown as Table 23.1.

Note that the form shown in Table 23.1 asks about wellness before well-being, and about the well-being and wellness of colleagues. This is for the reasons described in the previous section.

The form shown in Table 23.1 is used as follows.

During the identification part of the interview, the interviewer records any identified psychosocial risk sources in the leftmost column of the form. When the identification part of the interview is complete, the interviewer gives the completed

Table 23.1 Form for recording effects of psychosocial risk sources

Psychosocial risk source	What effect is this psychosocial risk source having on	Big −ve (−2)	Small −ve (−1)	No effect (0)	Small +ve (+1)	Large +ve (+2)
	your wellness?					
	your well-being?					
	your colleagues' wellness?					
	your colleagues' well-being?					
	your wellness?					
	your well-being?					
	your colleagues' wellness?					
	your colleagues' well-being?					
	your wellness?					
	your well-being?					
	your colleagues' wellness?					
	your colleagues' well-being?					

Source: Prepared by Tony Boyle for this book.

form to the interviewee with a request to fill in the scoring parts of the form. When the interviewee has completed the scoring for the psychosocial risk sources the interviewer has recorded, the interviewer asks the interviewee if they would like to add any psychosocial risk sources that they had not mentioned earlier in the interview. The interviewees are also asked to score any added psychosocial risk sources. This gives the interviewee an opportunity to record psychosocial risk sources that they were unable or unwilling to raise verbally.

The interviewer will also have to use their judgement with regard to the truthfulness of the interviewee. Interviewees can

overplay the negative effects that psychosocial risk sources are having on them so that, for example, they can take part in any psychosocial initiatives that the organisation is providing
underplay the negative effects that psychosocial risk sources are having on them so that, for example, they are not seen to be a troublemaker
overplay the positive effects that psychosocial risk sources are having on them so that, for example, they are seen to be a good team player
underplay the positive effects that psychosocial risk sources are having on them so that, for example, they can obtain a benefit being offered by the organisation.

Judgements on truthfulness will be a subjective judgement, but the ability to make such judgements is one of the competences required for this type of assessment. As with the results from risk psychosocial risk source identification interviews, there is little point taking action on the results of a scoring system when the interviewer has no confidence in the truthfulness of the responses given.

The simple scoring scheme shown in Table 23.1 – −2 to +2 – can be used in a variety of ways, including the following:

Intra-individual comparisons. For example, the relative effects on the individual of the different risk sources listed in the leftmost column.

Interindividual comparisons. For example, the effects on different individuals of the risk sources listed in the leftmost column.

Overall effect of a risk source on a group of individuals. For example, if a group of ten individuals was exposed to role ambiguity, the overall score for the group would range from −20 (everyone's well-being reduced a lot) through zero (no one is affected by the role ambiguity) to +20 (everyone's well-being increased a lot by the role ambiguity).

The use of these scores is discussed in Chapter 24 'Psychosocial threat and opportunity management' where they are used as a means of deciding on how to manage specific threats and opportunities.

The other methods for worker-focused proactive identification of psychosocial risk sources described in the *Identification of psychosocial risk sources* section can all make use of a form such as that shown in Table 23.1 to extend the method to cover assessment of effects. For example, the form can be used during focus group meetings.

Having assessed the effects of a particular psychosocial risk source, decisions have to be made with regard to any action required. This is dealt with in Chapter 24 'Psychosocial threat and opportunity management'.

Risk source-focused

In general, the risk source-focused methods for psychosocial risk source identification can only be used if they can be extended to enable the use of a form such as the one shown in Table 23.1. For example, health and safety risk assessments can include interviews dealing with well-being and wellness and the completion of Table 23.1 type forms. However, other methods such as analysis of absence data, and reviewing health and safety incident, and nonconformity reports and work records cannot readily be extended in this way.

The form in Table 23.1 can, however, be used to collect information on the effects of specific psychosocial risk sources and this use is discussed next.

It has been mentioned at various points in earlier chapters that dealing with all psychosocial risk sources when first setting up a psychosocial management system is rarely a practical option, and various suggestions have been made for ways to select your initial set of psychosocial risk sources. When you have made your selection, you can use a form such as the one illustrated in Table 23.2 to check the current effects of your selected psychosocial risk sources. The psychosocial risk

Table 23.2 Form for recording effects of specified psychosocial risk sources

Psychosocial risk source	What effect is this psychosocial risk source having on	Big −ve (−2)	Small −ve (−1)	No effect (0)	Small +ve (+1)	Large +ve (+2)
Role ambiguity	your wellness at work?					
	your well-being at work?					
	your colleagues' wellness at work?					
	your colleagues' well-being at work?					
Poor communication	your wellness at work?					
	your well-being at work?					
	your colleagues' wellness at work?					
	your colleagues' well-being at work?					
Inadequate equipment availability	your wellness at work?					
	your well-being at work?					
	your colleagues' wellness at work?					
	your colleagues' well-being at work?					

Source: Prepared by Tony Boyle for this book.

sources used for illustration in Table 23.2 are the first hazards of a psychosocial nature recorded in Tables 1, 2, and 3 of ISO 45003,[3] and they are for illustrative purposes only.

The form shown in Table 23.2 can also be used on an ongoing basis in the same ways that the form in Table 23.1 is used. The only difference is that you are choosing the psychosocial risk sources to include in the leftmost column; they are not being chosen by the workers being interviewed or surveyed.

Proactive assessment of psychosocial risk sources is the preferred approach, but it must be backed up by reactive assessment which is dealt with in the next subsection.

Reactive psychosocial risk source assessment

Typically, reactive reporting processes in traditional health and safety are restricted to the reporting of adverse events. However, an ideal psychosocial reactive reporting process would also include the reporting of factors that are having, or could have, a positive effect on well-being or wellness.

The various methods described earlier for reactive psychosocial hazard identification can usually be extended to include reporting the effects on the individuals of the psychosocial risk source being reported.

The practicalities of psychosocial reactive reporting processes are discussed in Chapter 25 'Psychosocial measurement, analysis, and evaluation'.

Establishing the pattern of effects of psychosocial risk sources

Assuming that a group of individuals has been exposed to role ambiguity, and that some version of Table 23.2 has been used to assess the effects on their well-being and wellness, the following scenarios for worker well-being are possible.

All scores are zero. That is, the psychosocial risk source is having no effect on the well-being of any of the individuals exposed. In this scenario, there are only the unaffected.

All scores are negative. That is, the psychosocial risk source is having a detrimental effect on the well-being of all of the individuals exposed. In this scenario, there are only victims.

All scores are positive. That is, the psychosocial risk source is having a beneficial effect on the well-being of all of the individuals exposed. In this scenario, there are only beneficiaries.

There is a mixture of negative and zero scores. That is, the psychosocial risk source is having a detrimental effect on the well-being of some of the individuals exposed, but not all of them. In this scenario, there are victims and unaffected.

There is a mixture of positive and zero scores. That is, the psychosocial risk source is having a beneficial effect on the well-being of some of the individuals exposed, but not all of them. In this scenario, there are beneficiaries and unaffected.

Table 23.3 Form for recording pattern of effects of risk sources

Psychosocial risk source	What effect is this psychosocial risk source having on	Big −ve (−2)	Small −ve (−1)	No effect (0)	Small +ve (+1)	Large +ve (+2)
Role ambiguity	your wellness at work?			20		
	your well-being at work?	2	8	10		
	your colleagues' wellness at work?		2	18		
	your colleagues' well-being at work?	8	10	2		

Source: Prepared by Tony Boyle for this book.

There is a mixture of negative, positive, and zero scores. In this scenario, there are victims, beneficiaries, and unaffected.

These scenarios also apply to worker wellness, colleagues' well-being, and colleagues' wellness, but, for clarity of explanation, the following discussion is restricted to worker well-being.

In the last three scenarios just described, account will also have to be taken of the proportion of individuals in each category. For example, if there is a mixture of negative and zero scores the extremes are

one zero score and the rest of the scores are negative
one negative score and the rest of the scores are zero.

It can be helpful to use a form to record the pattern of individuals' scores for a particular psychosocial risk source, and an example of such a form is shown in Table 23.3. The completed form in Table 23.3 is based on a group of 20 individuals exposed to role ambiguity to illustrate how the form is used.

In practice, it is likely to be preferable to restrict the use of this technique to worker well-being. This is particularly helpful if your psychosocial risk sources are unlikely to have a significant effect on worker wellness.

Completing the type of form shown in Table 23.3 concludes the assessment process for the psychosocial risk source, you then move on to the management process dealt with in Chapter 24.

Systemic psychosocial threats

Introduction to systemic psychosocial threats

It is unfortunately the case that certain psychosocial risk sources are, or become, systemic psychosocial threats in organisations. Systemic, like most technical terms, has various definitions, but for the purposes of this book, a systemic psycho-social threat is one that is part of the organisation's culture – the way we do things round here.

There are various well-documented examples of systemic psychosocial threats. In the UK, for example, there have been reports of racism in the Metropolitan Police and bullying in various government departments. In a typical organisa-tion, there will be systemic psychosocial threats that occur only in parts of the organisation, and these will be referred to as local systemic psychosocial threats. Examples of these local systemic psychosocial threats are given later in this section.

The difficulty with these local systemic psychosocial threats is that dealing with them requires a range of actions by a wide range of individuals. If you have a bully in your organisation, you have a focus for your psychosocial threat elim-ination – if you have a culture of bullying, you may find it difficult to know where to start.

This section deals with the various issues that have to be addressed if systemic psychosocial threats are to be identified and assessed. The actions needed to deal with systemic psychosocial threats are discussed in Chapter 24 'Psychosocial threat and opportunity management'.

Identifying and assessing systemic psychosocial threats

The discussion that follows addresses the concerns in larger organisations where only part of the organisation is involved in a systemic psychosocial threat. However, the problems being addressed in part of a large organisation may also occur across the whole of a smaller organisation.

The sorts of findings from interviews and surveys, or even from informal discussions, that may suggest there is a local systemic psychosocial threat include the following.

My boss is a bully – but all the bosses are.
They deliberately don't set clear objectives.
It's mushroom management around here.
No one will give the bosses bad news.
You can't trust the people you work with to do the right thing.
Most of the men are sexist, but you get used to it.
Racist language is put down as 'friendly banter'.

When there are such findings, the risk source-focused assessment methods described earlier in the chapter can be used to determine the extent and severity of the effects of the threat. This can be done as a single risk source survey about, for example, bullying or sexism, but it is usually more useful to use the survey to cover a number of relevant psychosocial risk sources and allow an 'other' option to identify and assess psychosocial risk sources that you may not have considered relevant to the groups being surveyed.

How to manage systemic psychosocial threats is dealt with in Chapter 24.

Traditional risk assessment and well-being and wellness

Traditional health and safety risk assessment procedures do not take into account the possible effects on well-being and wellness. The authors have seen over the years examples of the devastating effect that a fatality or a serious injury can have on the well-being and wellness of colleagues of the victim. At the extreme, there are workers who suffered such severe post-traumatic stress disorder (PTSD) that they never worked again. However, the authors have never seen a health and safety risk assessment procedure that has taken this sort of effect into account.

It is possible to include these effects on well-being and wellness, and one such way is discussed next. For the purposes of this discussion, 'individuals affected' have been referred to, and these include co-workers and interested parties who

witness the accident

are first responders or are otherwise involved in the aftermath of the accident

are the managerial workers responsible for the injured worker, the accident site, and the activity during which the accident happened

investigate the causes of the accident and take part in any investigations and prosecutions by regulatory authorities

have a positive personal relationship with the injured individual

have to pass the site of the accident in the course of their work and are therefore repeatedly reminded of what happened.

Developing a psychosocial risk assessment matrix

The overall effect on well-being and wellness of individuals affected will depend on the likely number of individuals affected and the average (mean) severity of the effects on their well-being and wellness. This enables the preparation of a matrix in the same format as the matrices used in health and safety risk assessment, and Table 23.4 shows a suggested psychosocial risk assessment matrix.

Organisations should allocate values to the numbers on the axes so that the matrix suits their circumstances and their current health and safety risk assessment matrix. The values given for number of victims in Table 23.4 are for illustrative purposes only.

The average severity of the most likely effects on well-being and wellness is used on the severity axis in order to take into account individual differences in susceptibility to the psychosocial risk source, and organisations should provide descriptions of what is meant by the numbers. For example, a scale from 1 = No effect or very little effect to 5 = Effects bordering on, or reaching, clinical levels of harm. It is not appropriate to use the −2 to +2 scale described earlier in this chapter

Table 23.4 Psychosocial risk assessment matrix

		Average severity of the most likely effects on well-being and wellness				
		1	*2*	*3*	*4*	*5*
Likely number of victims	5 = >50	L	M	M	H	H
	4 = 21–50	L	M	M	H	H
	3 = 6–20	L	L	M	M	M
	2 = 2–5	L	L	L	L	M
	1 = 1	L	L	L	L	L

Source: Prepared by Tony Boyle for this book.

since there are unlikely to be positive effects on the well-being or wellness of the individuals affected.

Using a psychosocial risk assessment matrix

Determining the likely number of victims involves determining the numbers of individuals in the various categories of individuals affected listed earlier in this section, and any other individuals affected in particular circumstances.

In determining the average severity, it is important to take into account individual differences, in particular:

The differences between the assessor and the people affected. It is tempting to think 'this is how I would feel if the accident happened, therefore this is how the individuals affected will feel'. However, this is not an acceptable approach because it does not take into account the individual differences between you and the individuals affected.

The differences between the individuals who might suffer the accident. For example, an injury to, or the illness of, a long-known and well-liked colleague is likely to have more severe effects on the well-being of the affected individuals than an injury to someone they do not really know.

The differences between the individuals affected who you will be taking into account when estimating average severity. Individuals affected will react differently for a whole range of reasons, and the only way to find out how they might react is to ask them. However, this 'asking' has to be done in a structured way and requires certain competences if it is to be effective. The methods described earlier in this chapter can be used to assess the likely effects on well-being.

The value estimated for the psychosocial risk should be added to the value estimated for the health and safety risk to give an overall risk value. This may move the risk up one or more categories on the criteria scale given earlier, that is from low to medium or high, or from medium to high.

Like the vast majority of risk assessments, the assessment of psychosocial risk is subjective and health and safety professionals may be reluctant to adopt these techniques. However, Tony Boyle can remember the days before health and safety risk assessment was a feature of health and safety management, and the trials and tribulations of devising workable health and safety risk assessment processes that health and safety professionals could and would use. It seems that history may have to repeat itself in this respect if psychosocial risk assessment is to become as routine as traditional risk assessment.

References

1   British Standards Institution. *Risk management – guidelines*, BS ISO 31000, 2018. BSI 2018.
2   MobiSystems, Inc, *Oxford Dictionary*, version 15.8. Last accessed 17 January 2024.
3   British Standards Institution. *Occupational health and safety management – Psychological health and safety at work – Guidelines for managing psychosocial risks*, BSI ISO 45003, 2021. BSI 2021.

24 Psychosocial threat and opportunity management

Introduction

In a traditional health and safety management system, the title of this chapter would be *Risk control*. However, as was illustrated in Figure 1.2 – reproduced in this chapter as Figure 24.1 for ease of reference – risk control is only part of what is required in a psychosocial management system – opportunities also have to be taken into account.

In ISO 31000,[1] both threats and opportunities are dealt with in risk assessment, and the process for dealing with them is referred to as *risk treatment*. However, this term has not been used to avoid confusion between risk treatment and the various treatments used to deal with medical disorders and impaired well-being and wellness.

The term 'psychosocial threat and opportunity management' has been used to distinguish the processes needed for dealing with psychosocial risk sources from the processes used in the ISO 45001[2] risk control and the ISO 31000 risk treatment. However, all three sets of processes have some overlaps, and the chapter begins with a discussion of the need for objectives and criteria that is common to all three.

For the purposes of the psychosocial management system described in this book, psychosocial threat and opportunity management is, in effect, a change management process. If you are eliminating, or reducing the dose of, a psychosocial risk source, you are changing some aspect of an individual's activities or environment at work, and you should establish the likely effects of proposed changes to psychosocial risk sources before implementing them. The core of this chapter is the detailed requirements for this type of change management. However, it is also necessary to deal with perpetrators, victims, and beneficiaries as part of your psychosocial threat and opportunity management, and the requirements for this are also discussed in this chapter.

In summary, the contents of this chapter are as follows.

Traditional risk control
Psychosocial threat and opportunity objectives and criteria
Actions to deal with perpetrators, victims, and beneficiaries

DOI: 10.4324/9781003490555-26

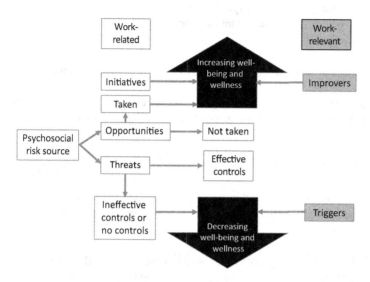

Figure 24.1 Influences on well-being and wellness.

Acting on the results of threat and opportunity assessment
Establishing likely effects of proposed changes

Each of these activities is dealt with in separate sections later in this chapter.

Traditional risk control

This section deals with the objectives organisations set for their psychosocial risk control and the criteria they use when setting these objectives.

Risk control objectives

Traditional health and safety risk assessment relies on two fundamental assumptions.

There is, in general, no need to take into account individual differences in vulnerability to the hazard. There are exceptions for particular classes of workers, for example pregnant workers and young workers are treated as special cases, but risk assessment within a particular class takes no account of individual differences within that class.
There are only threats from the hazard, not opportunities.

This means that risk can be expressed in terms of the likelihood of hazardous events and the severity of the most likely injury or ill health in the circumstances in which the hazardous event occurs. Typically, high, medium, and low risks are identified and organisations have risk control objectives as follows:

there will be no high risks in the organisation
medium risks will be kept under continual review and reduced to low when rea-
    sonably practicable

and the fact that low risks are accepted by the organisation is either stated or
implied.

For these objectives to be workable, there must be definitions of low, medium,
and high risk, and these definitions are the risk criteria discussed in the next
subsection.

Risk criteria

Risk criteria are usually described in a matrix in the form shown in Table 24.1.

The risk rating scale shown in Table 24.1 is then used to create risk criteria, for
example,

High > 15 (H) – the activity creating this risk must be stopped until risk control
    measures that reduce its risk to medium or low are implemented.
Medium 8–15 (M) – the activity creating this risk must be kept under review until
    risk control measures that reduce its risk to low have been implemented.
Low <8 (L) – no further risk control is required for this activity; the risk is accepted.

These risk criteria match up with the organisation's risk control objectives
described in the previous section.

However, if you accept that impaired well-being is sub-clinical mental ill health,
and impaired wellness is sub-clinical physical ill health, then the risk assessment
and control processes that use the ratings shown in Table 24.1, and their associated
objectives and risk criteria, preclude action being taken on well-being and wellness.
Impaired well-being and wellness will always be low risk and, therefore, no further
action will be required. This is recognised in ISO 45002[3], where one of the opportunities listed is

Table 24.1 Traditional health and safety risk criteria matrix[ii]

| | | Severity of the most likely injury or ill health in the circumstances | | | | |
		1	2	3	4	5
Likelihood of the	5	L	M	M	H	H
hazardous event	4	L	M	M	H	H
	3	L	L	M	M	M
	2	L	L	L	M	M
	1	L	L	L	L	L

Source: Prepared by Tony Boyle for this book.

improving well-being even where no significant risks have been determined.

It is worth restating that the ISO 45003[4] definition of psychosocial risk is the

combination of the likelihood of occurrence of exposure to work-related hazard(s) of a psychosocial nature and the severity of injury and ill-health that can be caused by these hazards.

This implies that you do not do anything about psychosocial hazards until they start to cause injury and ill health. As was pointed out earlier in this book, while this is a strategy you can adopt, it is not the one on which the psychosocial management system described in this book is based. The psychosocial threat and opportunity management processes described in this chapter are based on the assumption that the organisation is managing the psychosocial risk sources causing impaired well-being and wellness before these risk sources cause injury and ill health.

What has to be done to implement this strategy is to devise psychosocial risk source management processes that allow for action to be taken on severities of harm that would be considered too low to require action in traditional health and safety. In addition, these psychosocial risk processes must take into account individual differences in vulnerability and the existence of opportunities associated with psychosocial risk sources.

What these processes might look like is dealt with later in the chapter, but first it is necessary to deal with psychosocial threat and opportunity objectives and psychosocial threat and opportunity risk criteria.

Psychosocial threat and opportunity objectives and criteria

There is little point in setting up a psychosocial threat and opportunity management procedure without a clear, and agreed, statement of what you want to do with regard to psychosocial threats and opportunities. This section deals with the issues you will have to take into account.

As was discussed in Chapter 11 'The psychosocial management system terminology', the ISO 45003 definition of psychosocial risk is not suitable for the present purposes, and psychosocial risk was redefined as *the effect of uncertainty on psychosocial objectives*. To manage psychosocial risk, therefore, you need to decide what your psychosocial objectives will be with regard to psychosocial threat and opportunity management. Some of the broader issues to be taken into account were discussed in Chapter 22 'Psychosocial risk sources', but the present chapter focuses on the details required for practical psychosocial threat and opportunity management.

Psychosocial objectives are objectives which, if achieved, will maintain or improve the well-being and wellness of workers and interested parties. It would be possible, therefore, to have a psychosocial objective to 'maintain and improve the well-being and wellness of workers and interested parties'. However, ISO 45001 states that objectives should be *measurable (if practicable) or capable of performance evaluation*. As has been seen, well-being and wellness are relatively straightforward to measure – assuming the cooperation of the workers and interested parties within the scope of the psychosocial management system. This means that it is possible to set measurable objectives, for example,

All workers and interested parties with WHO 5 scores less than 52%[i] will be offered access to a Well-being counsellor – at no charge to the worker and in work time.
All workers and interested parties with specified wellness impairments (e.g., being overweight or having high blood pressure) will be offered access to appropriate remedial help.

Translating these objectives into objectives for psychosocial threat and opportunity management would produce the following objectives:

all psychosocial risk sources that significantly impair worker or interested party well-being or wellness will be subject to effective psychosocial risk control
all psychosocial risk sources that do not significantly impair worker or interested party well-being or wellness will be kept under review
all psychosocial risk sources that significantly improve worker or interested party well-being or wellness will be effectively exploited at all appropriate points in the organisation.

It then remains to define significant and effective.
If you are using WHO 5, you can do this easily. For example,

A significant decrease in well-being is a reduction of 10% or more in the WHO 5 score.
A significant increase in well-being is an increase of 10% or more in the WHO 5 score.
Effective in the context of psychosocial risk control is a control that increases an individual's WHO 5 score to 52% or more.

However, in practical psychosocial threat and opportunity management, it is likely that using the WHO 5 Index will be rather unwieldy, and what is needed is a simpler scale such as that introduced in Chapter 23 as Table 23.1. The first part of Table 23.1 is reproduced in this chapter as Table 24.2 for ease of reference.
Significant and effective can then be defined as follows:

A significant decrease in well-being is a reduction of one or more.
A significant increase in well-being is an increase of one or more.
Effective in the context of psychosocial risk control is a control that increases an individual's score to zero or more.

Table 24.2 Form for recording effects of psychosocial risk sources

Psychosocial risk source	What effect is this psychosocial risk source having on	Big −ve (−2)	Small −ve (−1)	No effect (0)	Small +ve (+1)	Large +ve (+2)
	Your wellness?					
	Your well-being?					

Source: Prepared by Tony Boyle for this book.

Actions to deal with perpetrators, victims, and beneficiaries

Chapter 10 'The people' provided the background information on perpetrators, victims, and beneficiaries, but a psychosocial threat and opportunity management process requires formal, agreed statements of the actions to be taken with regard to these three categories of individual. The content of these statements is discussed in the next three subsections.

Perpetrators

Dealing effectively with perpetrators requires the following.

Accurate identification of the perpetrators.
Detailed investigation of the causes of the perpetrators' behaviour.
The provision of remedial action to change perpetrators' behaviour and checking on the effectiveness of this remedial action.
Where necessary, proportionate punishment.

If these arrangements are not in place, or are not properly carried out, additional impairment of well-being and wellness can be caused. For example:

Where perpetrators are not identified, victims suffer not only from the perpetrator's behaviour but also from the knowledge that the organisation is doing nothing about the negative effects on their well-being and wellness. This is also the case when there is no remedial action or proportionate punishment.
A special case occurs when the perpetrators are top management, or senior managerial workers, but action is taken only with regard to workers at a lower level – the so-called 'deputy heads will roll' syndrome.

Unless there are already appropriate procedures in place for dealing with perpetrators of the psychosocial risk sources within the scope of your psychosocial management system, you should not attempt to identify perpetrators. You should wait until there is a documented procedure for dealing with them, and this procedure has been agreed and promulgated throughout your organisation. This is crucially important when the psychosocial risk source is, or may be, systemic. Unless everyone is aware that action will be taken, and the nature of this action, systemic psychosocial risk sources can only be dealt with in a piecemeal fashion, and this is unlikely to be effective.

Victims

Dealing effectively with victims requires the following.

Accurate identification of victims, including the identification of individuals falsely claiming to be victims.

The provision of treatment for the victims' impaired well-being and/or wellness and checks on the efficacy of this treatment.

Where appropriate, compensation for past impaired well-being and/or wellness.

As with the procedure for dealing with perpetrators, you should have an agreed procedure for dealing with victims that has been promulgated throughout your organisation before you begin to identify and deal with victims. As with the arrangements for dealing with perpetrators, this is particularly important for actual, or suspected, systemic psychosocial risk sources.

Beneficiaries

Dealing effectively with beneficiaries requires the following.

Accurate identification of beneficiaries, including the identification of individuals falsely claiming to be beneficiaries.

Where appropriate, compensation for loss of benefits if the psychosocial risk source is to be eliminated, or the dose reduced, and checks on the adequacy of this compensation.

It is particularly important to have an agreed procedure for dealing with beneficiaries because, for these individuals, eliminating or reducing their exposure to the psychosocial risk source will have a negative effect on their well-being and/ or wellness. This means that unless appropriate action is taken, this elimination or reduction will be contrary to your psychosocial threat and opportunity management objectives.

Acting on the results of threat and opportunity assessment

For the purposes of this section, it is helpful to divide the results of threat and opportunity assessments into four categories.

Assessment where all the responses were positive or zero, that is, there were only beneficiaries and unaffected.

Assessment where all the responses were zero, that is, there were only unaffected.

Assessment where all the responses were negative or zero, that is, there were only victims and unaffected.

Assessment where the responses were mixed, and there were beneficiaries, victims, and unaffected.

The actions required for the first two categories are the same, and they are dealt with in the first subsection below. The other two categories require different actions, and these are dealt with in separate subsections.

Only beneficiaries and unaffected

Where there are only beneficiaries and unaffected, the obvious action is to leave the psychosocial risk source in place but keep its assessment under review. This is a similar approach to that used for low risks in traditional health and safety risk control.

However, it may be the case that the psychosocial risk source is mandated for elimination, or elimination or dose reduction is considered desirable for some other reason. Where this is the case, it will be necessary to establish the likely effects on well-being and wellness of any proposed elimination or dose reduction. Establishing the likely effects of proposed changes is required for all of the categories of results of threat and opportunity assessment, so it is dealt with in a separate *Establishing likely effects of proposed changes* section later in this chapter.

Irrespective of the method used for establishing the likely effects of proposed elimination or dose reduction, the results will be one of the following.

The change will have a positive effect on the individuals' well-being and wellness. For example, some of the unaffected may become beneficiaries as a result of the change.

The change will have no effect on the individuals' well-being and wellness.

The change will have a negative effect on the individuals' well-being and wellness. For example, some of the unaffected may become victims as a result of the change.

For the first two results, there is no well-being or wellness reason for not proceeding with the elimination or dose reduction of the psychosocial risk source. However, if the elimination or dose reduction of the psychosocial risk source will have negative effects, then further action will be required to compensate beneficiaries who will have their well-being or wellness impaired, and any unaffected who may become victims. The nature of these actions will depend on your organisation's arrangements for dealing with victims, as discussed in the previous section of this chapter.

Only victims and unaffected

Where there are only victims and unaffected, establishing the likely effects of a proposed change will result in one of the following outcomes.

The change will have a positive effect on the individuals' well-being and wellness.
  For example, some of the victims may become unaffected or beneficiaries as a result of the change.
The change will have no effect on the individuals' well-being and wellness.
The change will have a negative effect on the individuals' well-being and wellness.
  For example, some of the unaffected may become victims as a result of the change.

These outcomes are similar in nature to the outcomes for the only beneficiaries and unaffected scenario described in the previous subsection, but the actions required are different.

Where the change will have a positive effect, the question to ask is whether the effect is sufficiently strong to satisfy your psychosocial threat and opportunity objectives. Where the effect is sufficiently strong, there is no well-being or wellness reason for not proceeding with the elimination or dose reduction of the risk source. However, if the effect is not sufficiently strong, you should proceed as if the change was having no effect, as described next.

Where the change will have no effect, or the change will have a negative effect, it will be necessary to investigate the reasons why this is the case. In effect, you have a psychosocial threat that is impairing individuals' well-being and/or wellness, and your proposed psychosocial risk control measure (removing the psychosocial threat or reducing its dose) is not going to work and may make matters worse. The techniques required for this type of investigation are dealt with in Chapter 27 'Psychosocial investigation'.

Beneficiaries, victims, and unaffected

Where there are beneficiaries, victims, and unaffected, there are various possible approaches, and three of them are described in this subsection under the following titles.

Dealing with outliers
Individual by individual approach
Greater good approach

Dealing with outliers

The ODE[5] defines an outlier as *a person or thing situated away or detached from the main body or system*, and for the present purposes an outlier would be

a victim in a group otherwise consisting of beneficiaries and unaffected
a beneficiary in a group otherwise consisting of victims and unaffected.

However, as the group size increases, it is possible to allow for more than one outlier in the group. A rule of thumb is to allow for up to 5% of outliers so that, for example, up to five outliers could be allowed for in a group of 100.

The approach when dealing with outliers is to

deal with majority of the group as only victims and unaffected, or only beneficiaries and unaffected, as the case may be, by following the guidance given in the earlier subsections, and

deal with the outlying beneficiaries or victims according to your organisation's agreed arrangements for dealing with beneficiaries and victims, or deal with them on an individual-by-individual basis, as described in the next subsection.

Individual-by-individual approach

Where there is a mixture of beneficiaries and victims but no preponderance of one category to enable the dealing with outliers approach, then an individual-by-individual approach is needed, and this is described next.

The practical problem to be solved is the fact that eliminating or reducing the dose of the psychosocial risk source will improve the well-being and/or wellness of some of the individuals currently exposed to the psychosocial risk source and reduce the well-being and/or wellness of some of the others.

This problem can only be resolved if you have detailed information on the reasons why eliminating or reducing the dose of the psychosocial risk source will have these effects and, because of individual differences, the only way to collect this information is to ask the individuals concerned. Collecting this information can be combined with questions about possible ways of solving the problem by asking individuals for their ideas on what could be done to solve the problem. This can be illustrated using role ambiguity as the psychosocial risk source.

Beneficiaries of role ambiguity may say that they like it because it allows them to choose the way they carry out their tasks and that any change that prevents this will impair their well-being.

Victims of role ambiguity may say that they do not like it because they never know whether they are 'doing the right thing' and that clarity on what is required will improve their well-being.

The solution could be to substitute flexibility for ambiguity. For example, a number of different, but all correct, ways of carrying out tasks could be specified. If these ways included all those currently used by beneficiaries, the beneficiaries would not suffer impairment, and victims could choose one or more of the ways and know that they are doing the right thing.

The solution or solutions identified may not please all of the individuals concerned, but it may please enough of them to allow the dealing with outliers approach to be adopted. What to do if no solution can be found is discussed in the next subsection.

Greater good approach

The greater good approach, also known as the least harm approach or, more cynically, the 'if all else fails approach', is used when none of the other approaches has worked or will work.

Where the options are simply to leave things as they are or to eliminate the psychosocial risk source or reduce its dose, then this approach compares the pattern of beneficiaries, victims, and unaffected as it is now, and how it is likely to be after the elimination or dose reduction. There will be beneficiaries, victims, and unaffected, both before and after, but they are likely to be different individuals, and within each category there will be changes, for example, individuals moving from a score of -1 to a score of -2 or *vice versa*.

Your decision on whether or not to take action should depend on the nature and extent of the likely changes in well-being and wellness.

If the main changes are improvements in well-being and wellness, then there is good reason for elimination or dose reduction, even if the improvements will be quite small.

If the main changes are reductions in well-being and wellness, then there is good reason for leaving things as they are. If the psychosocial risk source is one that has been mandated for elimination, it will be necessary to do further work to deal with individuals whose well-being or wellness is going to be adversely affected by the elimination or dose reduction.

When there are options in addition to simply leaving things as they are or eliminating the psychosocial risk source, or reducing its dose, the work required is more extensive, but the same principles apply. You establish the pattern of the likely changes in well-being and wellness for each option and implement the option that will produce the greater good, or do the least harm, as the case may be. As with elimination or dose reduction, action will be required to deal with individuals whose well-being or wellness is going to be adversely affected by the elimination or dose reduction.

The investigation techniques described in Chapter 27 'Psychosocial investigation' are likely to be required at various points during the greater good approach.

Establishing likely effects of proposed changes

In the discussions so far, assessing the current effect of a psychosocial risk source on an individual's well-being and wellness has been treated as a separate process from determining the likely effects on an individual's well-being and wellness of a change to a psychosocial risk source. For ease of reference, from now on the results of these two processes will be referred to as the before and after measures of an individual's well-being and wellness.

Table 24.3 Form for collecting information on effects of a proposed change

Proposed change			Big −ve (−2)	Small −ve (−1)	No effect (0)	Small +ve (+1)	Large +ve (+2)	Don't know
Remove role ambiguity	Wellness	Before change						
		After change						
	Well-being	Before change						
		After change						

Source: Prepared by Tony Boyle for this book.

Psychosocial before measures such as those described in Chapter 23 are an important part of a psychosocial management system since, for example, they are used to assess the current state of well-being and wellness of workers and interested parties. However, they have two disadvantages when they are used as both a before and after measure in psychosocial threat and opportunity management.

They are administratively difficult because you have to match up the before and after forms for named individuals and then compare the results on each of the pairs of forms.

They cannot be used for anonymous measuring because of the need to match up the before and after forms for named individuals.

For these reasons, when it is known, or suspected, that a change to a psychosocial risk source will be necessary, the before measurement should be replaced by a combined before and after measurement, and a form such as that shown in Table 24.3 can be used in this way.

There is an argument for not including the 'Don't know' column in the form shown in Table 24.3 because it provides an easy option for individuals who are unwilling to volunteer information on their well-being and wellness. You will have to make a judgement in any given set of circumstances whether to allow the 'Don't know' option.

As with the forms used for psychosocial threat and opportunity assessment, it will be necessary to provide the individuals involved in before and after measurement with clear instructions on how they should use the form.

Similarly, in the way that you need a form for recording the pattern of effects of risk sources at the end of a threat and opportunity assessment, you need a form for recording the pattern of likely shifts in well-being and wellness as a result of a

Table 24.4 Form for recording pattern of likely shifts in wellness

Wellness	Proposed change	Remove role ambiguity				
	After					
Before	*Big −ve (−2)*	*Small −ve (−1)*	*No effect (0)*	*Small +ve (+1)*	*Large +ve (+2)*	*Don't know*
Big −ve (−2)						
Small −ve (−1)						
No effect (0)						
Small +ve (+1)						
Large +ve (+2)						

Source: Prepared by Tony Boyle for this book.

proposed change. Forms such as those shown in Tables 24.4 and 24.5 can be used for this purpose.

Note the following about Tables 23.4 and 23.5:

Separate tables are used for wellness and well-being to facilitate analysis. It is possible to use a single table that includes wellness and well-being, but such tables tend to be too 'busy' and can result in error-prone analysis.

The tables are used in the same way as Table 23.3. That is, you record an individual's change by adding that individual to the relevant cell in Table 24.4 or 24.5 as the case may be. The most convenient way of doing this is to use the five-bar-gate approach and convert to numbers when you have entered all of your data – sometimes low-tech works best!

Tables 24.3, 24.4, and 24.5 are intended for use where there is only one option being tested – the elimination or dose reduction of the psychosocial risk source. However, there can be circumstances where you wish to test the likely effects of a number of different options. Where this is the case, a form such as that shown in Table 24.6 can be used.

You will have to prepare separate forms showing the pattern of likely shifts in well-being and wellness resulting from each of the proposed changes using the forms shown in Tables 24.4 and 24.5. Comparison of the content of these completed forms will show which, if any, of the proposed changes is the preferred option.

Table 24.5 Form for recording pattern of likely shifts in well-being

Well-being	Proposed change	Remove role ambiguity				
	After					
Before	*Big −ve (−2)*	*Small −ve (−1)*	*No effect (0)*	*Small +ve (+1)*	*Large +ve (+2)*	*Don't know*
Big -ve (−2)						
Small −ve (−1)						
No effect (0)						
Small +ve (+1)						
Large +ve (+2)						

Source: Prepared by Tony Boyle for this book.

Table 24.6 Form for collecting information on effects of different proposed changes

Proposed changes		*Big −ve (−2)*	*Small −ve (−1)*	*No effect (0)*	*Small +ve (+1)*	*Large +ve (+2)*	*Don't know*
	Wellness before change						
	Well-being before change						
Proposed change 1	Wellness after change						
	Well-being after change						
Proposed change 2	Wellness after change						
	Well-being after change						
Proposed change 3	Wellness after change						
	Well-being after change						

Source: Prepared by Tony Boyle for this book.

Notes

i   See Chapter 5 for details of the WHO index and the rationale for the 52%.

ii   In traditional health and safety, the axes of the matrix are often just labelled *likelihood* and *severity*, with no definition of 'likelihood of what' or 'severity of what'. The problems this creates and why the axes labels in Table 24.1 are used are discussed in Tony Boyle's *Health and safety: Risk management* book.[6]

References

1   British Standards Institution. *Risk management – Guidelines*, BS ISO 31000, 2018. BSI 2018.

2   British Standards Institution. *Occupational health and safety management systems – Requirements with guidance for use*, BSI ISO 45001, 2018. BSI 2018.

3   British Standards Institution. *Occupational health and safety management systems – General guidelines for the implementation of ISO 45001:2018*, BSI ISO 45002, 32023. BSI 2023.

4   British Standards Institution. *Occupational health and safety management – Psychological health and safety at work – Guidelines for managing psychosocial risks*, BSI ISO 45003, 2021. BSI 2021.

5   MobiSystems, Inc, *Oxford Dictionary*, version 15.8. Last accessed 17 January 2024.

6   Boyle T. *Health and safety: Risk management* (5th edition). Routledge 2019.

25 Psychosocial measurement, analysis, and evaluation

Introduction

There is no general agreement about what is meant by the three terms: measurement, analysis, and evaluation. Therefore, it is necessary to begin this chapter with a section describing how these terms will be used in this book. There is also much confusion over the pairs of terms numeric–non-numeric, qualitative–quantitative, and subjective–objective, and an attempt has been made to clear up this confusion in a section dealing with these pairs of terms. The chapter also has sections dealing with

what to measure and how to measure it
analysis
evaluation.

Terms and definitions

ISO 45001[1] defines measurement as a *process to determine a value*, but it gives no definitions for analysis or evaluation. The ODE[2] defines analysis as the *detailed examination of the elements or structure of something*, and it defines evaluation as *the making of a judgement about the amount, number, or value of something*. All of which is pretty abstract. The threat and opportunity management process discussed in Chapter 24 will be used to illustrate how these terms will be used in this book.

Measurement. You measure well-being and wellness and there are various instruments for carrying out these measurements. For example, the WHO 5 Index[3] is used for measuring well-being, and a tape measure is used for measuring waist size. Ideally, measurements should produce objective, numeric results, such as waist size, but measures of well-being are subjective and can be numeric or non-numeric.

Analysis. You analyse the results of your measurement in various ways depending on your purpose. If your purpose is, for example, to ensure that all your workers' well-being is positive, then your analysis will include identifying workers with negative well-being and, if necessary, the causes of their negative well-being.

DOI: 10.4324/9781003490555-27

Evaluation. Your evaluation is, effectively, deciding on what you are going to do about the results of your measurement and analysis. In the example being used, this will involve deciding on which workers will be offered remedial action, and the nature and extent of the remedial action to be offered.

There are descriptions of analysis and evaluation in ISO 31000[4] as follows.

The purpose of risk analysis is to comprehend the nature of risk and its characteristics including, where appropriate, the level of risk.

The purpose of risk evaluation is to support decisions. Risk evaluation involves comparing the results of the risk analysis with the established risk criteria to determine where additional action is required.

These more formal descriptions are helpful because they emphasise the importance of having criteria against which to evaluate the results of analysis. However, risk criteria are only one of the types of criterion required in psychosocial risk management and other types of criterion are discussed later in this chapter.

Pairs of terms

ISO 45001 and ISO 45003[5] both use the phrase *qualitative and quantitative* but provide no definitions. The ODE defines qualitative as *relating to, measuring, or measured by the quality of something rather than its quantity* and quality as *the standard of something as measured against other things of a similar kind.* The ODE definition of quantitative is *relating to, measuring, or measured by the quantity of something rather than its quality.*

The difference between the two types of measures can be illustrated using the WHO[6] definitions for overweight and obese, which are as follows:

A body mass index (BMI) over 25 is considered overweight, and over 30 is obese.

Describing someone as overweight is qualitative – they are heavier than other people – describing someone as having a BMI of 27 is quantitative – it is a measured (and calculated) quantity.

This example also illustrates the difference between numeric and non-numeric measures. Defining 'overweight' as 'having a BMI between 26 and 30' means that you have a numeric way of describing an overweight individual. This is in addition to the non-numeric, but still defined, term overweight. However, practitioners often allocate numeric values to qualitative measures for ease of analysis, as is done with the WHO 5 *well-being index* and the numeric scales used for psychosocial threat and opportunity assessment and management described in Chapters 23 and 24.

The third pair of terms is subjective–objective. This pair is best thought of as a way of measuring, rather than a type of measure. If you look at someone and decide they are overweight, that is subjective measurement. If you measure an individual's weight using scales, their height using a tape measure, and do the necessary calculation to arrive at their BMI, then that is objective measurement.

Note the following about these three pairs of words.

In an ideal world, all measures would be quantitative numeric measures, measured objectively. However, this is not possible in psychosocial risk management because all measures of well-being are qualitative and subjectively measured. In contrast, all wellness measures can be quantitative numeric measures, and they can be measured objectively.

Just because a measure is numeric does not mean it is quantitative. For example, as was seen in Chapter 24, the effects of psychosocial risk sources could be measured on a numeric scale, −2 to +2, or on a qualitative scale, large negative to large positive. Using a numeric scale makes analyses easier, but it does not make the measure quantitative.

When deciding on what you are going to measure as part of your psychosocial management system, you should be clear about the nature of your measures and aim for quantitative numeric measures where possible and try to identify ways in which they can be measured objectively. The use of the various types of measure is discussed in more detail in the next section.

What to measure and how to measure it

ISO 45001 requires organisations to determine what needs to be measured and, although this requirement is not carried over to ISO 45003, determining what you are going to measure is an essential part of setting up a psychosocial management system. In part, this is because there are so many things that you could measure that it is impractical to measure them all, and you have to be selective. This section describes the essential elements that have to be measured as part of a psychosocial management system and suggests possible additions to these elements. This description is based on the assumption that there is worker agreement to the measuring processes involved and that there are suitable arrangements for individual workers to 'opt out' if they wish.

When setting up a measuring process, it is helpful to divide the required measurements into two categories.

Measuring whether you are achieving what you set out to achieve.
Measuring whether you are doing what you said you would do in order to achieve what you set out to achieve.

Both types of measurement have to be in place because:

Saying you will achieve something and then not checking whether or not you are achieving it is poor management practice.

If you do not measure conformity with what you said you would do, then you will not know whether or not what you said you would do was relevant to your achievement. There are two main scenarios.

You may be achieving what you set out to achieve but not doing what you said you would do, in which case, what you said you would do is not relevant. For example, if you intended using a *Well-being and wellness handbook* as your main method of maintaining worker awareness of well-being and wellness issues, and you find that worker awareness of these issues is high despite the handbook not having been issued, then expenditure on preparing and distributing the handbook will not provide value for money. You need to find out what is maintaining worker awareness of well-being and wellness issues and make use of this instead.

You may not be achieving what you set out to achieve despite doing what you said you would do, in which case, what you said you would do is not the proper approach and should be changed. For example, if you are using a *Well-being and wellness handbook* as your main method of maintaining worker awareness of well-being and wellness issues, and worker awareness of these issues is poor despite them having read the handbook, then there is something wrong with the handbook, and you need to revise it or adopt another strategy for maintaining worker awareness of well-being and wellness issues.

The next two subsections deal with measuring what you want to achieve and measuring whether you are doing what you said you would do.

What you want to achieve

Different organisations will want to achieve different things with their psychosocial management system, which means that it is not possible to give a definitive list of measures for what organisations want to achieve. However, a useful rule of thumb is to identify all the things where a judgement will have to be made on success or failure, and what follows is an outline process for doing this.

It is best to begin with the intended outcomes of the psychosocial management system since these set out the fundamental things the organisation wishes to achieve with its psychosocial management system. The following intended outcomes were used for illustration in Chapter 15.

Maximise [optimise] the well-being and wellness of workers [and defined interested parties].

Minimise [reduce] [eliminate] the adverse effect of work and the workplaces on the well-being and wellness of workers [and defined interested parties].

Maximise [optimise] [promote] the positive effect of work and the workplaces on the well-being and wellness of workers [and defined interested parties].

The fulfilment of psychosocial legal requirements and other psychosocial requirements.

The achievement of psychosocial objectives.

All of these intended outcomes will have to have means of measurement in place, and the means for each of the outcomes are discussed next.

Well-being

Two possible measures of well-being have already been described, the WHO 5 *well-being index* and the five-point scale introduced in Chapter 23 'Psychosocial threat and opportunity assessment'. However, there is a range of other well-being measures that could be used, including the following.

WHO-10 *well-being index.*[7] As its title suggests, this measure is an extended version of the WHO-5 *well-being index* described in Chapter 3. It can be used to obtain more detailed information on the factors contributing to the state of an individual's well-being.

Warwick-Edinburgh *Mental Wellbeing Scale 7 item.*[8] This is one of a number of scales produced by academics for research purposes that can also be used in organisations. The seven statements in the scale are as follows:

I've been feeling optimistic about the future
I've been feeling useful
I've been feeling relaxed
I've been dealing with problems well
I've been thinking clearly
I've been feeling close to other people
I've been able to make up my own mind about things

Warwick-Edinburgh *Mental Wellbeing Scale 14 item.*[9] This is an extended version of the seven-point scale and is used in similar ways to the WHO-10 *well-being index* to obtain more detail of an individual's well-being.

There are numerous other instruments for measuring well-being, some of them intended for use in specific types of organisations such as health care. It is worth doing an online search, or having a discussion with someone with expertise in this topic, to see if there is a measure that would be particularly suitable for your organisation. You could also seek expert assistance with developing your own well-being measuring instrument tailored to the needs of your organisation.

The majority of measures of well-being can be used in a variety of ways, but they are all fundamentally self-report instruments – they rely on individuals giving honest responses to the statement or questions used in the instrument.

As has been seen in earlier chapters, these instruments can be used for a variety of purposes, including the following.

To measure an individual's well-being as a diagnostic aid or to test the effectiveness of an improver.
As part of a psychosocial process such as psychosocial threat and opportunity assessment or psychosocial threat and opportunity management.

To test the effectiveness of an initiative by doing a before and after survey of all or a sample of those taking part in the initiative.

To assess the general level of well-being across all, or part, of the organisation by asking all, or a sample of, workers and interested parties to take part.

Irrespective of the purpose for which they are used, an important feature is whether respondents will be identified. It is usually the case that more honest responses are obtained when surveys allow for anonymous responses, and this is the preferred option where anonymity will not make the measurement valueless. For example, a well-being survey across the organisation will produce valuable data even if the identities of individual respondents are not known, but this is not the case with, for example, a survey to identify victims of a psychosocial threat so that they can be compensated.

In general, it is better to get accurate data on well-being, and if you think this can only be done if anonymity is guaranteed, then you should make arrangements for ensuring anonymity. This may best be done by having an external organisation collect and analyse the data on your behalf, and there are organisations that specialise in this type of work. It is worth looking at the websites for these organisations as they provide a range of well-being-related products and services that you may find useful for your psychosocial management system.

Wellness

Measuring wellness is much more straightforward than measuring well-being since all the common aspects of wellness are quantitative numeric measures capable of objective measurement. The more common aspects of wellness and their associated measures were dealt with in Chapter 4 'The disorders', and these are probably adequate when setting up a psychosocial management system. However, other measures and measuring instruments can be added later, for example:

Body fat and muscle mass. These are typically measured by instruments referred to as 'body composition monitors' that provide a value for what is being measured and guidance on what constitutes 'healthy' values.

Heart performance. Pulse and blood pressure measuring instruments are commonly used, but there are also instruments for measuring other aspects of a heart's performance. For example, there are now reasonably priced instruments that provide an electrocardiogram (ECG).

Because measuring many aspects of wellness is straightforward, all that is necessary in this chapter is to consider the development and use of a wellness index.

As has been seen in earlier chapters, an individual's state of well-being can be described by a single number, often referred to as a well-being score, and the availability of this score facilitates various analyses. However, the authors know of no equivalent index for wellness, and an online search for 'wellness index' produces indices for well-being alone, mixed well-being and wellness indices, and indices covering a much wider range of issues such as spiritual well-being.

For practical purposes, in psychosocial risk management what is required is a wellness index based on the wellness factors that are within the scope of the psychosocial management system, and that provides a single value (score) for an individual that can be used in association with their well-being score. Examples of possible wellness indices are given next.

WAIST MEASUREMENT AND PULSE RATE

The weight measurement and pulse rate index shown in Table 25.1 can be used where only simple measuring instruments (a tape measure and timing device) are available. It produces a wellness score between 0 – 'all is well' – and 4 – 'action may be required'. However, the direction of the scale is arbitrary and you can reverse it if you wish, so that 4 is 'all is well', and 0 is 'action may be required'.

BLOOD PRESSURE AND BLOOD OXYGEN

Where suitable measuring instruments are available, blood pressure and blood oxygen levels can be added to the index shown in Table 25.1 to produce a wellness index that gives a score between 0 and 10 – or 10 and 0 if you choose to reverse the scale. This index is shown in Table 25.2.

OTHER MEASURES

It is possible to add other measures to the index shown in Table 25.2, for example, lung function and blood sugar levels. However, you should only do this if you can ensure consistency of measurement across your organisation, for example, by using the same type of spirometry measuring instrument for all lung function tests.

Table 25.1 Weight measurement and pulse rate index

Measure		*0*	*1*	*2*	*Score*
Waist circumference[i]	**Men**	Below 94 cm (37 in)	Between 94 and 102 cm (37–40 in)	Over 102 cm (40 in)	
	Women	Below 80 cm (31.5 in)	Between 80 and 88 cm (31.5–34.6 in)	Over 88 cm (34.6 in)	
Resting pulse rate		60–100 per minute		Less than 60 or over 100 per minute	

Source: Prepared by Tony Boyle for this book.

Table 25.2 Four factor wellness index

Measure		0	1	2	Score
Waist circumference[i]	**Men**	Below 94 cm (37 in)	Between 94 and 102 cm (37–40 in)	Over 102 cm (40 in)	
	Women	Below 80 cm (31.5 in)	Between 80 and 88 cm (31.5–34.6 in)	Over 88 cm (34.6 in)	
Resting pulse rate		60–100 per minute		Less than 60 or over 100 per minute	
Blood pressure	**Systolic**	90 to 120	<90 or 121 – 180	Over 180	
	Diastolic	60 to 80	Under 60 or 81–110	Over 110	
Blood oxygen		Over 95%	92–95%	Under 92%	

Source: Prepared by Tony Boyle for this book.

Legal and other requirements

ISO 45001 defines the term *legal requirements and other requirements* as

> *legal requirements that an organization has to comply with and other requirements that an organization has to or chooses to comply with*

and it defines *requirement* as a

> *need or expectation that is stated, generally implied or obligatory.*

There are two notes to the definition of requirement.

> *Note 1 to entry: 'Generally implied' means that it is custom or common practice for the organization and interested parties that the need or expectation under consideration is implied.*

> *Note 2 to entry: A specified requirement is one that is stated, for example in documented information.*

These definitions mean that legal and other requirements cover a wide variety of topics and potentially a very large number of things to measure. To make this manageable, when setting up your psychosocial management system, you can use the following rules of thumb.

There will be a 'legal register' that lists all of the relevant legislation and describes the key requirements of each piece of legislation, and responsibility for keeping this legal register up-to-date is clearly allocated and conformity monitored.

A need or expectation will only become a management system 'other requirement' when it has been agreed by relevant interested parties and been recorded in the relevant part of the management system documented information. In ISO 45001 terminology, only *specified requirements* are allowed as *other requirements*.

In the authors' experience, the vast majority of management system *other requirements* are in the 'What you said you would do' category rather than the 'What you want to achieve' category, but the following requirements are relevant in this section.

The compliance with legal requirements of relevance to psychosocial risk management. Some of these requirements will be familiar from traditional health and safety, for example, work at height, but others, such as discrimination, are typically dealt with by HR personnel.

The needs and expectations (requirements) of workers and interested parties dealt with in Chapter 16 'Needs and expectations'.

The achievement of psychosocial objectives. This is dealt with in the next subsection.

Psychosocial objectives

Clause 6.2 of ISO 45003 is *Objectives to address psychosocial risk*, and it consists of the following paragraph.

> *The organization should:*
> *a) establish measurable objectives consistent with the policy;*
> *b) develop and implement plans to ensure that these objectives can be achieved.*

This is a very succinct version of the ISO 45001 clause 6.2, which is *OH&S objectives and planning to achieve them* and which imposes many more requirements. However, the key difference between the ISO 45001 and ISO 45003 clauses is that ISO 45003 suggests organisations should *establish measurable objectives*, while ISO 45001 requires that OH&S objectives *be measurable (if practicable) or capable of performance evaluation.*

In Chapter 15, two types of objective were described – project objectives and system objectives – and it was suggested that, in the context of psychosocial management system, system objectives are to be preferred. The discussion which follows concentrates on how to make system objectives measurable.

The most obvious, and best, method is to incorporate the measure in the description of the objective. For example, all objectives to do with well-being or wellness should specify the well-being or wellness measure or measures to be used. This can be an externally developed measure such as the WHO 5 *well-being index* or an internally developed measure such as the *Four factor wellness index* illustrated earlier in this chapter.

If there is not a measure readily available, try to devise one as was done with the *Four factor wellness index*. Where possible, base your devised measure on research or other valid evidence, as was done with the wellness index, but do not be afraid of devising subjective measures that will provide you with the data you need. For example, you can devise a one to five scale for obtaining the views of workers and interested parties on a whole range of well-being and wellness issues such as providing access to well-being counsellors, or removing unhealthy diet choices from the work canteen menu and in-house vending machines.

When a value word, for example, adequate or sufficient, has to be used in an objective, always specify who has the authority to make the judgement on adequacy or sufficiency as the case may be. For example, if the objective is to have adequate documented information, the Head of well-being and wellness may be the person who makes the final judgement on the adequacy of a specific document, and if the objective is to have sufficient funding for the psychosocial management system, top management may be the ones who decide what is sufficient.

A good rule of thumb with regard to objectives is never set an objective unless you are absolutely clear how, and by whom, a decision can be made on whether or not that objective has been achieved.

What you said you would do

The first step in making decisions on what to measure with regard to what you said you would do is to go through the *Description* of the proposed management system and the documented information it references (see Chapter 17 'The psychosocial management system manual') and identify all the things where a judgement will have to be made on success or failure of implementation.

When doing this, it is useful to put on your auditor hat and constantly ask yourself

what has the organisation said it will do, and
how can I check whether or not the organisation is doing what it said it would do.

The processes for carrying out this sort of audit work are well defined in ISO 19011:2018 *Guidelines for auditing management systems*,[10] and Tony Boyle has summarised the use of these processes in the context of health and safety in *Health and safety: Risk management*.[11] The key points are as follows:

The organisation's *Description* of its management system and the documented information referenced in the *Description* are *audit criteria*, defined in ISO 19011 as the *set of requirements against which objective evidence is compared.*

It is necessary to check the adequacy of the organisation's documented information by comparing it with relevant requirements. For example, are all the documents and records required by ISO 45001, and suggested by ISO 45003, in place, and does the documented information follow the guidance in ISO 10013?[12]

It is useful to prepare what ISO 19011 refers to as *documented information for the audit*, and the following are particularly useful for checking whether an organisation is doing what it said it would do

checklists for reviewing documents
checklists for auditing the implementation of procedures
checklists for physical conditions.

The authors are experienced health and safety auditors and, in practice, they have their auditor hats on all the time they are preparing documented information for a management system. That is, they try not to describe a requirement unless they can see a way of auditing it and arriving at a decision about whether or not it has been met. The authors recommend that you adopt the same way of working – while you are writing, continually ask yourself 'will I be able to audit this?'.

If *documented information for the audit* is available in the form of checklists, then numeric measures can be devised simply by allocating a value for each positive response. At its simplest, you give one mark for each positive response, no mark for a negative response, and calculate a percentage score when you have completed the checklist. This simple approach can be elaborated in various ways to provide more sensitive measures. For example, where some items on the checklist are more important than others, they can be given a weighting greater than one that reflects their importance.

This approach to measurement can be summarised as follows.

Identify clearly what you are going to do, for example, by agreeing a procedure and work instruction.

Record what you say you are going to do in the form of a checklist with a weighting allocated for each item.

Complete the checklist at specified intervals and use the scores obtained as a measure of conformity with what you said you would do.

Analysis

As was mentioned earlier in this chapter, the type of analysis you carry out on your measurements will depend on your purpose. There are many possible purposes, but they are all used to turn your measurements (data) into information which ISO 9000[13] defines as *meaningful data*. For example, if you have WHO 5 *well-being* index scores for 100 workers, then you have data. However, for these data to be of use, you need to decide on a purpose and analyse your data in appropriate ways. The two most common types of analysis are trend analysis and pattern analysis, and these are discussed in the next two subsections.

Trend analysis

Trend analysis is typically used to determine whether things are getting better or worse, and it involves comparing measurements taken at different times. For example, you can collect the WHO 5 *Well-being* scores for 100 workers each year, calculate the mean score, and compare these means to determine whether there is an increase or decrease. Note the following about this type of analysis.

It does not have to be the same 100 workers each year. So long as you pick a random sample of workers each year, your comparisons of the mean scores will be valid.

The mean is not the only value that can be calculated for the 100 scores. For example, you can calculate the standard deviations if you want to know about changes in the spread of the scores.

Trend analysis techniques can be used on a one-off basis to make before and after comparisons.

Pattern analysis

Pattern analysis, more formally known as epidemiological analysis, is used to identify patterns in data that may provide information. Typical pattern analysis is a trial-and-error process carried out by comparing your data with other data. For example, if your data are the WHO 5 *Well-being* scores for 100 workers, then you could make the following comparisons.

Scores for workers at different levels, and in different functions, in your organisation.
Scores for workers at different geographical locations.
Scores for workers of different ages, and male and female workers.

A practical problem with pattern analysis of well-being scores is that, in general, the usefulness of the analysis improves with increases in the amount you know about the individuals involved in the analysis. However, pattern analysis can be a very powerful tool and you should, if necessary, arrange for it to be carried out by personnel with the authority to access the required confidential data about the individuals involved.

Tony Boyle has written extensively about analysis, including the use of performance indicators, in the *Measuring performance* chapter of *Health and safety: Risk management*, and if you need to know more about analysis, it is suggested that you start there.

Evaluation

Evaluation is comparing the results of your analysis with predetermined criteria and using the outcome of this comparison to help you decide what, if any, action is required. For example, you could have the well-being criterion:

Any worker with a WHO 5 *Well-being* score lower than 6 (an arbitrary value used for illustration) will be offered well-being counselling.

If this criterion was in place, you would go through the scores of your 100 workers and contact any worker with a score lower than 6. However, this type of criterion can only be used successfully when workers have agreed to be identified. Where anonymity is required, other criteria will have to be used.

Note

i These are the guidelines for people of white European, black African, Middle Eastern, and mixed origin. There are different guidelines for men and women of African Caribbean, South Asian, Chinese, and Japanese origin, and a separate index would be required for these groups. See Chapter 3 for further guidance on waist circumference.

References

1 British Standards Institution. *Occupational health and safety management systems – Requirements with guidance for use*, BSI ISO 45001, 2018. BSI 2018.
2 MobiSystems, Inc, *Oxford Dictionary*, version 15.8. Last accessed 17 January 2024.
3 This index no longer appears on the WHO websites, but it has been widely used, and copies in various formats are available on the internet.
4 British Standards Institution. *Risk management – Guidelines*, BS ISO 31000, 2018. BSI 2018.
5 British Standards Institution. *Occupational health and safety management – Psychological health and safety at work — Guidelines for managing psychosocial risks*, BSI ISO 45003, 2021. BSI 2021.
6 www.who.int/health-topics/obesity#tab=tab_1. Last accessed 22 February 2024.
7 This index no longer appears on the WHO websites but it has been widely used and copies in various formats are available on the internet.
8 https://warwick.ac.uk/fac/sci/med/research/platform/wemwbs/. Last accessed 22 February 2024.
9 https://warwick.ac.uk/fac/sci/med/research/platform/wemwbs/. Last accessed 22 February 2024.
10 British Standards Institution. *Guidelines for auditing management systems*, BSI ISO 19011, 2018. BSI 2018.
11 Boyle T. *Health and safety: Risk management* (5th edition). Routledge 2019.
12 British Standards Institution. *Quality management systems – Guidance for documented information*, BSI ISO 10013, 2021. BSI 2021.
13 British Standards Institution. *Quality management systems – Fundamentals and vocabulary*, BSI ISO 9000, 2015. BSI 2015.

26 Psychosocial monitoring, auditing, and corrective action

Introduction

This chapter deals with a group of management system processes that can be informally described as processes for 'keeping things on track'. Monitoring, auditing, nonconformity, correction, and corrective action are all defined terms, and the formal definitions are given at relevant points later in this chapter. However, what follows is an informal description of the processes by way of introduction.

Monitoring is individuals checking their own activities, or the activities of individuals for whom they are responsible. The most widespread form of monitoring is probably first-line managerial workers checking the activities of non-managerial workers, and this type of monitoring is often referred to as supervision.

Auditing is an independent check of the activities being carried out. By definition, you cannot audit your own activities or the activities of individuals under your control. A key difference between auditing and monitoring is that auditors do not have to do anything about any problems they identify, while monitors do have to take action to resolve any problems they identify.

Nonconformity is, in the measurement terminology used in Chapter 25, not achieving what you said you would achieve, or not doing what you said you would do. A core function of both monitoring and auditing is the identification of nonconformities.

Correction is putting things right. If you have not achieved an objective, correction is taking the action necessary to achieve the objective. If you are not doing what you said you would do, correction is changing individuals' behaviour in ways that ensure you are doing what you said you would do.

Corrective action is identifying the causes of nonconformities and taking action to ensure that these nonconformities do not happen again. Accurately identifying the causes of nonconformities and devising appropriate corrective action require the investigation and analytical skills dealt with in Chapter 27 'Psychosocial investigation'.

Each of the five topics listed above is dealt with in a separate section in the rest of this chapter. However, Tony Boyle has covered these topics in some detail in the

DOI: 10.4324/9781003490555-28

context of traditional health and safety in *Health and safety: Risk management.*[1] For this reason, the present chapter only deals with the issues of relevance to psychosocial risk management, and it is assumed that appropriate arrangements are already in place for dealing with traditional health and safety issues.

Monitoring

Monitoring is defined in Annex SL[2] and ISO 45001[3] as

determining the status of a system, a process or an activity

Note 1 to entry: To determine the status, there may be a need to check, supervise or critically observe.

This definition allows for monitoring at three levels.

Across the whole organisation, by monitoring conformity with the psychosocial management system requirements.

Across a specific psychosocial process, such as psychosocial threat and opportunity assessment, to determine conformity with the process requirements.

The activities of specific managerial and non-managerial workers to determine conformity with the requirements for those activities.

At each level, in addition to checking conformity, there should be checks on effectiveness and efficiency. Effectiveness is the *extent to which planned activities are realized and planned results achieved* (ISO 45001, from Annex SL), and efficiency is the *relationship between the result achieved and the resources used* (ISO 9000[4]). However, it is preferable to think of effectiveness as whether or not something is working, and efficiency as whether or not it is value for money. This makes the two concepts easier to explain and discuss, and the authors have not encountered problems with using this informal approach.

In practice, the monitoring of conformity with the psychosocial management system requirements will be the responsibility of the Head of well-being and wellness, and the responsibility for monitoring processes will be the responsibility of the process owner. These individuals should ensure that they are competent auditors (see the next section for information on audit competences) and apply good practice audit techniques to their monitoring activities. Because they are checking things for which they are responsible, they are monitoring, not auditing, but good practice audit techniques are equally valuable for monitoring activities.

What follows is a discussion of the third level of monitoring, checking the activities of specific managerial and non-managerial workers. As a reminder, only the aspects of this type of monitoring of relevance to psychosocial issues are dealt with – it is assumed that any necessary health and safety monitoring arrangements are already in place. What to do about the results of monitoring are dealt with in the *Correction* and *Corrective action* sections later in this chapter.

The main psychosocial monitoring activities are as follows.

Checking their own well-being and wellness. All workers should monitor their own well-being and wellness and take appropriate action when either their well-being or wellness is impaired.

Checking the well-being and wellness of direct reports. Most individuals are able to arrive at an informal assessment of the well-being and wellness of other individuals, especially if they know them well. However, this informal assessment is usually inadequate for psychosocial monitoring purposes, and managerial workers who have direct reports should be provided with competences in well-being and wellness assessment, at least to the level of identifying individuals who may require treatment for impaired well-being or wellness.

Checking that all required behaviours are being carried out in a competent manner. This should include the individual's own behaviours, the behaviours of direct reports, and, as necessary, the behaviours of interested parties.

Checking that there are no occurrences of prohibited behaviours. As with required behaviours, this should include their own behaviours and behaviours of direct reports and interested parties.

Implementation and effectiveness of other psychosocial threat controls. Where a psychosocial threat control is required for an activity or location, the individual who has responsibility for that activity or location should check that it remains in place and that it is having the intended effect.

Implementation and effectiveness of psychosocial opportunities. As with psychosocial threat controls, there should be checks that any arrangements for exploiting psychosocial opportunities remain in place and are having the intended beneficial effect.

New psychosocial threats and opportunities. As part of their day-to-day activities, individuals should check for the emergence of new psychosocial threats and opportunities, and changes to existing psychosocial threats and opportunities, and take, or initiate, appropriate action.

If psychosocial monitoring is to be effective, those carrying out the monitoring activities will require the following competences.

Assessing their own well-being and wellness and the well-being and wellness of others. For example, the correct use of whatever well-being measuring instrument your organisation has decided to use.

The actions required when they identify impaired, or improved, well-being or wellness. For example, referral to a well-being counsellor or any other support your organisation provides, and passing information on improvement to the Head of well-being and wellness.

The examination of documents to assess any contribution they may be making to psychosocial threats and opportunities. For example, role ambiguity in a work instruction.

The examination of records to identify any contribution the activities they record may be making to psychosocial threats and opportunities. For example, records of frequent long shifts or the frequent working of unsocial hours.

Observing work locations and work activities. These competences are particularly required for identifying the hazards of a psychosocial nature in the ISO 45003[5] *Work environment, equipment and hazardous tasks* category.

Questioning relevant individuals. This is a key competence in psychosocial monitoring because of the need to find out about individual's well-being, but it is also needed as a contribution to identifying psychosocial threats and opportunities and the effect these threats and opportunities are having on the well-being and wellness of the individuals exposed to them.

An important part of setting up a psychosocial monitoring procedure is devising and implementing arrangements for specifying, delivering, and assessing the required competences. Other arrangements for psychosocial monitoring, such as the frequency of monitoring and how the results of monitoring will be recorded, are similar to the arrangements for traditional health and safety monitoring.

Auditing

In Chapter 25, it was pointed out that the processes for carrying out audits are well defined in ISO 19011:2018 *Guidelines for auditing management system*[6], and the preparation of *documented information for the audit* was briefly outlined. What follows are the key points from ISO 19011, with a discussion of how they apply to psychosocial auditing.

ISO 45001 uses the ISO 19011 definition of audit as follows.

systematic, independent and documented process for obtaining audit evidence and evaluating it objectively to determine the extent to which the audit criteria are fulfilled

Note 1 to entry: An audit can be an internal audit (first party) or an external audit (second party or third party), and it can be a combined audit (combining two or more disciplines).

Note 2 to entry: An internal audit is conducted by the organization itself, or by an external party on its behalf.

Note 3 to entry: 'Audit evidence' and 'audit criteria' are defined in ISO 19011.

The discussion which follows is restricted to internal audits, either a single psychosocial audit or a combined audit with health and safety and/or HR.

All ISO 19011 audits have to have agreed and documented objectives, scope, and criteria as described below:

Objectives. These define what the audit is supposed to accomplish, and there is a wide range of possible objectives. However, they mainly fall into one of two categories – assessing conformity with audit criteria (see below) or assessing whether or not something has been achieved. These categories mirror the measurement categories of conformity and achievement discussed in Chapter 25.

Scope. This describes the extent and boundaries of the audit, and it is usually specified in terms of one or more of the following – physical locations, organisational functions, groups of workers, or a time period. In psychosocial audits, it is also necessary to specify whether well-being and wellness are in scope, or just well-being or wellness.

Audit criteria. These are the *set of requirements used as a reference against which objective evidence is compared* (ISO 19011). There are two broad categories of audit criteria.

External audit criteria. These are requirements set by outside organisations. For example, legal requirements in health and safety or HR legislation, requirements set by international documents such as ISO 45001 and ISO 45003, and codes of good practice published by, for example, mental health organisations.

Internal audit criteria. These are the requirements that the organisation sets for itself, and they should be defined in the organisation's documented information. Internal audit criteria are also divided into the conformity requirements and achievement requirements discussed in Chapter 25.

For any given audit, a subset of external and/or internal audit criteria has to be specified because it is usually impractical to cover all of an organisation's audit criteria in a single audit. When internal audit criteria are being used, a first step should be to check their adequacy against any relevant external audit criteria. For example, if your organisation has committed to conformity with ISO 45001, the audit should check that any internal audit criteria being used in the audit conform to the relevant ISO 45001 requirements. Similarly, if you are auditing a procedure for compliance with a particular piece of legislation, you should check that your procedure deals with all of the requirements of that piece of legislation before auditing conformity with the procedure itself.

When the audit objectives, scope, and criteria have been agreed, the next stage is to prepare what ISO 19011 refers to as the *documented information for the audit*. This type of documented information was introduced in Chapter 25, and the following examples were given:

Checklists for reviewing documents
Checklists for auditing the implementation of procedures
Checklists for physical condition

Another generally useful type of *documented information for the audit* is forms, such as:

Forms to accompany the checklists referred to in the previous paragraph. These forms are used to remind auditors to record relevant information such as the name of the auditor, the date and time of the audit, and details of what was audited, for example, the name of the document or procedure being used as an audit criterion, and the location where physical checks were carried out.

Forms for recording the results of interviews. The simplest of this type of form reminds auditors to record things like the date and time of the interview and the names and roles of the individuals involved in the interview. There is then a blank sheet of paper for recording what is said. However, interview forms can be made more useful by replacing the blank sheet of paper with some form of *aide memoire* for the auditor. This can range from a list of the topics to be covered during the audit interview to a so-called structured interview where the *aide memoire* is a detailed list of questions to be asked and, for some structured interviews, possible follow-up questions to be asked depending on the interviewee's response.

Forms for recording minutes of meetings. The types of forms for minutes are similar to those for interviews. They range from only providing spaces for recording such things as date, start and finish times, and names and roles of attendees followed by a blank sheet of paper, to detailed point-by-point agendas to be covered during the meetings.

The key difference between the *documented information for the audit* for a health and safety audit and the *documented information for the audit* for a psychosocial audit is the need to allow for discussion and/or measurement of the well-being and/or wellness of workers and interested parties as part of the psychosocial audit. It is easy to write suitable requirements into the *documented information for the audit*, but ensuring that auditors carrying out psychosocial audits have the relevant competences may be more difficult.

ISO 19011 deals with a range of audit activities such as audit planning, sampling, opening and closing meetings, and communication during the audit. However, these activities are similar in health and safety and psychosocial audits, and they have not been dealt with in this book. The three audit activities that need to considered are

Collecting and verifying information
Generating audit findings
Determining audit conclusions

In ISO 19011, audit evidence is *records, statements of facts or other information, which are relevant to the audit criteria.* However, only verified information is allowed as audit evidence. This requirement for verification is problematic in psychosocial audits since, for example, there is no means of verifying an individual's self-reported state of well-being. However, if verbal self-reports of well-being are recognised as a special case, and the auditors have the interview competences to identify patently untruthful statements, then individuals' verbally self-reported state of well-being can be treated as *statements of fact.* Similarly, completed well-being forms such as the WHO 5 *well-being index* can be recognised as valid *records.*

Audit findings are created by the auditors by comparing the audit evidence with the audit criteria or, as ISO 19011 describes them, audit findings are *the results of evaluation of the collected audit evidence against the audit criteria.* At their simplest, audit findings are conformities and nonconformities – if the collected audit evidence shows that a requirement in an audit criterion is being met, then the audit finding is conformity; if the requirement is not being met, then the audit finding is nonconformity. This simple conformity–nonconformity approach can be modified in various ways, for example, by having different degrees of severity of nonconformity. However, for the present purposes, the simple conformity–nonconformity approach is adequate. Assuming that the audit criteria have been adequately drafted, and the problems with self-reporting of well-being have been resolved, the generation of audit findings can be done using the techniques used in health and safety audits.

In ISO 19011, the audit conclusion is *the outcome of an audit, after consideration of the audit objectives and all audit findings.* Although ISO 19011 refers to *audit conclusion,* there can, in practice, be many audit conclusions. The first audit conclusion is usually the extent of conformity with the audit criteria and, if appropriate checklists have been used, this conformity can be expressed in percentages. Other audit conclusions will depend on the audit objectives but, in the context of a psychosocial audit, audit objectives could be set that enable the following audit conclusions.

The extent to which impaired well-being and wellness of workers and interested parties were being identified and addressed.
The effectiveness of existing arrangements for dealing with psychosocial threats and opportunities.
Opportunities for improvement of the psychosocial management system.
More, generally, whether the intended outcomes of the psychosocial management system are being achieved.

It is important that the audit conclusions give a fair summary of the auditee's performance with regard to the audit criteria. The authors have seen far too many sets of audit conclusions that are long lists of minor failures with no mention of the much, much longer lists of things, the auditee is doing well. All auditors, but particularly psychosocial auditors, should remember that for the majority of auditees, an audit is a powerful psychosocial risk source and typically a psychosocial threat.

Nonconformity

Annex SL and ISO 45001 define nonconformity as the

non-fulfilment of a requirement

and conformity as

fulfilment of a requirement.

As a reminder, a requirement is a *need or expectation that is stated, generally implied or obligatory.*

ISO 45001 adds the following note to its definition of nonconformity:

Nonconformity relates to requirements in this document [that is, ISO 45001] *and additional OH&S management system requirements that an organization establishes for itself.*

There are two important aspects of nonconformities that should be taken into account – the degree of nonconformity and the importance of the requirement that is not being fulfilled. These two aspects are dealt with in the next two subsections.

Degree of nonconformity

Some requirements are simply binary – you are either conforming or not. For example, if the requirement is that *documents should be reviewed on or before the review date*, then this has either been done or not been done. Checking for this non-conformity is very easy because all you have to do is compare the review date with the date you make your check – you do not have to read the document. Note, however, that if the requirement is that *documents must be kept up to date*, then you will have to read the document, and you will need background information, for example, changes in relevant legislation, to enable you to check whether or not it is up-to-date.

All requirements can be treated as binary, but for the majority of requirements this is usually unfair. To continue with the example in the previous paragraph, a document can range from being so severely out of date that using it could have serious consequences to being out of date on a single unimportant item that would have no practical consequences. Both documents are nonconforming but not to the same degree.

For this type of nonconformity, a scoring system can be developed and, as ISO 19011 puts it,

Nonconformities can be graded depending on the context of the organization and its risks. This grading can be quantitative (e.g. 1 to 5) and qualitative (e.g. minor, major).

An alternative quantitative scale is a percentage score, but any scoring system must include, where necessary, definitions of what the scores mean in practice, for example

1 = The document is so out of date that it must not be used.
3 = This document is out of date and must be used with caution.
5 = This document is out of date in ways that do not affect its use in practice.

Scores 2 and 4 on this scale would be used for documents with intermediate degrees of outdatedness.

A major use of nonconformity scoring systems is to enable those carrying out the checks, for example, auditors, to give a fair picture of the state of nonconformity. For example, an auditee will be provided not only with information on the number of nonconformities but also the degree of severity of these nonconformities. This is particularly important when comparisons are going to be made between one auditee and another. It can be the case that both auditees have the same number of nonconformities but, using the 1–5 scale described earlier, one auditee has mainly 1 scores while the other auditee has mainly 5 scores. Using only numbers of nonconformities will result in the two auditees being unfairly judged as being performing equally well.

So far, out-of-date documents has been used as the example of a nonconformity – this was done for simplicity and the arguments apply to all types of nonconformity. However, it can be argued that scoring systems are particularly necessary for important requirements, and the importance of requirements is discussed in the next subsection.

Importance of requirement

In the present context, the importance of a requirement is defined in terms of the impact nonconformity with the requirement would have on the well-being and wellness of workers and interested parties. Using this definition

requirements such as up-to-date documents would be of low importance
requirements such as assessing the likely effect of changes on well-being and wellness would be of medium importance, and
requirements such as maintaining controls for significant psychosocial threats would be of high importance.

It is of course the case that all nonconformities are important in some sense, but resources for dealing with nonconformities are usually limited, and rating the nonconformities in the sort of way just described provides a method for deciding which nonconformities to tackle first.

As with the degree of nonconformity, the importance of the requirement can be graded quantitatively (for example 1–5) or qualitatively (for example unimportant to very important).

It can be useful to devise a combined scale that gives a single value, and a scale of this type is illustrated in Table 26.1.

The scale shown in Table 26.1 can be used to create criteria for action as follows.

I (Immediate) – Immediate action required to restore conformity with the requirement.
U (Urgent) – Urgent action required to restore conformity with the requirement.
RD (Resource Dependent) – Action to be taken to restore conformity with the requirement as soon as resources allow.

Table 26.1 Combined degree of conformity and importance of requirement scale

		Degree of conformity				
		1	*2*	*3*	*4*	*5*
Importance of requirement	5	RD	U	U	I	I
	4	RD	U	U	I	I
	3	RD	RD	U	U	U
	2	RD	RD	RD	U	U
	1	RD	RD	RD	RD	RD

Source: Prepared by Tony Boyle for this book.

Irrespective of the way a nonconformity is identified, or its nature and extent, dealing with it will require correction and corrective action, and these two processes are dealt with in the next two sections.

Correction

Annex SL defines correction as

action to eliminate a detected nonconformity

and requires organisations to *take action to control and correct* nonconformities that occur.

This definition of correction is not carried over into ISO 45001 or ISO 45003,[6] but the requirement to control and correct nonconformities is carried over into ISO 45001.

In practical terms, correction is action to put things back to the way they should be. For example,

If the nonconformity is an out-of-date document, the correction is to update the document.
If the nonconformity is failure to maintain a psychosocial threat control measure, the correction is to reinstate the measure.

In general, organisations are good at correction and pride themselves on how promptly they deal with nonconformities. However, the authors have long argued that many of the problems with traditional health and safety management arise from this focus on correction – what can be referred to as a 'correction culture'. What organisations should have is a 'corrective action culture' that deals with the causes of nonconformities and prevents their recurrence, as well as putting them right when they occur. Corrective action is dealt with in the next section.

Corrective action

Annex SL defines corrective action as

> *action to eliminate the cause of a nonconformity and to prevent recurrence.*

ISO 45001 has a modified form of this definition, and an explanatory note as follows.
Corrective action is

> *action to eliminate the cause(s) of a nonconformity or an incident and to prevent recurrence*
>
> *Note 1 to entry: This constitutes one of the common terms and core definitions for ISO management system standards given in Annex SL of the Consolidated ISO Supplement to the ISO/IEC Directives, Part 1. The definition has been modified to include reference to 'incident', as incidents are a key factor in occupational health and safety, yet the activities needed for resolving them are the same as for nonconformities, through corrective action.*

The Annex SL requirements for corrective action are as follows:

> b) *evaluate the need for action to eliminate the cause(s) of the nonconformity, in order that it does not recur or occur elsewhere, by*
>   *reviewing the nonconformity*
>   *determining the causes of the nonconformity, and*
>   *determining if similar nonconformities exist, or can potentially occur;*
> c) *implement any action needed;*
> d) *review the effectiveness of any corrective action taken;*

These requirements are carried over into ISO 45001, but they are complicated by the introduction of 'incident' in the ISO 45001 definition of corrective action. These complications are discussed in Chapter 27, which deals with psychosocial investigation.

For the present purposes, the key features of the corrective action process are as follows:

The causes of the nonconformity have to be identified, and in the context of the psychosocial management system it is assumed that this requires a psychosocial investigation.

The investigation of a nonconformity is not limited to that nonconformity. The investigation must determine *if similar nonconformities exist, or can potentially occur.*

The corrective action process does not end with the implementation of the corrective action; there must be follow-up to *review the effectiveness of any corrective action taken.*

In the authors' view, organisations that have this sort of corrective action process in place have a 'corrective action culture', but this sort of culture is much rarer than the 'correction culture' described in the previous section.

The key features of a corrective action process are very similar to the key features of an incident investigation process. Since most organisations have a well-developed health and safety incident investigation process that can be adapted for psychosocial investigations, the corrective action and incident investigation processes have been dealt with together in Chapter 27 on psychosocial investigation.

References

1   Boyle T. *Health and safety: Risk management* (5th edition). Routledge 2019.
2   *ISO/IEC Directives, Part 1 Consolidated ISO Supplement – Procedure for the technical work – Procedures specific to ISO (Thirteenth edition, 2022). Annex SL (normative) Harmonised approach for management system standards. Appendix 2 (normative) Harmonized structure for MSS with guidance for use.*
3   British Standards Institution. *Occupational health and safety management systems – Requirements with guidance for use*, BSI ISO 45001, 2018. BSI 2018.
4   British Standards Institution. *Quality management systems – Fundamentals and vocabulary*, BSI ISO 9000, 2015. BSI 2015.
5   British Standards Institution. *Occupational health and safety management – Psychological health and safety at work – Guidelines for managing psychosocial risks*, BSI ISO 45003, 2021. BSI 2021.
6   British Standards Institution. *Guidelines for auditing management systems*, BSI ISO 19011, 2018. BSI 2018.

27 Psychosocial investigation

Introduction

Investigations are an important element of a health and safety management system and ISO 45001[1] requires organisations to investigate incidents and nonconformities. The techniques for these investigations are well specified – but not always well applied – and in this chapter they will be referred as health and safety investigations.

Health and safety investigations are needed in a psychosocial management system to investigate issues that do not involve the well-being or wellness of workers and interested parties. However, where the well-being or wellness of workers and interested parties is involved, additional investigation techniques are required and the investigations involving well-being and wellness will be referred to as psychosocial investigations.

In many ways, psychosocial investigations are more akin to criminal investigations than accident investigations because, for example, like criminal investigations, they have to deal with perpetrators and victims. For this reason, the techniques used for police investigations are a more suitable model for psycho-social investigation, and the material in this chapter draws heavily on the guidance material published by the UK's College of Policing.[2]

The first section of this chapter discusses the overall approach to psycho-social investigation, and the second section deals with the PEACE approach to interviewing that is particularly suited to the interviews needed in psychosocial investigations. There is then a section dealing with causal factor analysis, and the chapter ends with a discussion of the ISO 45001 requirements and the ISO 45003[3] guidance on incidents and investigation.

Investigation

In this section, the authors describe their adaptation of the criminal investigation process to suit the purposes of psychosocial investigation. Figure 27.1 shows the steps in this psychosocial investigation process, and each of these steps is dealt with in a separate subsection.

DOI: 10.4324/9781003490555-29

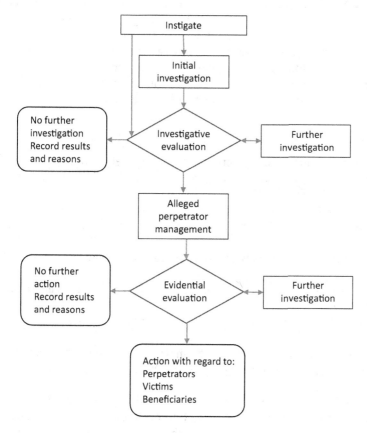

Figure 27.1 The psychosocial investigation process.

Instigation

Investigations can be instigated proactively or reactively. Proactive instigation occurs when the investigators choose what to investigate, and reactive investigation occurs when the need for a psychosocial investigation is identified by someone else.

The most common type of reactive instigation is usually victims or witnesses reporting occurrences of psychosocial risk sources and, where these reports are made verbally to an individual, the report should be considered as the first part of the investigation. To ensure that best use is made of the report, individuals who may receive such reports should be competent in collecting information of relevance to any subsequent investigation. These competences are, of course, in addition to the competences required to deal sensitively with the victim or witness making the report.

As is shown in Figure 27.1, where there is already information on the subject of the investigation, as might be the case with an investigation instigated as a result of a psychosocial threat and opportunity assessment, the investigator can move straight on to the investigative evaluation phase. Where very little information is available, as is likely to be the case with nonverbal or anonymous reports of the occurrence of a psychosocial risk source from victims or witnesses, an initial investigation will be required and this is dealt with in the next section.

Initial investigation

The purpose of the initial investigation is to collect sufficient information to determine whether a full psychosocial investigation is required. Typical questions to answer include the following.

Are there victims? If so, how many, and what is the nature and extent of their victimisation?

Are there beneficiaries? If so, how many, and what is the nature and extent of the benefits?

Are there perpetrators? If there are, how many, and what is the nature of their alleged behaviour?

Are there witnesses to the perpetrators' alleged behaviour, other than any victims or beneficiaries?

Are any immediate actions required? For example, treatment for victims' impaired well-being, or temporary suspension of perpetrators.

Initial investigation is useful for two main reasons. First, there are always likely to be malicious or mistaken reports of the occurrence of psychosocial risk sources, and an initial investigation enables these to be screened out. Second, it provides an opportunity to implement immediate action to address the concerns of victims.

As is shown in Figure 27.1, further investigation may be needed before sufficient information is available to enable the investigators to move on to the investigative evaluation stage. A major part of this further investigation will be interviews with witnesses and victims. However, the techniques to be used for these interviews are the same as the techniques to be used for all interviews in the psychosocial investigation process, and these techniques are dealt with in the *PEACE interviews* section later in this chapter.

Investigative evaluation

The primary purpose of the investigative evaluation is to decide what further action, if any, will be required. Because there is such a wide range of possible psychosocial risk sources, there is a correspondingly wide range of possible actions, but they typically fall into one of the following categories.

No further action. This will be the conclusion when, for example, there has been a genuine misunderstanding with regard to individuals' actions, and any impairment to well-being or wellness has been minor and transient.

Action by functions other than the psychosocial investigation function. This will be the conclusion when, for example, HR personnel have to arrange immediate treatment for victims with impaired well-being, or temporarily suspended an alleged perpetrator from their role.

Action by the psychosocial investigation team. This will be the conclusion when, for example, there is initial evidence that an alleged perpetrator has been creating a psychosocial threat, and further investigation is required. Note that action by the psychosocial investigation team and action by functions other than the psychosocial investigation function, for example HR, are not mutually exclusive. For example, treatment of victims and investigation of an alleged perpetrator's behaviour can run in parallel.

Irrespective of the nature of the decisions made, there should be a detailed and accurate record of the actions taken during the initial investigation and the investigative evaluation, the results of these actions, and how these results led to the decisions reached.

Alleged perpetrator management

In the context of police investigation, deciding that someone is a suspect

> requires there to be some reasonable, objective grounds, based on known facts or information, which are relevant to the likelihood that the offence has been committed and the person to be questioned committed it.[4]

A similar test should be applied to deciding on whether an individual can be deemed an alleged perpetrator.

Evidential evaluation

Evidential evaluation begins with the drawing up of a plan for the proposed investigation. This plan should include the following.

The objectives of the investigation. These may be quite specific and limited, for example, establish whether the alleged perpetrator carried out the alleged action, and to establish what will be required with regard to the victims of the alleged perpetrator. However, the objectives can be extended in various ways, including investigations into whether the actions alleged are being carried out by other perpetrators elsewhere in the organisation.

The investigative techniques to be used to achieve the objectives. The principal technique will be PEACE interviews, but examining CCTV footage, checking computers and mobile devices, and surveys of potential victims are examples of additional techniques that might be required.

The resource requirements of the investigation, in particular, the availability of investigators with the relevant competences.

These three aspects of the investigation plan should be considered together to ensure that the objectives can be met with the available resources. It is better to complete successfully an investigation with limited objectives than to only partially complete an investigation with objectives that were too ambitious.

When the investigation plan has been prepared, the investigation enters the *Further investigation* phase with the collection of evidence using the techniques decided upon. However, you should remember the saying that 'no plan survives first contact with the enemy' and be prepared to amend the plan if necessary.

Further investigation is carried out until a decision can be reached on each of the investigation's objectives. With regard to the behaviour of an alleged perpetrator, the possible decisions are:

The perpetrator carried out the alleged actions, and this resulted in a significant impairment of the well-being or wellness of one or more victims.

The perpetrator carried out the alleged actions, but they did not result in a significant impairment of the well-being or wellness of other individuals.

The perpetrator did not carry out the alleged actions, but some individuals are suffering significant impairment of the well-being or wellness from some other cause.

The perpetrator did not carry out the alleged actions, and there is no significant impairment of the well-being or wellness of other individuals.

There is insufficient evidence to reach a decision.

The actions required to deal with each of these decisions should already have been agreed by the organisation and ideally described in the *Well-being and wellness handbook*. The investigators' function ends with preparing detailed documented information on the conduct of the investigation and its results – usually referred to as an investigation report.

Other points on investigation

The discussion above was intended to highlight the key differences between the techniques used for a traditional health and safety 'accident investigation' and the techniques needed for a psychosocial investigation. However, the discussion was only an introduction to these techniques, and it is strongly recommended that you make a detailed study of the relevant College of Policing material. In addition, or alternatively, you could attend a training course dealing with this sort of investigation. An internet search will provide a list of organisations that provide relevant training.

You may also wish to consider having psychosocial investigations carried out on your behalf. This may be appropriate when the in-house investigators could be seen as insufficiently independent of the issues involved, or for systemic psychosocial risk sources that require large-scale investigations that cannot be carried out with in-house resources. As with investigation training, there are organisations that provide these investigative services, usually as one of a suite of different types of investigative services. There is a relevant British Standard that you should refer to before selecting an organisation to provide investigative services BS 102000:2018 *Code of practice for the provision of investigative services.*[5]

Although the investigation technique just described focuses on perpetrators, the technique should also be used for investigating other psychosocial issues, including the following.

Psychosocial nonconformities not involving a perpetrator.
As has been discussed earlier, limitations are likely to have been placed on the scope of the psychosocial management system so that, for example, some psychosocial hazards have been excluded. Where there is evidence to suggest that one of these psychosocial hazards is having a significant effect on the well-being or wellness of workers or interested parties, whether the effect is positive or negative, a psychosocial investigation should be carried out to enable a decision on whether the psychosocial hazard should now be within the scope of the psychosocial management system.

When an unintended change has taken place, there should be a psychosocial investigation of the consequences for the well-being or wellness of workers and interested parties who were affected by the change. Change is dealt with in detail in Chapter 31.

PEACE interviews[i]

PEACE is an acronym for a systematic interview process with the following stages:

Planning and preparation
Engage and Explain
Account – Clarification and challenge
Closure
Evaluation

The process is widely used and, when used correctly, increases the likelihood of obtaining relevant information and, in some cases, confessions. The five stages of the PEACE interview process are dealt with in the next five subsections.

Planning and preparation

This phase involves the creation of a written interview plan. In deciding on the contents of this plan, the interviewer should take into account the following.

The information about the investigation already available from other sources.
The objectives of the interview.
The personal characteristics of the interviewee.
When the interview should be carried out – immediately, or after further information has been obtained from elsewhere.
Where the interview should be carried out – some locations are less threatening than others.
Whether there will be one interviewer or two.

The interview plan is used by the interviewer(s) as an *aide memoire* during the interview.

Engage and explain

The engage part of this phase is the establishment of a rapport with the interviewee to facilitate further exchanges of information.

The explain part of the phase involves the interviewer explaining relevant features of the interview to the interviewee and checking that the interviewee understands these features. Typical topics to be covered include:

The reasons for the interview.
The objectives of the interview and the topics to be covered.
The practicalities of the interview, for example, timings and the means of recording what is said.
Where necessary, the organisation's definitions of well-being and wellness.

Account – clarification and challenge

This phase is the one during which the interviewee's account of the circumstances under investigation is obtained. The clarification and challenge are the interviewer's actions to ensure the account is accurate and comprehensive, and the primary interviewer action is effective questioning.

Closure

This phase is intended to ensure an orderly end to the interview with the interviewer summarising what the interviewee has said, giving the interviewee an opportunity to comment on what has been said and telling the interviewee what will happen next.

Evaluation

Evaluation has three purposes.

Determining how the interviewee's account fits in with the rest of the investigation and considering the implications if it does not.

Deciding whether any further action is necessary with regard to the interviewee and the investigation more generally.

Providing an opportunity to reflect on the interviewer, or interviewers' performance.

Other points on interviewing

It is impossible to overestimate the importance of good interview technique in ensuring the effectiveness of psychosocial investigations. Training in PEACE interviewing is provided by a number of organisations, and if you have not already done so you should attend one of these training courses. Remember, there is a huge difference between being able to carry out a conversation – for which no training is required – and carrying out an interview – which cannot be done without appropriate training.

Although PEACE interviewing is particularly important for interviews with perpetrators and victims, the approach should ideally be used for all psychosocial interviews.

Causal factors

As has been pointed out in earlier chapters, a typical weakness in investigations is failure to identify causes. Investigators find out what happened, but not why it happened, and if you do not know why something happened, you do not have the information you need to stop it happening again.

There are various techniques that can be used to overcome this weakness and the authors' preferred options are the following.

The five whys. This is a very simple technique that involves repeatedly asking 'Why?' until asking why no longer makes sense. Although it is called the five whys, the number of times you ask why is not fixed – sometimes you need fewer than five whys and sometimes more than five. The five whys should be used routinely during your investigation interviews and the subsequent analysis of investigation findings to ensure that you get as much information as you can on the causal factors.

Events and causal factor analysis (ECFA). The output from this process is a diagram showing the chronological sequence of events being investigated and the causal factors associated with these events. ECFA is particularly useful for keeping track of complex investigations and for communicating information about investigations – most people find a diagram easier to 'take in' than pages of text.

There is extensive online guidance on the five whys, ECFA and other causal factor analysis techniques, and many providers of training courses covering these techniques.

ISO 45001 requirements and ISO 45003 guidance

Clause 10.2 of ISO 45001 (*Incident, nonconformity and corrective action*) includes the following requirements:

> *b 1) investigating the incident or reviewing the nonconformity.*

However, the *reviewing the nonconformity* is carried over from Annex SL, which does not use the term investigate, and elsewhere in ISO 45001 the *reviewing the nonconformity* is dropped. For example, bullet point e) 7) of clause 5.4 *Consultation and participation of workers* is

> *investigating incidents and nonconformities and determining corrective actions*

and, as was seen earlier, the note to the ISO 45001 definition of corrective action is

> *Note 1 to entry: This constitutes one of the common terms and core definitions for ISO management system standards given in Annex SL of the Consolidated ISO Supplement to the ISO/IEC Directives, Part 1. The definition has been modified to include reference to 'incident', as incidents are a key factor in occupational health and safety, yet the activities needed for resolving them are the same as for nonconformities, through corrective action.*

ISO 45003 further muddies the waters with the following end to clause 10.2. *NOTE A nonconformity occurs whenever there is an actual or potential lack of conformity to the requirements of the organization's OH&S management system. An incident occurs whenever there is an actual, or potential for, injury or ill health to a worker.* It can be argued that this note is an oversimplification. For example, not wearing required PPE is a nonconformity with the OH&S management system that has *actual, or potential for, injury*, which makes it an incident as well as a nonconformity.

However, the ISO 45001 and ISO 45003 requirements with regard to incident investigation and nonconformity investigation cannot straightforwardly be carried over to a psychosocial management system and the reasons for this are discussed in the next two subsections.

Incident investigation

ISO 45001 defines incident as follows

> *occurrence arising out of, or in the course of, work that could or does result in injury and ill health*

> *Note 1 to entry: An incident where injury and ill health occurs is sometimes referred to as an 'accident'.*

Note 2 to entry: An incident where no injury and ill health occurs, but has the potential to do so, may be referred to as a 'near-miss', 'near-hit' or 'close call'.

Note 3 to entry: Although there can be one or more nonconformities related to an incident, an incident can also occur where there is no nonconformity.

From now on, incidents as defined by ISO 45001 will be referred to as health and safety incidents to differentiate them from psychosocial incidents.

Health and safety incidents cannot be used as the basis for investigations in a psychosocial management system because they are defined in terms of the occurrence, or possible occurrence, of injury or ill health. In a psychosocial management system, you need a definition based on well-being and wellness. What follows is the authors' view of what a definition of a psychosocial incident might be and the reasons for this view.

It would be possible to create a definition of psychosocial incident simply by substituting 'impaired well-being and wellness' for 'injury and ill health' to give the following.

occurrence arising out of, or in the course of, work that could or does result in impaired well-being and wellness.[ii]

However, this definition takes no account of the fact that an occurrence that does, or could, result in impaired well-being and wellness for some individuals could also result in improved well-being and wellness for other individuals. This is an extension of the fact that psychosocial risk sources create both threats and opportunities. To take this into account, the definition of psychosocial incident could be

occurrence arising out of, or in the course of, work that could or does result in a significant change in well-being and wellness.

This definition does, of course, mean that you can only use the term psychosocial incident in practice if

you can measure the effect it has, or could have had, on well-being and wellness and
you have an agreed definition of *significant change.*

These are not issues that arise with health and safety incidents because it is usually obvious whether injury or ill health has, or could have, occurred and, if it is not obvious, or the severity of the injury or ill health is not obvious, it is not the responsibility of the health and safety investigator to establish the relevant facts. In contrast, investigators of psychosocial incidents have to identify and measure the effects of the psychosocial incident they are investigating. However, techniques are available for measuring these effects and defining significant change, and these are discussed in Chapter 23 'Psychosocial threat and opportunity assessment' and Chapter 24 'Psychosocial threat and opportunity management'.

Although you may wish to have a definition of a psychosocial incident in order to match the ISO 45001 terminology, for practical purposes the definition is of little value. More useful approaches are to define psychosocial nonconformity, as discussed in the next subsection, or use the ISO 31000[6] terminology introduced in Chapter 11 'The psychosocial management system terminology'. That is, a *psychosocial event*, defined as

> *occurrence or change of a particular set of circumstances affecting psychosocial result(s)*

and a *psychosocial result*, defined as

> *outcome of an event affecting psychosocial objectives.*

Nonconformity investigation

A nonconformity is a *non-fulfilment of a requirement* and since there are different types of requirements in a management system, there is a need for different types of investigation. For example, as was mentioned earlier in this chapter, health and safety investigations will be required for nonconformities not involving well-being or wellness, and psychosocial investigations will be required when well-being or wellness is involved. However, there is generally no need to change definitions with regard to nonconformity when setting up a psychosocial management system.

Notes

i   There is a piece of legislation, the *Police and Criminal Evidence Act* 1984, that applies primarily in England and Wales. Among other things, this Act sets out how the police should conduct interviews, and these interviews are referred to as PACE interviews. A PACE interview can be conducted using the PEACE interview process.

ii   The ISO 45001 definition of injury and ill health has the following note.
Note 2 to entry: The term 'injury and ill health' implies the presence of injury or ill health, either on their own or in combination.
This note would also apply to impaired well-being and wellness.

References

1   British Standards Institution. *Occupational health and safety management systems – Requirements with guidance for use*, BSI ISO 45001, 2018. BSI 2018.
2   www.college.police.uk/app/investigation/investigation-process. Last accessed 10 April 2023.

3   British Standards Institution. *Occupational health and safety management – Psychological health and safety at work – Guidelines for managing psychosocial risks*, BSI ISO 45003, 2021. BSI 2021.

4   www.college.police.uk/app/investigation/managing-investigations. Last accessed 11 April 2023.

5   British Standards Institution. *Code of practice for the provision of investigative services*, BS 102000, 2018. BS 102000.

6   British Standards Institution. *Risk management – Guidelines*, BS ISO 31000, 2018. BSI 2018.

28 The role of top management

Introduction

ISO 45001[1] defines top management as

> person or group of people who directs and controls an organization at the highest level

and there are two relevant notes to this definition

> Note 1 to entry: Top management has the power to delegate authority and provide resources within the organization, provided ultimate responsibility for the OH&S management system is retained.

> Note 2 to entry: If the scope of the management system covers only part of an organization, then top management refers to those who direct and control that part of the organization.

There are various requirements on top management set out in ISO 45001, and ISO 45003[2] adds to these requirements with its guidance on what top management should do with regard to psychosocial risk management. The requirements and guidance are set out in the following clauses of ISO 45001 and ISO 45003.

5.1   Leadership and commitment
5.2   OH&S policy
5.3   Organizational roles, responsibilities and authorities
9.3   Management review

The content of the first three of these clauses is dealt with in separate sections later in this chapter, and management review is dealt with in Chapter 29. In addition, there are further references to top management in ISO 45003, and these are dealt with in a separate section of the present chapter.

An important point to make is that although top management is allocated activities in ISO 45001 and ISO 45003, it is rarely the case that they carry out these

DOI: 10.4324/9781003490555-30

actions in person. For example, top management is responsible for the organisation's OH&S policy, but this is usually drafted by the Head of OH&S and agreed by top management, occasionally with minor changes. In the discussions which follow, it is assumed that the Head of well-being and wellness and the Head of HR will be carrying out the required activities on behalf of the top management. The majority of activities top management has to carry out in person will, therefore, involve checking that the Head of well-being and wellness and the Head of HR are meeting their allocated responsibilities. This is discussed in a separate section called *The practicalities.* Readers who are familiar with the ISO 45001 requirements with regard to top management activities may wish to skip to this section.

The chapter ends with some of the authors' personal reflections on top management.

5.1 Leadership and commitment

ISO 45001 states that *Top management shall demonstrate leadership and commitment with respect to the OH&S management system*, and the ISO 45003 equivalent is *Top management should demonstrate leadership and commitment to managing psychosocial risk and to promoting well-being at work.*

There is a list of things that top management must do to demonstrate leadership and commitment and these can be divided into two categories.

Things that have a readily measurable outcome, for example, *ensuring that the OH&S policy and related OH&S objectives are established.*
Things that do not have a readily measurable outcome, for example, *supporting other relevant management roles to demonstrate their leadership.*

Each of the items in the first category is dealt with in a separate subsection, followed by a subsection dealing with the second category.

OH&S policy

Top management must ensure *that the OH&S policy and related OH&S objectives are established and are compatible with the strategic direction of the organization.* However, clause 5.2 of ISO 45001 and ISO 45003 deal with the OH&S policy in detail and further discussion will be found in the *OH&S policy* section later in this chapter.

Integration

The ISO 45001 requirement is that top management has to ensure *the integration of the OH&S management system requirements into the organization's business processes.* ISO 45003 adds to this with *reinforce the sustainability of managing psychosocial risk by including it in strategic plans and existing systems, processes and reporting structures.*

This requirement can create problems for some organisations. For example, organisations with certification to ISO 9001[3] or ISO 14001[4] may not wish to integrate OH&S requirements into their quality or environmental management system for fear of losing their quality or environmental certification because of OH&S nonconformities. However, the increasing use of integrated management systems (IMSs) may help with ISO 45003 integration. Note that, although ISO 45003 is guidance, not a standard, it can be suitable for certification.

The authors' experience with integration is that it fails to be implemented because health and safety is seen as a 'bolt on extra' by managerial workers, and health and safety professionals pander to this view by, for example, having safe systems of work, rather than work instructions that cover all aspects of the relevant task, including quality, environment, and health and safety.

Although it usually has to be done qualitatively, the extent of integration in an organisation can be assessed by examining its documented information and interviewing a sample of managerial and non-managerial workers. It is also usually quite easy to identify opportunities for integration, although getting the top management to agree to the implementation of these opportunities may be more difficult.

Resources

The ISO 45001 requirement is that top management has to ensure t*hat the resources needed to establish, implement, maintain and improve the OH&S management system are available* and the ISO 45003 version is to *determine the resources needed and make them available in a timely and efficient manner.*

As with integration, identifying required resources is relatively easy, and it is usually done by the Head of OH&S who then puts in a bid to the top management. The same approach can be used for the psychosocial management system with the Head of well-being and wellness identifying the resource requirements, with input from the Head of HR where necessary.

Protecting workers

The ISO 45001 requirement is that top management has to protect *workers from reprisals when reporting incidents, hazards, risks and opportunities*, and ISO 45003 makes two additions

> *protect workers from reprisals and/or threats of reprisals for reporting incidents, hazards, risks and opportunities;*
> *communicate how whistleblowers, victims, witnesses and those who report or raise workplace psychosocial risk concerns will be protected.*

The Head of well-being and wellness and the Head of HR will have joint responsibility for implementing and maintaining the protection processes and checking that they work in practice. The ISO 45003 guidance with regard to communication can be met using the type of *Well-being and wellness handbook* described in Chapter 21 'Awareness and communication'.

Intended outcomes

The ISO 45001 requirement is that top management ensures *that the OH&S management system achieves its intended outcome(s)* and there is related, but more specific, guidance in ISO 45003, that is, *obtain and provide feedback to determine the effectiveness of managing and preventing psychosocial risk within the OH&S management system, both in implementation and operation.*

In the psychosocial management system described in this book, the Head of well-being and wellness is responsible for ensuring that intended outcomes are in place for the psychosocial management system and that these intended outcomes have been agreed by the top management. It is also the responsibility of the Head of well-being and wellness to ensure that these intended outcomes continue to be met, and to keep the top management informed of the status with regard to intended outcomes.

Continual improvement

In ISO 45001, top management is responsible for *ensuring and promoting continual improvement.* However, as with achieving the intended outcomes, in the psychosocial management system being described in this book, the Head of well-being and wellness ensures that opportunities for continual improvement are identified and taken. Where necessary, this will be done in consultation with the top management, and the Head of well-being and wellness will keep the top management informed of progress.

Consultation and participation

The ISO 45001 requirement is that top management ensures that *the organization establishes and implements a process(es) for consultation and participation of workers*, and ISO 45003 has three additional points of relevance to this requirement:

remove barriers that can limit worker participation, and aim to enhance participation

actively engage workers in a continual dialogue on the management of psychosocial risk

support and encourage workers to actively participate in the management of psychosocial risk in the workplace.

Processes for consultation and participation were discussed in Chapter 19, where it was pointed out that top management should consult with their direct reports on well-being and wellness issues. However, you have to take great care in allocating other responsibilities for consultation and participation to top management, especially if these responsibilities require a significant amount of top management's time. A case can be made for actions such as top management briefly dealing with well-being and wellness issues during meetings on other topics. However, if this is set as a psychosocial requirement and the top management do not fulfil this requirement, or fulfil it badly, this can result in detrimental effects on the psychosocial management system.

Health and safety committees[i]

In ISO 45001, top management is responsible for *supporting the establishment and functioning of health and safety committees.* There is reference to health and safety committees in ISO 45003 but no suggestion in ISO 45003 that a well-being and wellness committee should be set up. Elsewhere in ISO 45003, there are suggestions for well-being and wellness activities for the health and safety committee, for example, in clause 5.4 *Consultation and participation of workers.*

In Chapter 19 'Consultation and participation', an outline of possible terms of reference for a well-being and wellness committee was given together with suggestions with regard to the membership of this committee. In an ideal world, a member of the top management would chair this committee or a member of the top management would attend each meeting. This has a number of advantages, including top management demonstrating commitment to well-being and wellness and the opportunity for top management to enable the committee to take into account business issues of which they would not otherwise be aware. The problem arises if top management is given a role in the well-being and wellness committee and they fail to carry out that role. It is better to have a committee without the top management's involvement that is achieving its terms of reference, even if these terms of reference are limited, than a committee that is supposed to have the top management's involvement but does not.

No readily measurable outcome

ISO 45001 has the following requirements that have no readily measurable outcome

> *taking overall responsibility and accountability for the prevention of work-related injury and ill health, as well as the provision of safe and healthy workplaces and activities*
> *communicating the importance of effective OH&S management and of conforming to the OH&S management system requirements*
> *directing and supporting persons to contribute to the effectiveness of the OH&S management system*
> *supporting other relevant management roles to demonstrate their leadership as it applies to their areas of responsibility.*

To be fair to ISO 45001, only the first of these requirements is self-imposed. The other three are direct carry-overs from Annex SL.[5]

It is of course possible to ask top management what, if anything, they are doing to meet these requirements and to conduct surveys to obtain workers' views on these topics. However, it is difficult to see how the validity of either of these measures could be checked, and this makes the results they achieve of limited value.

ISO 45003 has the following guidance

> *identify, monitor and be aware of its roles and responsibilities with respect to managing psychosocial risks*
> *empower workers and ensure they are competent to fulfil their roles and responsibilities to identify and manage psychosocial risk.*

Ensuring that workers *are competent to fulfil their roles and responsibilities to identify and manage psychosocial risk* is essential and has a measurable result. However, like other measurable results, the activities required are not carried out by the top management. The other aspects of the ISO 45003 guidance do not have readily measurable results.

5.2 OH&S policy

ISO 45001 requires that *Top management shall establish, implement and maintain an OH&S policy*, and ISO 45003 gives various suggestions as to what the top management should do when establishing the OH&S policy.

As with leadership and commitment, the ISO requirements with regard to the OH&S policy can be divided into those that can readily be measured and those that cannot. A similar division occurs in the ISO 45003 guidance, and there are additional complications arising from the possible need for a separate well-being and wellness policy and the role of other policies the organisation might have. The relevant issues are discussed in the subsections that follow.

Commitments

Both ISO 45001 and ISO 45003 say that the OH&S policy should include certain commitments and it is, of course, easy to check whether or not these commitments have been included.

The OHSAS 45001 commitments are:

> *to provide safe and healthy working conditions for the prevention of work-related injury and ill health*
> *to fulfil legal requirements and other requirements*
> *to eliminate hazards and reduce OH&S risks*
> *to continual improvement of the OH&S management system*
> *to consultation and participation of workers, and, where they exist, workers' representatives.*

The ISO 45003 commitments are

*to preventing ill health and injuries related to psychosocial risk and promoting
well-being at work*
*to fulfil legal requirements and other requirements related to health, safety and
well-being at work, including a commitment to manage psychosocial risk.*

It is easy to include these commitments in an OH&S policy or a combined
OH&S and well-being and wellness policy – the devil is in the detail of meeting
these commitments. The required detail is described in Chapter 15.

OH&S objectives

ISO 45001 requires that the OH&S policy *provides a framework for setting the
OH&S objectives*, but it is not immediately obvious what this means in practice.
ISO 45003 makes matters worse with its suggestion that the OH&S policy should
*provide a framework for setting and reviewing, evaluating and revising objectives
for the management of psychosocial risk*. As was seen in Chapter 15, it can be
argued that an ISO 45001 or ISO 45003 compliant policy can be prepared without
mentioning objectives in the policy itself. However, a commitment to achieving
psychosocial objectives could be included in your well-being and wellness policy.

Appropriateness

Annex SL requires that policies are *appropriate to the purpose of the organization*.
ISO 45001 elaborates this requirement in two places in clause 5.2 as follows.
The OH&S policy must be

*appropriate to the purpose, size and context of the organization and to the spe-
cific nature of its OH&S risks and OH&S opportunities*
relevant and appropriate.

ISO 45003 repeats the *appropriate to the purpose, size and context of the organization* and adds that the OH&S policy should *be reviewed periodically to ensure it
remains relevant and appropriate to the organization.*
As with the framework for setting OH&S objectives, it is not immediately clear
what criteria can be used to judge whether or not a policy is *appropriate to the purpose of the organization* – the Annex SL requirement. It is even less clear which
criteria can be used with the additional ISO 45001 requirements and ISO 45003
guidance.

Communication

ISO 45001 has two very straightforward requirements with regard to communication of the OH&S policy – it has to *be communicated within the organization*, and
be available to interested parties, as appropriate.

ISO 45003 muddies the waters somewhat with *The OH&S policy should ... be communicated to all workers so that they are aware of their rights and responsibilities.* It can be argued that this implies that the OH&S policy should include details of workers' *rights and responsibilities* which goes far beyond the ISO 45001 requirements with regard to the contents of an OH&S policy.

One or more policies

ISO 45003 suggests that top management should

> *determine if there is a need for a separate policy about managing psychosocial risk,* and
> *consider how other policies (e.g. human resources, corporate social responsibility) support and are consistent with the OH&S policy to achieve common objectives.*

These two topics should be considered together because it is possible that the need for a separate well-being and wellness policy can be avoided by appropriate amendments to both the OH&S policy and the HR policy. However, see Chapter 15 for a discussion on the appropriateness or, otherwise, of having a separate well-being and wellness policy.

Other ISO 45003 guidance

ISO 45003 has two other items of guidance in its clause 5.2.

> *The OH&S policy should promote and enhance a working environment consistent with the principles of dignity, mutual respect, confidentiality, cooperation and trust in the OH&S management system.*
> *The organization should consult workers and, where they exist, worker representatives in the development of a policy to manage psychosocial risk and, where relevant, consult other interested parties.*

The problems arising from the difficulty of checking conformity with the first of these items of guidance have been discussed in Chapter 15, where it was suggested that it be omitted from well-being policies and amended OH&S policies.

The second item of guidance is an extension of the ISO 45001 requirement to *emphasize the consultation of non-managerial workers ... on establishing the OH&S policy* and consultation was discussed in Chapter 19.

5.3 Organizational roles, responsibilities, and authorities

The first requirement in clause 5.3 of ISO 45001 is

> *Top management shall ensure that the responsibilities and authorities for relevant roles within the OH&S management system are assigned and communicated at all levels within the organization and maintained as documented information.*

In practice, as with most other aspects of top management's activities in OH&S, most of the work needed to meet this requirement will be done by the OH&S team, and fulfilment of this requirement in the context of a psychosocial management system has been dealt with in other chapters. There is a note in ISO 45001 that appears to acknowledge that this will be the case.

NOTE While responsibility and authority can be assigned, ultimately top management is still accountable for the functioning of the OH&S management system.

ISO 45003 has a rephrased version of this ISO 45001 requirement as follows.

Top management is responsible for the functioning of the OH&S management system and should clarify roles, responsibilities and authorities for managing psychosocial risk in the workplace.

The only other ISO 45001 requirements are

Top management shall assign the responsibility and authority for:

a) *ensuring that the OH&S management system conforms to the requirements of this document;*
b) *reporting on the performance of the OH&S management system to top management.*

There is no further guidance on this issue in ISO 45003. In the context of well-being and wellness, psychosocial management system can be substituted for OH&S management system in this requirement.

ISO 45003 additional references

In ISO 45001, there are no references to top management outside the three clauses discussed earlier and clause 9.3 *Management review.* This is not the case in ISO 45003, and this section deals with the additional references to top management in ISO 45003.

7.2 Competence

Paragraph 7.2.2 begins

The organization should establish the competence requirements for:

a) *top management and workers with line management responsibility.*

The authors have long argued that a major weakness in traditional health and safety is the failure to specify, deliver, and assess the relevant competences for top management. When setting up a psychosocial management system, you should give serious thought to what you want your top management to do, and this is discussed in the later section *The practicalities.*

7.3 Awareness

Paragraph 7.3.2 begins

> *When developing awareness of psychosocial risk, the organization should take into account:*
>
> *a) the importance of top management support for reporting psychosocial hazards and protection from reprisals for such reporting.*

As with the competence issues discussed in the previous subsection, the requirements for top management's awareness of well-being and wellness issues require serious thought, and these issues are also dealt with in the later section *The practicalities.*

7.4 Communication

Clause 7.4 of ISO 45003 includes the following.

> *When communicating, the organization should:*
>
> *a) demonstrate top management commitment to other workers, to increase knowledge and use of processes;*
> *b) provide opportunities for feedback to top management from workers on actions, programmes and policies intended to facilitate worker involvement;*

It is not immediately clear what bullet point (a) means, and it can be doubted that it has any practical meaning at all – fortunately it is guidance and not a requirement.

Bullet point (b) is covered by the sorts of reporting arrangements discussed in earlier chapters and the activities of the Head of well-being and wellness in analysing these reports and passing the results of these analyses to the top management.

The practicalities

Like politics, top management well-being and wellness activities are the art of the possible. The authors have set out earlier, in rather tedious detail, the ISO 45001 requirements with regard to the top management and the ISO 45003 guidance with regard to the top management. However, if you present top management with this information, you are unlikely to get a positive response – polite maybe, but not positive. Nevertheless, you have to get the top management 'on board', and what follows is one suggestion for doing this.

The suggested approach assumes that your top management has agreed to the establishment of a psychosocial management system and has assigned you the responsibility and authority for establishing this management system.

Before you begin to develop your psychosocial management system, you should address the following top management issues.

- Your top management will already be extremely busy doing their day job and, however concerned they are about the well-being and wellness of their workers, they will have little time to do anything about it. You need to find out if any of the members of your top management are willing and able to devote more than the minimum amount of time to dealing with well-being and wellness issues.
- A key objective of your top management will be to ensure the continuing viability of their organisation, and this will involve careful control of expenditure, particularly expenditure that has no corresponding financial benefit. You should try to find out what, if any, resources will be available for altruistic well-being and wellness issues, and the top management's appetite for business case well-being and wellness initiatives. Altruism was discussed in Chapter 15, and business cases are used to show that particular expenditure on well-being or wellness will produce a measurable benefit for the organisation.
- Individual members of your top management may have their own well-being and wellness issues. Theirs is a highly stressful role and, although there is usually a degree of self-selection, members of your top management may be suffering impaired well-being or wellness. This is a delicate area because some members of the top management in this position may think 'I'm going through it so why should I care if other workers are suffering as well', while others will see it as an opportunity to volunteer for treatment options 'to see if they are suitable for our organisation'.
- In some organisations, members of the top management are a significant psychosocial risk source because of, for example, their bullying behaviour or their imposition of unreasonable work demands. This is another delicate area because, as has been described elsewhere, some managerial workers, for example, see bullying simply as a robust management style. The clear definition of prohibited and required behaviours, as discussed in earlier chapters, and the top management acceptance of these definitions, is the first step in dealing with this issue.

If necessary, you should research your top management's current views on, and involvement in, well-being and wellness issues. This can be straightforward if

- you have access to a sympathetic member of your top management who can provide you with the necessary information
- members of the top management respond to your emails requesting information
- your top management agree to a short meeting to discuss the issues.

Otherwise, you will have to get your information 'second-hand', for example, from the top management's direct reports.

Irrespective of the current involvement of your top management in well-being and wellness issues, there are two key objectives you have to achieve.

Your top management must be aware of their responsibilities within the psychosocial management system, and which of these responsibilities have been allocated to the Head of well-being and wellness, the Head of HR, or some other function.

The top management must discharge those responsibilities that have been allocated to them, and not to others.

It is possible to prepare written top management work instructions, setting out top management responsibilities and describing how these responsibilities should be discharged. However, whether such a work instruction is needed will depend on the top management responsibilities within your psychosocial management system. For example, no *Top management well-being and wellness work instruction* will be needed if the only activity top management has to carry out personally is management review.

Where there is no *Top management well-being and wellness work instruction*, you should prepare a succinct description of any responsibilities that top management has to carry out personally, and a separate description of the top management responsibilities that are being carried out on their behalf. In an ideal world, your top management will maintain their awareness of the content of this documented information and carry out the allocated actions effectively and in a timely manner.

Personal reflections

Tony Boyle was one of the people who set up the consultancy Hastam, and he was a member of its top management for 30 years. Hastam is not a large organisation, but over its 30 years it has created numerous and significant psychosocial risk sources for its top management. Tony has drawn on these experiences at various points in other chapters.

In addition, during his years as an occupational psychology consultant and a health and safety consultant, he met and worked with the top management of many organisations. These organisations included 'household name' organisations in manufacturing and construction, major local authorities, hospital trusts, and national and international charities. As you might expect, there was a huge variety in the top management he met. For example, in the context of health and safety, the range was from 'it's nothing to do with me and I don't care' to a genuine, clearly demonstrated commitment to doing whatever was necessary to keep people safe. As with his own experiences as a member of top management, Tony has drawn on the results of his encounters with top management in other organisations when writing this book.

Note

i Both ISO 45001 and ISO 45003 refer to the health and safety committee. It is not clear why it is not the OH&S committee.

References

1 British Standards Institution. *Occupational health and safety management systems – Requirements with guidance for use*, BSI ISO 45001, 2018. BSI 2018.
2 British Standards Institution. *Occupational health and safety management – Psychological health and safety at work – Guidelines for managing psychosocial risks*, BSI ISO 45003, 2021. BSI 2021.
3 British Standards Institution. *Quality management systems – Requirements*, BS EN ISO 9001:2015. BSI, 2015.
4 British Standards Institution. *Environmental management systems – Requirements with guidance for use*, BS EN ISO 14001:2015. BSI, 2015.
5 *ISO/IEC Directives, Part 1 Consolidated ISO Supplement – Procedure for the technical work – Procedures specific to ISO (Thirteenth edition, 2022). Annex SL (normative) Harmonised approach for management system standards. Appendix 2 (normative) Harmonized structure for MSS with guidance for use.*

29 Management review

Introduction

The ISO 45001[1] requirement for management review is

Top management shall review the organization's OH&S management system, at planned intervals, to ensure its continuing suitability, adequacy and effectiveness.

Management review is important for two reasons. First, it is a top management responsibility, and second, it is the only ISO 45001[1] process that has to be carried out at *planned intervals*.

As was discussed in Chapter 28, the involvement of top management is essential if a management system is to continue to be effective. However, the individuals who have day-to-day responsibility for maintaining and improving the management system should ensure that top management only have to do the bare minimum, or as much as they are willing to do. This is particularly the case with management review because effective management review requires extensive work on, for example, data collection and analysis. The nature of this work and how it can be done are discussed later in the chapter.

The second point about *planned intervals* is important because it enables management review to be used as a mechanism for preventing what can be referred to as 'management system drift'. This is management system processes being allowed to fall into disuse, or to run without any check on their effectiveness. Putting management review at the heart of the psychosocial planning process provides a means of preventing management system drift, and this is discussed in Chapter 30: 'Psychosocial planning and continual improvement'.

The present chapter deals with the following topics.

The management review process
Inputs to the management review
Outputs from the management review[i]
Other points about management review
Documented information for management review

DOI: 10.4324/9781003490555-31

The management review process

In management system terms, management review is a relatively straightforward process, and during a psychosocial management review top management should

review the psychosocial data and information available to them and, if necessary, ask for further data or information

compare the available psychosocial data and information with relevant criteria, such as the intended outcomes of the psychosocial management system and the psychosocial objectives

make decisions on the *continuing suitability, adequacy, and effectiveness* of the psychosocial management system[ii]

mandate corrections, corrective actions, and actions to ensure continual improvement

ensure that documented information is available as evidence of the results of the psychosocial management reviews, and that these results are appropriately promulgated.

However, in practice, almost all of the work required by psychosocial management review is carried out by the Head of well-being and wellness, with inputs from the Head of HR as necessary. Typically, the top management then have a meeting to consider the work the Head of well-being and wellness has carried out and either agree it *in toto* or in an amended form. However, there can be occasions when the Head of well-being and wellness is told to 'go back to the drawing board'.

By its very nature, management review is a repetitive process, but this chapter deals with a single management review consisting of

data and information collection and analysis by the Head of well-being and wellness

preparation by the Head of well-being and wellness of suggested corrections, corrective actions, and actions to ensure continual improvement

a top management meeting to consider the work of the Head of well-being and wellness

preparation of documented information and promulgation of results by the Head of well-being and wellness.

For brevity in the sections that follow 'you' has been used, rather than 'the Head of well-being and wellness'.

Inputs to the management review

ISO 45001 has a list of required inputs to the OH&S management review, and this list can be made appropriate for a psychosocial management review, usually by simply substituting 'psychosocial' for 'OH&S'. The ISO 45001 management review inputs, amended where necessary to suit psychosocial management reviews, and what you should do about them, are dealt with in the subsections that follow. The final subsection deals with the additional guidance in ISO 45003.[2]

Previous management reviews

You should check the status of actions from previous management reviews well before the review meeting so that you have an opportunity to implement correction and corrective action if necessary. However, if your planning process is effective, you should already have arrangements in place for doing this – see Chapter 30 for details of the psychosocial planning process.

You should prepare a statement setting out

which actions from previous management reviews have been carried out with, if appropriate, information on their effectiveness

any actions from the previous management reviews that have not been carried out with, as necessary, the reasons why they have not been carried out, any corrections and corrective actions taken, and the results of these actions.

External and internal issues

This requirement is to include changes in external and internal issues that are relevant to the psychosocial management system, including

the needs and expectations of interested parties
legal requirements and other requirements
threats and opportunities.

You will see that these topics are the ones that are covered by the SWOT analyses described in Chapter 18. You should ensure that your preparatory work for a management review meeting includes a detailed psychosocial SWOT analysis. There are further links between SWOT analysis and management review, and these are described in Chapter 30 'Psychosocial planning and continual improvement'.

Policy and objectives

You should determine the extent to which the well-being and wellness policy and the psychosocial objectives are being met. Your views with regard to the well-being and wellness policy will, of necessity, be qualitative, but if earlier recommendations on setting objectives have been taken into account, your assessment of achievement of objectives should be quantitative.

Trend analyses

Trend analysis was discussed in Chapter 25, where it was pointed out that it is typically used to determine whether things are getting better or worse, and that it involves comparing measurements taken at different times.

ISO 45001 requires the results of a wide range of trend analyses to be used as management review inputs, and the list below gives the ISO 45001 requirements adapted for use with psychosocial management review.

Incidents, nonconformities, corrective actions. The value, or otherwise, of using psychosocial incidents was discussed in Chapter 27: 'Psychosocial investigation'. If you are recording psychosocial incidents, you should maintain trend analyses based on numbers of incidents and their severity. Trend analysis of nonconformities should be based on their number and a qualitative estimate of their severity, and trend analysis of corrective actions should be based on their number and a qualitative estimate of their effectiveness.

Continual improvement. You should have set targets for continual improvement by, for example, establishing continual improvement psychosocial objectives. Trend analysis of continual improvement involves determining the extent to which your continual improvement psychosocial objectives have been met.

Monitoring and measurement results. Monitoring and measurement were dealt with in earlier chapters, and if the guidance in these chapters has been followed, the results from monitoring and measurement should be suitable for trend analyses of these data.

Results of evaluation of compliance with legal requirements and other requirements. Compliance with these requirements is a subset of more general monitoring and measurement, and the results can be treated in the same ways.

Audit results. Trend analyses of audit results have to be carried out with great care because all audits are based on samples, including a sample of workers, a sample of locations, and a sample of activities. In theory, if these samples were truly random, then direct comparisons between successive audits could be made, but truly random sampling is rarely possible. However, successive audits can be compared on such things as percentage conformity, number and severity of nonconformities, and the conclusions of the auditors with regard to whether or not the psychosocial management system is effectively implemented and maintained.

Consultation and participation of workers. Where you have set objectives of relevance to consultation and participation, trend analysis can be carried out by comparing the extent to which these objectives were achieved over successive periods of time. In addition, where consultation and participation of workers are included in psychosocial monitoring and measurement processes, trend analysis of the relevant subsets of data can be carried out. Where neither of these two options is available, it will be necessary to devise a method or methods for the qualitative assessment of trends in the consultation and participation of workers.

Psychosocial threats and opportunities. Trends in the numbers of psychosocial threats and opportunities can be determined and made available for management reviews. However, it is probably more important to identify trends in the nature of psychosocial threats and opportunities – particularly the emergence of new psychosocial threats and opportunities. Where evidence suggests that a particular psychosocial threat or opportunity is no longer in place, the known, or suspected, reasons for this change should be reported.

The results of trend analysis are usually presented as diagrams, for example, histograms or graphs. Such uses are discussed in detail in Tony Boyle's *Health and safety: Risk management.*[3]

Resources

The requirement for this input is a report on the adequacy of resources for maintaining an effective psychosocial management system. You should be monitoring your psychosocial management system resource requirements as part of your planning process – see Chapter 30 for details – and the input to the management review should be a summary of current resources and your views on their adequacy.

Communications with interested parties

ISO 45001 requires *relevant communication(s) with interested parties* as an input to management reviews. Reports on this input will vary depending on the scope of the psychosocial management system – which interested parties are included – and the nature of these interested parties – for example, suppliers of well-being and wellness products and services, and regulatory bodies. While you can report on the number of communications, reporting on the nature of the communications, and who they were with, is usually more important.

Opportunities for continual improvement

Opportunities for continual improvement are both an input and an output of management review. The input is suggestions for continual improvement, and the output is decisions on which, if any, of the suggestions to adopt. Identifying suggestions for continual improvement is one of the activities in the SWOT analyses described in Chapter 18, and there is additional discussion of continual improvement in Chapter 30: 'Psychosocial planning and continual improvement'.

ISO 45003

The ISO 45003 guidance largely mirrors the ISO 45001 requirements, but it also makes the following very important point.

> *Evidence-based decision-making is key for continually improving the effectiveness of the OH&S management system.*

The earlier notes on meeting the ISO 45001 management review input requirements were very much focussed on providing evidence on which the top management could base their decisions.

There is one suggestion for further inputs to the management review in ISO 45003, that is, *other data (e.g. support services, disability plans, compensation schemes)*. You should include in this category of *other data* reports on such things as psychosocial initiatives (their nature and effect), psychosocial treatments being offered to workers and interested parties (their nature and rates of uptake), and any other well-being or wellness activities not dealt with elsewhere.

Outputs from the management review

The Annex SL[4] requirements with regard to outputs (results) from the management review are succinct and straightforward.

> *The results of the management review shall include decisions related to continual improvement opportunities and any need for changes to the XXX management system*

and these requirements will be discussed in Chapter 30.

ISO 45001, however, requires a number of additional outputs from the management review, and these additional outputs are dealt with in separate subsections below. Rather surprisingly, ISO 45003 gives no additional guidance on the outputs from the management review process.

Intended outcomes

The management review outputs should include decisions related to

> *the continuing suitability, adequacy and effectiveness of the OH&S management system in achieving its intended outcomes.*

There appears to be an anomaly here because there is no requirement for information on the extent to which intended outcomes are being met to be included as an input to the management review. However, checking the extent to which intended outcomes of the psychosocial management system are being met prior to the management review meeting, and using of the results of these checks as an input to the management review meeting, is good practice.

Continual improvement

The management review outputs should include decisions related to *continual improvement opportunities*. As was mentioned earlier, in ISO 45001, continual improvement opportunities are both an input to and an output from the management review process. You can have a major influence on the input side of the continual improvement opportunities because you can collect and collate suggestions from workers and interested parties, generate your own suggestions, and provide as input to the management review meeting a carefully considered list of suggested improvements. The process for this careful consideration is dealt with in Chapter 30: 'Psychosocial planning and continual improvement'.

Your influence on the output side of the continual improvement opportunities is considerably less since this is top management making their decisions. However, you can attempt to influence these decisions by, for example, prioritising your list of suggestions and giving details of the costs and benefits of individual suggestions for continual improvement. These topics are also dealt with in Chapter 30.

Management system

The ISO 45001 requirement is for decisions related to

> *any need for changes to the OH&S management system;*
> *resources needed;*
> *actions, if needed;*
> *opportunities to improve.*

It can be argued that this is an over-elaborate requirement because *resources needed* and *actions, if needed*, apply to all of the outputs from the management review, and opportunities to improve the OH&S management system can be included in the suggestions for continual improvement, as discussed in the previous subsection.

So far as the psychosocial management system is concerned, it is preferable to use the Annex SL requirement, that is simply, *any need for changes to the XXX* [that is, the psychosocial] *management system.*

Integration

The ISO 45001 requirement is that the management review outputs should include decisions related to *integration of the OH&S management system with other business processes.* Integration of OH&S management system processes with other business processes is a good way of improving the likelihood that the OH&S management system processes will be implemented and maintained. This also applies to psychosocial management processes. However, if your top management is going to be making decisions about integration, you should ensure that the relevant data and information are included as inputs to the management review meetings dealing with this issue.

Strategic direction

This requirement is for decisions related to *any implications for the strategic direction of the organization.* Typically, you will not have sufficient information about the strategic direction of your organisation to make suggestions on this topic. In addition, while certain aspects of OH&S may have implications for an organisation's strategic direction, this is less likely to be the case with well-being and wellness issues.

What you can do, however, is to make sure that your top management is reminded of this requirement by, for example, including it in the documented information you supply for their management review meeting.

Other points about management review

The other points to make about management review fall into two categories.

The remaining ISO 45001 requirements and ISO 45003 guidance.
Use of the management review process for purposes other than top management reviews.

ISO 45001 and ISO 45003

In line with Annex SL, ISO 45001 requires organisations to *retain documented information as evidence of the results of management reviews.*[iii] This could simply be minutes of the management review meeting, but a more structured approach is described in the final section of this chapter.

The other ISO 45001 requirements and ISO 45003 guidance deal with the promulgation of the results of management reviews as follows.

Top management shall communicate the relevant outputs of management reviews to workers, and, where they exist, workers' representatives.

(ISO 45001)

Top management should communicate relevant results of the management review in relation to psychosocial risk to workers and other interested parties, as appropriate.

(ISO 45003)

In practice, you will probably be allocated responsibility for the promulgation of results, but whatever the arrangements, they should be included in your management review procedure.

Other uses of management review

Management review is a process, and although Annex SL, and all of the management systems based on Annex SL, confine its use to top management as a group, it can be a useful tool for individual senior managers and the Head of well-being and wellness and the Head of HR.

The discussion that follows focusses on the use of the management review process by the Head of well-being and wellness as part of psychosocial planning.

As has been described earlier in this chapter, the management review process involves extensive data and information collection and analysis in order to identify continual improvement opportunities and any need for changes to the psychosocial management system.

It is usually the case that the actions required to exploit some of the opportunities, and to make some of the changes, are within the scope of the authority of the Head of well-being and wellness. For example, these actions could be correcting typographical errors or otherwise improving documented information, or reallocating financial resources within the budget allocated to the Head of well-being and wellness. However, depending on the nature and extent of the responsibility and authority the top management has delegated to the Head of well-being and wellness, the scope for making changes without further reference to the top management may be much wider.

Irrespective of their scope, the Head of well-being and wellness should use the management review techniques described in this chapter as a tool in the psychosocial planning process dealt with in Chapter 30.

Documented information for management review

The suggested documented information for top management review is

A paragraph in the *Psychosocial management system manual* such as the one given in Chapter 17, that is

9.3 Management review
Each year the top management reviews the psychosocial management system to ensure its continuing suitability, adequacy, and effectiveness. This review is carried out in accordance with WI51 *Top management well-being and wellness work instruction.*
A section in the *Top management well-being and wellness work instruction* and suggested content for this section is given below.
A form for recording the results of the review meeting.

Top management well-being and wellness work instruction

The contents of section 9.3 *Management review* of the *Top management well-being and wellness work instruction* should cover the following topics.

The purpose of the review, for example, to ensure the continuing suitability, adequacy, and effectiveness of the psychosocial management system. If appropriate, include the ISO 45001 information on suitability, adequacy, and effectiveness.
When the reviews should be carried out (to satisfy the *planned interval* requirement).
A list of the things to consider at each review meeting. In practice, this will be all, or a chosen subset, of the inputs to management reviews discussed earlier in this chapter, plus any inputs you have added to suit your own psychosocial

management system. If appropriate, include the ISO 45001 information on *consider and take into account*, that is

The word 'consider' means it is necessary to think about but can be excluded, whereas 'take into account' means it is necessary to think about but cannot be excluded.

An explanation that, prior to each review meeting, the Head of well-being and wellness and the Head of HR will provide top management with the information they need to consider and take into account.

A list of the required outputs of the management review. As with inputs, this will be all, or a subset, of the decisions on the output topics discussed earlier in this chapter, plus any additional decisions required by your psychosocial management system.

An explanation that, prior to each review meeting, the Head of well-being and wellness and the Head of HR will provide top management with their considered views on possible outputs from the management review.

The arrangements for communicating the relevant outputs of the management review to workers, workers' representatives, and interested parties. For example, this responsibility has been assigned to the Head of well-being and wellness.

The need to *retain documented information as evidence of the results of management reviews*. For example, by ensuring that the *Well-being and wellness management review* form is completed at the end of the review meeting. This form is discussed in the next subsection.

Form

The minimum needed in a form for recording the results of a top management review would be a list of the decisions made. However, it is more useful to have a form that records more detail and makes use of technology to facilitate the management review meeting itself. A possible form of this type is discussed next.

As has been described earlier in the chapter, the Head of well-being and wellness carries out the following actions for each of the inputs to the management review.

Collects and analyses the relevant data and information – for example, data on the achievement of psychosocial objectives.

Evaluates the data and information against the relevant criteria – for example, which psychosocial objectives are being achieved and which, if any, are not being achieved.

Makes suggestions for action where necessary – for example, correction and corrective action when a psychosocial objective is not being achieved.

Makes suggestions for continual improvement.

Continuing with the psychosocial objectives example, the form for recording the results of a top management review of psychosocial objectives could have a three-column table as shown in Table 29.1.

Table 29.1 Form for recording management review of psychosocial objectives

Topic	Input	Output
Psychosocial objectives	This cell is completed by the Head of well-being and wellness prior to the management review meeting, and it contains the following. The results of the evaluation, that is, which psychosocial objectives are being achieved and which are not. Any suggestions for action. Hyperlinks to the data, information, and criteria used for the evaluation.	This cell is completed during the management review meeting by the top management, or someone acting on their behalf. However, there could be suggested outputs provided by the Head of well-being and wellness.

Source: Prepared by Tony Boyle for this book.

This format means that, if they wish, top management can complete the management review quite quickly – effectively by agreeing to the suggestions made by the Head of well-being and wellness recorded in the third column of Table 29.1 – but where there are matters they wish to query, they have ready access to the relevant data, information, and criteria.

In the full version of the form, there would be a separate row in the table for each of the inputs to the management review, so that a completed form would be a comprehensive record of the work done to prepare for the review meeting, the views of the Head of well-being and wellness, and the decisions made by the top management.

Since the third column of the form will contain the outputs from the management review, it can also be used as the basis for the promulgation of the results of the review.

Notes

i The definition of process used in ISO 45001 is *set of interrelated or interacting activities that uses or transforms inputs into outputs*. Since management review is a process, ISO 45001 refers to its outputs. However, the definition of process in Annex SL has been changed to *set of interrelated or interacting activities that uses or transforms inputs to deliver a result*. The ISO 45001 definition has been used for the purposes of this chapter.

ii ISO 45001 gives the following guidance on *suitability, adequacy and effectiveness. The terms used in relation to management review should be understood as follows:*

a) *'suitability' refers to how the OH&S management system fits the organization, its operation, its culture and business systems;*

b) *'adequacy' refers to whether the OH&S management system is implemented appropriately;*

c) *'effectiveness' refers to whether the OH&S management system is achieving the intended outcome.*

iii This is another area where Annex SL has changed terminology since ISO 45001 was published. The equivalent in ISO SL is *Documented information shall be available as evidence of the results of management reviews.*

References

1   British Standards Institution. *Occupational health and safety management systems – Requirements with guidance for use*, BSI ISO 45001, 2018. BSI 2018.
2   British Standards Institution. *Occupational health and safety management – Psychological health and safety at work – Guidelines for managing psychosocial risks*, BSI ISO 45003, 2021. BSI 2021.
3   Boyle T. *Health and safety: Risk management* (5th edition). Routledge 2019.
4   *ISO/IEC Directives, Part 1 Consolidated ISO Supplement – Procedure for the technical work – Procedures specific to ISO (Thirteenth edition, 2022). Annex SL (normative) Harmonised approach for management system standards. Appendix 2 (normative) Harmonized structure for MSS with guidance for use.*

30 Psychosocial planning and continual improvement

Introduction

Two types of psychosocial planning are dealt with in this book.

The planning you need to do to develop and implement a psychosocial management system. This type of psychosocial planning is dealt with in Chapter 32 'The psychosocial management system development plan'.

The psychosocial planning that is a continual process within the psychosocial management system and is dealt with in clause 6 *Planning* of ISO 45001[1] and ISO 45003.[2] It is this clause 6 planning that is dealt with in this chapter.

The ISO 45001 planning requirements and the ISO 45003 planning guidance are complex, and rather confusing, and the last section of this chapter describes these requirements and the guidance and their complexities. However, the requirements for psychosocial planning suggested in this book are much simpler and it is these requirements that are dealt with next.

Overview

Planning within the psychosocial management system has to be a continual process, and one way of ensuring continual planning is to base it around twice-yearly SWOT analyses and top management reviews. This is the approach described in this chapter, but, since many other approaches are possible, what has to be done has been described in some detail so that you have the information you need to develop your own approach.

The main stages in a full planning cycle are as follows.

Review the external criteria such as ISO Standards and legal requirements.
Determine whether your existing documented information is meeting the requirements of these external criteria.
Determine whether you are conforming with the requirements set out in your procedures and work instructions – is your organisation doing what it said it would do?

DOI: 10.4324/9781003490555-32

Assess the extent to which meeting the requirements set out in your procedures and work instructions is having the desired effect – is what your organisation said it would do working?

Assess the extent to which you are achieving the intended outcomes of your psychosocial management system, your well-being and wellness policy, and your psychosocial objectives – is your organisation achieving what it set out to achieve with regard to well-being and wellness?

Check that actions decided upon during earlier planning cycles have been carried out as specified and, where appropriate, check on their effectiveness and efficiency.

Identify actions that will ensure continual improvement of the psychosocial management system and/or the well-being and wellness of workers and interested parties.

Each of these stages is concerned with identifying changes and specifying the actions needed to deal with these changes. However, dealing with changes is a separate process and it is dealt with in Chapter 31 – the present chapter deals only with identifying changes and specifying the actions.

The following seven sections deal in turn with the seven stages in the planning cycle outlined earlier.

External criteria

So far as the psychosocial management system is concerned, external criteria can be put into the following categories.

International standards and guidance of direct relevance to the psychosocial management system. These include

ISO 45001:2018 *Occupational health and safety management systems Requirements with guidance for use*

ISO 45002:2023[3] *Occupational health and safety management systems – General guidelines for the implementation of ISO 45001:2018*

ISO 45003:2021 *Occupational health and safety management – Psychological health and safety at work – Guidelines for managing psychosocial risks*

ISO 10013:2021[4] *Quality management systems – Guidance for documented information*

ISO 19011:2018[5] *Guidelines for auditing management systems*

Other standards and guidance that you may choose to take into account, for example

PAS 3002:2018[6] *Code of practice on improving health and wellbeing within an organization*

BS 76000:2015[7] *Human resource – Valuing people – Management system – Requirements and guidance*

Advice and guidance supplied by relevant organisations such as

the World Health Organization
mental health and well-being organisations
physical health and wellness organisations.

At this stage in the planning process, you should seek answers to the following questions.

Have there been any changes to the external criteria that you currently take into account?

Should you make changes to the list of external criteria that you currently take into account, either by adding new ones or by removing existing ones?

When the need for action is identified, the action should be accurately specified and recorded. However, this is the case for all actions, and for this reason specifying and recording actions are dealt with in a separate section later in this chapter.

Documented information

This stage of the planning process involves checking that your organisation's documented information meets the relevant requirements of your agreed list of external criteria. Typical requirements for documented information were discussed in Chapter 12, but as a reminder, there are two main types of documented information.

Documents. These include the description of the psychosocial management system, procedures, work instructions, forms, and checklists.

Records. These are principally records of what has been done and the results achieved – typically recorded on a form or checklist.

External criteria impose requirements for both types of documented information. For example, requirements for a process to have a written procedure, and the required content of an OH&S policy, and by implication, any Well-being and wellness policy.

One set of external criteria that is often missed in this stage of the planning process is the spelling, grammar, and readability of the documents. Reviewing documents may identify misspellings and poor grammar that can readily be corrected, but readability is more difficult. However, there is little point in having procedures and work instructions that intended users cannot understand because the documents are too 'difficult' for them. What follows is a brief explanation of readability and how you can measure the readability of documents.

One of the very many individual differences is an individual's reading ability. In general, the more intelligent and better educated a person is, the better their reading skills. There are various ways of describing reading skills but 'reading age' is commonly used. Reading age is what an average child can read and understand at a particular age and, for example, the average nine-year-old would have a reading age of nine. When a psychologist says that an adult has a reading age of nine, it means that they have the reading ability of an average nine-year-old child.

What is not commonly understood is that the average adult reading age is nine. Newspaper publishers know this, and the reading age for a tabloid newspaper is eight or lower, while the reading age for a broadsheet is 12 or higher. When you are writing documents for an average population, you should ensure the documents have a reading age of nine or below. If you have reason to suspect that the reading age of your target audience is below average, then you should ensure the documents have a reading age of seven or below.

There is special software that you can use to measure reading age, and there are various other measures of readability. For example, Word automatically measures the following six readability characteristics.

Sentences per paragraph. The fewer sentences there are per paragraph, the more readable the document.

Words per sentence. Short sentences are more readable than long sentences.

Characters per word. Sentences consisting of short words are more readable than sentences consisting of, or containing, long words.

Flesch reading ease. This is a number between 1 and 100, with 1 being unreadable and 100 being extremely easy to read.

Flesch-Kincaid Grade Level. This gives the American school grade required to read the document. This can be converted into school grades for other countries if required.

Passive sentences. Passive sentences are harder to read than active sentences. For example, 'You will remember that ...' is easier to read than 'It will be remembered that ...'

You should make a habit of checking the readability of what you write and making alterations to your text when the measures of readability suggest that your text may not be suitable for your target audience.

In a comprehensive psychosocial management system, it will not be possible to check all of your documented information during every planning cycle. You should, therefore, set up a 'rolling programme' of documented information checks that enables you to check all of your documented information over, for example, four or five planning sessions. However, this programme can be overridden when you have reason to believe that a particular item of documented information requires immediate review.

Conformity

This stage of the planning process is where you check that you are doing what your documented information says you should be doing. As with the review of documented information, you cannot make all of the necessary checks during every planning session, and you should also have a 'rolling programme' for checks on conformity.

The following techniques can be used for checking conformity.

Examination of monitoring records. For example, the following checks can be made on a sample of inspection checklists.

Are they completed on time, and competently?

If they contain details of nonconformities, is information on correction and corrective action available?

Was the correction suitable and sufficient?

Was the investigation of the causes of the nonconformity carried out competently, and did it result in effective corrective action to address the identified causes?

Examination of other relevant records. Other relevant records include those kept for health and safety reasons – duration of exposure to health and safety hazards and the results of health surveillance, for example – and those kept by HR – working hours and shift rotations, for example. Checks for nonconformity involve comparing the content of these records with any criteria set for well-being and wellness reasons. For example, your organisation may set a lower level of exposure to noise than the level set for health and safety reasons in order to maintain workers' well-being and wellness, and you may do well-being and wellness surveys in addition to legally required health surveillance.

Examination of audit results. The audit results will identify nonconformities, and you can make further checks on the auditee's response to the identified nonconformities. These checks are similar to those just described for inspection checklists, that is, the appropriateness of the auditee's correction and corrective action.

Inspections and interviews. The planning team can conduct their own inspections of workplaces, and their own interviews with workers and interested parties, to check for nonconformities.

Irrespective of the method used to identify the nonconformity, the following actions are required when a nonconformity is identified.

Determine whether there has been timely and appropriate correction and competent corrective action.

When there has been timely and appropriate correction and competent corrective action, no further action is required – the system is working as intended.

When there has been a lack of either correction or corrective action, this is, in itself, a nonconformity and must be treated as such.

Where there has been no, or inadequate, correction and/or corrective action, specify and record appropriate correction and corrective actions to deal with the original nonconformity.

Specify and record corrective actions to identify and deal with the reasons why there was no, or inadequate, correction and/or corrective action to deal with the original nonconformity. Where this will require extensive investigation, specify and record the need for a psychosocial investigation – see Chapter 27 'Psychosocial investigation' for details.

Note that this stage of the planning process can result in a need to go back to an earlier stage in the planning process. For example:

A nonconformity can be occurring because of inadequate guidance on external documented information which makes it necessary to seek out additional external criteria that will supply this guidance, for example, further advice from well-being or wellness organisations.

A nonconformity can be occurring because of poorly drafted procedures or work instructions. When this occurs, the documented information phase has to be revisited, and the relevant documented information revised and re-issued.

Desired effect

It can be the case that, despite your best efforts, what you have asked workers and interested parties to do is simply not appropriate. Over the authors' careers, they have seen many of their brilliant ideas fail miserably and no matter how good a procedure or work instruction looks on paper, it is the practical effect it produces which matters.

You should approach checking on desired effects both reactively and proactively by investigating any reports of procedures or work instructions that are not having their desired effect, and having a rolling programme of checks on a sample of procedures and work instructions. It is also worthwhile including a periodic review of workers' and interested parties' awareness of all, or sections of, the *Well-being and wellness handbook*.

Achievement

Checking whether you are achieving what you said you would achieve is similar to checking whether procedures and work instructions are having the desired effect, but the criteria are different. For the purpose of this stage of the planning process, achievement criteria can be put into two categories.

Criteria where achievement can be measured quantitatively. These criteria include measurable psychosocial objectives, activities which have to be carried out at planned intervals, and actions that had to be carried out by a specified date. Checks on achievement of these criteria involve collection of the relevant data and the evaluation of these data against the relevant criterion.

Criteria where achievement can only be measured qualitatively. These criteria include achievement of the *Well-being and wellness policy*, psychosocial objectives that are not measurable, and activities the achievement of which can only be judged subjectively. Checks on achievement of these criteria involve collection of the opinions of relevant workers and interested parties and the evaluation of these opinions against the relevant criterion.

As with checking for desired effect, you should approach checking on achievement both reactively and proactively. Reactively by investigating any reports of achievement criteria that are not being met, and proactively by having a rolling programme of checks on a sample of achievement criteria.

Previous actions

The output of the planning process is a list of actions to be taken, and you should check that these actions have been carried out as specified and recorded in previous planning rounds. When they have not been carried out, you should treat it as a nonconformity and investigate the causes and take the necessary corrective action.

Continual improvement

So far, the planning process has dealt only with checking that the psychosocial management system is operating as intended and that the actions decided upon in earlier planning sessions are being carried out as specified and are working out as planned. This aspect of planning is often overlooked, but it is very important. Over their years of working in health and safety, the authors have investigated many accidents, some with very serious consequences, that had, as their primary cause, a failure to do the basics well, or in some cases, at all. In the organisations involved, the planning process was driven by a desire 'to do something new' and this led to resources being diverted from 'what you need to do' to 'what would be nice to do'. You should avoid falling into this trap by ensuring that each cycle of your planning process begins with the types of review just described, and you should move on to continual improvement only when you are satisfied that all is as it should be, or you have specified and recorded the actions necessary to make sure everything is as it should be.

When resources are available for continual improvement, they can be used in the following ways.

Improve the psychosocial management system. In general, you can improve the psychosocial management system by making it more effective or making it more efficient, and there are many ways of improving effectiveness and efficiency.

Extend the psychosocial management system. This is done by revising the scope to include, for example, additional psychosocial risk sources or additional categories of interested parties.

Improve well-being and/or wellness of workers and interested parties. This can be done via initiatives or by improving existing arrangements for maintaining well-being and wellness.

Irrespective of the nature of proposed continual improvement, it should not be implemented until there is conformation that existing arrangements are in place and operating as intended.

Specifying and recording actions

The actions that are the output of the planning process are what are referred to as project actions, that is, they are intended to achieve a one-off result. This result could be, for example, to get an existing process back on track or to set up a new process. The following information has to be specified for each project action.

The result to be achieved.
The actions and resources required to achieve the result.
The completion date.
The person who has accepted responsibility for ensuring the intended result is achieved by the specified completion date.

Once the specification has been agreed, it should be the subject of a check against available resources. In particular, are the competences needed to carry out the required actions in place, do the competent individuals have the necessary time to carry out the required actions, and, if there are financial requirements, will these be available? The final stage of the planning process is recording the required actions and relevant information about the action, such as the person responsible and completion date. It can also be useful to record notes on the reasons why any action was thought necessary and why a particular action was chosen.

You can use a word processor or spreadsheet for this recording, but there is a wide range of computer software and mobile device apps designed for use during planning, and some of the software and apps are free. You should look at a sample of these and, if appropriate, use them to record information about your planning activities. Particularly useful are software and apps that also facilitate tracking of actions. Checking that planned actions are being carried out as intended, and in a timely manner, is essential, and software and apps that allow the recording of the completion of actions and provide notifications of overdue actions can be very helpful.

Planning in ISO 45001 and 45003

As was mentioned in the Introduction section of this chapter, the planning requirements in ISO 45001 are complex and confusing, and to make sense of them it is necessary to go back to the Annex SL[8] planning requirements, which are threefold.

Planning how to achieve objectives (clause 6.2)
Changes to the *XXX management system ... shall be carried out in a planned manner* (clause 6.3) This clause was inserted after ISO 45001 was published. The equivalent in ISO 45001 is clause 8.1.3 *Management of change.*

Planning the actions needed to address the following risks and opportunities

> *give assurance that the XXX management system can achieve its intended result(s);*
> *prevent, or reduce, undesired effects*
> *achieve continual improvement.*

These requirements are shown diagrammatically in Figure 30.1.

When you create an equivalent diagram for the ISO 45001 requirements, you get Figure 30.2.

The addition of planning for *emergency situations* is necessary in the context of OH&S, and there is an argument to be made for including actions to *address legal requirements*. However, the complexities made necessary by the ISO 45001 treatment of risks and opportunities make the ISO 45001 planning requirements difficult to navigate.

The picture is further complicated by the extensive guidance on planning given in ISO 45003. The following notes are a summary of this guidance.

Clause 4.1 includes *the organization should ... determine how the assessment of psychosocial risks will be used to make effective action plans.* It appears that this means that the results from the assessment of psychosocial risks should be an input to the planning process.

Clause 6.1.1.2 gives a list of uses for the planning process, that is to

> *a) establish appropriate objectives;*
> *b) determine how to achieve the objectives for the management of psychosocial risk and fulfil legal requirements and other requirements;*
> *c) demonstrate a commitment to continual improvement that, where possible, goes beyond fulfilling legal requirements.*

Bullet points (a) and (b) should, it can be argued, be in clause 6.2 *Objectives to address psychosocial risk*, and no guidance is given on what to do if there are no well-being and wellness legal requirements.

Clause 6.1.1.3 gives a list of things that should be taken into account during the planning process. These have already been covered elsewhere in this chapter or in the chapter on SWOT analysis. The exception is *how to actively involve workers through consultation and participation.*

Clause 8.1.1.1 suggests that the *organization should plan, implement, control and maintain processes to adequately and effectively manage psychosocial risks and new opportunities,* and gives a list of suggested actions or activities for doing this. The list is, in essence, the activities for managing health and safety hazards reworded to suit hazards of a psychosocial nature.

Clause 8.3 *Rehabilitation and return to work* includes *c) talking with an affected worker to understand and plan for reasonable work adjustments to support return to work.*

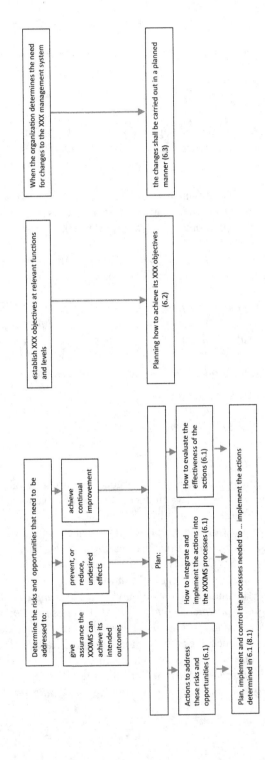

Figure 30.1 Annex SL planning requirements.

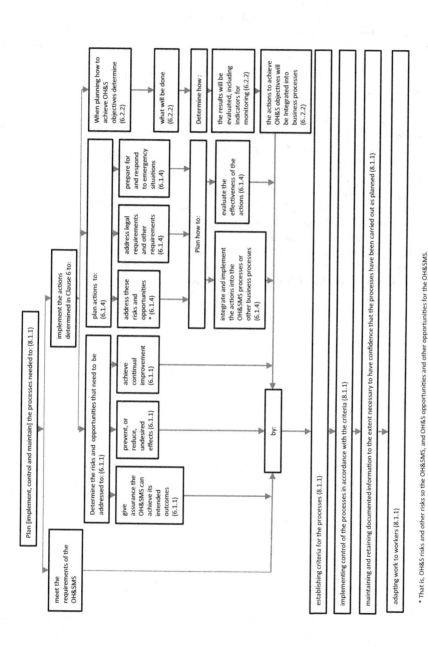

Figure 30.2 The ISO 45001 planning requirements.

References

1   British Standards Institution. *Occupational health and safety management systems – Requirements with guidance for use*, BSI ISO 45001, 2018. BSI 2018.
2   British Standards Institution. *Occupational health and safety management – Psychological health and safety at work – Guidelines for managing psychosocial risks*, BSI ISO 45003, 2021. BSI 2021.
3   British Standards Institution. *Occupational health and safety management systems – General guidelines for the implementation of ISO 45001:2018*, BSI ISO 45002, 2023. BSI 2023.
4   British Standards Institution. *Quality management systems – Guidance for documented information*, BSI ISO 10013, 2021. BSI 2021.
5   British Standards Institution. *Guidelines for auditing management systems*, BSI ISO 19011, 2018. BSI 2018.
6   British Standards Institution. *Code of practice on improving health and wellbeing within an organization*, BSI PAS 3002, 2018. BSI 2018.
7   British Standards Institution. BS 76000:2015 *Human resource – Valuing people – Management system – Requirements and guidance*, BSI 76000, 2015. BSI 2015.
8   ISO/IEC Directives, Part 1 Consolidated ISO Supplement. *Procedure for the technical work – Procedures specific to ISO (Thirteenth edition, 2022). Annex SL (normative) Harmonised approach for management system standards. Appendix 2 (normative) Harmonized structure for MSS with guidance for use.*

31 Change, procurement, and emergencies

Introduction

This chapter deals with the three ISO 45001[1] management system processes that have not been dealt with in previous chapters. There is no strong links between these three processes – they are put together in the same chapter simply because there is not enough to say about each one to warrant a separate chapter for each.

There are separate sections dealing with change, procurement, and emergencies, and, as with the other processes dealt with in this book, the focus is on the well-being and wellness issues associated with the processes.

Change

As was discussed in Chapter 19, there are two types of decisions that can lead to changes – psychosocial management system decisions and business decisions. It should be possible to deal with the changes arising from psychosocial management system decisions in an orderly manner since the decision-making is in the control of the psychosocial management system personnel. However, changes arising from business decisions may be more difficult to deal with since the psychosocial management system personnel may not have access to the relevant data and information and, in extreme cases, may not find out about the change until after it has happened. However, the well-being and wellness aspects of the change processes are similar for both types of change, and these processes are described next.

ISO 45001 deals with two types of change – unintended change and planned change.[i] The requirement with regard to unintended change is

The organization shall review the consequences of unintended changes, taking action to mitigate any adverse effects, as necessary.

ISO 45003[2] does not refer to unintended changes but it has the following guidance on planned changes.

DOI: 10.4324/9781003490555-33

The organization should establish, implement and maintain a process(es) for communication and control of changes that can impact health, safety and well-being at work.

Unintended changes can occur for a variety of reasons and reviews of their consequences can produce a variety of results, including the identification of a need for planned changes. Other sources of planned change include corrections and corrective actions. However, irrespective of the origin of the need for a change, the same process has to be followed and Figure 31.1 shows this process. There are the following explanatory notes on Figure 31.1.

From a psychosocial point of view, the first question to ask during the review of an unintended change is whether it had an effect on well-being or wellness. Where there has been an effect on well-being or wellness, you should determine the nature and extent of the effect and what, if any, actions are required. This determination should follow the guidance in Chapter 27 'Psychosocial investigation'. Note that, in addition to investigating the current state of well-being and wellness of those affected by the unintended change, it may also be necessary to investigate the effects on well-being and wellness during the change process itself. Typically, investigation of well-being and wellness during the change process will be required when the change process was protracted, or involved circumstances that were different from those before and after the change.

The position is similar for planned changes. From a psychosocial point of view, planned changes can be ignored if, in your opinion, they can have no effect on the well-being or wellness of the workers or interested parties within the scope of your psychosocial management system. You will, however, have to ensure that there is monitoring of the effects of planned changes to check that your opinion was correct.

When, in your opinion, a planned change could have an effect on well-being or wellness, a psychosocial threat and opportunity assessment should be carried out to determine the nature and extent of the foreseeable effects. This assessment should follow the guidance in Chapter 23 'Psychosocial threat and opportunity assessment'.

If the psychosocial threat and opportunity assessment suggests that there will be negative effects on well-being or wellness, then you should try to find ways of revising the proposed change to remove the aspects of the change that will have the negative effects on well-being or wellness. If necessary, the revised change should be the subject of a psychosocial threat and opportunity assessment to check that the revised proposed change will not have negative effects on well-being or wellness.

Where a proposed change cannot be revised in ways that remove negative effects on well-being or wellness, you will have to make a decision as to whether a decision on its implementation should be referred to top management. The need for top management involvement will be determined by the nature and extent of the negative effects on well-being and wellness and the importance of the change for the functioning of the organisation. Where there are only limited negative effects on well-being or wellness, the actions required for the change can be added to the type

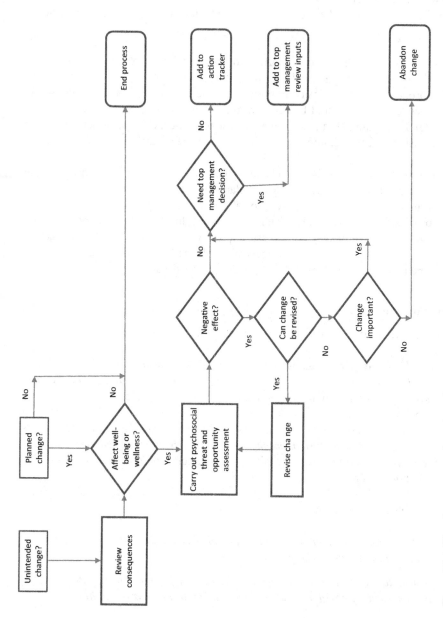

Figure 31.1 Planning processes for unintended and planned changes.

of action tracker described in Chapter 30 and arrangements made for monitoring the psychosocial effects of the change. However, where there are likely to be significant negative effects on well-being or wellness, the importance for the change for the functioning of the organisation has to be taken into account. The extremes are as follows:

The proposed change is not important for the functioning of the organisation in which case the change can be abandoned.

The proposed change is very important for the functioning of the organisation in which case it should be referred to the top management for a decision. In Figure 31.1 this referral is via the top management review, but where an urgent decision is required, immediate referral will be necessary.

One final point on planned changes. The discussion above is based on the assumption that you know about the planned change in advance and have the opportunity to carry out a psychosocial threat and opportunity assessment of the proposed change and any revisions to it. Where this is not the case and a planned change goes ahead, it may be necessary to carry out a psychosocial investigation into the well-being and wellness effects of the planned change and, if necessary, the well-being and wellness effects of the change process itself.

Procurement

Clause 8.1.4 of ISO 45001 is *Procurement* and it has three subclauses.

General. This requires organisations to *control the procurement of products and services in order to ensure their conformity to its OH&S management system.*

Contractors. The two main requirements in this subclause are to *coordinate its procurement process(es) with its contractors, in order to identify hazards and to assess and control the OH&S risks* and to *ensure that the requirements of its OH&S management system are met by contractors and their workers.*

Outsourcing. This subclause requires organisations to *ensure that outsourced functions and processes are controlled.*

Outsource is defined in ISO 45001 as

make an arrangement where an external organization performs part of an organization's function or process

Note 1 to entry: An external organization is outside the scope of the management system, although the outsourced function or process is within the scope.[ii]

This definition and the note are carried over from Annex SL[3], and the *General* subclause in ISO 45001 would appear to match the Annex SL requirement with regard to products and services, but processes are dealt with in the *Outsourcing* subclause where functions are added to match the outsourcing definition.

ISO 45001 uses the term contractor at various points and defines contractor as

external organization providing services to the organization in accordance with agreed specifications, terms and conditions

Note 1 to entry: Services may include construction activities, among others.

It is not clear why ISO 45001 restricts contractors to organisations providing services. It can be argued that it is perfectly possible to have a contractor that provides a product or products. In ISO 9000,[4] a provider (also referred to as a supplier) is defined as

organization that provides a product or a service

and Note 2 to this entry is

In a contractual situation, a provider is sometimes called 'contractor'.

The position is further complicated by Note 3 to the ISO 45001 definition of *worker*

The work or work-related activities performed under the control of the organization may be performed by workers employed by the organization, workers of external providers, contractors, individuals, agency workers, and by other persons to the extent the organization shares control over their work or work-related activities, according to the context of the organization.

However, unless you need to deal with these complexities to ensure conformity with ISO 45001, they can be ignored in your psychosocial management system. The factors to be taken into account with regard to procurement in a psychosocial management system are as follows.

Existing procurement procedures should be the subject of psychosocial threat and opportunity assessment using the same processes you use for the organisation's other procedures.

Proposed procurement procedures should be dealt with as a particular type of change and dealt with in the ways described in the previous section of this chapter.

In addition, when the procurement is for products or services that are under the control of the psychosocial management system, there should be checks on whether products are fit for purpose and on the competence of service deliverers. Where there is extensive psychosocial procurement, or sensitive or specialised well-being or wellness services are being procured, it may be necessary to have a separate documented psychosocial procurement procedure.

Emergencies

ISO 45001 requires organisations to *prepare for and respond to potential emergency situations*, and ISO 45003 gives a list of examples of emergencies as follows

> *natural disaster, emerging infectious diseases, suicide of a colleague, incidents, crises, terror, threats, robbery, dismissals, shut-downs, fire.*

This is an interesting list since it includes occurrences such as *suicide of a colleague, threats,* and *dismissals* that would not feature as health and safety emergencies. In your own psychosocial emergency planning, you should not only take these emergencies into account but also the other types of potentially traumatic events discussed in earlier chapters.

One of the emergency planning requirements in ISO 45001 is *the provision of first aid,* and ISO 45003 also suggests that organisations should *prepare for inclusion of appropriate care in the planned response to emergency situations.* There is no guidance in ISO 45003 on what constitutes *appropriate care,* but they are likely to include the sorts of treatment discussed in Chapter 8 'The improvers'. This is borne out by the inclusion of *appropriate specialists* and *additional advice and support* in the following ISO 45003 guidance

> *use competent workers, emergency services or other appropriate specialists to respond to the emergency situation and seek additional advice and support as necessary.*

Key points to take into account when preparing a psychosocial emergency plan are:

What will be considered a psychosocial emergency. You need to make decisions such that you have a manageable list of psychosocial emergencies for which to plan.

Who will be taken into account when dealing with the effects on well-being and wellness if a psychosocial emergency arises. Typical health and safety emergency plans include first aid provision by the organisation and rapid access to medical treatment for those more seriously injured, but there is no provision for dealing with those affected by, but not injured during, the emergency. In a psychosocial emergency plan, a much wider range of individuals will have to be taken into account, and you will need to decide how wide this range will be in your psychosocial emergency plan.

The sorts of well-being and wellness treatments that will be made available to the individuals who will be taken into account in your psychosocial emergency plan. For each treatment to be provided, you will also have to plan how individuals will access it, and how it will be delivered competently and in a timely manner.

The arrangements needed for testing the emergency plan.

The arrangements for checking individuals' well-being and wellness at appropriate intervals after a psychosocial emergency has occurred.

Notes

i These ISO 45001 requirements are set out in clause 8.1.3 *Management of change.* However, Annex SL has amended the change requirements with changes to the management system dealt with in clause 6.3 *Planning of changes*

> *When the organization determines the need for changes to the XXX management system, the changes shall be carried out in a planned manner*

and planned and unintended changes in 8.1 *Operational planning and control*

> *The organization shall control planned changes and review the consequences of unintended changes, taking action to mitigate any adverse effects, as necessary.*

ii Annex SL defines outsource but it does not use it in the text. The only text relevant to procurement in Annex XL is in clause 8.1 *Operational planning and control – The organization shall ensure that externally provided processes, products or services that are relevant to the XXX management system are controlled.*

Note that functions are omitted in this text although they are included in the definition of outsourcing.

References

1 British Standards Institution. *Occupational health and safety management systems – Requirements with guidance for use*, BSI ISO 45001, 2018. BSI 2018.
2 British Standards Institution. *Occupational health and safety management – Psychological health and safety at work – Guidelines for managing psychosocial risks*, BSI ISO 45003, 2021. BSI 2021.
3 *ISO/IEC Directives, Part 1 Consolidated ISO Supplement – Procedure for the technical work – Procedures specific to ISO (Thirteenth edition, 2022). Annex SL (normative) Harmonised approach for management system standards. Appendix 2 (normative) Harmonized structure for MSS with guidance for use.*
4 British Standards Institution. *Quality management systems – Fundamentals and vocabulary*, BSI ISO 9000, 2015. BSI 2015.

32 The psychosocial management system development plan

Introduction

This chapter is about identifying the work you need to do before your psychosocial management system can 'go live' and preparing a psychosocial management system development plan for approval by your top management. You will probably also need an implementation plan, often called a 'roll out plan', but these plans vary so widely that they are not dealt with in detail in this chapter.

In the context of a psychosocial management system, preparing a development plan requires the activities shown in Figure 32.1. The rest of this chapter deals separately with each of these main activities, beginning with drafting the psychosocial management system manual.

Preparing the manual

A *Psychosocial management system manual* of the type discussed in Chapter 17 sets out what the organisation wants to achieve with regard to psychosocial risk management and the well-being and wellness of workers and interested parties. Because of this, it is the best document to use as the basis for a psychosocial management system development plan, and the manual outlined in Chapter 17 has been used to illustrate suggestions for developing a psychosocial management system development plan.

This section of the chapter deals with the practicalities of drafting and recording the documented information needed to prepare a development plan. The section is subdivided as follows.

Assumptions. In order to provide examples, it has been necessary to make certain assumptions and these are set out in this subsection.
Activities. This subsection describes the main activities required to produce a fit-for-purpose manual.
Managing documented information. This subsection provides practical suggestions for managing the documented information associated with preparing a manual.

DOI: 10.4324/9781003490555-34

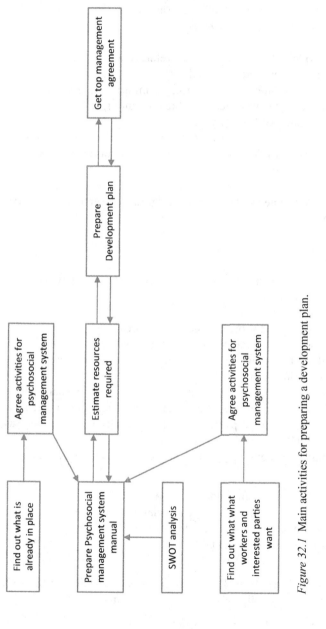

Figure 32.1 Main activities for preparing a development plan.

Assumptions

The following assumptions have been made.

There is a single person in charge of preparing the psychosocial management system development plan – referred to as 'you' for the rest of this chapter – and that you have the following competences.

Able to explain the well-being and wellness concepts dealt with in Part I of this book to workers and interested parties.

Able to conduct interviews to collect the information needed to prepare a psycho-social management system suitable for your organisation.

Able to conduct SWOT analyses.

Able to prepare documented information. In this context, 'prepare' means draft, discuss with workers and interested parties, revise as necessary, and obtain an agreed version.

It is also assumed that you have the time and the authority to carry out the necessary work.

Activities

In order to ensure that your manual is fit for purpose, you will have to carry out the following activities.

Find out what psychosocial processes are already in place and agree which, if any, of these will become psychosocial management system processes. This is to avoid 're-inventing the wheel' and/or 'treading on people's toes', and it was discussed in Chapter 14.

Be clear about what you want from your psychosocial management system, and find out what other workers, particularly top management, and interested parties want from a psychosocial management system. This was discussed in Chapter 15.

Draft initial versions of the documented information described in Chapter 15, that is:

Purpose of the organisation
Intended outcomes of the psychosocial management system
Scope of the psychosocial management system
Well-being and wellness policy
Psychosocial objectives

Carry out an initial SWOT analysis as described in Chapter 18 and produce initial versions of the following documented information.

Strengths, weaknesses, opportunities, and threats.
Categories of workers in the organisation and their requirements (needs and expectations) – see Chapter 16 for details.

Interested parties and their requirements (needs and expectations) – see Chapter 16 for details.

Threats and opportunities that need to be addressed to

give assurance that the psychosocial management system can achieve its intended outcomes

prevent, or reduce, undesired effects, and

achieve continual improvement.

Psychosocial legal register – see Chapter 25 for details.

Opportunities for improvement. At this stage, these could be opportunities that could be taken even if there was no formal psychosocial management system.

Managing documented information

The authors' preference when developing a psychosocial management system development plan is to keep the documented information in stand-alone folders and files on their computer, and this is what they do unless a client organisation's document control procedure prevents it. Initially, they set up the folders and files described in the next four subsections.

Manual folder

The principal file in this folder is the *Psychosocial management system manual* and, as discussed in Chapter 17, this has three sections, *Introduction, Preliminaries*, and *Description*. The *Psychosocial management system manual* file is used to record the most up-to-date version of the manual, liberally sprinkled with to-do notes in red font.

Procedures folder

The Procedures folder is used for the psychosocial management system procedures referenced in the *Description* section of the *Psychosocial management system manual*. This folder contains a separate sub-folder for each of the referenced procedures. For the manual discussed in Chapter 17, the sub-folders would be

P01 *Well-being and wellness consultation and participation procedure*
P02 *Psychosocial threat and opportunity assessment procedure*
P03 *Psychosocial planning and continual improvement procedure*
P04 *Psychosocial competence procedure*
P05 *Psychosocial awareness procedure*
P06 *Psychosocial communication procedure*
P07 *Psychosocial procurement procedure*
P08 *Psychosocial monitoring, measurement, analysis and evaluation procedure*
P09 *Psychosocial audit procedure*
P10 *Psychosocial nonconformity and corrective action procedure*

As work progresses, the following are added to the procedure sub-folders:

Proposed text for the procedure. It is helpful to draft the *Purpose* and *Scope* sections of the procedures early on so that these are available for discussion. Notes are added to the *Activities* section as relevant material becomes available.

Any task-based work instructions that will be referenced in the procedure, and notes on the content of these work instructions if any relevant information is available. If appropriate, any forms associated with the task-based work instructions are added to the sub-folder.

Role work instructions folder

The role work instruction folder is used to record the role work instructions that are referenced in the *Psychosocial management system manual* and any documented information associated with these work instructions. For example, the results from the initial SWOT analysis would be recorded in the *Head of HR well-being and wellness work instruction* because the Head of well-being and wellness has been allocated responsibility for carrying out these analyses. This file is also used for committee terms of reference because committee membership is a role in the psychosocial management system. The list of the referenced role work instructions and terms of reference for the manual discussed in Chapter 17 is as follows.

WI51 Top management well-being and wellness work instruction
WI52 Middle manager well-being and wellness work instruction
WI53 First-line manager well-being and wellness work instruction
WI54 Head of well-being and wellness work instruction
WI55 Head of HR well-being and wellness work instruction
Terms of reference for the Well-being and wellness committee

Well-being and wellness handbook folder

As has been described in previous chapters, the *Well-being and wellness handbook* is a succinct description of what your organisation wants to happen with regard to well-being and wellness, and it is central to maintaining worker awareness of psychosocial issues. For these reasons, it is preferable to start on the handbook as soon as possible, and to discuss drafts as widely as possible. The results of these discussions can be very helpful in establishing what is going to be practical and what is not.

Estimating resources

As indicated by the arrows in Figure 32.1, the work done on estimating resources may cause you to make changes to your draft manual – typically because you think that the resources for what you would ideally like to do are not going to be available. You probably already have your own processes for estimating resources, but what follows is basic guidance on what the estimating resource process needs to achieve.

For each resource requirement you identify, you should ask and answer the following four questions.

What? You need an accurate description of the nature of the resource requirement as a basis for your costing.

How many or how much? You need an accurate description of the size of the resource requirement, for example, how many workers require a particular competence, or how many hours it will take to prepare a work instruction.

Unit cost? For example, how much does it cost to provide a single worker with a required competence, and what is the hourly rate for the person preparing the work instruction.

Total cost? The 'how many or how much' multiplied by the unit cost.

Where you think the total cost is acceptable, the requirement can be included in the psychosocial management system development plan you will be sending to top management. However, where you think the total cost is too high, you need to take one of the following actions.

Remove the requirement from your *Psychosocial management system manual.* This option can be used when, for example, the requirement is a 'nice to have' rather than an essential element of your psychosocial management system.

Reduce the amount in your development plan. This can be done by having a 'pilot study' rather than immediate full development. This option is useful when you believe what you are planning to do will be cost-effective, and a pilot study will enable you to demonstrate this.

Plan for a review. The fact that what you want to do is too costly at present does not mean that it will always be too costly. You can keep such items in your plan by recording that you will review them annually, recalculate the costs and benefits, and make a new decision on what to do about them.

You will also have to keep a 'running total' of planned expenditure by adding up the total costs for all of the things you include in your psychosocial management system development plan.

Preparing the development plan

Because organisations differ from each other in many ways, there is a wide range of different psychosocial management systems, and a correspondingly wide difference in plans for their development. This means that it is not possible to provide a single development plan that will suit all organisations. However, what is possible is to suggest the content for a generic development plan based on a chronological sequence of activities, and this generic plan is discussed in this section.

For ease of description, the development plan has been set out as a series of phases but, in practice, these phases will overlap, and circumstances may arise that make it sensible to reorder the phases. You will obviously have to record your plan and there is a note on recording plans before describing the phases.

Recording the development plan

As was described in Chapter 30, there is a range of computer software and mobile device apps designed to help with planning and these are very useful, particularly for large or complex plans. However, a word processor or spreadsheet can also be used, and the last section of this chapter consists of an example of an outline psychosocial management system development plan.

One other point on recording your development plan. As you add each item to your plan, it is useful to go back to the four folders described in the *Managing documented information* section earlier in this chapter, that is, the Manual folder, the Procedures folder, the Role work instructions folder, and the Well-being and wellness handbook folder, and add any relevant information. For example, if you have decided that members of the psychosocial management system team will attend a PEACE interviewing course to improve their interviewing skills, then you could make the following additions.

Record in your Procedures file that demonstrated competence in PEACE interviewing techniques is a requirement for psychosocial management system team members carrying out, for example, psychosocial threat and opportunity assessment, psychosocial investigations, and psychosocial audits. This can be done by having a sentence such as 'Do not use this work instruction unless you are competent in PEACE interview techniques' in the relevant work instructions.

Record in the Head of well-being and wellness and Head of HR work instructions in your Role work instructions file that demonstrated competence in PEACE interviewing techniques is a requirement for these roles. If appropriate, you could also specify this as a requirement for members of the Well-being and wellness committee.

You should do this revisiting of files for each of the phases described below.

Phase 1 – Psychosocial team competences and handbook

The aims of this phase are to ensure the following.

All the members of the psychosocial management system team have the relevant competences.

All of the required psychosocial management system competences are available, either from members of the psychosocial management system team or via consultants or other specialists.

There is a clear statement of your organisation's position with regard to well-being and wellness, preferably in the form of an agreed *Well-being and wellness handbook*. However, if you are not using a handbook, you will have to prepare some other form of documented information to record the required information.

You should record in your plan the activities that will be necessary to ensure the required competences are delivered and tested, and that the agreed statement can be understood by all members of its target audiences.

Phase 2 – Establishing the baselines

The aim of this phase is to ensure that you know from where you are starting. The reasons for doing this are as follows.

If you have set any form of target, for example, a psychosocial objective, you need to be assured that you are not already meeting this target, or are so close to it that additional work would not be cost-effective. If you do not do this, you could end up wasting resources, and bringing your psychosocial management system into disrepute.
Where you are proposing action for continual improvement, you need to establish a baseline if you are to be able to demonstrate that continual improvement has been achieved.

The activities required in this phase will obviously depend on what you want to achieve, but a central activity will be measuring the current state of the well-being and wellness of your workers and interested parties.

Competences in establishing baselines include data collection, analysis, and evaluation, and these competences should have been put in place in phase 1.

Phase 3 – Worker competence provision arrangements

The aim of this phase is to put in place the arrangements for delivering, assessing, and maintaining the psychosocial competences required by top management, managerial workers, non-managerial workers, and interested parties.

Typical activities for this phase include:

Identifying organisations that deliver relevant competences, checking their competence in delivery and assessment of competence, and establishing likely costs of using their services. This activity should be linked with the development of P07 *Psychosocial procurement procedure.*
Preparing training course material and assessment methods for competences that are to be delivered in-house.
Ensuring that the individuals who will deliver in-house courses are competent in competence delivery and assessment.

It is particularly important during this phase to give sufficient attention to the arrangements for maintaining the psychosocial competences of workers and interested parties and ensuring that you set up system objectives rather than project objectives.

Phase 4 – Other provisions

The aim of this phase is to ensure that arrangements are in place for the delivery of any equipment and services your organisation will be providing as part of its psychosocial management system. Examples of these include the following.

Equipment for measuring aspects of wellness (for example blood pressure monitors) or improving wellness (for example treadmills).
Counselling services, either by in-house personnel or by an external provider.
Well-being and wellness treatment services, either by in-house personnel or by an external provider.
Mental health first aid provision.

You should check that you have dealt with all of the equipment and services your organisation says it will be providing.

Phase 5 – General awareness

The aim of this phase is to ensure that arrangements are in place for making all workers and interested parties aware of the nature and purposes of the psychosocial management system and, in particular, what the organisation expects them to do with regard to well-being and wellness.

Some organisations have well-developed arrangements for drawing up and implementing Communication plans, usually referred to as 'Comms plans', and where this is the case you should 'plug in' to these arrangements. Otherwise, you will have to prepare and record your own Communication plan to achieve the aim of this phase. The simplest initial communications plan would be a programme to make all workers and interested parties aware of the contents of the *Well-being and wellness handbook*.

Phase 6 – Other procedures

The aim of this phase is to ensure that arrangements are in place for all of the procedures required by the psychosocial management system that have not been dealt with in earlier phases. The possible exception is the *Psychosocial audit procedure* since audits will not be required until some time after implementation. However, you should include in your development plan any work that will be required to ensure that the other psychosocial procedures can 'go live'.

You should also record information on how levels of awareness will be maintained and continually measured.

Example outline plan

Top managements vary in their requirements with regard to detail, but the authors' experience is that they prefer less rather than more, and a useful rule of thumb is not to provide more information than can be set out on a single sheet of A4. Table 32.1 illustrates this sort of information provision using the phases described in the previous section.

Explanatory notes for Table 32.1.

Although the plan is divided into six phases, this is an arbitrary choice for the purposes of illustration. You may prefer to use monthly or quarterly divisions with lists of activities to be carried out in each month or quarter.

It is important that the first two phases – provision of competences for the psychosocial management system team and establishing base lines – are positioned early in any plan you prepare. This is because the team competences will be

Table 32.1 Outline psychosocial management system development plan

Phase		Activities	Cost
1	Provision of competences for psychosocial management system team	PEACE interview courses Mental health first aid courses Data collection and analysis courses	
2	Establish baselines	Worker well-being and wellness survey Interested party well-being and wellness survey	
3	Worker competence provision arrangements	Preparing training course materials Train the trainers courses Identify external providers	
4	Other provisions	Equipment purchases Identify external providers of well-being and wellness products and services	
5	General awareness	Preparing *Well-being and wellness handbook* Drafting Comms plan	
6	Other procedures	Testing psychosocial threat and opportunity assessment techniques Preparatory meeting of the Well-being and wellness committee **Total**	

Source: Prepared by Tony Boyle for this book.

required for effective development of later phases, and knowledge of existing baselines will allow a more focussed approach to developing other procedures and work instructions.

The activities listed for each phase are only illustrative examples, in practice you are likely to have many more activities. Where appropriate, you should also have background information about each of your listed activities which you can provide promptly when top management asks for it. For example, you should have available course outlines for the courses listed in phase 1 and details of the proposed well-being and wellness surveys listed in phase 2.

The cost column is shown as containing a single figure, but you may prefer to, or be required to, provide the sort of costing information discussed in the *Estimating resources* section earlier in this chapter. For example, for the courses listed in phase 1, you could provide the number of people who will be attending each course, the time required for course attendance, the cost of each course, and the cost of the attendee's travel and subsistence expenses. Similarly, you could provide costing for a range of alternative well-being and wellness surveys in phase 2, from a small-sample in-house email survey to a full survey conducted by an external organisation using a variety of data and information collection techniques, including interviews with workers and interested parties. Where you provide costs for different options in this way, you should also provide clear information on the additional benefits to be achieved from more expensive options.

Getting top management agreement

In an ideal world, you will have found out what your top management want from a psychosocial management system, and how much they are willing to pay for it, and you will deliver a development plan that meets their wishes. You may encounter this ideal world when preparing your own development plan but things do go wrong, for example:

There have been changes in top management personnel during the preparation of the development plan, and the new personnel want different things from the management system, or in extreme cases, no management system at all.

There have been changes in the financial status of the organisation during the preparation of the development plan, typically a deterioration, that means the resources promised for the development of a management system are now required elsewhere.

There have been external changes that require major revisions to the proposed management system. The introduction of ISO 45001[1] and the phasing out of BS 18001[2] was the latest in a series of changes to OH&S management systems that forced the authors to change course during the preparation of management systems for client organisations.

It is best to think of the development plan you submit to your top management as an opening bid, and be prepared for them insisting on changes – most of which you will not like. What is not a sustainable option is pressing on with a development plan that does not have the support of your top management.

References

1   British Standards Institution. *Occupational health and safety management systems – Requirements with guidance for use*, BSI ISO 45001, 2018. BSI 2018.
2   British Standards Institution. *Occupational health and safety management systems – specification*, BS OHSAS 18001:2007. BSI, 2007.

Index

Printed in the United States
by Baker & Taylor Publisher Services